'*The Changing Face of Imperialism* combines the analyses from a set of most competent Indian thinkers. An enlightening collection which simultaneously reminds the reader of the continuities of that major facet of capitalism through the successive phases of its global deployment and gives its full importance to the changes associated with the dominance of contemporary finance capital. An essential reading to understand the challenges of our time.'

Samir Amin, Director, Third World Forum, Dakar
and former Director, Institut Africain de Développement
Économique et de Planification (IDEP) and Professor
at the Universities of Poitiers, Dakar and Paris

'A very timely volume which going against the current forcefully reminds us that imperialist surplus appropriation continues to occur in the contemporary world though formal colonies are long gone. The authors of this volume are globally renowned specialists in their respective areas and the volume has successfully brought them together to make an important common point.'

Aditya Mukherjee, Professor of Modern History,
Jawaharlal Nehru University, New Delhi, India

The Changing Face of Imperialism

This volume reiterates the relevance of imperialism in the present, as a continuous arrangement, from the early years of empire-colonies to the prevailing pattern of expropriation across the globe. While imperialism as an arrangement of exploitation has sustained over ages, measures deployed to achieve the goals have gone through variations, depending on the network of the prevailing power structure. Providing a historical as well as a conceptual account of imperialism in its 'classical' context, this collection brings to the fore an underlying unity which runs across the diverse pattern of imperialist order over time. Dealing with theory, the past and the contemporary, the study concludes by delving into the current conjuncture in countries including Latin America, the United States and Asia.

The Changing Face of Imperialism will provide fresh ideas for future research into the shifting patterns of expropriation – spanning the early years of sea-borne plunder and the empire-colonies of nineteenth-century to contemporary capitalism, which is rooted in neoliberalism, globalization and free market ideology.

With contributions from major experts in the field, this book will be a significant intervention. It will be of interest to scholars and researchers of economics, politics, sociology and history, especially those dealing with imperial history and colonialism.

Sunanda Sen is former Professor of Economics, Jawaharlal Nehru University, New Delhi, India. She researches contemporary capitalism, international finance, economic history and development. Her publications include over 70 articles in reputed journals and ten books, including *Dominant Finance and Stagnant Economy* (2014), *Globalisation and Development* (2008, 2013) and *Unfreedom and Waged Work* (with Byasdeb Dasgupta, 2009).

Maria Cristina Marcuzzo is Professor of Economics, University of Rome, 'La Sapienza', Italy, and Fellow of the Italian Academy of Lincei. She has worked on classical monetary theory, the Cambridge School of Economics, Keynesian economics and, more recently, on Keynes's investments in financial markets. She has published about 100 articles in journals and books, and authored/edited 20 volumes.

The Changing Face of Imperialism
Colonialism to Contemporary Capitalism

Edited by
**Sunanda Sen and
Maria Cristina Marcuzzo**

Routledge
Taylor & Francis Group

LONDON AND NEW YORK

First published 2018 by Routledge

2 Park Square, Milton Park, Abingdon, Oxfordshire OX14 4RN

52 Vanderbilt Avenue, New York, NY 10017

Routledge is an imprint of the Taylor & Francis Group, an informa business

First issued in paperback 2019

British Library Cataloguing-in-Publication Data
A catalogue record for this book is available from the British Library

Library of Congress Cataloging-in-Publication Data
A catalog record for this book has been requested

ISBN: 978-1-138-08271-7 (hbk)
ISBN: 978-0-367-89070-4 (pbk)

Typeset in Sabon
by Apex CoVantage, LLC

Contents

List of figures   x
List of tables   xii
Notes on contributors   xv
Preface   xvii

Introduction   1
SUNANDA SEN AND MARIA CRISTINA MARCUZZO

PART I
The conceptual basis of imperialism   13

1 Imperialism, the 'old' and the 'new': departures
   and continuities   15
   SATYAKI ROY

2 Marx's *Capital* and the global crisis   37
   JOHN SMITH

3 Reflections on contemporary imperialism   61
   PRABHAT PATNAIK

4 The particularity of imperialism in the stage of
   neoliberal globalisation and global capitalism:
   a dialogue between Nikolai Bukharin and Aimé Césaire   78
   ANJAN CHAKRABARTI

5 Is imperialism a relevant concept in today's world?   104
   SUBHANIL CHOWDHURY

PART II
Patterns of contemporary imperialism   129

6 Latin America in the new international order:
   new forms of economic organisations and old
   forms of surplus appropriation   131
   NOEMI LEVY ORLIK

7 Latin America and imperialism   160
   AMIYA KUMAR BAGCHI

8 Did US workers gain from US imperialism (1985–2000)?   171
   GERALD EPSTEIN

PART III
Imperialism and the colonial context   199

9 India's global trade and Britain's international dominance   201
   UTSA PATNAIK

10 Unrequited exports of labour from India in
   late-nineteenth and early-twentieth centuries:
   Britain's financial interest in plantation colonies   226
   SUNANDA SEN

11 Labour laws and the global economy: the discourse of
   labour control and welfare in India, 1919–1947   247
   SABYASACHI BHATTACHARYA

PART IV
Contemporary capitalism and the Indian economy   265

12 Financialisation in contemporary capitalism: an
   inter-sectoral approach to trace sources of instability
   in finance, real estate and business services in India   267
   SUKANYA BOSE AND ABHISHEK KUMAR

13 Contemporary imperialism and labour: an analytical note   295
BYASDEB DASGUPTA

14 'Emerging' Third World capitalism and the new
   imperialism: the case of India   310
SURAJIT MAZUMDAR

Index   331

Figures

2.1 Share of developing nations in world exports of
manufactured goods   40
2.2 Share of developing nations in manufactured goods
imports of developed nations   41
2.3 Global industrial workforce   44
4.1 Changing share of world GDP   93
5.1 Share of groups of countries in world GDP
based on PPP   109
5.2 Share of BRICS and its constituents in world GDP
based on PPP   111
5.3 Index of average wage of BRIC with respect to United
States for 2010   112
5.4 GDP growth rates in developed countries   114
5.5 US current account and growth rates of GDP
across countries   115
5.6 Share of US dollars and Euro in world foreign
exchange reserves   117
6.1 Terms of trade of the Latin America region
and specific countries   148
6.2 Main components of the financial account of specific
Latin American countries and the United States   150
6.3 Main components of the primary account of specific
countries of Latin America and United States   151
6.4 Net income composition from direct and portfolio
investment of specific countries in Latin America
and the United States   152
6.5 Interest rate and sovereign bonds in different countries
of Latin America and the United States   153
6.6 Real exchange rate index of different countries in
Latin America (1990 = 100)   154

8.1	Real military spending in the United States	178
8.2	Spot price of oil	188
8.3	Real price of oil	188
10.1	Emigration to Mauritius and British Caribbean	230
10.2	Destination of emigration in shares	230
10.3	Emigration to Mauritius	231
10.4	Import of raw sugar from various colonies	232
10.5	Average import price of sugar in shillings per cwt.	236
10.6	Triangular trade – Britain and plantation colonies	241
12.1a	Quarterly growth rate (rolling)	270
12.1b	Quarterly growth rate (rolling)	270
12.2	Share of finance, insurance, real estate and business services (FINREBS)	271
12.3a	Components of FINREBS (Rs Billion) at 2004–2005 prices	273
12.3b	FINREBS, 2012–2013	274
12.4	Co-integration test with FINREBS rolling recursive trace statistics	282
14.1	Share of private organized sector and public sector non-departmental enterprises in NDP at current prices, 1990–1991 to 2012–2013	313
14.2	India's trade, invisibles and current balances as percentages of GDP, 2000–2001 to 2014–2015	320

Tables

5.1 Military expenditure of the top 15 countries in the
world along with their share in total military expenditure 119
6.1 Financial market evolution in Latin America 140
6.2 Financial sector size in term of country's GDP (%) 142
6.3 GDP main components of the Latin American and
Caribbean region and economic growth rates 144
6.4 Latin American and Caribbean trade balance by
technological intensities 146
6.5 Income distribution by deciles (% of total income) 155
8.1 Military and military-related expenditure, 2001
and 2002, billions of US dollars 179
8.2 Military expenditure in a sample of countries,
1985–2000 180
8.3 Average military expenditure shares and the military
cost of US imperialism 1985–2000 181
8.4 Approximate distribution of US military budget 182
8.5 Share of total income and total federal taxes by
income quintiles of households 1979, 1985 and 1997 183
8.6 Tax costs to 'working class' of US imperialist military
expenditure 1985–2000, billions of US dollars 183
8.7 Current account balance as share of GDP, average
and minimum over the period 1970–2000 185
8.8 Disruptions in world petroleum supply 189
8.9 Cost of oil price hikes due to political disruption 190
8.10 Counter-factual cost to worker of no US military
action in Persian Gulf, 1985–2000 190
8.11 Do US workers gain from the iron fist? 191
9.1 Britain's trade volumes 1750–1754 to 1800–1804:
special trade and general trade 208

9.2 Britain's imports by commodity groups, 1784–1786 to
1824–1826, three year averages in £ million 209
9.3 Commodity structure of Britain's imports from Asia
and the West Indies 1784–1786 to 1854–1856 211
9.4 Britain's imports from Asia, the West Indies and
Ireland by commodities, 1784–1786 to 1824–1826,
£ million 212
9.5 Britain's imports from Europe and from its colonies
1784–1786 to 1854–1856, three year average, £ million 213
9.6 Britain's trade balance with Europe and the United
States 1784–1786 to 1854–1856, three year average,
£ million 214
9.7 Britain's trade with Asia and the West Indies and trade
balance as share of GDP, 1784–1786 to 1854–1856,
three year averages in £ million 216
9.8 Britain's trade balance with Ireland 1784–1786
to 1824–1826 217
9.9 Investment: Great Britain 1761–1860 and United
Kingdom 1851–1860 219
9.10 Britain's trade deficit with Europe and the United
States compared with transfer from Asia, the West
Indies and Ireland 221
12.1 Summary of backward linkage (direct and indirect):
inter-sectoral and inter-temporal comparison 277
12.2 Summary of forward linkage (direct and indirect):
inter-sectoral and inter-temporal comparison 280
12.3 Causality between FINREBS and other sectors,
sample: 1996:Q2–2014: Q3 284
14.1 Share of 15 largest economies in world GDP on
PPP basis (percentages) 312
14.2 Distribution of net fixed capital stock of the corporate
sector between public and private sectors: 1991–2013
(percentage shares) 313
14.3 Distribution of factor incomes in the private organised
sector/private corporations 314
14.4 Concentration of corporate profits 315
14.5 Illustrative list of MNCs in different sectors in India 316
14.6 Export to sales ratios of FDI and non-FDI companies
(percentages) 317
14.7 R&D intensity of Indian business groups and
independent companies, 2012–2013 (Rs. million) 318

14.8   Share of manufacturing, construction and services
         in private organized net domestic product (NDP)
         (percentage shares)   319
14.9   India's foreign trade (million US dollars)   321
14.10   India's merchandise trade balance with selected
         countries (million US dollars)   322
14.11   Pattern of net issues for financing private corporate
         business deficit (percentage shares)   323
14.12   Assets, sales and exports of foreign affiliates in
         selected host countries (millions of dollars)   324

Notes on contributors

Amiya Kumar Bagchi is Founder-Director and Emeritus Professor at the Institute of Development Studies, Kolkata, India. His latest book is *Colonialism and Indian Economy* (2010).

Sabyasachi Bhattacharya is founding President of Association of Indian Labour Historians. His most recent publication is *The Colonial State: Theory and Practice* (2016).

Sukanya Bose is Assistant Professor at the National Institute of Public Finance and Policy, New Delhi, India. Her latest work is on 'Resource requirements for Right to Education (RTE): Normative and the Real'.

Anjan Chakrabarti is Professor of Economics, University of Calcutta, India. He has published extensively in the field of Marxian theory, financial economics, political philosophy, development and Indian economics.

Subhanil Chowdhury is an economist at the Institute of Development Studies, Kolkata, India. His areas of interest are development economics, labour and political economy.

Byasdeb Dasgupta is Professor at Department of Economics of University of Kalyani, West Bengal, India. His latest book is *The Indian Economy in Transition* (co-authored with Anjan Chakrabarti and Anup Dhar, 2015).

Gerald Epstein is Professor of Economics and founding Co-Director of the Political Economy Research Institute (PERI) at the University of Massachusetts, Amherst, United States.

Abhishek Kumar is a research scholar at the Indira Gandhi Institute of Development Research, Mumbai, India. His research interests include macroeconomics and monetary economics.

Noemi Levy Orlik is Senior Professor, Economic Faculty, Universidad Nacional Autónoma de México. She has written widely on issues of development and finance in Latin America.

Surajit Mazumdar is at the Centre for Economic Studies and Planning at Jawaharlal Nehru University, New Delhi, India, and works on the political economy of Indian economic development.

Prabhat Patnaik is Professor Emeritus at Jawaharlal Nehru University, New Delhi, India. He is the co-author (with Utsa Patnaik) of *A Theory of Imperialism* (2016).

Utsa Patnaik is Professor Emeritus, Jawaharlal Nehru University, India and National Fellow, Indian Council of Social Science Research. She has co-authored (with Prabhat Patnaik) *A Theory of Imperialism* (2016).

Satyaki Roy is Associate Professor at the Institute for Studies in Industrial Development, New Delhi, India. He is the author of *Small and Medium Enterprises in India: Infirmities and Asymmetries in Industrial Clusters* (2013).

John Smith is a writer and activist based in northern England. He teaches International Political Economy at Kingston University, United Kingdom.

Preface

The collection of essays in the present volume originates from a conference titled 'Imperialism Old and New', which was held in Delhi in February 2015. The conference was a sequel to a project undertaken by one of the editors and some authors from the present volume. The project, funded by the ICSSR, was housed in Jamia Millia Islamia University in Delhi. We thank both these organisations for their generous help.

Some of the papers in the volume include those which were presented in this conference. The final versions include thorough revisions, which have added further insights and perspectives to the original paper.

We expect that the present volume will be able to throw some fresh light on the well-researched topic of imperialism. It will provide further research on the theme of imperialism, touching its conceptual, historical and the current context. We hope our efforts to put these papers together will provide analytical inputs for future research in this area.

Sunanda Sen
New Delhi
September
2017

Maria Cristina Marcuzzo
Rome
September
2017

Introduction

Sunanda Sen and
Maria Cristina Marcuzzo

The title of the present volume is indicative of the relevance of imperialism as a concept, or more appropriately, as a continuous arrangement since the early years of empire-colonies to the current pattern of expropriations, on the part of those who wield power vis-à-vis the weaker ones.

Varied interpretations of imperialism are there in the literature, on what it stands for, or even on whether the notion has any relevance at all in contemporary capitalism. Interpretations as above, however, do not lessen the significance of what can be observed as the common ground underlying the alternate positions. The unity, which runs across the diverse pattern of expropriations under imperialism, makes it even more relevant to put together a new set of research dealing with different approaches to what can be characterised as imperialism. We attempt, in this book, a similar exercise, putting together papers dealing with alternate interpretations, of imperialism and its changing pattern over space and time.

Continuities, in the run of imperialism over centuries and the engulfing of newer regions, incorporate within its fold, the changing parameters of authority and suppression. Aspects, as are highlighted in the literature, provide alternate interpretations of the changing pattern of oppression, often reflecting the dynamics underlying a pattern which is rather similar. In this the attempts to characterise what has been called 'new imperialism' under contemporary capitalism provides an explanation of its evolution in its new incarnation.

Earlier formulations of 'imperialism' can be found in the writings of Hobson, Hilferding and Lenin. Analyses, as above, were framed in the context of the imperial relations between the ruling nations and their colonies. Political subjugation of the latter, captured by force or by commerce, provided the groundwork for their economic domination in the interest of the ruling nations. Forms of such arrogation varied, across regions and over time, between the early years of European invasions of South America, the slave trade across oceans, the use of plantation islands by importing indentured labour from colonies and the structured governance of colonies to drain off surpluses by using trade and financial channels. As indicated in the related literature, it was from nineteenth century onwards that imperialism in its early form was found to rest on the formal control of the colonies by the respective empires. The pattern, however, has considerably changed since then. While imperialism as an arrangement of exploitation has continued over time, measures deployed to achieve the goals have gone through variations, much depending on the network of the power structure. The formal makeover for change came up with decolonisation at the end of the Second World War, introducing new relations between some of the advanced countries and their former colonies. While social democratic governments in the West were trying to generate a stable capitalist order within the region, their links with the developing region were reworked in a neo-colonial frame where overseas development assistances (ODAs) were fetching economic mileages with loan tying in general or with the PL480s used by the United States to access captive external markets in order to dispose of its surplus farm products. Trade between the advanced industrialised countries and the rest of the world, especially the primary producing countries, was conducted at a terms of trade which added further to the gap between the rich and the poor nations. Much of those were facilitated by the machinations of imperialism in its new incarnation.

Predictions in the Marxist literature, on the limits to expanded reproduction under capitalism, turned out to be a reality by the last quarter of the twentieth century, in particular with the continued stagnation in the real economy of the major advanced countries. With growing inequalities, primitive accumulation led way to disproportionate stocks of wealth concentrated among a few, in turn calling for measures which could protect as well as augment those. Thus began the era of finance-led capitalism with state patronage, providing the space for changes in institutions which could ease out financial markets and generate handsome returns as rentier income. As in the earlier period of imperialism with empire-colony relations, external markets under new imperialism continued to provide opportunities for further accumulation and expanded reproduction of wealth under finance capital. It is important to observe that it was the revival of methodological individualism as the philosophical basis of official policies which provided the ideology behind the opening up of markets and the remodelling of institutions in favour of finance. With free flow of financial assets providing opportunities for speculation, a large part of transactions in the market were no longer subject to national jurisdictions. Classic examples include the expanse of shadow banking which has overtaken, in a large number of countries, the pace of credit flows under the surveillance of the central banks. Also, one recalls the sub-prime crisis in recent times, which led the world economy to severe disruptions.

Unleashing new imperialism in contemporary capitalism rests on several tools to protect and enhance financial assets. There is a need to avoid depreciation of values of financial assets (in real estate, stock markets or even in commodity stocks) by using deflationary policies in the real economy. In addition, the predatory state facilitates accumulation by using its power to dispossess those who have lost the ability to resist, be it with land acquisition, labour flexibility or even displacement of indigenous manufacturing. Imperialism in its new form operates not only across but also within nations, with the same pattern of unequal relations in the market-led exchange between the stronger and weaker partners. Corporate-led finance continues to innovate further avenues to prosper by using new instruments, like mergers or privatisations of publicly owned property. Deregulation of markets with rising uncertainty has also generated newer opportunities to make money by hedging financial assets, as indicated by the rising values of derivative instruments which, incidentally, never generate real activities. Simultaneously, there emerge powerful alliances within corporate houses, between shareholders and managers geared to lucrative short-term investments in financial assets, as against long-term growth in the real economy. Mobile capital in the financial oligarchy today has an international presence, not only in the private sphere of financial markets but also in official multinational institutions like the IMF and the WTO. Dominance of finance replicates itself in the functioning of above institutions, as ordained by the rich and powerful nations.

As in its old form under colonialism, new imperialism continues in contemporary capitalism by using unequal power relations. The changes in the form of political arrangement, from colonial to a neo-colonial order, have replaced the regal authority by the so-called liberal order of the market. The latter is based on the ideological precepts of methodological individualism, which further strengthens the process of appropriation, using the efficient growth paradigm as justification. One can conclude that not much has changed between the days of political subordination under old imperialism and the ideology-driven advances of markets for arrogation by the powerful, in this age of new imperialism of current times.

The book

Part I of the book is devoted to addressing theoretical issues, which may appear to be rather abstract in nature but, in fact, serve to illuminate the various angles from which the notion of imperialism can be examined and evaluated. It contains five papers containing the conceptual basis of arguments in the volume.

Of the latter, Satyaki Roy's starting point is that we do not have a single theory of imperialism applicable to all times, but several which correspond to multiple historical manifestations of imperialism in the post-competitive phase of capitalism. So the author takes us through the interpretations of imperialism that comprehend global hegemony in the context of colonial domination and war (Luxemburg, Hilferding, Bukharin, Lenin) to the theories of New Imperialism in the post-colonial phase, the latter explaining how in the context of globalisation hegemony emerges as Empire.[1]

Roy sees, in the recent theoretical developments, attempts to reconcile the tension between the non-territorial forms of domination emerging in the context of globalisation and the role of the nation-state. Earlier theories of imperialism focussed on the conflicts between nations representing interests of national capitals, but in the context of globalisation and universal capitalism, nation-states are no longer the organizing unit. So the question at the core of the paper is whether global capitalism renders the notion of imperialism irrelevant. The author argues that while the notion of capitalism has still many insights to offer, theories of the Empire are less so, because those ignore the diversities of interests that still exist in the capitalist world. The characterisation of imperialism today cannot be limited to a rivalry between advanced capitalist countries nor an expression of conflict between developed and underdeveloped nations; it has to encompass the power structure and internal articulation of global capitalism. While the division of the world between core and periphery is no longer based on geography, it is still a structural element of the global economy.

John Smith's paper dwells on the present situation of the working class worldwide (workers as 'global labour'). It looks at the effects of the efforts by firms in Europe, North America and Japan to cut costs and boost profits by replacing higher-waged domestic labour with cheaper foreign labour, achieved either through emigration of production ('outsourcing') or through immigration of workers. Neoliberal globalisation is the new imperialist stage of capitalist development, where imperialism is characterised by the exploitation of 'southern' labour by northern 'capital'. The current structure of the world trade sets firms in low-wage countries competing with each other in offering goods produced by their workers to the global market. In 2010, 79 percent or 541 million of the world's industrial workers lived in 'less-developed regions'. This is up from 34 percent in 1950 to 53 percent in 1980 – compared to the 145 million industrial workers, or 21 percent of the total, which in 2010 lived in northern countries.

Smith takes issue with the dependency theories, which sought to explain the persistence of imperialist exploitation, following the dismantling of territorial empires, on the basis of the unequal exchange between developed nations and the Third World, and expressed in declining terms of trade of their raw material exports vis-à-vis manufactured imports from core nations. As held by Smith, it generates large-scale transfer of wealth from the former to the latter.

The globalisation of production, Smith argues, has transformed the typical social relation between capital and labour, also sharpening competition between workers of the north and the south. The fundamental driving force of today's imperialism is the high degree of exploitation prevalent in export-oriented industries of low-wage nations; this constitutes a third way (after extending the working day or through technological upgrading) in which capitalism managed to increase surplus value.

Prabhat Patnaik takes us from the original formulation of Lenin, who associated imperialism with monopoly capitalism as the result of the process of centralisation of capital in industry and among banks, through the different phases which have developed since then to the present form of imperialism, the latter marked by the hegemony of international finance capital, globalisation and the pursuit of neoliberal policies.

The author takes issue with those interpretations of imperialism as 'a political project undertaken by the State of the leading imperialist country, the US, for globalising its brand of capitalism through enlisting the support of other advanced capitalist States'. The argument put further in this chapter is that taking the leading country's state as the driving force behind imperialism, means attributing to the state an *autonomy*, which none of the present capitalist countries have. According to the author, today's imperialism is marked by the retreat of the state in obedience to the need of international finance. The paper conveys also the message that the only political option is a selective de-linking of the national economy from the global economy, in forms which will have to be diverse in different regions in the world. As we will notice in the following pages, this volume is, in fact, focused in the attempt to highlight the regional differences, both historically and in present times, at least in areas which include Latin America, the United States, Europe and India. The particularity of imperialism today is the topic addressed in Anjan Chakrabarti's chapter. Along with class domination-induced imperialism in the nation state (which is what it is defined as 'external' imperialism), the author introduces the notion of 'internal' imperialism as the domestically induced policy of conquest of the world by the so-called underdeveloped/developing or postcolonial nations. Neoliberal globalisation has re-shaped the international division of labour and intra-national division of labour by mechanisms of offshoring, outsourcing and subcontracting, so that globalisation has been able to fragment activities across time zones, spaces and enterprises *within* the nation states. The methodology of the analysis draws on Bukharin (1915) and his notion of policy of conquest. Thus, for Chakrabarti, today's imperialism is a policy of conquest through force and violence over the 'outside' of the capitalist world.

Subhanil Chowdhury's chapter departs from the classical notion of imperialism based on the division of the world into two clear segments, with one consisting of the advanced capitalist countries oppressing the other (third world). Imperialism, seen as a thwarting capitalist development in the developing countries, is no longer true in today's world, at least for a set of significantly large countries, such as India and China. The share of the advanced capitalist countries in world GDP has been declining consistently (from 60 percent in 1992 to 51 percent in 2011), while the share of developing and emerging economies has increased (from around 35 percent in 1992 to 49 percent in 2011). The 'third world' countries, now located within the overall circuit of global capital, have access to global finance, markets and technology, and their big bourgeoisie have become major players in the international market. The increase in the share of world GDP for developing countries is due mainly to the growth of China and India, but also to the emergence of BRICS. However, the significant factor remains that the workers in these countries are way behind those of the United States, in terms of their wages, and their lives are not on par with those of the workers in developed countries. Through the policies of reforms and globalisation, we witness a process of enrichment of the ruling classes, while the vast masses of people remain detached from these capitalist processes and remain impoverished.

Part II of the book focuses on the patterns of imperialism in Latin American countries and the United States where the varieties, as predicated in previous part, can be seen in all clarity. In the present era of finance capital domination, the United States ceased to be the global producer of manufactured goods and the major supplier of advanced technological innovations. Instead, the country has gone through a de-industrialising process, with foreign capital flows pouring into its financial system. From the 1980s onwards, the US financial system has broadened and diversified, moving its operations from credit creation to financial trading, creating shadow banks composed of mutual and pension funds, finance companies, real estate investment trusts, hedge funds and so on. The present variety of imperialism couples *financialisation* with *neomercantilism*, that is, the policies situating net exports as the driving force of economic growth and the external market, together with reduced internal markets, competitive (undervalued) exchange rates and low wages. This variety of imperialism as domination through *financialisation* and *neomercantilism* is the background of all the three chapters in Part Two, which looks at the region where it originated (the United States) and examines how it impacted on Latin America and other world regions.

Noemi Levy examines the performance of six Latin American economies: Argentina, Brazil, Colombia, Chile, Mexico and Peru; these countries were chosen because of their different sizes and distinct economic specialisations. The latter, however, did not make for a remarkable difference in the process of *financialisation* and *neomercantilism* in these economies. The author shows that the region failed to adopt a successful *neomercantilist* model: the region as a whole did not benefit from the new international division of labour, which shifted the manufacturing industry from the United States to developing economies. The liberalisation process gave unfavourable results because these countries either specialised in raw materials or assembly manufacturing exports; and in neither of the above-mentioned countries did investment spending play an important role in their export specialisation (with the exception of Mexico, because of its specialisation in high-tech manufactured goods). The conclusion is that the neoliberal model, deregulating and globalising the production finance and commercial structures, while imposing an export-led growth model, has changed the Latin American region with further concentration of the distribution of income as happened within these countries.

The imperialist nature of the relationship between the United States and Latin America is the core of Amiya Bagchi's chapter, which reviews and reveals instances and circumstances of the US domination through military and political control, with complicity of the domestic elite.

Arguments in Bagchi's chapter tallies with the next chapter by Gerald Epstein on the role of military spending in the years antecedent to the wave of terrorists' attacks in 2001. Epstein views the facet of US imperialism as the velvet glove as opposed to the iron fist, which accompanied the rise of neoliberal policies and globalisation. The paper attempts various measures to quantify the effects of military expenses on net earnings and consumption of the 60–80 percent bottom income of US population, and arrives at the conclusion that

> workers do not, on balance, gain from US imperialism, at least since 1985 . . . the situation was probably different in the 1950s, 1960s and 1970s. At that time, US workers had much more power to extract rents from U.S. capitalists. Therefore, they had much more power to get a piece of the imperialist pie. Oil prices were extremely low and very stable. Taxes were more progressive. Trade competition was not as intense.

Parts III and IV of this book relate to India. The chapters there look to the colonial and contemporary conditions and examine in which way imperialism as a category is useful to interpret its past and present.

Utsa Patnaik's chapter provides the general framework of British domination by providing data on the exceptionally large magnitude of India's export earnings which were appropriated by Britain, showing the important role the colony was made to play in providing real and financial resources for sustaining the growth and operation of the entire British Empire. Britain largely re-exported imported tropical goods to obtain imports from temperate lands, which entered as wage goods (corn) and raw materials (cotton, iron) into its domestic production and without which a large part of its domestic output and exports, especially cotton cloth, would not have been possible. The author provides calculations of regional trade balances for the late eighteenth to the mid-nineteenth century, using basic data series prepared by the economic historians of Britain.

> The conclusion is that Britain, the world capitalist leader at the centre of the global payments system was crucially dependent on the rising export earnings of India. . . . Britain ran rising deficits on current account (merchandise plus invisibles) with the Continent, North America and the regions of recent settlement, while also lending to these regions, thus running up very large balance of payments deficits. It would have been impossible for it to do so without access to the rising foreign exchange earnings of its colonies, which were entirely appropriated by Britain to settle its own deficits and to export capital.

Sunanda Sen looks at another aspect of the imperialist relationship between India and Britain in colonial times. Providing a component in the tremendous increase in world trade volume between 1850 and 1913, there comes the 'trading in indentured labour'. Faced with a shortage of labourers at the end of slavery, the planters in the British colonial islands pressured the British government to find way to supplement labour cheaply. The desperately poor and famine-stricken populations of Asia and India, in particular, became the target of an organised large-scale emigration of indentured labourers from India to plantation colonies, whose dependence on coerced labour persisted throughout most of the nineteenth century for sugar production. It can also be seen that the waves in immigrant flows were singularly linked to the fortunes of sugar plantations. A triangular network involving labour (indentured), commodities (both raw materials and processed) and finance characterised the relationship between Britain and the colonies between the late nineteenth and early twentieth centuries. Thus was the variety of imperialism, which was rooted first in slave trade and later in movements of indentured labour and 'proved a lucrative source of earning surpluses which were appropriated by the commercial and financial interests of imperial Britain'.

Indenturing of labour from India (and China) continued till the 1920s, which was followed by the commencement of a new era in labour welfare and labour control in colonial India. This is the theme of Sabyasachi Bhattacharya's chapter that looks at the interaction between the International Labour Organisation (ILO) and the welfare and labour legislation in India between 1919 and 1929. The post-First World War time saw the emerging global economic system, the growth of transnational capital and the internationalisation of the labour market, which required the devising of an international normative on labour. One of the aims was to make sure that the higher level of wages and benefits in the developed countries did not become an impediment in competing with less developed countries with a lower wage cost. The colonial state in India put on the statute books an impressive number of labour laws. Although their application was ineffective, they show the pressure coming from Britain, where lobbying was active to promoting labour legislation in India as cheapness of Indian labour was perceived as a threat.

Even prior to large scale employment of immigrant labour in the advanced countries the factor of wage cost differential and the resultant disadvantage to the countries with higher wages and labour regulations loomed large in the calculations of metropolitan industrial interests. Standardisation of labour regulations through an international legal/normative regime was one of the means of reducing this disadvantage.

The chapters in the final Part IV address the issues connected with liberalisation and deregulation in contemporary India, which are seen as part of a process producing a variety of imperialism, very different from the colonial past, but no less damaging in terms of its effects on income distribution, poverty and social inequality.

The opening piece by Sukanya Bose and Abhishek Kumar looks at the role of finance and services in the Indian economy by first examining the contrasting evidence coming from empirical studies on the role of above in fostering growth. The main hypothesis of the authors is that several service sectors, namely, banking, insurance, real estate and business services, did not feed into growth of industrial sectors and vice-versa. The linkages of these sectors with the rest of the economy have 'probably been weak such that the expansionary phase of this sector has not been accompanied by a revival of overall economic growth'. The hypothesis is put to test in the paper by using empirical exercises, whose results provide confirmation at large that the kind of finance-led growth India has witnessed in the recent period does not seem to be embedded in the real economy, thus making the finance-driven growth in the current phase of finance capitalism unsustainable.

Byasdeb Dasgupta looks at the Indian labour market and the effects of the neoliberal reforms, in particular the dismantling of the welfare state and of the system of labour protections. The author looks in particular to the features of flexible labour regime in contemporary India.

Surajit Mazumdar's closing piece brings together various threads of the analysis of imperialism presented in the previous chapters, with particular reference to India. He starts by reviewing the elements explaining remarkable growth of the country in the last three decades making India a prosperous economy relative to all the advanced countries barring the United States (in PPP terms) and pointing out how this growth has been greatly beneficial only to some segments of Indian society. As a result, the distribution of income within the sector has moved very sharply in favour of corporate profits, to the disadvantage of India's working population, most of which is in agriculture and in the informal non-agricultural sectors.

The structure of the Indian economy has been dramatically changed by globalisation and neoliberal reforms, favouring the maintenance of its relative subordination in the world economy. Rather than a story of success, present-day Indian capitalism exhibits inherent weakness, such as vulnerability of the external payments front and a great degree of dependence on volatile capital flows as well as on the US economy. This in turn circumscribes India's capacity to play an *autonomous* leading role on the global stage whether as a partner or as a rival of the advanced economies. Another instance of the changed face of todays' imperialism.

Note

1 N. Bukharin, *Imperialism and the World Economy* (1915), New Delhi: Aakar Books, 2010; Hilferding, R. Das Finanzkapital (1910), *Finance Capital: A Latest Phase of Capitalism* translated by Bottmore T., Routledge and Kegal Paul (1981); Lenin V.I, *Imperialism: The Highest Stage of Capitalism* (1917), Penguin 2010; Luxembourg, R., *Accumulation of Capital* (1913), Routledge and Kegal Paul 1951.

Part I

The conceptual basis of imperialism

1 Imperialism, the 'old' and the 'new'

Departures and continuities

Satyaki Roy[1]

Marx did talk about capitalism emerging as a world system and the role of foreign trade in hastening the falling tendency of the rate of profit. In *Capital I*, Marx refers to a process that creates a division of the world suited to centres of industries and how advanced capitalism chiefly exploits the agricultural field of production, which supplies raw materials through relative productive advantages. Marx also indicated how an international credit system helps in overcoming the barrier to circulation and sphere of exchange. These are all ingredients in brewing a theory of imperialism that Marx could not take up in detail. Setting the design for capital in *Grundrisse*, he expressed his intention to deal with 'The colonies. Emigration. . . . The international relation of production. International division of labour. International exchange. Export and import. Rate of exchange. . . . The world market and crises.'[2] The unfinished task was taken up by later Marxists during the first half of the twentieth century, which became the springboard for diverse theories of imperialism thereafter. Imperialism conceived as intrinsic to systemic necessity of realising unconsumed surplus at the core; imperialism as modes of reproducing unequal exchange; imperialism as territorial expansion for cheap resources, markets or avenues to invest where the rates of profit are relatively higher; imperialism as the political superstructure of monopoly capital and expanding finance, and also as an outcome of a terminal phase of capitalist cycle; and so on. Hence, we do not have a single theory of imperialism which is applicable for all times in the post-competitive phase of capitalism, nor do we find an abstract rationale to favour one theory over the other. In fact, we can have an abstract theory of capitalist accumulation that Marx had offered, but the abstract theory of accumulation, expectedly, does not deal with irregularities, frictions and concrete domains of power which have always been intertwined with and overdetermined by the realities of accumulation. It is the unevenness of capitalism that creates the pretext of power-driving accumulation in a specific space and time. As a result, we come across multiple historical manifestations of imperialism which were explored and debated by scholars and activists.

The focus of this essay is to present a critical review of the major Marxian theories of imperialism by tracing out the debates and examining the development of their basic tenets. Imperialism as a category in Marxian literature is theorised as a tendency specific to the post-competitive phase of capitalism. But the modes of hegemony embedded in the complex articulation of accumulation and power do change over time. Therefore, characterisation of imperialism in different points of time focussed on concrete questions related to the specificities of the monopoly stage and its larger impact on the dynamics of capitalism, how it motivated expansion and resulted in stagnation at different points of time, how conflict between advanced capitalist countries eventually led to a worldwide conflict between developed and developing nations, and finally, in the post-colonial phase, how global hegemony entails a different architecture of power internalised through the nation state.

At the outset, I must mention that my reading of imperialism in this essay is thematic. I trace the continuities and departures that evolved in the realm of theory. Many of the ideas that emerged in a particular historical context might have seemed to be submerged in a new debate, but they again surfaced in new incarnations later. In this essay, I intend to comprehend those traits and trajectory of ideas and contextualise them in relation to the relevant debates. Two broad sets of theories are taken on board – first, theories of imperialism that comprehended global hegemony in the context of colonial domination and war, often categorised as 'old' and emerged mostly in the inter-war years and immediately after that. Luxemburg, Hilferding and Bukharin-Lenin are important markers in this tradition. The second set of theories, termed 'new', talk about imperialism in the post-colonial phase and see how, in the context of globalisation, the hegemony emerges as empire. Harvey, Arrighi and Wood are important thinkers in this phase. This comes against the backdrop of more recent attempts by some Marxists to render imperialism in the post-globalisation phase as defunct.[3] Other than excavating the rich repertoire of ideas that emerged in the debates on imperialism, my critical review additionally has the underlying purpose of highlighting and defending the notion of imperialism which cannot be reduced to either neoliberalism, globalisation or capitalism, even as in the contemporary these combine into a historical conjecture.

Realisation crisis and imperialism

I begin with Luxemberg's discussion on accumulation and the theory of imperialism that follows, because it is unique in conceiving imperialism as intrinsic to capitalism and not as related to a particular stage of capitalism, which had been the predominant notion within Marxian discourse during pre- and post-war phase of inter-capitalist rivalry. This idea of theorising imperialism as a systemic necessity has been generic in Marxian literature, but in case of Luxemberg, it was argued more as a logical conclusion rather than related to concrete moments of history. I also, however, argue that Luxemburg's theory of imperialism, even though taking off from a critique of Marx's reproduction scheme, is essentially rooted in particular historical conjectures and debates related to praxis.

Capitalism as a class-divided society is a demand constraint system because workers are paid less than the value of their product, and capitalists consume proportionately less than the workers of what they receive as surplus. This leads to a persistent gap in realising the produced value. Luxemburg argued that Marx's reproduction scheme could not take care of this realisation problem; hence, the idea of conceiving capitalism as a closed system is unrealistic. In fact, Luxemberg's idea of imperialism is derived from a systemic necessity, as capitalism always requires a non-capitalist periphery to realise the unconsumed surplus at the core.[4] And the intrusion has to be by use of force, because she assumed pre-capitalist 'outside' as a natural self-contained economy that has little surplus to offer on exchange. The drive to annihilate non-capital is also to source cheap raw materials and labour for the production at the core. Luxemburg did not see either the possibility of consuming the surplus produced at the core in the form of investment in the means of production or being absorbed due to proportional increase of both consumption and investment at the core. In other words, her analyses of extended reproduction and the necessity of inside/outside dialectics of capitalism is derived from the argument of underconsumption or underinvestment and has nothing to do with the specific phase of capitalism. In spite of the fact that there would always be a possibility of underinvestment in capitalism, nevertheless, Luxemburg built her theory on the impossibility of adequate investment opportunity at the centre and the need to intrude upon the non-capitalist periphery. Luxemburg defined imperialism as

> the political expression of the accumulation of capital in its competitive struggle for what remains still open of the non-capitalist

environment . . . [which] grows in lawlessness and violence, both in aggression against the non-capitalist world and in ever more serious conflicts among the competing capitalist countries.[5]

It essentially rests upon a theory of capitalist crisis that becomes imminent as the pre-capitalist periphery shrinks and the rivalry between capitalist powers intensifies further.

The critique of Luxemburg's theory of crisis primarily rests on the fact that while capitalism as a system is always fraught with tendencies of deficient demand, such tendencies could not be taken as inevitable. And the requirements of individual capital cannot be confused with the needs of capitalist system as a whole. Joan Robinson wrote in the introduction of *Accumulation* that Luxemburg's primary emphasis was not on the possibility that capitalists might not choose to buy each other's products and thus sustain demand, but on the absurdity (in her eyes) of supposing that they could *ever* do so.[6] Otto Bauer's critique, first of all, showed using reproduction schemes that it is incorrect to argue that realisation in expanded reproduction is impossible with rising organic composition of capital, and also, there is no point assuming that accumulation of money capital by individual capitalist should take place simultaneously. Bauer, however, acknowledged the fact that accumulation in a closed capitalist system, although possible, reaches a limit and that limit can be extended by imperialism. He contested Luxemburg's position that capitalism would not be able to reproduce itself when all the non-capitalist realm is being internalised. Rather he argued that

> Capitalism will break down, not when the last peasant and the last *petit bourgeois* on the entire earth are converted into wage labourers, so that no extra market is open to capitalism. It will be brought down much sooner, by the growing indignation of the working class, constantly increased, schooled, united and organised by the mechanism of the capitalist production process itself.[7]

Tugan-Baranovski, while confronting Russian populism, also made a similar theoretical point, that capitalism is not a system that is meant to satisfy human needs, but it is driven by the quest for profit. The extreme imagery of accumulation by producing machines for the production of machines while consumption being reduced was made precisely to argue that capitalism is essentially an inhuman system and the proposition to replace it by a new one could not be derived from some immutable objective laws that inevitably give rise to a breakdown of the system.

Luxemburg's theory of imperialism as a structural inevitability was primarily driven by a political need of countering Kautsky's revisionist position. Kautsky initially held that imperialism emerges as a result of capitalists' compulsive quest for non-capitalist markets. He also distinguished 'work colonies' that were European settlements and 'exploitation colonies' where plunder of the native population was the rule.[8] The former was important in absorbing exports from the imperial countries, while the latter could be conceived as the sphere of primitive accumulation of capital. This was quite similar to what Luxemburg also pointed out, but the implications drawn were contrary to each other. Kautsky assumed that capitalists of the world would unite rather than fight with each other, thereby giving rise to ultra-imperialism, which would be the regime of 'common exploitation of the world by internationally united finance'.[9] Luxemburg's theory of imperialism was motivated to counter this revisionist position and to argue the imminent need of overthrowing capitalism in the midst of imperialist war. Hence, Luxemburg's characterisation of imperialism, although emerging from an abstract critique of reproduction scheme, it was overdetermined by concrete moments of history and praxis.

Monopoly stage of capitalism

Theories of imperialism within the Marxist tradition primarily evolved during the pre-war phase and later immediately after the interwar years. The challenge was to explain the conflict and war between advanced capitalist countries in terms of class analysis. Imperialism was generally identified with the monopoly stage of capitalism and the rise of finance capital. However, theories of monopoly capitalism that evolved in different points of history address different challenges in the context of the concrete. Hobson and Hilferding explain the monopoly stage as a problem of expanding capitalism giving rise to conflicts and war between advanced capitalist countries. The later characterisation of monopoly capitalism that follows from Baran and Sweezy proposes the monopoly stage as a stage of capitalist stagnation. It actually opened up a new focus in understanding global hegemony and that of a conflict between advanced and underdeveloped nations.

J.A. Hobson,[10] who was a liberal, developed a theory of imperialism based on underconsumption or excess savings occurring in the stage of monopoly that drives capital beyond the national boundaries to seek for places having potentials for higher returns. He analysed the monopoly stage of capitalism giving rise to excess savings relative to investment, the latter being constrained by the level of growth which in turn is determined by the supply of labour and fixed proportions of production. As a result of excess savings, interest rates would fall at home and the decline, when compared to higher profitability or lesser risks of investment in other countries, would drive the outflow of capital. This external move for higher profitability of investment is endemic at the monopoly stage, because excess savings pull down the returns at home. Similar to other underconsumptionist theories, Hobson's argument pays little attention to why the possibilities of investments and capital intensive trajectories would not be able to pull the economy back from chronic lack of demand. Expanding further, Hilferding was the first Marxist to provide a comprehensive analyses of imperialism.[11] Hilferding's observation and theorising of finance capital were crucial to the understanding of imperialism. The rise of finance capital as a fusion of industrial and financial capital and their mutual reinforcing nexus epitomised in the new avatar MNCs became one of defining features of the monopoly stage of capitalism. Hilferding interprets how credit helps in keeping 'idle money' at the minimum, and since bank credit has significant advantages over merchant capital, banks increasingly emerged to be prominent suppliers of credit to industry. The nature of credit also changes from a mere source of short-term finance which Hilferding called 'circulating credit' to the provision of funds for long-term investment projects as 'investment credit'. Consequently, banks took growing interest in firm's long-run prospects rather than having limited concern about immediate solvency. This change, however, manifests through an important shift in the distribution of aggregate surplus value. The share of interest increases at the expense of entrepreneurial profit, reflecting the growing power of the banks in the economy as a whole. Hilferding underlined the concentration and centralization taking place in banks that take hold of the idle money and insisted upon cartelisation of industries to avoid defaulter. The rise of joint stock companies and their mutual interlocking creates possibilities of a higher concentration of capital. Together with bank capital, it builds a kingdom of influence with the state as its protector. Hilferding, therefore, argued that the function of protectionism had been completely transformed. 'From being a means of defence against the conquest of the domestic market by foreign industries it has become a means for the conquest of foreign markets by domestic industry'.[12] Therefore, rivalry between advanced countries increases together with oppression of the pre-capitalist nations. Militarism, oppression and racism becomes the necessary ingredients of the ideology of imperialism. Hilferding describes the oligarchic rule: 'Finance capital, in its maturity, is the highest stage of the concentration of economic and political power in the hands of the capitalist oligarchy. It is the climax of the dictatorship of the magnates of capital.'[13]

There are two major strands of inter-related arguments that characterise monopoly stage of capitalism in the post-Second World War phase. They emerge from Baran and Baran and Sweezy:[14] one is primarily close to Hobson's underconsumptionist position that monopoly capital is not likely to generate enough investment to sustain demand, and the second is that monopolies, unlike in the phase of competitive capitalism, hold back growth of output and advancement of technology in order to retain higher prices and protect technology rents. Sweezy's position was that decline in consumption share in output demands growth of investment at a higher pace than that of consumption, but this structural necessity remains unfulfilled because of the limits set by the technological relation of fixed proportions between investment and new output of consumer goods. This discrepancy results in gap between actual investment and potential investment thereby giving rise to a chronic shortage of demand unless being taken over by external stimuli like state investment, waste production and so on. Baran's thesis emphasized the near impossibility of diffusion of capitalism in the underdeveloped countries. Underdevelopment can be explained with reference to peasant agriculture, merchant capital and the presence of monopoly capital. It is a typical situation characterised by little investable resources, as output is low or drained away or invested in unproductive spheres; even if not diverted, there is not much incentive to invest because of the lack of demand. Low available surplus for investment, together with a low incentive to invest, gives rise to low-growth equilibrium. Therefore, in Baran and Sweezy, the realm of conflict shifted from rivalry between advanced nations to a polarity between developed and underdeveloped countries.

Imperialism and worldview of liberation

Theories of imperialism in the Marxian tradition had never been delinked from the world of revolutionary praxis. In fact, the most influential contributions that synthesised theories into a radical worldview emerged from the immediate need to offer the working class a guide to action. Bukharin and Lenin, as leaders of the Bolshevik party, the only party that did not join the ruling classes when the world war broke out, proposed an understanding of the world economy from the vantage point of praxis. It was Trotsky who argued that the growth of productive forces in capitalism could no longer be limited to the confines of the nation state any more. Capitalism is increasingly emerging as a global system managed by a network of nation states. He made the point also that backward countries like Russia would have a very different past and future compared to advanced countries, but because of this uneven and combined development, revolutionary changes of the democratic stage had to be telescoped to a socialist revolution.[15] However, Trotsky never explained imperialism, except viewing it as conflicts between capitalist powers for markets. But these tendencies of internationalisation to be a contradictory phenomenon were further explicated by Bukharin. He argued that such tendencies are accompanied by a contradictory phenomenon that explains the rise of imperialism.[16] The two conflicting tendencies were, on the one hand, capitalism emerging as a world system and, on the other hand, a growing national consolidation where monopoly capital got mingled with the nation state giving rise to state monopoly capitalism. Bukharin identifies the rise of this 'new Leviathan', a quasi-totalitarian state capitalism that leaves no room for social transformation by any parliamentary means. The metamorphosis of state-monopoly capitalism evolves with a new qualitative unity of the national ruling class that not only shares the gains of monopoly power within themselves but also bribes the working class and facilitates labour aristocracy. Bukharin argued, similar in line with Luxemburg and Trotsky, who stated that the stage of imperialism cannot be transformed as the revisionists suggested and the working class not only has to seize control over the state power but smash all its apparatus by a dictatorship that is committed to building a new society.

The small pamphlet on imperialism written by Lenin is considered to be one of the most influential perspectives within Marxists and even to some non-Marxists, since it provides critical insights in the understanding of relations and conflicts between nations.[17] The analyses of imperialism as a specific stage of capitalism was not something novel in Lenin. Rather, he put together many of the arguments made by Hobson and Hilferding in defining the specific features of the monopoly stage of capitalism and the rise of finance capital. But what made this small pamphlet far more significant than many other treatises was envisioning a world order that provides a framework to understand rivalries between capitalist nations in the global plane and also the emerging perspectives for resistance and revolutions. It is a comprehensive analyses of capitalist imperialism that laid down the foundations of radical interventions in the age of monopoly capitalism.[18] Lenin's imperialism is also a radical departure from the sterile evolutionary perspectives of the Second International. The Marxism of Second International was primarily a doctrine that relegates politics into the backseat and foregrounds 'scienticism' in the name of 'necessary laws of capitalist development'. Lenin's point of departure was that he could think of possibilities of revolution in countries where the contradiction between productive forces and production relations has not reached its highest point. And this he could do precisely because of perceiving the imperialist chain in the global system of capitalist relations and through that opening, the possibility of identifying and breaking the weakest links. The striking feature of Lenin's pamphlet is this that it reinstates the importance of politics in driving radical changes. Instead of human agencies being conceived as passive observers of immutable laws, Lenin opened up the possibility of radical interventions that could mutually constitute the economic contradictions into a radical rupture.

Lenin defined imperialism as

> capitalism at that stage of development at which the dominance of monopolies and finance capital is established; in which the export of capital has acquired pronounced importance; in which the division of the world among the international trusts has begun, in which the division of all territories of the globe among the biggest capitalist powers has been completed.[19]

Imperialism and colonialism were also there in pre-capitalist societies but the present capitalist imperialism is a stage beyond competition and also marked by the change from the dominance of capital in general to the dominance of finance. It is primarily a result of concentration and centralisation of capital in industry and banking, and finance capital is 'capital controlled by banks and employed by industrialists'.[20] Once the division of the economic territory within the nation is complete, monopoly capital tries to increase its terrain of influence by exporting capital to other countries. In sum, Lenin's characterisation of imperialism encapsulates the emerging features of the new phase of capitalism that, although they tried to avoid competition and anarchy through centralised integration and planning, ultimately gave rise to fierce competition between few. And this is the backdrop of conflicts between nations that cannot be resolved, leaving the system unchanged. The other important dimension of imperialism according to Lenin is that capitalism at this stage is characterised as decaying, parasitic or moribund. And this conclusion by Lenin does not reference growth rates or possibilities of chronic depression looming large, as in Baran and Sweezy later, but in a far deeper sense. It is decaying because the contradiction between socialisation of production and private appropriation reaches an acute level in this stage. The separation between money capital and productive capital, between rentiers and entrepreneurs is far more complete in this stage compared to the competitive phase. This gives rise to rentier or usurer states who grow on the basis of rents earned from the debtor countries. Lenin used the term moribund not because growth was slowing in advanced capitalist countries, but rather, he was reflecting on the nature of growth which is increasingly becoming dependent on clipping coupons.

Theories of imperialism in Marxist lineage are primarily linked to a specific phase of capitalism. Lenin's imperialism is conjectural where the changing nature of economic relations and conflicting class relations give rise to a complex process of interrelations between nations. This perspective, for the first time, shifts the focus from conflicts between advanced countries to the struggle for liberation in the underdeveloped world. World politics and class conflicts were, for the first time, viewed as an integrated whole in a theory of imperialism and anti-imperialism. The politics of changing societies were integrated with the politics of liberation struggle against imperialist countries of the world. And the prominence of politics gave a new perspective to revolutionary praxis that completely demolished the evolutionary perspective of waiting for the ripe moment of growth of productive forces.

Cyclical crisis and post-colonial imperialism

The relatively recent strand of literature that talks about 'new' imperialism is primarily motivated to reconcile the tension between the non-territorial forms of domination emerging in the context of globalisation and the role of nation state. Despite the decline of the colonies, hegemonic power could continue to maintain an inter-state network of power. There has been a rise of the transnational corporations reorganising capital–labour relations at a global plane, thereby giving rise to new dynamics of the capital–state relationship in the absence of colonial expansion. It views imperialism as historically determined but, at the same time, not being identified as a definite stage of monopoly capitalism.

Harvey's account of imperialism reflects a double dialectics: (a) between the territorial logics and capitalist logics of power; and (b) between inner and outer relation of capitalist state.[21] The argument is that the logic of capital, which is driven by the immediate concerns of profit of one or more capitalists, can flow seamlessly across regions. The territorial logic of power that is driven by the collective concerns of the capitalist class, represented by the state, however, does not allow an unbounded expansion. Therefore, the logic of capital dialectically confronts the territorial logic of power, given that both these logics primarily emanate to serve the profit motive of capital. Harvey argues that capitalism addresses the problem of over-accumulation through the spatio-temporal fix, that is, either by deploying surplus in creating new industries or markets or by creating infrastructure as a temporal fix to employ unused capital for future returns. And this intrinsic need to compress time and space in order to reduce the turnover time of capital give rise to the expansionist tendencies of capital. The exercise of power works through an unstable mix of domination, consent and emulation. The other dimension of the dialectics relates to the changing mix of accumulation by expanded reproduction and accumulation through dispossession. Harvey argues that the liberal assumptions of free market that Marx took as a premise of his critique limit 'primitive accumulation' as a formative phase in the emergence of capitalism. Once it is established, it is the silent economic rules of expanded reproduction that take over. Harvey, somewhat close to Luxemburg, talks about a non-temporal version of accumulation through dispossession, which is a continuous process within capitalism once we relax the liberal assumptions of defined contract. And at the present moment, capitalism is more dependent on accumulation through dispossession, which includes denial of various ownerships of properties, rights and entitlements that existed in the realm of non-capital. Predominance of accumulation through dispossession over accumulation through expanded reproduction characterises imperialism of the present phase and also determines the location of resistance that increasingly shifted from the workplace to those related to community and livelihood.

The conflict between the logic of capital and that of territorial power gives rise to larger states that, in successive phases, internalises elements for which the earlier forms of state had to depend on external forces. Arrighi, in a longer time frame, discusses the genesis of state in relation to the rise and fall of systemic cycles of accumulation.[22] Arrighi distinguished colonialism/expansionism from imperialism as the former being related to territorial expansion while the latter is related to the political expansion of the nation state and not the nation. The domination can take both formal and informal forms, and finance works more through indirect ways of free trade of goods, services and people. Arrighi views capitalism as a strategic alliance between the finance capital and the state and not as a class process. Following Braudel he argued that finance capital is nothing new in the twentieth century, rather it attains dominance signalling the maturation of every systemic cycle since the Genoese–Iberian cycle, stretching from the fifteenth through the early sixteenth century. Capital assumes a higher stage of abstraction in finance which is not qualified by concrete conditions of production. It is far more flexible and mobile and aspires for freedom from territorial barriers. Pollin, however, argues that interpreting circuit of capital in terms of distinct phases of long historical periods undermines the entirety of the process of production and financialisation in the capitalist production relations.[23] A similar critique of Arrighi comes from Robinson, who argues that the framework identifies capital only as finance, and the states that control finance are the only determinants of the dynamics of the system.[24] It does not see capitalism as a production relation rather a state–capital relationship; hence, an inter-state system continues to be the organising principle of capitalism according to this framework. To both Harvey and Arrighi, imperialism refers to a specific phase in capitalist accumulation, as a response to a crisis emerging in the form of over-accumulation; it presupposes a network of credit in order to deploy funds in more profitable ventures and a freedom aided by a centre of power that can be captured by a system of nation states.

Empire with or without imperialism

In the context of the post-colonial world, the debate on imperialism in Marxist tradition was primarily focused on two central themes: (a) the impossibility of diffusion of capitalism in underdeveloped countries, theorised in the context of monopoly stage which seems no longer tenable; in fact, the imperatives of capital are far more universal, and in spite of the fact that asymmetries exist, hegemony cannot be captured by conflicts mapped between advanced and underdeveloped parts of the world; and (b) the role of nation states in organising capitalism; this is important because earlier theories of imperialism were primarily predicated on conflicts between nations representing interests of national capitals and if in the context of universal capitalism, nation states seize to be the organising unit, then we have global capitalism or an empire with the notion of imperialism having little or no relevance. We engage with the debate based on works of Hardt and Negri's *Empire* that virtually denounces the existence of imperialism, Ellen Meksins Wood's *Empire of Capital* that reinstates the primacy of nation states in the context of universal capitalism and also identifies hegemony of US imperialism in a hierarchical network of nation states, and finally, William Robinson's theory of transnational capitalist class and the rise of global capitalism that also characterises present-day world as capital organised by an emergent capitalist class that hardly has any roots in nation states.

Hardt and Negri, in their famous work *Empire*, argued that sovereignty of the nation state was the defining principle of imperialism that European powers relied upon while exercising hegemony over foreign land.[25] Therefore, according to Hardt and Negri, imperialism was really an extension of the sovereignty of the European nation states beyond their own boundaries. They further argue that this sovereignty of the nation state is being replaced by a different type of sovereignty which is de-centred and de-territorialised, constructed by a complex combination of national and supranational entities that work on the basis of a common logic of rule giving rise to Empire. The crux of the argument is that imperialism is dead and is replaced by the Empire:

> Our basic hypothesis, however, that a new imperial form of sovereignty has emerged, contradicts both these views. The United States does not, and indeed no nation state can today, form the centre of an imperialist project. Imperialism is over. No nation will be world leader in the way modern European nations were.[26]

Their account of Empire is a Foucauldian image where flows of people, information and wealth creates an all-embracing power that could hardly be monitored from a centre. Therefore, conventional dichotomies between core and periphery or the ruling class, and the proletariat, are increasingly being replaced by far more intricate patterns of inequality.

The problem of this theorisation of de-territorialised capital lies precisely on the homogenisation of classes to an abstract level. Hardt and Negri talk about a subjectivist theory where capital in abstract confronts the 'multitude', which is also an amorphous category representing the exploited. The process of class rule requires no mediation by the nation state, and since there is no 'outside' to capitalism, there is no weakest link or vulnerable extremities potent with possibilities of rupture. Rather the 'empire' can be attacked at any point by the multitude. The point which is relevant to the present discussion is that Empire conceives a seamless collaboration of capital and ignores the contradiction between capitals that might not always be linked to national connotations. In other words, both the categories of 'empire' and 'multitude' are ambiguous, with little empirical relevance, and fail to capture the complex negotiations that take place within the capitalist class and also within various layers of the proletariat. Ignoring the contradictions within the capitalist forces implies a denial of the basic realities of uneven capitalist development and rivalries between capitals. The fact that heterogeneities and conflicts between capital exists, which the theory of empire essentially denies, does not however resolve the question whether conflicts are mediated by nation states or not. The conflict of the logic of capital and the logic of territory as mentioned in Harvey's analyses of new imperialism rests on the appreciation of the relevance of nation state and inter-state relations which still remains to be the locus of conflict between politics and economics of capital.

Ellen Meiksins Wood conceives a different empire of capital.[27] The argument being that capitalism is the system which, unlike pre-capitalist societies, separates the exploitative power from the coercive power of the state. In other words, the economic power in capitalism does not require a monopoly over political rights and the internationalisation of capitalist imperatives make the subordinate states subservient to global capital without any explicit political control. Wood further argues that earlier theories of imperialism were, at the core, adherents of Luxemburg's key proposition that imperialism emerges out of conflict between advanced capitalist countries to get a hold of pre-capitalist peripheries, and they hardly recognised the fact of diffusion of capitalism giving rise to universal capitalist order. In fact, long ago, Bill Warren, in his controversial book *Imperialism Pioneer of Capitalism*, rejected the Leninist thesis that the monopoly stage is a degenerate stage and argued that capitalism in the imperialist stage continues to play its progressive role in advancing productive forces not only in the developed countries but also in developing countries by relative diffusion.[28] The post-war notions of underdevelopment and neocolonialism informed by dependency arguments follow from the same idea of degenerate capitalism that Lenin propounded. He argued that the degenerate thesis is fundamentally flawed, and the diffusion of development took place in colonial countries in two ways: industrialisation and rapid transformation of agriculture. Warren argued that imperialist moves were not at all external responses to internal stagnation, as had been the dominant formulation of the monopoly stage. Instead, they are the outcomes of Schumpeterian atavism, an essentially political phenomenon not always driven by economic goals. This was highly contested, given the realities of underdeveloped countries, and Warren only tried to cover up the facts of decline by relying on uneven development of capitalism. But in the post-colonial context, Wood's thesis of diffusion of capitalism and rise of a universal imperative is acceptable, given the fact of expansion of capitalist relations on erstwhile peripheries. Such diffusion led to a new hierarchy of nation states dominated by a regime of infinite war by US imperialism. This war is no longer targeted towards territorial domination but an unending control over extra-economic application of force.

Contesting this view, Robinson argues that the relevance of nation state is challenged because of the rise of a transnational capitalist class that has no baggage of national interests.[29] The transnational capital is grounded on global markets and global circuits of capital. This proposition does not, however, negate the importance of nation states but argues that inter-state system seizes to be the organising principle of capitalist expansion. In other words, in this analysis, homogeneity of capital is not invoked as in the theory of empire, but it rejects the role of nation state and also imperialism because of the rise of a ruling transnational class represented by a group of nations. The crux of the argument is that the transnationally oriented faction of the capitalist class has attained hegemony over the national factions of capitalists in most countries in the world. Robinson further argues that the interventions, as well as invasions, on foreign land are in most of the cases led by the United States, but that is precisely not to serve the US capital alone but to maintain the hegemony of global capital. The US state, in this case, acts as a surrogate global state, a point of condensation for pressures from dominant groups to resolve the problems of global capitalism. There is no doubt of the fact that something of the sort of transnational capitalist interest is cropping up, and if we speculate a complete subordination of capitals with regional and national interests to such global capital, then there would be no reason to stick to the term imperialism which is essentially pegged on the reality of uneven development and rivalry between capitals.

There has always been a returning back of the theory of 'ultra-imperialism' first propounded by Kautsky in the early twentieth century during the first wave of globalisation. The crux of the argument is derived from the increasing concentration and centralisation of capital at a global scale giving rise to a cartelisation of foreign policy, and consequently, eternal peace. Lenin, of course, did not deny the logical tendency towards a single world trust but refuted such a possibility foreseeing the growing class struggle and conflicts between nations and capitals.

Theory of empire bears resemblance to such ideas that ignore the diversities of interests that still exist and would continue to exist in the capitalist world. Empire recognises the conflict between capital and multitude and talks about the sovereignty of the omnipresent abstract capital. In other words, the theory of empire wishes away conflicts between capitals, thereby closely resembling with the notion of ultra-imperialism. Lenin was categorical in appreciating the ebbs and flows of contradictions and the form they take in periods of truce and war: 'inter-imperialist' or 'ultra-imperialist' alliances, no matter what form they may assume, whether of one imperialist coalition against another, or of a general alliance embracing *all* the imperialist powers, are *inevitably nothing* more than a 'truce' in periods between wars. In the context of the current conjuncture, the apparent peace is analysed by Patnaik in the introduction to Lenin's *Imperialism*.[30] Patnaik argues that of course the nature of the finance capital now is very different from the one Lenin talked about. It is far less rooted in national interests and cannot be qualified by national identities. Furthermore, the finance capital today is not just a merger of bank and industrial capital as Lenin talked about but attains a far larger autonomy than earlier times. Patnaik notes that finance capital, which is in dominance today operates in the context of an apparent peace, a situation not ridden by inter-imperialist rivalry and this is quite different from Lenin's time. But this unprecedented unity, he argued, is only a temporary truce between blocks of global capital that are aided by nation states.

Notwithstanding the fact that global finance in dominance facilitates a smooth and seamless mobility, it will be a mistake to ignore the remarkable changes in the production structure as well. The division of labour in the production process has undergone a change since 1940s. The entire production process of a specific industry is laid down across the globe depending on the distribution of endowments in regions. In other words, regions are no longer producers of the entire product, but they perform specific tasks in the entire production process.[31] And, since the value addition takes place through the entire chain, there are conflicts between nations and producers to get a larger share of the accumulated profit. However, it becomes imperative to keep these conflicts in check such that the entire chain does not get disturbed.

Departures and continuities

The notion of imperialism has to be problematised in the context of new realities. Its characterisation today could neither be limited to a rivalry between advanced capitalist countries nor an expression of conflict between developed and underdeveloped nations. The current phase of globalisation entails the expansion of capitalist relations to the fullest, which contradicts the argument of impossibility of diffusion of capitalism in the monopoly phase. Capitalist relations, in fact, invade every corner of the globe and all spheres of life. This invasion works through a mix of coercion and consent, articulated through economic and non-economic means. It also altered the earlier mapping of power and works through institutions that internalise the imperatives of global capital. The challenge is to comprehend the concrete of this articulation of power and how in the current context with the reorganisation of capital–labour relations and modes of accumulation, institutions change their role or evolve into new forms that work as nodes of global hegemony. The rest of this concluding section identifies the departures and continuities in theories of imperialism that can provide some pointers for further analyses.

The division of the world defined by their role in the process of accumulation and appropriation had been a key element in characterising particular phases of capitalist imperialism. Ernest Mandel characterised the point of departure by the changes that took place in the distribution of direct production of surplus and the primitive accumulation.[32] In the epoch of free concurrence capitalism, the production of surplus value was more or less confined to Western Europe and North America, while the act of primitive accumulation continued in several other parts of the world. The division of the world according to the nature of accumulation and distinctive dominance of the production of surplus value, which integrated pre-capitalist periphery into the needs of expanded reproduction of metropolitan capital is Mandel's world of imperialism. Harvey, on the contrary, talks of new imperialism in which accumulation through dispossession is not linked to periphery only but becomes the dominant mode of accumulation in the current phase of imperialism. Capital is increasingly de-territorialised and there seems to be a delinking between social and geographical polarisation. In other words, the conceptual divisions of the world between core and periphery or North–South or First, Second and Third Worlds are increasingly becoming a social relationship rather than signifying geopolitical divisions. In terms of production, appropriation and distribution of surplus value, this implies a sea change. Earlier there was clear division of countries who were producing the surplus value and those appropriating the produced surplus. And the appropriators used to dictate the process of production in the producing countries. This conceptual mapping of nation states in relation to the production and distribution of surplus value no longer remains valid. Instead, the production and appropriation of surplus value is far more distributed across the globe, and the appropriators and receivers of subsumed class payments do not show any geographic or racial pattern. There is no doubt of the fact that the magnitude of surplus value appropriated is far more concentrated within the advanced countries even today, but that might be because of historical reasons and not because of exercising control flowing from the power of particular nation states.

Export of capital has been identified as one of the defining features of imperialism. Lenin remarked 'Typical of the old capitalism, when free competition held undivided sway was the export of goods. Typical of the latest stage of capitalism when monopolies rule, is the export of capital.'[33] Warren argued that the empirical facts Lenin used in his *Imperialism*, primarily derived from Hobson's and Hilferding's work, were not a correct representation of the global trends of investment flows. Export of capital by advanced capitalist countries was consistently happening long before they reached the monopoly phase in terms of industrial structure. In fact, Britain and France started exporting capital as early as 1820s and 1850s, respectively, and Kuznets also showed that the rate of growth of cumulated foreign capital between the 1820s and 1870s was higher than that between 1870s and the First World War. Export of capital was always a significant feature of capitalism, and there was no sharp rise during late nineteenth century, and it was not a feature of decaying capitalism. During 1874–1914, Warren argues that foreign trade was far more important than foreign investment flows and the challengers of the hegemonic power at that time, United States, Japan, Russia, Italy, Portugal and Spain, were net importers of capital, hence, export of capital during that time was not a distinctive feature of capitalism. Furthermore, the division of world between imperialist powers was complete by the end of the nineteenth century, but the rise of monopoly and control over economies in advanced countries only came in the first decade of the twentieth century. In a more contemporary context, Magdoff argues that export of capital accounts for a miniscule share of the US investment, and such figures do not capture the actual control exercised by the amount of capital mobilised or leveraged by the United States across the globe.[34] Further, the export of capital cannot be explained by any intrinsic necessity derived to counter the falling tendency of the rate of profit, the need to invest surplus capital or the incessant drive to get hold of cheap labour. The decision to invest abroad is driven by comparing profitability at the margin and not determined by any falling or rising trends of profit.

The most contentious terrain in the discourse of imperialism is the role of the nation state. There is no doubt that theories of imperialism that evolved in the twentieth century were largely predicated on the idea of rivalry between nation states. In fact, the role of the nation state has undergone remarkable changes. It is now less an aid to protect the interest of the domestic capital against foreign intruders and more of an apparatus to internalise the interests of the global capital. This is precisely the reason why the present world cannot be characterised by conflicts between nations and competition between nation states. Capitalism is no longer organised on national lines; the world is not a mere collection of nation states articulated through trade and markets; and it is far more interpenetrative: inter-firm trades largely outweigh inter-country trades, and expansion of capitalism is primarily dependent on the fragmentation of existing political institutions based on national territories. There is no doubt, of course, that capitalism and imperialism cannot do away with extra-economic forces; hence, they cannot dispense with the state, but this state as institutionalised class relations need not be territorial, as it historically evolved earlier. Rather the diffusion of capitalist relations are articulated by supranational institutions that emerge as the new regulators of global circuits of capital.

The emergence of a transnational capitalist class that has no national commitments is increasingly putting their weights on nation states, and this has important implications in the context of class struggle. The beneficiaries of financialisation across the world become more tuned with the interests of global finance, bringing the oppressors at various levels much closer to each other. The oppressed classes, on the other hand, in various nation states become much more similar than ever before. In this context, the contradiction is precisely that the legitimacy of the nation state demands a commitment to the people of a specific country and, at the same time, the state has to play its role in protecting the interest of the global capital. Leo Panitch puts it succinctly: 'The state now takes the form of a *mediator* between the externally established policy priorities and the internal social forces to which it also still remains accountable.'[35] Therefore, the struggle against imperialism seems to have far greater correlation with the struggle against the domestic ruling class.

Conflicts of capital are more fundamental than conflicts between nations in the Leninist interpretation of imperialism. The debate on the possibility of ultra-imperialism or of 'empire' in its modern incarnation is primarily a negation of the fact of uneven development in capitalism. But once we appreciate the fact of differences of interest within capital, the question of mediation comes into being. The nation states that were mediating on behalf of the national capital had increasingly internalised the rules of global capital in the garb of neo-liberalism. But it is yet to see how various other spatial identities apart from nations would unfold at supranational levels representing regional interests of capital. Therefore, even if we assume a nascent global capitalist class in the making, it would be moving far from reality to think of capital being completely freed from regional lineage.

Moreover, to assume that all other capitalist interests are subsumed to the interest of the global capitalist class would be erroneous. There is no doubt of the fact that oppressors of the world at various levels are far more integrated and interdependent than ever before but the complex network of hierarchies that characterise the current phase of capitalist domination is always potent with fissures and ruptures that might not have a national character as it used to be earlier. Internationalisation of exploitation works through what Mezaros mentioned as the diminishing differential rate of exploitation.[36] The conflicts of the world are more apparent today in terms of classes than between nations and distributional tensions are far more uniform across the globe. It is perhaps the age of new imperialism that is caught between the nation and the globe sometime using the proxy of an elite club of nations but actually striving for an appropriate mediator often invoking a supranational discourse relating to development and liberty that articulates the new rhetoric of imperialism.

Notes

1 The author would like to thank Sunanda Sen, Anjan Chakrabarti, Amiya Kumar Bagchi and Chirashree Dasgupta for their valuable comments and suggestions at different phases of the work.

2 Karl Marx, 'The Method of Political Economy', in *Grundrisse, Foundations of the Critique of Political Economy*, Section 3, London: Penguin Book, 1993, p. 108.

3 William I. Robinson, 'The New Transnationalism and the Folly of Conventional Thinking', *Science and Society*, 2005, 69(3): 316–28; Michael Hardt and Antonio Negri, *Empire*, London: Harvard University Press, 2000.

4 For her idea of imperialism see Rosa Luxemberg, *The Accumulation of Capital*, London: Routledge & Kegan Paul (first published in German in 1913), 1951.

5 Rosa Luxemberg, 'Protective Tariffs and Accumulation', in *The Accumulation of Capital*, p. 446.

6 Joan Robinson's introduction to Luxemberg's, *The Accumulation of Capital*, pp. 13–28.

7 Cited in M.C. Howard and J.E. King, 'Capital Accumulation, Imperialism and War: Rosa Luxemburg and Otto Bauer', in *A History of Marxian Economics Vol.1*, Princeton, NJ: Princeton University Press, 1989, p. 120.

8 See Karl Kautsky, 'Work Colonies', in *Socialism and Colonial Policy*, 1907, www.marxists.org/archive/kautsky/1907/colonial/ (accessed on 14 February 2013).

9 For a detailed discussion, see Howard and King, ch. 6 in 'Capital Accumulation, Imperialism and War', pp. 123–4 and V. I. Lenin, 'Division of the World Among Capitalist Associations', in *Imperialism: The Highest Stage of Capitalism*, LeftWord Books, 2000.

10 John A. Hobson, *Imperialism: A Study*, London: University of Michigan Press (first published in 1902), 1938.

11 Rudolph Hilferding, *Finance Capital: A Study of the latest Phase of Capitalist Development*, London: Routledge & Kegan Paul (first German edition published in 1910), 1981.

12 Rudolph Hilferding, 'The Reorientation of Commercial Policy', in *Finance Capital*, p. 310.

13 Rudolph Hilferding, 'The Proletariat and Imperialism', in *Finance Capital*, p. 370.

14 Paul A. Baran, *The Political Economy of Growth*, Harmondsworth: Penguin (first published in 1957), 1973; Paul A. Baran and Paul Sweezy, *Monopoly Capital*, Harmondsworth: Penguin (first published in 1966), 1968.

15 Leon Trotsky, *Our Revolution: Essays on Working Class and International Revolution 1904–17*, Westport, CT: Hyperion Press, 1973.

16 Nikolai Bukharin, *Imperialism and World Economy*, London: Merlin Press (first Russian edition published in 1917), 1972.

17 Vladimir Lenin, *Imperialism the Highest Stage of Capitalism*, LeftWord Books, 2000 (First published in mid-1917 in pamphlet form).

18 See in this context, Amiya Kumar Bagchi, 'Towards a Correct Reading of Lenin's Theory of Imperialism', *Economic and Political Weekly*, 1983, 18(31): PE2–PE12.

19 Vladimir Lenin, 'Imperialism, as a Special Stage of Capitalism', in *Imperialism the Highest Stage of Capitalism*, LeftWord Books, 2000, p. 114.

20 Rudolph Hilferding in 'Finance Capital and the Financial Oligarchy', in Lenin's, *Imperialism the Highest Stage of Capitalism*, p. 74.

21 David Harvey, *The New Imperialism*, New York: Oxford University Press, 2003.

22 Giovanni Arrighi, *The Long Twentieth Century*, London: Verso, 1994.

23 Robert Pollin, 'Contemporary Economic Stagnation in World Historical Perspective', *New Left Review*, 1996, 1(219).

24 William I. Robinson, 'Giovanni Arrighi: Systemic Cycles of Accumulation, Hegemonic Transitions, and the Rise of China', *New Political Economy*, 2010, 11(1), 1–14.

25 Hardt and Negri, *Empire*.

26 Ibid., Preface pp. xiii–xiv.

27 Ellen Meiksins Wood, *Empire of Capital*, London, New York: Verso, 2003.

28 Bill Warren, *Imperialism Pioneer of Capitalism*, London: NLB and Verso, 1980.

29 William I. Robinson and Jerry Harris, 'Towards a Global Ruling Class? Globalization and the Transnational Capitalist Class', *Science & Society*, 2000, 64(1) Spring: 11–54; William I. Robinson, 'Transnational Processes, Development Studies and Changing Social Hierarchies in the World', *Third World Quarterly*, 2001, 22(4) August: 529–63; Robinson, 'The New Transnationalism and the Folly of Conventional Thinking', 316–28.

30 Prabhat Patnaik, 'Introduction', in *Imperialism: The Highest Stage of Capitalism*, New Delhi: LeftWord Books, 2000.

31 Ray Hudson, 'Uneven Development in Capitalist Societies: Changing Spatial Divisions of Labour, Forms of Spatial Organization of Production and

Service Provision, and Their Impacts on Localities', *Transactions of the Institute of British Geographers*, New Series, 1988, 13(4): 484–96.

32 Ernest Mandel, *Late Capitalism*, London: NLB, 1975.

33 Vladimir Lenin, 'Export of Capital', in *Imperialism the Highest Stage of Capitalism*, p. 88.

34 Harry Magdoff, *Imperialism Without Colonies*, New Delhi: Aakar Books with Monthly Review Press (first published in 2003), 2007.

35 Leo Panitch, 'Globalisation and the State', *The Socialist Register*, 1994, 30: 69.

36 Istvan Mezaros, *Beyond Capital: Toward a Theory of Transition*, London: Merlin Press, 1995.

2 Marx's *Capital* and the global crisis

John Smith[1]

The deepest roots of the financial whirlwind currently on world tour are to be found not in finance but in capitalist production. The series of financial heart attacks that began on 9 August 2007[2], were provoked by the adverse side effects of two ingredients of the elixir that gave capitalists in the dominant nations a respite, for several decades, from the systemic crises of the 1970s. These were an enormous expansion of domestic, corporate and sovereign debt helped to prop up demand and maintain GDP growth, and the globalisation of production and the shift of much of it to low-wage countries, which allowed northern capitalists to cut costs and restore sagging profits by substituting relatively expensive domestic labour with cheap labour. But stratospheric accumulation of debt has destabilised the global financial system, while the shift of production to low-wage countries has resulted in large structural trade imbalances and equal and opposite capital account imbalances – creating a reverse, perverse Marshall Plan, in which poor countries lent their hard-currency export earnings to rich countries (at zero or negative real interest rates) to finance the rich nations' ever-expanding demand for cheap food and manufactured goods. For many commodities and production tasks, outsourcing is a way to reduce costs without having to invest, further depressing the share of capital expenditure in GDP, further increasing reliance on debt to replace feeble corporate demand for investment goods. Debt and outsourcing has turned out to be a poisonous brew, and the two-headed monster it helped to suppress, overproduction of commodities and overaccumulation of capital, can now only be contained by even more concentrated doses of the same toxic concoction that brought on the crisis in the first place. The greatest of all the global imbalances is the one between the enormous swollen mass of financial assets, that is, claims on new wealth, and the faltering ability of the productive system to feed all those hungry mouths. So, to avert a massive cancelation of asset values and a chaotic reassignment of claims on social wealth, central banks are adopting increasingly desperate and extreme policies, each time raising the stakes higher, to the point where in June 2016, Bill Gross, founder of the world's largest bond trading company, said that the trillions of dollars of bonds now paying negative interest rates are 'a supernova waiting to explode'.[3]

In public and academic debates on the causes and nature of the crisis, debt mountains and credit bubbles have received vast attention, yet the less-obvious but even more important ways in which the southwards shift of production is implicated in capitalism's return to systemic crisis barely receives a mention. This essay analyses the causes and consequences of globalisation of production, its shift to low-wage countries and how Marx's *Capital* may help to explain this phenomenon. Its fundamental driving force is what some economists call 'global labour arbitrage':[4] the efforts by firms in Europe, North America and Japan to cut costs and boost profits by replacing higher-waged domestic labour with cheaper foreign labour, achieved either through emigration of production ('outsourcing', as used here) or through immigration of workers.

By uprooting several billion workers and farmers in southern nations from their ties to the land and their jobs in protected national industries, neoliberal capitalism turned towns and cities into refugee camps for people fleeing the countryside, accelerating the expansion of a vast pool of super-exploitable labour. Suppression of its free movement across borders has interacted with this hugely increased supply to produce a dramatic widening of international wage differentials between industrialised and developing nations, vastly exceeding price differences in all other global markets. This steep wage gradient provides two different ways for northern capitalists to increase profits: through the emigration of production to low-wage countries, or the immigration of low-wage migrant workers for exploitation at home. Immigration and outsourcing, therefore, are bound together, two sides of the same coin.

Reduction in tariffs and removal of barriers to capital flows have spurred the migration of production to low-wage countries, but militarised borders and rising xenophobia have had the opposite effect on the migration of workers from these countries – not stopping it altogether, but inhibiting its flow and reinforcing migrants' vulnerable, second-class status. And so, factories freely cross the US–Mexican border and pass with ease through the walls of Fortress Europe, as do the commodities produced in them and the capitalists who own them, but the human beings who work in them have no right of passage. This is a travesty of globalisation – a world without borders to everything and everyone except for working people.

Global wage differentials, in large measure resulting from suppression of the free movement of labour, provide a distorted reflection of global differences in the rate of exploitation (simply, the difference between the value generated by workers and what they are paid). The southwards shift of production signifies that the profits of firms headquartered in Europe, North America and Japan, the value of all manner of financial assets derived from these profits, and the living standards of the citizens of these nations have become highly dependent on the higher rates of exploitation of workers in so-called 'emerging nations'. Neoliberal globalisation must therefore be recognized as *a new, imperialist stage of capitalist development*, where imperialism is defined by its economic essence: the exploitation of southern living labour by northern capitalists.

Part One of this essay presents the results of empirical analysis of the global shift of production to low-wage nations and identifies its key feature: imperialist super-exploitation;[5] Part Two seeks to explain this in terms of Marx's theory of value, first by visiting the debate in the 1960s and 1970s between dependency theory and its 'orthodox' Marxist critics, concluding with some critical reflections on Marx's *Capital* and Lenin's theory of imperialism.

Part one: globalisation and imperialism

The globalisation of production and of producers

Globalisation of production is reflected in an enormous expansion of the power and reach of transnational corporations, the great majority of which are owned by capitalists resident in imperialist countries. The United Nations Conference on Trade and Development (UNCTAD) estimates that 'about 80 per cent of global trade . . . is linked to the international production networks of TNCs [transnational corporations]', either as in-house foreign direct investment (FDI), or as 'arm's-length' relations between 'lead firms' and their formally independent suppliers.[6]

Export-oriented industrialisation (or, from a northern perspective, 'outsourcing') is the only capitalist option for poor countries not endowed with abundant natural resources. Under its aegis, 'developing nations' share of global manufactured exports rose from around 5 percent in the pre-globalisation period to close on 30 percent by the turn of the millennium (see Figure 2.1), while in just 10 years, the share of manufactured goods in the south's exports tripled, stabilising in the early 1990s at more than 60 percent. Figure 2.2 shows this dramatic transformation from the perspective of imperialist countries.

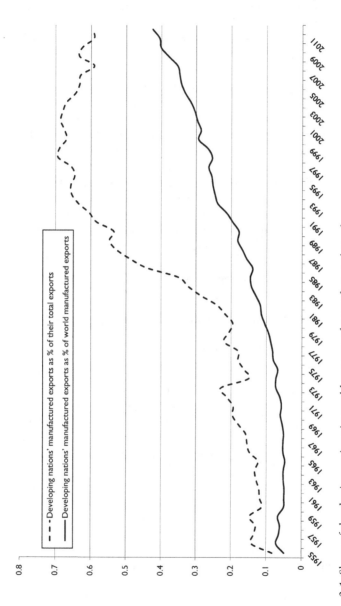

Figure 2.1 Share of developing nations in world exports of manufactured goods

Sources: *UNCTAD Statistical Handbook*, http://unctadstat.unctad.org. 1955–1995 data is from UNCTAD, 'Handbook of Statistics – Archive: Network of Exports by Region and Commodity Group – Historical Series', http://unctadstat.unctad.org (accessed on 18 July 2009), no longer online (data is in possession of author).

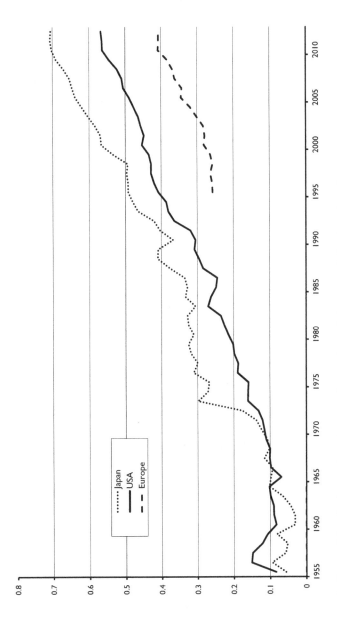

Figure 2.2 Share of developing nations in manufactured goods imports of developed nations

Sources: *UNCTAD Statistical Handbook*, http://unctadstat.unctad.org. (see note to chart 1 for 1955–1995 data).

In 1970, barely 10 percent of their manufactured imports came from what was then called the Third World; by the turn of the millennium, this share – of a greatly expanded total – had quintupled.[7] The US auto industry vividly illustrates this. In 1995, Canadian firms exported nearly three times more components to the United States than did Mexico, parity was achieved in 2008, and by 2015, Mexico's component exports were more than twice those of Canada.[8] The relocation of production processes to low-wage countries has been at least as important to European and Japanese firms as to those in North America. As *The Economist* noted, 'Japanese electronics companies continue to flourish in American markets precisely because they have moved their assembly lines to China',[9] while a study of EU–Chinese trade concluded that 'the possibility of offshoring the more labour-intensive production and assembly activities to China provides an opportunity to our own companies to survive and grow in an increasingly competitive environment'.[10]

The result is a highly peculiar structure of world trade, in which northern firms compete with other northern firms, their success hinging on their ability to cut costs by outsourcing production; firms in low-wage countries fiercely compete with each other, all seeking to exercise the same 'comparative advantage', namely, their surfeit of unemployed workers desperate for work. But *northern firms do not generally compete with southern firms.*[11] This simple, often-overlooked fact is obviously true of relations between parent companies and their wholly owned subsidiaries (that is, of FDI), but it is also true of the increasingly favoured arm's length relationship – between Primark and its Bangladeshi suppliers and between General Motors and the Mexican firms who manufacture more and more of its components, the relationship is complementary, not competitive, even if it is highly unequal. There are many exceptions, from solar panels to steel, where northern firms compete directly with southern firms, and indeed this peculiar structure is riven with contradictions, but the overall pattern is clear: there is north–north rivalry between TNCs in Europe, North America and Japan, including to see who can make the biggest cuts in production costs through outsourcing; meanwhile, competition among their suppliers has reached race-to-the-bottom proportions, *but there is a general absence of head-to-head north–south competition.* So it is in product markets and between firms – but, in contrast, labour markets are characterised by increased competition across national borders, militarisation of these same borders, wage repression and, everywhere, an accelerating decline in labour's share of GDP.

The globalisation of production has transformed not just the production of commodities but of social relations in general, and especially of the social relation that defines capitalism: *the capital–labour relation*ship, which has increasingly become a relationship between northern capital and southern labour. The enormous and continuing growth of the industrial workforce in low-wage nations (corresponding to the ILO's 'less-developed regions' in Figure 2.3) during the era of export-oriented industrialisation is portrayed in Figure 2.3, revealing that in 2010, 79 percent, or 541 million, of the world's industrial workers lived in 'less-developed regions'. This is up from 34 percent in 1950 and 53 percent in 1980 – compared to the 145 million industrial workers or 21 percent of the total, who in 2010 lived in imperialist countries.

However, with the partial exception of China – a special case because of its 'one-child' policy, extraordinarily rapid growth, and, not least, its as-yet incomplete transition from socialism to capitalism – no southern economy has grown fast enough to provide jobs to the millions of young people entering the labour market and the millions fleeing rural poverty.

'Global labour arbitrage' – key driver of the globalisation of production

As mentioned earlier, the suppression of international labour mobility has interacted with a greatly increased supply to produce a dramatic widening of international wage differentials, which, according to World Bank researchers, 'exceed any other form of border-induced price gap by an order of magnitude or more'.[12] The steep wage gradient provides two different ways for northern capitalists to increase profits – through the emigration of production to low-wage countries, or the immigration of workers from those countries. The International Monetary Fund (IMF) made this connection quite precisely: 'The global pool of labour can be accessed by advanced economies through imports and immigration', significantly observing that, 'Trade is the more important and faster-expanding channel, in large part because immigration remains very restricted in many countries.'[13]

What the IMF calls 'accessing the global labour pool' others have dubbed as 'global labour arbitrage', whose essential feature, according to Stephen Roach, is the substitution of 'high-wage workers here with like-quality, low-wage workers abroad'.[14] Roach, then head of Morgan Stanley's Asian operations, argued that 'a unique and powerful

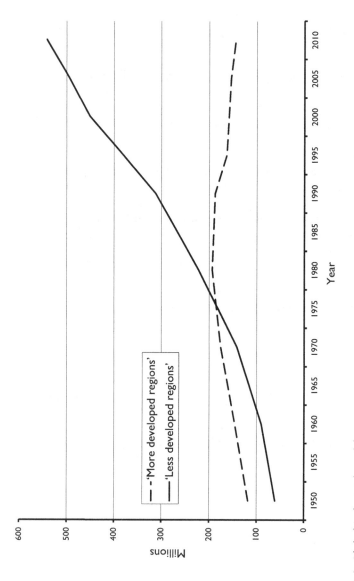

Figure 2.3 Global industrial workforce

Sources: Data from 1995 to 2008 was obtained from LABORSTA, http://laborsta.ilo.org, and *Key Indicators of the Labour Market (KILM)*, 5th and 6th editions, http://ilo.org. Data from 1950 to 1990 is obtained from ILO, 'Population and Economically Active Population', accessed in 2004, no longer online (data is in possession of author).

confluence of three mega-trends is driving the global arbitrage'. These are 'the maturation of offshore outsourcing platforms . . . E-based connectivity . . . [and] cost control'.[15] Of these, 'cost control' – that is, lower wages – is 'the catalyst that brings the global labour arbitrage to life'. Expanding on this, Roach explains:

> In an era of excess supply, companies lack pricing leverage as never before. As such, businesses must be unrelenting in their search for new efficiencies. Not surprisingly, the primary focus of such efforts is labour, representing the bulk of production costs in the developed world. . . . Consequently, *offshore outsourcing that extracts product from relatively low-wage workers in the developing world has become an increasingly urgent survival tactic for companies in the developed economies.*
>
> (my emphasis)[16]

This is a much richer description of neoliberal globalisation's driving force than the one offered above by IMF technocrats. We might ask, though, why Roach says 'extracting product' instead of 'extracting value' – capitalists, after all, are not interested in the product of labour but in the value contained in it. The answer, we suspect, is that 'extracting value' would make it even more explicit that these low-wage workers create more wealth than they receive in wages, in other words *that they are exploited* – a heretical notion for a mainstream economist. Roach's observation also begs the question – just how do 'companies in developed economies' 'extract product' from workers in Bangladesh, China and elsewhere? The only visible contribution these workers make to the bottom line of firms in 'developed economies' is the flow of repatriated profits from FDI, but not one penny of H&M's or General Motors' profits can be traced to their independent suppliers in Bangladesh or Mexico; all of it appears instead as value added by their own activities. This conundrum, inexplicable to mainstream economic theory and therefore ignored, can only be resolved by redefining value-added as *value captured*; in other words, a firm's 'value-added' does not represent the value *it* has produced, but the portion of total, economy-wide value it succeeds in capturing through exchange, including value extracted from living labour in far-flung countries. Not only is value capture not identical to value creation, as mainstream theory maintains, but there is no correlation between them – banks, for example, generate no value but capture a great deal of it. Since a country's GDP is, by definition, nothing else than the sum of its firms' added value, GDP statistics systematically diminish the real contribution of southern nations to global wealth and exaggerate that of the 'developed' countries, thereby veiling the increasingly parasitic, exploitative and imperialist relationship between them. I call this 'the GDP illusion'.[17]

Part two: theories of exploitation

Dependency theory and its critics

The dependency debate in the 1960s and 1970s saw the first and last sustained attempt to found the theory of imperialism on Marx's theory of value. The rise of 'dependency theory', which sought to explain the persistence of imperialist exploitation following the dismantling of territorial empires, was inspired by the anti-colonial and anti-imperialist struggles that swept through Africa, Asia and Latin America following the Second World War.

Dependency theory – really a spectrum of theories, or of political perspectives, since it sought to give theoretical expression to a movement for change involving hundreds of millions of people – viewed the world from a southern perspective, as it appears to and is experienced by the peoples of poor nations, whether they be impoverished workers and farmers or domestic capitalists wishing to retain a larger share of the surplus value extracted from them. Dependency theory's leading exponents were overwhelmingly Latin American, Asian, African; citizens of which they and all politically conscious people in those continents saw as neo-colonies, nations that had attained formal independence but remained politically and economically subordinated to the former colonial powers. What united this diverse array of reformists and revolutionaries was a perception that unequal exchange between developed imperialist nations and what was then known as the Third World (the Soviet Union and its allies constituted the Second World) – expressed in declining terms of trade of their raw material exports vis-à-vis manufactured imports from imperialist nations – generates a large-scale transfer of wealth from the former to the latter, spurring development of the dominant nations and underdevelopment in southern nations. The primary difference between dependency's proponents lay between those like Arghiri Emmanuel, author of *Unequal Exchange: A Study in the Imperialism of Trade*, and Fernando Henrique Cardoso (later a neoliberal Brazilian president) who sought a path for independent capitalist development in the south, while Marxists like Samir Amin, André Gunder Frank and Ruy Mauro Marini argued in different ways that capitalism, being intrinsically imperialist, is itself the obstacle.

Dependency theory rose and fell in the period prior to the neoliberal era, a time when 'developing countries' exported raw materials and imported manufactured goods and when the globalisation of production was still in the egg. The hatching of this egg – the rapid export-oriented industrial development in South Korea and Taiwan in the 1970s – partly explains its downfall, since these early instances of industrial take-off appeared to refute its insistence that imperialist domination blocked industrial development in the south. This is ironic, since the south's manufactured exports were soon to suffer the same declining terms of trade as its raw material exports, although without the wild fluctuations, and proliferating global value chains, export processing zones and others, would soon be generating larger south to north flows of value than at any time in history.

Recognition of the plunder of wealth on a vast scale through unequal exchange was a breakthrough, yet was fiercely resisted by many Marxists based in Europe and North America, who argued that workers and farmers were, if anything, more intensively exploited in the north than in the south – since 'the more the productive forces are developed, the more the proletarians are exploited'.[18] Despite their differences on other matters, there was broad agreement among northern Marxists that, as Nigel Harris argued,

> the higher the productivity of labour, the higher the income paid to the worker (since his or her reproduction costs are higher) and the more exploited he or she is – that is, the greater the proportion of the workers output [that] is appropriated by the employer,[19]

an argument based on a seemingly faithful reading of Marx's *Capital* and one that will be questioned in the final section of this essay.

Dependency theory opened up questions which northern Marxists were (and are) not comfortable with – about if, how and how much some of the proceeds of unequal exchange are shared with workers in imperialist countries, and whether wide and growing differences in wages and living standards between workers in imperialist nations and southern nations reflect a higher rate of exploitation in the latter and its mitigation in the former. Meanwhile, the transformations of the neoliberal era have fatally undermined the Euro-Marxist argument. It cannot be seriously argued that the global shift of production to low-wage countries is a minor event that changes little. On the contrary, not only has outsourcing had a major effect on capitalist profits and capital accumulation, it has transformed social relations in general and the capital–labour relation in particular: since goods consumed by workers in the north are, to an ever-greater extent, produced by southern low-wage labour (the production of labour power itself has been globalised!), wages and productivity in low-wage countries substantially determine consumption levels and the rate of exploitation in imperialist countries.

Still, these arguments continue to be advanced to the present day. Thus, Alex Callinicos argues that dependency theory's 'critical error is not to take into account the significance of high levels of labour productivity in the advanced economies',[20] while Joseph Choonara believes 'it is a misconception that workers in countries such as India or China are more exploited than those in countries such as the US or Britain'.[21] Yet extreme rates of exploitation in Bangladesh garment factories, Chinese production lines and South African platinum mines is a palpable, directly observable fact, one that is experienced every day in the flesh by hundreds of millions of workers in low-wage countries; we need a theory that explains this, not one that makes it invisible. 'Communism is not a doctrine but a *movement*; it proceeds not from principles but from *facts*', said Frederick Engels.[22] Wide international differences in the rate of exploitation, the huge global shift of production to where this rate is highest, and the tremendous southwards shift in the centre of gravity of the industrial working class are the new, big facts from which we must proceed. These are the defining transformations of the neoliberal era, and they must be studied if we are to understand the nature and dynamics of the global crisis. Instead of scouring Marx's *Capital* for quotes to use to dismiss twenty-first century super-exploitation (and the imperialist order resting on it), we must test Marx's theory against these new facts and vice versa, critically developing his theory in order to understand this latest stage of capitalism's imperialist development.

Marx's Capital *and the theory of imperialism*

As noted earlier, by and large, imperialist countries and low-wage countries produce and export different commodities. To understand the significance of this, consider what happens when two firms produce the same commodity, for example, steel. Let us assume (a) that workers in more productive and less productive steel mills are all paid the same wage, (b) that they all work with the same intensity, and (c) that the market price of steel is determined by the average socially necessary labour time required for its production (ignoring, in other words, the difference between the capital–labour ratio in the steel industry and in the wider economy, which, as Marx explained in Volume 3, cause prices of production to move away from socially necessary labour time). In this case, all labour expended in both steel mills enters into the calculation of the socially necessary average; the capitalist owners of the more productive steel mill will reap surplus profit; and the owners of the less productive will reap below-average profits. Should the latter be forced into bankruptcy, the average socially necessary labour time to produce a ton of steel will fall and with it, the price and surplus profits of the surviving capitalist.

In one of the two references in *Capital* to the difference between the individual value of a commodity and its social value, Marx says: 'The exceptionally productive labour operates as intensified labour; it creates in equal periods of time greater values than average social labour of the same kind'.[23] According to this, where an individual capitalist introduces an innovation which reduces necessary labour, I understand 'exceptionally productive labour operates as intensified labour' to mean that the effect, from the point of view of this individual capitalist, is *as if* his workers were working more intensively than average. The two cases are analogous, but they are not identical, and the differences between them are important. Since value is a social relation rather than a thing, what matters in the calculation of the rate of surplus value is the social value of the commodities produced, not their individual value, yet it must be remembered that the social value is determined not exclusively by the productivity of labour in the more advanced steel mill but by the average productivity of labour in the steel sector as a whole, and the higher rate of surplus value in the more advanced steel mill depends on the survival of less-productive steel mills – or, as Marx says in the continuation of the quote mentioned earlier, 'this extra surplus value vanishes as soon as the new method of production is generalised, for then the difference between the individual value of the cheapened commodity and it social value vanishes'.[24]

So, the difference between labour productivity in one mill and another is crucial to considering their profitability and rates of surplus value, but such productivity differences are irrelevant when considering the rates of surplus value between different sectors, since now we are no longer comparing individual values with social values, we are comparing one social value with another. This matters a lot, because the steel sector is a special case. In general, as stated earlier, trade between imperialist nations is in similar goods, while, in contrast, trade between imperialist and developing nations are in different goods. To illustrate the difference between the special case and the typical case, let us now imagine that in the car park of our two steel mills, two hamburger-flippers are employed to provide steelworkers with their lunch, and both steel mills and hamburger-flippers operate with the average level of productivity for their respective branches of production. Assuming uniform wages among hamburger-flippers and steel-workers (that is, a uniform value of labour power), the rate of surplus value in all four is identical – since in none of them is the productivity of labour higher or lower than the average for their respective sectors.

To take another step towards real life, let us now assume that the fast-food workers are forced, by unemployment, segmented labour markets, racial discrimination and other circumstances, to accept lower wages than those paid to steelworkers. The rate of surplus value will now be higher in the fast-food sector than in the steel mills, some which may be passed on to steelworkers in the form of cheaper sandwiches or will be entirely captured by their employers if wages can be lowered accordingly. Here, steel mills substitute for imperialist economies and the fast-food sector substitutes for export-oriented industries in low-wage countries, and this becomes a stylised picture of contemporary relations between imperialist and low-wage economies, within which super-exploitation has a central place.

On the face of it, Marx's statement that

exceptionally productive labour operates as intensified labour; it creates in equal periods of time greater values than average social labour of the same kind' contradicts his statement elsewhere that 'variations in productivity have no impact whatever on the labour itself represented in value. . . . The same labour, therefore, performed for the same length of time, always yields the same amount of value, independently of any variations in productivity.[25]

The contradiction between Marx's two statements is only apparent because, in the first of these quotes, Marx deals exclusively with productivity differences between individual firms in a given sector, that is, between firms producing identical commodities but in different amounts of time, showing how the law of value asserts itself through the attempts of individual capitalists to violate it, while in the second of these quotes he ignores such differences and talks directly about the general law.

This is important because the Euro-Marxist rejection of dependency theory, super-exploitation, Lenin and others, rests on two flimsy pillars – an unwarranted generalisation of Marx's observation that exceptionally productive labour generates more value in a given amount of time than labour of average productivity, extending to the entire global economy a factor that is specific to capitals producing the same commodities in direct competition with each other. The second is that they found their rejection of super-exploitation and the 'unequal exchange' arising from it on passages from Marx's *Capital* that, on superficial reading, appear to support their view. For example, Marx devotes a short chapter of *Capital* to 'National Differences in Wages', which concluded that even though England's workers receive higher wages than in Germany or Russia, they may be subject to a higher rate of exploitation: 'it will frequently be found that the daily or weekly wage in the first nation is higher than in the second while the relative price of labour, that is, the price of labour as compared both with surplus value and the value of the product, stands higher in the second than in the first.'[26] This is exactly the argument used by Bettelheim, Harris, Choonara and others, but there are three reasons why Marx's argument does not apply to contemporary north–south relations.

First, each of the nations used by Marx for his comparisons – England, Germany and Russia – were rival oppressor nations, each of them busy acquiring colonial empires of their own. The formally free nations of today's global south cannot be regarded merely as 'less-developed' capitalist nations, analogous to Germany and Russia in the nineteenth century. Second, late-twentieth century trade between imperialist and 'developing' nations is qualitatively different from late-nineteenth century trade between England, Germany and Russia. Back then, not only did each worker consume domestically produced goods, each capitalist consumed domestically reared labour power – this was an age before global value chains, outsourcing and other modern features, although pioneers and precursors of global wage arbitrage-driven outsourcing can be found in Marx's day. Third, Marx's example assumed that capitalists in countries like Germany and England competed in the production of similar goods, whereas, as noted earlier, this is not so of contemporary north–south trade.

Marx's *Capital* investigated the capitalist form of the value relation, in order to discover how capitalist profit could arise if every commodity sold at its value. Before the commodification of labour power, when the producers owned their means of production, merchant profits could only arise from buying cheap and selling dear, that is, by profiting from market imperfections, thereby violating the equality of exchanges and, therefore, the law of value. Capitalists make their profits differently, without violating the law of value – by employing those who have only their labour power to sell and paying them less than the value they produce. This does not violate the principle of equal exchange, since the value of labour power (whose monetary expression is the wage) is what it costs to produce it, not what this labour power itself produces. If the commodities daily consumed by a worker and their family require four hours of labour for their production, everything beyond four hours that this worker works is 'surplus labour' used to expand the wealth of the capitalist.

Marx investigated the origin and nature of surplus value, whereas the task before us is to theoretically comprehend capitalism's current, imperialist stage of development. The level of abstraction required for Marx's project is evident from his statement that

> Even though the equalisation of wages and working hours between one sphere of production and another, or between different capitals invested in the same sphere of production, comes up against all kinds of local obstacles, the advance of capitalist production and the progressive subordination of all economic relations to this mode of production tends nevertheless to bring this process to fruition.[27]

Marx treated the divergence of wages as the result of temporary or contingent factors that ceaselessly mobile capital and labour would erode over time, which could be safely excluded from analysis:

> Important as the study of frictions ["local obstacles" obstructing the equalisation of wages] is for any specialist work on wages, they are still accidental and inessential as far as the general investigation of capitalist production is concerned and can therefore be ignored.[28]

Such a level of abstraction is clearly inappropriate for our current, urgent task; in today's hideously divided world, the premise of equality between workers assumed by Marx is profoundly violated and cannot be dismissively ascribed to 'local obstacles'.

'The Third Form of Surplus Value Increase'[29]

In the first volume of *Capital*, Marx analysed, in depth, two ways in which capitalists strive to increase the rate of exploitation: by lengthening the working day, thereby increasing 'absolute surplus value'; and by reducing necessary labour time through increasing the productivity of workers producing consumption goods, thereby increasing 'relative surplus value'. In several places he alludes to a third: surplus labour time can also be extended 'by pushing the wage of the worker down below the value of his labour power', but, rigorously excluding everything not essential to the general theory, he adds, 'Despite the important part which this method plays in practice, we are excluded from considering it here by our assumption that all commodities, including labour power, are bought and sold at their full value'.[30]

'Pushing the wage of the worker down below the value of his labour power', is again mentioned two chapters later, during a discussion of the consequences for workers when 'machinery . . . gradually seizes control of the whole of a given field of production', with the result that a 'section of the working class . . . rendered superfluous . . . swamps the labour market, and makes the price of labour power fall below its value'.[31] The contemporary relevance of this hardly needs stating. A huge section of the working class in the global south has been 'rendered superfluous' by the inability of modern production methods to soak up enough labour to prevent rising unemployment, and this alone, even before we take into account the much harsher labour regimes prevalent in low-wage countries, exerts a powerful force that makes 'the price of their labour power fall below its value'.

In the third volume of *Capital*, while discussing 'counteracting factors' inhibiting the tendency of the rate of profit to fall, Marx makes another brief reference to this third way to increase surplus value. One of these counteracting factors, the 'Reduction of Wages Below their Value', is dealt with in just two short sentences:

> like many other things that might be brought in, it has nothing to do with the general analysis of capital, but has its place in an account of competition, which is not dealt with in this work. *It is nonetheless one of the most important factors in stemming the tendency for the rate of profit to fall.*[32]

Not only did Marx leave to one side the reduction of wages below their value, he made a further abstraction that, while necessary for his 'general analysis of capital', must also be relaxed if we are to analyse capitalism's current stage of development: 'The distinction between rates of surplus value in different countries and hence between different national levels of exploitation of labour are completely outside the scope of our present investigation'.[33] Yet, precisely this must be the starting-point for a theory of contemporary imperialism. Wage- and arbitrage-driven globalisation of production does not correspond to absolute surplus value – long hours are endemic in low-wage countries, but the length of the working day is not the outsourcing firms' primary attraction. Nor does it correspond to relative surplus value – necessary labour is not, in the main, being reduced thorough the application of new technology. Indeed, northern firms have turned to outsourcing as an alternative to investment in new technology – contributing to their investment strike, which long predated (and portended) the financial crash. It does, however, correspond to super-exploitation, 'the hidden common essence defining imperialism. . . . not because the Southern working class produces less value, but because it is more oppressed and more exploited'.[34]

Lenin and imperialism

To develop his general theory of the capital relation, Marx, as we have seen, presumed equality and free mobility of capital, leading to the formation through competition of an average rate of profit, and equality, predicated on its free mobility, of labour. The systematic violation of equality between proletarians, deriving from the systematic inequality between nations, was central to Lenin's theory of imperialism, who argued that 'the division of nations into oppressor and oppressed [is] the essence of imperialism'.[35] Lenin's *Imperialism, the Highest Stage of Capitalism*, written in the midst of the First World War, was a guide to action, an attempt to lay bare the reasons for the capitulation of the mass socialist parties on the eve of world war, to show that the war itself was no aberration or accident and that it proved the objective necessity of world social revolution and the transition to a communist mode of production. He identified those essential characteristics of capitalism's imperialist stage which were evident at its birth, in particular the concentration of wealth and the rise of finance capital, its oppression of and predation on weak nations, and its rampant militarism. Lenin could not have included a conception of how value is produced in globalised production processes because these were only to emerge in a later phase of capitalist development. The result is an inevitable disconnection, persisting right to this day, between Lenin's theory of imperialism and Marx's theory of value. Reconnecting them is a considerable task, here we have space only for a brief note on what Lenin regarded as two defining features of capitalism's imperialist stage: monopoly and the export of capital.

Marxists in imperialist countries have often ignored Lenin's insistence on the economic and political centrality of the division of the world into oppressed and oppressor nations, dwelling instead on his arguments on inter-imperialist rivalry and 'in its economic essence imperialism is monopoly capitalism'.[36] Monopoly is used quite promiscuously in both bourgeois and Marxist literature to describe phenomena pertaining to production, distribution, brand loyalty, finance, concentration of capital, political and military power and much else.

Most of these pertain to the distribution of value, not to its production, which does not necessarily mean they are less important. A value theory of imperialism must distinguish between the two and, moreover, recognise that the source of imperialist profits is not to be found in any form of monopoly – however big a role monopolistic corporations may play in helping to generate these conditions – but in the exploitation of living labour.

In *Imperialism*, Lenin argued that 'The export of capital, one of the most essential economic bases of imperialism . . . sets the seal of parasitism on the whole country that lives by exploiting the labour of several overseas countries and colonies'.[37] This resonates powerfully with contemporary global capitalism, where imperialist transnational corporations share the spoils of super-exploitation with myriad service-providers and their own employees, and where the biggest cut of all is taken by the state. There is, however, an obvious problem with applying Lenin's searing insight to contemporary imperialism. Companies like Apple and H&M *export no capital* to Bangladesh and China – their iPhones and garments are produced by arm's-length production processes.[38]

The riddle can be solved by focusing on the essence of the matter, not the form (the *export* of capital being the form). The imperialists, Lenin argued, were compelled to export part of their capital in order to exploit the labour of workers overseas because the imperialists' accumulated wealth had reached such proportions that the gigantic mass of surplus value required to convert their wealth into capital, that is, self-expanding wealth, far outstrips what can be extracted from its domestic workforce. As Andy Higginbottom argues, capital export is intimately connected to oppression of nations: 'The export of capital means that there must be a new type of capital – labour relation, between Northern capital and Southern labour, it means the *export of the capital – labour relation under terms of national oppression*'.[39] What is new and could not have been anticipated by Lenin is that capitalism's evolution, especially since 1980, has provided transnational corporations with ways to capture surplus value from workers in low-wage countries which does not require them to 'export' their capital to those countries – which is why arm's-length outsourcing is now a more important source of profits than FDI, portfolio investments and debt (the three components of capital export) combined.

To conclude this all-too-brief discussion of Lenin's contribution to the theory of imperialism, the outstanding task is the forging of a concept that unites its economic essence (monopoly capitalism) and political essence (the division of the world into oppressed and oppressor nations), in terms of the law of value developed by Karl Marx in *Capital*. This is the path to a new synthesis of Marx's theory of value and Lenin's theory of imperialism, a Marxism–Leninism worthy of the name.

Conclusion

Analysis of the empirics of neoliberal globalisation reveals global labour arbitrage, arising from the higher degree of exploitation prevalent in export-oriented industries in low-wage nations, to be its fundamental driving force. The central finding from our brief review of Marx's *Capital* is that this super-exploitation corresponds to the third form of surplus value increase, whose importance was stressed by Marx yet which he excluded from his general theory. Here is the only possible solid foundation for a renaissance of Marxism on a world scale. This central finding also allows us to see the place of the neoliberal era in history. In *Grundrisse*, Marx comments,

> As long as capital is weak, it still relies on the crutches of past modes of production. . . . As soon as it feels strong, it throws away the crutches, and moves in accordance with its own laws. As soon as it begins to sense itself and become conscious of itself as a barrier to development, it seeks refuge in forms which, by restricting free competition, seem to make the rule of capital more perfect, but are at the same time the heralds of its dissolution and of the dissolution of the mode of production resting on it.[40]

This is reminiscent of Lenin's argument that

> capitalism only became capitalist imperialism at a definite and very high stage of its development, when certain of its fundamental characteristics began to change into their opposites, when the features of the epoch of transition from capitalism to a higher social and economic system had taken shape and revealed themselves in all spheres.[41]

The rise of capitalism depended on the most barbaric forms of what Marx called 'primitive accumulation', such as the transportation of millions of African slaves, colonial plunder and opium trafficking. When capitalism reached its adult stage and took full control over the production process, competition flourished and the inner laws of capital became expressed most fully. Finally, in its epoch of decay, capitalism increasingly relies on forms other than free competition – monopoly, vastly increased state intervention in all aspects of economic life, 'accumulation through dispossession',[42] and imperialism – for its survival, but at the cost of distorting the operation of its laws and erecting new barriers to the expansion of the productive forces. How does this chronology relate to the three forms of surplus value increase discussed in this essay? In immature capitalism, increasing absolute surplus value – extending the working day to and beyond physical limits – was predominant. Once capital took control of the production process, relative surplus value – technology improvements to reduce the time needed to produce workers' consumption goods – became the predominant form, though at all times this depended on the persistence of much more brutal and archaic forms of domination, especially in the subject nations. In the neoliberal era, capitalists have enormously increased their recourse to global labour arbitrage, cutting costs and increasing profits by outsourcing production to low-wage countries. This constitutes a third way to increase surplus value, and its rapid growth is a defining feature of the neoliberal era. The proletarians of the semi-colonial countries are its first victims, but broad masses of working people in the imperialist countries also face destitution.

Capitalism now confronts its greatest ever crisis, one that will end, in the words of the *Communist Manifesto*, 'either in a revolutionary reconstitution of society at large, or in the common ruin of the contending classes'.[43] The massive reinforcements to the global working class, overwhelmingly youthful and highly female, in all corners of the earth, is a cause for us to rejoice and our enemies to fear. Along with the increased presence of migrant workers and of women in the working classes in imperialist countries, the transformations of the past decades have dramatically changed the face of the world working class, which now much more closely resembles the face of humanity, and they improve its prospects of prevailing in coming battles. No longer is the working class primarily white, male and located in imperialist countries.

Marx pointed out many times that as a purely economic movement, workers are at a huge disadvantage – we must sell our labour power or starve; we are forced to compete for work with those who have none. The onset of capitalism's greatest crisis means that the workers' movement can fight defensive battles but can only advance, anywhere, by fusing the economic struggle with the struggle for political power; by beginning the process of converting itself into a revolutionary political movement; and by gathering around itself all oppressed, exploited and marginalised peoples.

Neoliberal globalisation's transformations have sharpened competition between workers in the north and south and reveal ever more clearly that 'national' solutions proposed by labour leaders in imperialist countries strengthen xenophobia and lead towards fascism. If North American and European workers do not wish to compete with their sisters and brothers in Mexico, China, India and others, they must join with them in the struggle to abolish the racial hierarchy of nations and the tremendous disparities associated with it to achieve an authentic globalisation – a world without borders – in which no one has more right to a job, an education or a life than anyone else. The path of socialism is nothing else than the struggle to eradicate the gigantic differences in living standards and life chances that violate the principle of equality between proletarians. As Malcolm X said, 'Freedom for everybody, or freedom for nobody'.

Notes

1 The arguments presented here are further developed in John Smith, *Imperialism in the Twenty-First Century: Globalisation, Super-Exploitation and Capitalism's Final Crisis*, New York: Monthly Review Press, 2016.
2 Unsure who was holding US subprime mortgage securities, on 9 August 2007, European banks suddenly stopped lending to one another, compelling the European Central Bank to make an emergency transfusion of €94.8 bn ($131 bn) into the Eurozone's banking system. When US markets opened a few hours later, the US Federal Reserve followed with an injection of $24 billion into the US banking system. Writing in the *Financial Times* soon afterward, Martin Wolf called this 'the moment when credit dried up even to sound borrowers. Panic had arrived' ('Fear Makes a Welcome Return', *Financial Times*, 14 August 2007).
3 Cited in Robin Wigglesworth and Joel Lewin, 'Bill Gross Warns Over $10tn Negative-Yield Bond Pile', *Financial Times*, 9 June 2016.
4 Stephen Roach, 'Outsourcing, Protectionism, and the Global Labor Arbitrage', Morgan Stanley Special Economic Study, 2003: 6, www.neogroup. com/PDFs/casestudies/Special-Economic-Study-Outsourcing.pdf (accessed on 22 March 2017).
5 For the purposes of this essay, 'super-exploitation' denotes rates of exploitation that are higher than the global average. These, it is argued here, are prevalent in export-oriented industries in low-wage nations.
6 UNCTAD, *World Investment Report 2013*, Geneva: United Nations, 2013, p. 153.
7 The trace for Europe, generated by subtracting intra-EU manufactured imports from the EU total, begins in 1995, because data is only continuous since the EU enlargement of that year.
8 Source: UNCTADStat, 'Merchandise Trade Matrix – Detailed Products, Imports in Thousands of Dollars, Annual, 1995–2015', http://unctadstat. unctad.org/wds/TableViewer/tableView.aspx?ReportId=24740 (accessed on 22 April 2017).
9 'The Great Unbundling', *Economist*, 18 January 2007.
10 Ari Van Assche, Chang Hong and Veerle Slootmaekers, 'China's International Competitiveness: Reassessing the Evidence', LICOS Discussion

Paper Series, Discussion Paper No. 205, 15, http://neumann.hec.ca/pages/ari.van-assche/papers/competitiveness.pdf (accessed on 22 March 2017).

11 For proof of this, see Ricardo Hausmann, César Hidalgo, et al., 'The Atlas of Economic Complexity', http://atlas.cid.harvard.edu/media/atlas/pdf/HarvardMIT_AtlasOfEconomicComplexity_Part_I.pdf (accessed on 9 April 2017).

12 Michael Clemens, Claudio Montenegro and Lant Pritchett, 'The Place Premium: Wage Differences for Identical Workers Across the US Border', Policy Research Working Paper 4671, 2008: 16, New York: World Bank.

13 IMF, *World Economic Outlook, April 2007*, Washington, DC: IMF, p. 180.

14 Stephen Roach, 'More Jobs, Worse Work', *New York Times*, 22 July 2004.

15 Roach, 'Outsourcing, Protectionism, and the Global Labor Arbitrage'.

16 Roach, 'Outsourcing, Protectionism, and the Global Labor Arbitrage', p. 6.

17 John Smith, 'The GDP Illusion', *Monthly Review*, 2012, 64(3): 86–102.

18 Charles Bettelheim, 'Theoretical Comments', appendix to Arghiri Emmanuel, *Unequal Exchange: A Study in the Imperialism of Trade*, London: NLB, 1972, pp. 302, 271–322.

19 Nigel Harris, 'Theories of Unequal Exchange', *International Socialism*, 1986, 2(33): 119–20.

20 Alex Callinicos, *Imperialism and Global Political Economy*, Cambridge: Polity Press, 2009, pp. 179–80.

21 Joseph Choonara, *Unravelling Capitalism*, London: Bookmarks Publications, 2009, p. 34.

22 Frederick Engels, 'The Communists and Karl Heinzen', in Karl Marx and Frederick Engels (eds.), *Collected Works, Vol. 6*, New York: International Publishers, [1847] 1975, p. 303.

23 Karl Marx, *Capital*, vol. 1, London: Penguin, [1867] 1976, p. 435. Later in vol. 1 (ibid., p. 530) Marx says: 'machinery produces relative surplus value, not only by directly reducing the value of labour power, and indirectly cheapening it by cheapening the commodities that enter into its reproduction, but also, when it is first introduced sporadically into an industry, by converting the labour employed by the owner of that machinery into labour of a higher degree, by raising the social value of the article produced above its individual value, and thus enabling the capitalist to replace the value of a day's labour-power by a smaller portion of the value of a day's product'.

24 Marx, *Capital*, vol. 1, p. 435.

25 Marx, *Capital*, vol. 1, p. 137.

26 Marx, *Capital*, vol. 1, p. 702.

27 Karl Marx, *Capital*, vol. 3, London: Penguin, [1894] 1991, pp. 241–2.

28 Marx, *Capital*, vol. 3, p. 242.

29 Phrase cited from Andy Higginbottom, 'The System of Accumulation in South Africa: Theories of Imperialism and Capital', *Économies et Sociétés*, 2011, 45(2): 284, www.iippe.org/wiki/images/e/ee/CONF_SOA_Higginbottom.pdf (accessed on 22 March 2017).

30 Marx, *Capital*, vol. 1, p. 430–1.

31 Marx, *Capital*, vol. 1, p. 557.

32 Marx, *Capital*, vol. 3, p. 342; my emphasis.

33 Marx, *Capital*, vol. 3, p. 242.

34 Higginbottom, 'The System of Accumulation in South Africa: Theories of Imperialism and Capital', 268.

35 V.I. Lenin, 'The Revolutionary Proletariat and the Right of Nations to Self-Determination', in *Collected Works*, vol. 21, Moscow: Progress Publishers, [1915] 1964, p. 407.

36 V.I. Lenin, 'Imperialism, the Highest Stage of Capitalism', in *Collected Works*, vol. 22, Moscow: Progress Publishers, [1916] 1964, p. 266.

37 Lenin, 'Imperialism, the Highest Stage of Capitalism', vol. 22, p. 77.

38 Export of capital comes in three forms: FDI, portfolio investment (in shares and financial securities which, unlike FDI, do not give the investor a controlling influence) and loan capital.

39 Higginbottom, 'The System of Accumulation in South Africa', 284. The disinterment of the third form of surplus value – it was buried in full sight! – is a major breakthrough, made in his *The Third Form of Surplus Value Increase*, paper at the Historical Materialism conference, London, 27–29 November 2009, www.academia.edu/11418979/Third_form_of_extrac tion_surplus_value (accessed on 22 March 2017).

40 Karl Marx, *Grundrisse*, London: Penguin, [1858] 1973, p. 651. I am grateful to Walter Daum for pointing out the relevance of this passage.

41 Lenin, 'Imperialism, the Highest Stage of Capitalism', p. 265.

42 David Harvey, 2003, *The New Imperialism*, Oxford: Oxford University Press, p. 77.

43 Engels, 'The Communists and Karl Heinzen', p. 482.

3 Reflections on contemporary imperialism

Prabhat Patnaik

Phases of imperialism

Lenin dated the imperialist phase of capitalism, which he associated with monopoly capitalism, from the beginning of the twentieth century, when the process of centralisation of capital led to the emergence of monopoly in industry and among banks.[1] The coming together (coalescence) of the capitals in these two spheres led to the formation of 'finance capital' which was controlled by a financial oligarchy that dominated both these spheres, as well as the state, in each advanced capitalist country. The struggle between rival finance capitals for 'economic territory' in a world that was already completely partitioned, not just for the direct benefits that such 'territory' might provide, but more importantly for keeping rivals out of its potential benefits, necessarily erupted, according to him, into wars, which offered each belligerent country's workers a stark choice: killing fellow workers across the trenches, or turning their guns on the moribund capitalism of their own countries, to overthrow the system and march to socialism.

We can distinguish between three different phases of imperialism since then. The first phase, of which the Second World War was the climax, corresponded almost exactly with Lenin's analysis: rivalry between different finance capitals to repartition an already partitioned world bursting into wars which in turn led to the formation of a socialist camp. The precise course of events through which this general trend unfolded after Lenin's death included an acute economic crisis (the Great Depression of the 1930s), to which the disunity among capitalist powers contributed, which in turn created the conditions for the emergence of fascism that unleashed the Second World War and that represented in Dimitrov's words the 'open terrorist dictatorship of the most reactionary, most chauvinistic and most imperialist elements of finance capital'.[2]

The Second World War greatly weakened the position of financial oligarchies. The working class in the advanced capitalist countries which had made great sacrifices during the War emerged much stronger from it and unwilling to go back to the old capitalism. (A symptom of this was the defeat of Winston Churchill's Tory Party in the post-war elections in Britain and the enormous growth of the Italian and French Communist Parties.) The socialist camp had grown significantly and was to grow even further with the victory of the Chinese Revolution. Capitalism had to make concessions to survive, and two concessions in particular were significant: one was decolonisation, where it was so reluctant to proceed that even after the formal process was completed it refused voluntarily to yield control over third world resources, as evident in the cases of Iran (where Mossadegh was overthrown in a CIA coup after nationalising oil) and Egypt (where an Anglo-French invasion was launched after Nasser nationalised the Suez Canal). The other was state intervention in 'demand management' in advanced countries to maintain high levels of employment, which until then had never been experienced in capitalist economies. State intervention in demand management, in turn, was made possible through the imposition of controls over cross-border capital flows, and also over trade flows. A new international monetary system where the dollar was declared 'as good as gold' (exchangeable against gold at $35 per ounce) and which allowed such restrictions on trade and capital flows, came into being. It reflected the new reality of the domination of US imperialism, and a muting of inter-imperialist rivalries in the new scenario. This was the second phase of modern imperialism.

The conditions for the third phase, within which we are currently located, were created by this second phase itself. The dollar's being 'as good as gold' meant in effect that the United States was handed a free and unlimited gold mine: it could print notes and the rest of the world was obliged to hold such notes since they were 'as good as gold'. As a result, the United States did print notes to finance, among other things, a string of military bases all over the world with which it encircled the Soviet Union and China. These notes started pouring into European banks which then started lending all over the world. They wanted to lend even more as the torrent of notes increased during the Vietnam War. Capital controls were a hindrance, in their way, and were therefore gradually removed. The International Monetary System, under which the dollar was officially convertible to gold, could not be sustained and was abandoned in the early 1970s, though the pre-eminent position of the dollar as the form in which a large chunk of the world's wealth was held remained. But the easing of capital controls and increased mobility of finance across the globe brought into being a new entity, international finance capital.

This third phase of modern imperialism is marked by the hegemony of international finance capital, which is the driving force behind the phenomenon of globalisation, and the pursuit of neoliberal policies in the place of Keynesian demand management policies in the advanced countries and of Nehru-style 'planning' (or what some development economists call *dirigiste* policies) in the third world.

Finance capital then and now

In this third phase of imperialism, there has been such an immense growth of the financial sector within each capitalist economy and of financial flows across the globe that many have talked of a process of 'financialisation' of capitalism, rather like 'industrialisation' earlier. While this may be an accurate description of the processes involved, it does not draw attention to the entity that has come into centre stage, namely, international finance capital. This entity differs from finance capital of Lenin's time in at least three ways.

Firstly, while Lenin had talked about the 'coalescence' of finance and industry and referred to finance capital as capital 'controlled by banks and employed in industry', which tended to have a *national* strategy for expanding 'economic territory' that would also serve the needs of its industrial empire, the new finance capital is not necessarily tied to industry in any special sense. It moves around the world in the quest for quick, speculative gains, no matter in what sphere such gains accrue. This finance is not *separate* from industry, since even capital employed in industry is not immune to the quest for speculative gains, but industry does not occupy any special place in the plans of this finance capital. In other words, not only does capital-as-finance function as capital-as-finance, but even capital-in-production also functions as capital-as-finance; capital-as-finance on the other hand has no special interest in production. This is basically what the process of 'financialisation' involves, namely, an enormous growth of capital-as-finance, pure and simple, and its quest for quick speculative gains.[3]

Secondly, finance capital in Lenin's time had its base within a particular nation, and its international operations were linked to the expansion of that nation's 'economic territory'. But the finance capital of today, though of course it has its origins in particular nations, is not necessarily tied to any 'national' interests. It moves around globally, and its objectives are no different from those of finance capital that has its origins in some other nation. It is in this sense that distinctions between 'national' finance capitals become misleading, and we can talk of an international finance capital, which, no matter where it originates from, has this character of being detached from any particular 'national' interests, having the world as its theatre of operations, and not being tied to any particular sphere of activity, such as industry.

Thirdly, such uninhibited global operation requires that the world should not be split up into separate blocs or into economic territories that are the preserves of particular nations and are out of bounds for others. The interests of international finance capital, therefore, require a muting of inter-imperialist rivalry. If this process of muting of inter-imperialist rivalry began in the post-war period as an outcome of the overwhelming economic and strategic strength of the United States among capitalist powers, it gets sustained in the current phase by the very nature of international finance capital.

To say this is not to suggest that contradictions do not exist among these powers, or that they are not engaged in intense competition in world trade, of which the present currency wars (which amount to a 'beggar-my-neighbour' policy) are a reflection.[4] But such contradictions are kept in check by the need of globalised finance to have the entire globe as its unrestricted arena of operations. Certainly, the idea of these contradictions bursting into open wars *among the advanced capitalist countries*, or even proxy wars among them, appears farfetched in the foreseeable future.

Many have seen in this fact a vindication of Karl Kautsky's theory of 'ultra-imperialism', which referred to the possibility of a peaceful and 'joint exploitation of the world by internationally united finance capital', as against Lenin's emphasis on inter-imperialist rivalry and the inevitability of wars. But the world has moved beyond the Kautskyan perception as well, so that using his concept of 'ultra-imperialism' in today's context is misleading for at least two reasons. Firstly, 'internationally-united finance capital' of Kautsky is not the same as 'international finance capital' of today. We are not talking about unity among a handful of 'national' finance capitals of major capitalist countries, but we are talking about an international phenomenon which goes beyond 'national' finance capitals and is no longer confined to a handful of powerful countries. It is both composed of finance capitals of different national origins, including from third world countries, and also moves around the entire globe pursuing its own interest and no particular national capitalist interest. Secondly, Lenin's emphasis on wars as accompanying imperialism remains as valid today as it was in his time. World wars among imperialist countries may not appear on the horizon; but other kinds of war arising from the phenomenon of imperialism, of which the Iraq war, the war in Afghanistan and the earlier war in the Balkans are examples, continue.

Globalisation of finance and the nation state

In the current phase of imperialism, finance capital has become international, while the state remains a nation state. The nation state, therefore, must willy-nilly bow before the wishes of finance, for otherwise finance (both originating in that country and brought in from outside) will leave that particular country and move elsewhere, reducing it to illiquidity and disrupting its economy. The process of globalisation of finance, therefore, has the effect of undermining the autonomy of the nation state. The state cannot do what it wishes to do, or what its elected government has been elected to do, since it must do what finance wishes it to do.

It is in the nature of finance capital to oppose any state intervention, other than that which promotes its own interest. It does not want an activist state when it comes to the promotion of employment, or the provision of welfare, or the protection of small and petty producers; but it wants the state to be active exclusively in its own interest. It brings about, therefore, a change in the nature of the state, from being an apparently supra-class entity standing above society, and intervening in a benevolent manner for 'social good', to one that is concerned almost exclusively with the interests of finance capital. To justify this change which occurs in the era of globalisation under pressure from finance capital, *the interests of finance are increasingly passed off as being synonymous with the interests of society.* If the stock market is doing well, then the economy is supposed to be doing well, no matter what happens to the levels of hunger, malnutrition or poverty. If a country is graded well by credit-rating agencies, then that becomes a matter of national pride, no matter how miserable its people are.

The point, however, is that this 'inverted logic', this apparent illusionism, is not just a misconception or false propaganda; it has an element of truth and is rooted in the actual universe of globalisation. It is indeed the case that if finance lacks 'confidence' in a particular country and flows out of it, then that country will face dire consequences through a liquidity crisis, so that pleasing finance, no matter how oppressive it is, is a pre-condition for economic survival *within this system.* This 'inverted logic', therefore, is the direct offshoot of a real-life phenomenon, namely, the hegemony of international finance capital. It cannot be overcome by appealing to some 'correct logic' or some 'correct priorities of the state'; it requires the transcendence of the hegemony of international finance capital. It requires in short not 'reform' within a system dominated by finance capital but an overcoming of the system itself.

Finance capital's insistence upon a non-activist state, except when the activism is in its own interest, takes in particular the form of imposing fiscal austerity upon the state. In the old days, 'sound finance' on the part of the state that was favoured by finance capital consisted of balancing its budget. At present, it takes the form, pervasively, of a 3 percent limit on the size of the fiscal deficit relative to GDP. This is the limit legislated across the world from the EU to India and sought to be enforced. (The one exception among capitalist countries is the United States which alone among these countries enjoys a degree of fiscal autonomy. But this is because its currency is still considered de facto, though no longer de jure, to be 'as good as gold'; hence, it constitutes the medium in which much of the world's wealth is held; capital flight out of the United States, owing to displeasure on the part of finance over the size of its fiscal deficit, therefore, will be resisted by the entire capitalist world, a fact that speculators themselves are well aware of.)

Since the nation state pursuing trade liberalisation has to cut customs duties and, therefore, must restrict excise duties (so as not to discriminate between domestic and foreign capitalists) and since in the interests of 'capital accumulation' it keeps taxes on corporate incomes, and hence, for reasons of *inter se* parity personal incomes, low, the limit on the fiscal deficit causes an *expenditure deflation* on its part. And this provides the setting for 'privatising' not only state-owned assets 'for a song' but also welfare services and social overheads like education and health.

All this is usually referred to as constituting a 'withdrawal of the state' and its rationale is debated in terms of 'the state' versus 'the market'. Nothing could be more wrong than this. *The state under neoliberalism does not withdraw*; it is involved as closely as before, or even more closely than before, in the economy, but its intervention is now of a different sort, namely, exclusively in the interests of finance capital.

The events in several advanced capitalist countries in the wake of the world financial crisis, in 2008, underscore this point. The state in those countries incurred a fiscal deficit in order to shore up the banks which had financed speculative bubbles earlier and had now fallen heavily with the bursting of the bubbles. To cut the fiscal deficit, however, the state had to truncate its welfare state measures, at the expense of the working masses. The state, in short, intervened in favour of finance capital, but withdrew from intervention in favour of the working people. In India itself, despite significant hunger and malnutrition, the state hoards vast stocks of foodgrains because their release through the public distribution system would raise the fiscal deficit, hence, offend finance capital.

Not surprisingly, both Keynesian demand management in the advanced capitalist countries and third world *dirigisme* become untenable in the era of globalisation. The nation state in the era of globalisation, in short, becomes a custodian of the interests of international finance capital, which has the obvious effect of attenuating and diminishing political democracy, since, no matter which political formation the people elect, the same economic policies continue to be pursued.

The global financial community

The restrictions on the activities of the nation state are imposed not just by the fear of a capital flight. A whole ideological apparatus, and with it a whole army of ideologues, gets built for supporting neoliberal policies. Since finance capital itself becomes *international* in character, the controllers of this international finance capital constitute, to borrow Lenin's expression, a *global financial oligarchy*. This global financial oligarchy requires for its functioning an army of spokesmen, media persons, professors, bureaucrats, technocrats and politicians located in different countries.

The creation of this army is a complex enterprise, in which one can discern at least three distinct processes. Two are fairly straightforward. If a country has got drawn into the vortex of globalised finance by opening its doors to the free movement of finance capital, then willy-nilly even well-meaning bureaucrats, politicians and professors will demand, *in the national interest*, a bowing to the caprices of the global financial oligarchy, since not doing so will cost the country dearly through debilitating and destabilising capital flights. The task in short is automatically accomplished, to an extent, once a country has got trapped into opening its doors to financial flows.

The second process is the exercise of peer pressure. Finance ministers, governors of central banks and top financial bureaucrats belonging to different countries, when they meet, tend increasingly to constitute what has been called an 'epistemic community'.[5] They begin increasingly to speak the same language, share the same world view and subscribe to the same prejudices, the same theoretical positions that have been aptly described as the 'humbug of finance'.[6] Those who do not are under tremendous peer pressure to fall in line, and most eventually do. Peer pressure may be buttressed by the more mundane temptations that Lenin described, ranging from straightforward bribes to lucrative offers of post-retirement employment, but, whatever the method used, conformism to the 'humbug' that globalised finance dishes out as true economics becomes a mark of 'respectability'.

But even peer pressure requires that there should be a group of core ideologues of finance capital who exert and manipulate this pressure. The 'peers' themselves are not free-floating individuals but have to be goaded into sharing a belief system. There has to be, therefore, a set of key intellectuals, ideologues, thinkers and strategists who promote this belief system, shape and broadcast the ideology of finance capital, and generally, look after the interests of globalised finance. They are not necessarily capitalists or magnates; but they are close to the financial magnates, and usually share the 'spoils'. The financial oligarchy proper, consisting of these magnates, together with these key ideologues and publicists of finance capital, constitute the 'global financial community'. The function of this global financial community is to promote and perpetuate the hegemony of international finance capital. And this global financial community insinuates its way into the political systems of various countries, initially as IMF and World Bank-trained 'advisers' into economic ministries and, subsequently, as cabinet ministers and even office-bearers of established political parties.

Reforms are undertaken everywhere in the education system to rid it of the vestiges of any worldview different from what the global financial community propagates. They play an important role in the ideological hegemony of finance capital. The process of privatisation and commoditisation of education facilitates the instituting of such reforms.

Contradictions of globalisation

The neoliberal regime imposed upon the world by the ascendancy of globalised finance capital entails a number of serious contradictions which bring the system to an impasse. What we are witnessing at present is such an impasse. There are at least four contradictions which need to be noted.

The first is the fact that free movement of goods and services and of capital (though not of labour) has made it difficult to sustain the wage difference between the advanced and backward economies that had traditionally characterised capitalism. Since broadly similar technologies are available to all economies (and the free movement of capital ensures this), commodities produced with the cheaper labour that exists in the third world economies can outcompete those produced in the advanced countries. Because of this, wages in the advanced countries cannot rise, and if anything, tend to fall,[7] in order to make their products more competitive, to move a little closer towards the levels that prevail in the third world, levels which are no higher, thanks to the existence of substantial labour reserves, than those needed to satisfy some historically determined subsistence requirements. Advanced country workers, in other words, can no longer escape the baneful consequences of third world labour reserves (which were created through colonial and semi-colonial exploitation that caused 'deindustrialisation' in, and imposed a 'drain of surplus' from, the dominated economies). And, even as wages in the advanced countries cease to increase at the prevailing levels of labour productivity, labour productivity in the third world countries moves up at the prevailing level of wages, towards the level reached in the advanced countries. This is because the wage differences that still continue to exist, induce a diffusion of activities from the former to the latter *and hence, a reduction in the share of wages in the total world output.*

Such a reduction in the share of wages in world output also occurs for yet another, analytically distinct, reason: as technological progress in the world economy raises the level of labour productivity *all around*, the wages of workers do not increase in tandem, again owing to these wages being tied to the existence of substantial labour reserves in the world economy.

As a result, taking the world economy as a whole, there is both an increase in income inequalities, and, as a consequence, a growing problem of inadequate aggregate demand: since a dollar in the hands of the working people is spent largely on consumption while a dollar in the hands of the capitalists is partly saved, any shift in income distribution from wages to profits tends to depress demand and create a 'realisation problem'. Credit financed expenditure and expenditure stimulated by speculative asset price 'bubbles' provide only temporary antidotes to this tendency towards over-production at the world level, but with the bursting of such 'bubbles' and the inevitable termination of such credit financing, the basic underlying crisis of the world economy reappears with all its intensity.[8]

The second contradiction under the neoliberal regime arises from this. Any deficiency of aggregate demand resulting in unemployment and recession naturally affects the high-wage and, therefore, high-cost producers in the advanced countries more severely than those in the low-wage countries like India or China. Countries like the United

States therefore, experience, as a result of this world tendency towards over-production, *not only higher levels of unemployment but also continuous and growing current account deficits on their balance of payments.* In short, acute unemployment, particularly in the hitherto high-wage economies and the so-called problem of 'world imbalances' (whereby countries like China have continuous and growing current account surpluses while the United States has growing deficits and hence gets increasingly indebted) are both caused by the neoliberal regime imposed upon the world by globalised finance capital. While US multinational corporations and US financial interests demand neoliberal regimes everywhere, the fall-out of this demand is stagnant, or even reduced, wages and reduced employment for the US workers.

If the state in the advanced economies like the United States could intervene to promote demand, then unemployment there could be reduced. But as we have seen, the regime of globalised finance entails a rolling back of state intervention in demand management. Of course, the state of the leading economy, the United States, whose currency, being almost 'as good as gold', enjoys a degree of immunity from the caprices of international finance capital in this respect, still retains some fiscal autonomy and can still undertake demand management, since capital flight away from its currency will not be too serious. But since the leading-currency country itself is getting progressively indebted, its ability to undertake demand management also suffers. The incapacity of the capitalist state to undertake demand management as earlier constitutes the third contradiction of the neoliberal regime, within which, therefore, there is no effective solution to the problem of global over-production and global imbalances.

Neoliberalism, in short, pushes capitalism towards a protracted crisis for several co-acting reasons: it creates a tendency towards over-production in the world economy by engendering inequalities in world income distribution; it enfeebles capitalist nation states for undertaking demand management; and it also undermines the capacity of the leading state for playing a similar role, but for a different reason, namely, by saddling it with continuous and acute current account deficits.

It may be thought that the crisis we are talking about is primarily concerned with the advanced capitalist world, which will continue to remain sunk in it for a long time to come (and if by chance there is a new 'bubble' that temporarily lifts it out of this crisis, its inevitable collapse will plunge it back into crisis) that the third world, especially countries like India, are immune to it. This, however, is where the fourth contradiction of neoliberal capitalism becomes relevant. *This relates to the fact that the bourgeois-led state in the third world withdraws from its role of supporting, protecting and promoting the peasant and petty producers' economy, as the domestic big bourgeoisie and financial interests become closely integrated with international finance capital under the neoliberal regime, leading to a fracturing of the nation and the development of a deep hiatus within it.* The abandonment of this role which the bourgeois-led state had taken upon itself during the dirigiste period as a part of the legacy of the struggle for decolonisation, causes a decimation of petty production, the unleashing of a process of primitive accumulation of capital (or what may be more generally called a process of 'accumulation through encroachment').[9] Multinational retail chains like Walmart come up to displace petty traders; agribusiness comes in to squeeze the peasantry; land grabbing financiers come in to displace peasants from their land; and petty producers of all descriptions everywhere get trapped between rising input prices caused by withdrawal of state subsidies and declining output prices caused by the withdrawal of state protection from world commodity price trends. When we add to all this the rise in the cost of living, because of the privatisation of education, health and several essential services, which affects the entire working population, we can gauge the virulence of the process of primitive accumulation that is unleashed.

The current period, therefore, is one where it is not only the advanced capitalist countries that are beset with crisis and unemployment, but even apparently 'successful', 'high growth' countries like India. The former are affected by the problem of inadequate demand, the latter by both the fall-out of the former's crisis (via its effects on peasants' prices and export activities) and also by the additional problem of distress and dispossession of petty producers and the unemployment engendered by it. Both segments of the world economy, therefore, get afflicted by acute social crisis.

Some other perspectives on contemporary imperialism

We have discussed contemporary imperialism so far on the basis of Lenin's analysis, that is, taking his analysis as our point of departure. In contemporary writings on imperialism, however, we come across certain other perspectives. Let us examine some of these.

One such perspective sees imperialism not in terms of the immanent economic logic of capitalism, which, through the process of centralisation of capital, gives rise first to the finance capital that Lenin had analysed, and subsequently to international finance capital; instead it emphasises imperialism as a political project undertaken by the state of the leading imperialist country, the United States, for globalising its brand of capitalism through enlisting the support of other advanced capitalist states. It, therefore, sees a continuity in the imperialist project in the post-war period, in terms of a persistent attempt by the US state to build an 'informal empire' by taking other capitalist states on board. This project might have been thwarted in some periods (such as the dirigiste period in the third world) and advanced rapidly in others (such as the more recent 'era of globalisation'). But through all these vicissitudes, it is essentially a conscious, planned political project.

The difference between this perspective and the one outlined earlier is methodological, hence, quite fundamental. By taking the leading country's state as the driving force behind imperialism, it attributes not just a *relative autonomy* to the state but in fact an *absolute autonomy*. The state, it admits, acts within an economic milieu, but it does not see economics as driving politics. In fact, it rejects such a proposition as being 'reductionist'. It, therefore, departs from the fundamental understanding of capitalism as being a 'spontaneous' or self-driven system that is unplanned, and therefore incapable of resolving its own basic contradictions.

An immediate consequence of this position is to underestimate the current impasse of capitalism. More generally, the methodological flaw in the approach that attributes autonomy to politics is that it cannot anticipate events, but can only explain them post facto. There are no foreclosed options for capitalism in any given situation imposed by the intrinsic economic logic of the system; the state as an autonomous agency can always mould the system to overcome whatever predicament it may happen to be in. Whether it will be able to do so or not can only be known after the event. This approach, therefore, is not conducive to conscious revolutionary praxis founded upon the building of revolutionary class alliances on the basis of anticipating the course of movement of society as a whole.

A very different perspective is provided by the influential work by Hardt and Negri,[10] which talks of a transition from 'modern' imperialism based on nation states to a 'post-modern' global Empire, a transnational entity comparable to ancient Rome. With the rise of the Empire, there is an end to national conflicts. The Empire is total: victorious global capitalism completely permeates our social lives, appropriates for itself the entire space of 'civilisation' and presents its 'enemy' only as a 'criminal', a 'terrorist' who is a threat not to a political system or a nation but to the entire ethical order.

Unlike the standard Leftist position, however, which struggles to limit the destructive potential of globalisation by preserving the welfare state for instance, Hardt and Negri see a revolutionary potential in this dynamic; the standard left position from their perspective, therefore, appears to be a conservative one, fearful of the dynamics of globalisation. In this sense, they can claim an affinity to Marx who did not advocate limiting the destructive potential of capitalism but saw in it an enormous advance for mankind which *had to be carried forward through the transcendence of capitalism itself.*

But even if this affinity is granted for argument's sake, there is nonetheless a basic difference even in this regard between Marx on the one hand and Hardt and Negri on the other. This difference is the fact that while Marx saw not only the necessity for the transcendence of capitalism but also the fact that the system produced the instrument, namely, the proletariat, through which it could be carried out, Hardt and Negri's practical proposals for going beyond contemporary globalisation come as a damp squib.

The authors propose political struggles for three global rights: the right to global citizenship, the right to a minimal income and the right to a re-appropriation of the new means of production (that is, access to and control over education, information and communication). Instead of concrete strategies of struggle, we thus end up with mere pious wishes.

Take, for instance, the right to a minimal income. The immanent tendency of capitalism to produce 'wealth at one pole and poverty at another' is manifesting itself at present through a vicious process of absolute immiserisation, caused by an unleashing of primitive accumulation of capital that is not accompanied by any significant absorption of the impoverished into the ranks of the proletariat. The demand for a minimal level of income in this context is meaningless unless we are willing to transcend capitalism and struggle for an alternative system which is free of any immanent tendency to produce such absolute impoverishment. The logic of this alternative system, the nature of this alternative system and the roadmap for getting to this alternative system (which we call socialism) must therefore be worked out if we are serious about the right to a minimal level of income. The demand for such a right within capitalism then can only play the role of a *transitional demand* (in Lenin's sense), which is unrealisable within the system but which can act as a mobilising, educating and illuminating device.

To argue, *in general*, for a minimal level of income, therefore, is an illusion if it is considered achievable within capitalism, and a mere pious wish if the contours of a society within which it is achievable are not analysed. To detach this demand from the struggle for socialism is reflective of a theoretical flaw, which afflicts *Empire*. The book, notwithstanding its several insights, does not have any analysis of the tendencies immanent in globalisation, does not examine the economics of the system and does not see its 'spontaneity'; its self-driven character that both create its own grave-diggers and give rise to conjunctures for revolutionary political praxis.

Georg Lukacs once said that the remarkable property of Marxism was that every idea that apparently went beyond Marx was in fact a reversion to something pre-Marxian. Hardt and Negri's post-Marxist analysis paradoxically ends up regressing to a position that is even pre-utopian socialist.

The struggle against imperialism

The nature of the crisis, as argued earlier, differed somewhat between the first and third worlds. In the former it is primarily a crisis of insufficiency of aggregate demand, which manifests itself in terms of unemployment and unutilised capacity, while in the latter (especially in countries like India), this aspect of the crisis, though very much present, is reinforced by the impoverishment of the peasants and petty producers through a process of primitive accumulation of capital and of the workers too as a consequence of it. It follows that class alliances behind the struggle will be different in the two theatres.

In the former, the working class, the immigrants, the so-called 'underclass', together with the white-collar employees and the urban middle class, will combine to provide resistance, as is happening in Greece, France, Ireland and England, though of course, as also happens in all such situations, there is a parallel growth of fascism promoted by finance capital that seeks to thwart and disrupt this resistance. In the latter, it is the peasants, petty producers, agricultural labourers, marginalised sections like the tribals and dalits, and the working class that will combine to provide the resistance, while segments of the urban middle class, who are not yet affected by crisis and continue to benefit from whatever growth has been ushered in by globalisation, may for the time being remain followers of the big bourgeoisie and financial interests.

The crucial difference thus relates to two segments: the peasants and petty producers who are a significant anti-imperialist force in the third world but are of less significance in the first, and the urban middle class, which is a militant force in the first world but vacillates or tails the big bourgeoisie in the third world. (Latin America is different in this respect both in having a relatively small peasantry and in having an urban middle class that has experienced acute distress caused by its longer history of globalisation and unrestrained neoliberalism.)

Given this difference, a coordinated global resistance is not on the horizon, in which case the struggle against imperialist globalisation must take diverse forms in diverse regions. In countries like India, at any rate, it must entail forming a worker–peasant alliance around a national agenda based on a judicious de-linking from the global order.

The proposal for a selective de-linking of the national economy from the global economy will be objected to by many, since it appears to involve a retreat to 'nationalism' from a regime of globalisation. True, globalisation is dominated by international finance capital and is carried out under the aegis of imperialism, but the way to fight it, many would argue, is through coordinated international actions by the workers and peasants. Nationalism, even anti-imperialist nationalism, they would hold, represents a retreat from such international struggles, hence, a degree of shutting oneself off from the world, which has potentially reactionary implications.

There are two basic arguments against this position. Firstly, internationally coordinated struggles, even of workers, is not a feasible proposition in the foreseeable future. And, when we see the peasantry as being a major force in the struggle against imperialist globalisation in countries like India, so infeasible is the international coordination of peasant struggles that one cannot help feeling that those who insist on such international coordination are altogether oblivious of the peasant question. In other words, any analysis that accords centrality to the alliance of workers and peasants as the means of embarking on an alternative strategy, cannot but see the struggle against imperialist globalisation as being nation-based, with the objective of bringing about a change in the class-nature of the nation state.

Secondly, as already mentioned, such de-linking is essential for bringing about an improvement in the living condition of workers in any country. The workers who struggle for such an improvement cannot possibly be asked to wait until a new world state has come into being that is favourably disposed to the interests of workers and peasants.

Any delay on the part of the left in third world countries like India in working towards such a worker–peasant alliance against imperialist globalisation will have serious consequences for another reason: the peasants will not wait for the left to organise them; they will turn to all kinds of fundamentalist organisations to spearhead their resistance against the new global order if the left does not step in. It is possible to detect to a certain extent the class support of peasants and petty producers behind certain strands of Islamic fundamentalism, just as the same class support lies behind the rise of an Evo Morales in Bolivia. Which trajectory is followed in a particular country depends inter alia upon how quickly the left moves to organise the peasantry as a militant force aligned with the working class against imperialist globalisation.

But, leaving aside pragmatism, does not a retreat into a national agenda represent a conservative, defensive reaction of the sort that Hardt and Negri had criticised, as opposed to seizing the dynamics of globalisation for a revolutionary carrying forward of the process? Is not a retreat to a national agenda against the march of history, an un-dialectical act of setting the clock back? The answer to this question lies in the fact that the forward march of history is ensured by the lead provided by a force that comprehends 'the historical process as a whole', a force that brings the revolutionary class outlook to the working class and organises the peasantry around it. The march of history is not reducible to formulae about whether the *terrain of* resistance is national or international; it depends upon whether the leading force in the resistance is *internationalist* or reactionary.

The crisis of capitalism, as argued earlier, is likely to be a protracted one. It will pass through many phases and many twists and turns, some even adverse to the left, just as during the unfolding of the 1930s crisis. But it is pregnant with historical possibilities of a socialist transition for mankind if the left makes proper use of this conjuncture, as Lenin did earlier.

Notes

1 V.I. Lenin, *Imperialism, the Highest Phase of Capitalism*, with an Introduction by P. Patnaik, New Delhi: Leftword Books, 2000, p. 42.
2 Georgi Dimitrov, *Against Fascism and War*, New York: International Publishers, 1986, p. 2.
3 For a discussion of contemporary finance in an advanced capitalist economy, see Paul M. Sweezy and Harry Magdoff, *Stagnation and The Financial Explosion*, New York: Monthly Review Press, 1987; see also John Bellamy Foster, *Naked Imperialism*, New York: Monthly Review Press, 2006.
4 Since exchange rate depreciations are typically against the US dollar, the United States itself is increasingly resorting to direct protectionism in various forms. For a discussion of these 'beggar-my-neighbour' policies, see Prabhat Patnaik, 'Capitalism and Its Current Crisis', *Monthly Review*, New York, January 2016.

5 I first came across this term in the course of a talk by the Argentinian economist Arturo O'Connell.
6 Joan Robinson uses this term to describe the view that fiscal deficits should be avoided (beyond a small ceiling at the most) under all circumstances. See Joan Robinson, *Economic Philosophy*, Harmondsworth: Penguin Books, 1966.
7 Joseph Stiglitz finds that, adjusted for price rise, a typical male American worker's income in 2011 was lower than in 1968; see Joseph Stiglitz, 'Inequality is Holding Back the Economic Recovery', *New York Times*, 13 January 2013.
8 Patnaik, 'Capitalism and Its Current Crisis'.
9 Prabhat Patnaik, 'The Economics of the New Phase of Imperialism', in *Re-Envisioning Socialism*, New Delhi: Tulika Books, 2011.
10 Michael Hardt and Antonio Negri, *Empire*, Cambridge, MA: Harvard University Press, 2000.

4 The particularity of imperialism in the stage of neoliberal globalisation and global capitalism

A dialogue between Nikolai Bukharin and Aimé Césaire[1]

Anjan Chakrabarti

> The scientific significance of N.I. Bukharin's work consists particularly in this, that he examines the fundamental facts of world economy relating to imperialism as a whole, as a definite stage in the growth of most highly developed capitalism.[2]

> Capitalism has attempted to tame the working class and to subdue social contradictions by decreasing the steam pressure through the aid of a colonial valve. But having accomplished this task for a moment, it thus prepared the explosion of the whole capitalist boiler.[3]

Taking off from Nikolai Bukharin's classic *Imperialism and World Economy*, we integrate some of his insights into a class-focused Marxian framework to rethink the relevance and particularity of imperialism as a category in the contemporary.[4] Bukharin's long lasting contribution is methodological as Lenin suggests. The 'colonial valve' that Bukharin invokes is the equivalent of *outside* of capitalism, without which, he insists, one cannot comprehend the historical form of imperialism in the early twentieth century. It is notable that he uses the category of outside in a spatial sense. Bukharin is put to dialogue with Aimé Césaire who insists on, alongside class, the importance of the 'Negro' question in the context of capitalism under post-colonial condition. The Negro question is the equivalent of the outside in Césaire. However, unlike Bukharin, Césaire considers this outside primarily as a standpoint, that is, forming the perspective of/from the 'Negro' location. From our vantage point, the aspects of colonial valve/spatial (Bukharin) and the Negro/perspectival (Césaire) are different ways of emphasising the importance of the outside to global capitalism.

In this essay, I deploy the class-focused framework[5] to bring these two elements (colonial valve/spatial; Negro question/perspective) together to formulate *a theory of outside*. This realm of outside is what we name as *world of the third*.[6] This outside in turn helps unpack the contemporary particularity of imperialism in its connection with capitalism. Along with class domination that the hitherto nation state-induced imperialism has been credited with (which is what we call 'external' imperialism), we unpack imperialism is also the *domestically induced policy of conquest of world of the third carried out at the behest of global capital*. This is 'internal' imperialism, encapsulating how independent nations (sometimes called underdeveloped/ developing or postcolonial) initiate on behalf of global capital a policy of conquest of world of the third *from within*. This domestic policy, in turn, is related to attempts to adapt to the contradictions of global capitalism in developed nations and in maturing capitalisms like India. In its contemporary form, imperialism represents an overdetermined and contradictory relation between its 'internal' and 'external' forms.[7]

Situating the problem of imperialism

Nikolai Bukharin[8] argued that imperialism must be analysed in its historical context and that it must be seen as a 'policy of conquest' through force and violence, though every policy of conquest is not imperialism. For the latter to be imperialist, one needs to find out the basis of the policy of conquest which in turn must be traceable to the class characterisation of imperialism, especially the connection of the policy of conquest with that of global capitalism. If we take his methodology (and not the content specifying the particular historical context of his time) to be our point of reference and departure, then undoubtedly, imperialism in today's historical context has many tricky territories to counter.

If neoliberal globalisation is the category that encapsulates much of the erstwhile characteristics of imperialism, then why do we need imperialism? What is so distinct about imperialism today? If not, wither imperialism! We beg to differ. We contend that it is not an either/or choice.

Neoliberal globalisation is the polished condition of global capitalism, while imperialism embodies a 'tooth and claw' policy of conquest through force and violence. The two are constitutive components of global capitalism that make and remake the world. Only in their connectivity is the complex and contradictory nature of capitalism unpacked in the present historical stage. That is why it may not be correct to infer that neoliberal globalisation per se had usurped the erstwhile stage of imperialism to appear as the present higher stage of capitalism. During this long hundred-year period, imperialism has undergone shifts, modifications and relocations in order to preserve its core, bare minimum, content (as a policy of conquest on behalf of global capital) such that, in conjunction with neoliberal globalisation, it continues to be a necessary ally of capitalism. There is a need to conceptually extract the core content of imperialism from that of its forms – its manifested physiognomy – which could be historically divergent depending upon the ensemble of constituting effects that make up a particular conjuncture. In case we are unable to specify the relation of the core content with the physiognomy of imperialism, we shall perhaps fail to identify its particularity or relevance in the making and unmaking of (global) capitalism.

Following Bukharin's line, two conditions are necessary for the 'policy of conquest' to qualify as an instance of imperialism: it must encapsulate force and violence in some form and this force and violence must appear in direct connection with global capital through a policy of conquest of 'colony' (which will be qualified later). We posit this as the core content of imperialism. If one or the other is missing then that does not qualify as imperialism. The core content also explains why imperialism cannot be reduced to neoliberal globalisation, whether conceptually or in its historical form. Instead, a better frame to capture and analyse contemporary global capitalism is to identify imperialism and neoliberal globalisation as broadly its two conditions of existence, to unpack their respective features and effects, and to analyse their combined effects in any concrete instance.

The above discussion takes us to the stage of imperialism. The world has moved from domination of global capital (under colonialism) to nation capital (as nation states acquired formal independence) to back to global capital (under neoliberal globalisation).[9] How do we theorise contemporary imperialism in the absence of nation-based colonialism or predominantly nation-based capitalism? This makes the context different from what Bukharin or the post-Second World War imperialist literature dealt with. In Bukharin, for instance, the roles of 'world economy', 'national state' and 'finance capital' are central and interwoven in the characterisation of imperialism. These though appear as very different in today's historical context. To cite a few differences, the process of carving out the markets of world economy through wars and conquests has given way to neoliberal globalisation that is founded on a different principle of competitive market economy (created and shaped by state and global institutions) to be motored by supposedly independent and autonomous mass of rational ability machines or today's homo economicus. Nation-states, at least formally, pay heed to the principle of free competitive market of neoliberal globalisation and generally altered their policy paradigm and rule of law to accommodate this condition. Despite variations across nations, a new form of capitalism appeared under the scenario of neoliberal globalisation. This capitalism is unlike what informed Bukharin's 'finance capital', which was made up of highly centralised productive and unproductive capital[10] combined into trusts controlled by the state (the stage of monopoly capitalism) that competed over colonies to get access to raw materials and markets; for Bukharin, this 'colonial valve' serving as the outside of capital is critical for imperialism to exist as the pioneer of monopoly capitalism. Moreover, if the relation between the nation-state and global capital has altered (some even argue, not correctly in our opinion, in favour of total subsuming of nation-state to the logic/networks of capital and Empire), then we need to unpack the class character of imperialism of this new global order. This indeed was Bukharin's point. Finally, one needs to highlight the difference in the role of imperialism. During the early twentieth-century phase, Bukharin showed how the world economic order based on colonialism and the contradictions emanating from monopoly capitalism culminated in the imperialist policy of war and conflict between nation-states in developed capitalism to carve out the world. But, today, the form of imperialism is different. As David Ruccio avers contemporary imperialism:

> do not involve a political or economic carving up of the world . . . *not individual parts of the world but the world as whole, a project to recolonise the entire world*, to remake it, with the zeal of a humanising mission, precisely reminiscent of the 'Civilisation, Christianity, and Commerce' theme that, according to the legendary David Livingstone, was the basis of the European civilization. . . . And, just like the classical imperialisms, the new one involves subject peoples who are producing their own vigorous cultures and economies of opposition and resistance.
>
> (italics author's)[11]

It is a challenge to once again theorise imperialism and resistance to it within a historical conjuncture in which it is embedded with global capitalism and neoliberal globalisation, and where, while the relation between 'world economy', 'nation-state' and 'finance capital' remain, they are not the same as in Bukharin's time and these do not even mean the same thing. Therefore, the problem at hand: taking off from the 'thin' core content of imperialism forwarded by Bukharin, how do we go about theorising imperialism such that we can mark out the particularity and relevance of imperialism in the contemporary?

The particularity of imperialism and anti-imperialism

The task of theorising imperialism in the contemporary requires some preliminary comments and qualifications. We start with the question of global capital. It is our contention that the new global order has helped reshape the makeup and location of global capital such that (a) its theatre of operation is the entire globe, and (b) it is now cultivated from within the post-colonial nations.[12] Once detached from its erstwhile moorings in north–south division, global capital (productive and unproductive) can be located spatially within the centre of circuits that connect the global capitalist enterprises with the other local capitalist and non-capitalist enterprises through the local and global markets (henceforth, local–global markets). With global capital as the privileged centre, we call this spatialised domain as the *circuits of global capital*. Creation, solidification and expansion of global capital would imply growth and extension of the circuits of global capital. There is an outside to the circuits of global capital, both in a spatial and perspective sense. We have provisionally named it as world of the third. However, for imperialism to appear, world of the third needs to be displaced and re-located as third world. As we shall explore soon, *circuits of global capital – world of the third – third world* constitute the triad essential to capture the particularity of contemporary imperialism.

In so far as the particularity of the policy of conquest at the behest of global capital is concerned, the theatre of imperialism has decisively shifted from nation to nation confrontation to one functioning and appearing from within; it is the insidedness of imperialism as the generalised condition, or what we call *internal imperialism*, that distinguishes the present form of imperialism. This feature of internalness of imperialism, imperialism through the churning within nation itself, is irreducible to any other formulations of imperialism based on the political geography of nation state that functioned with the premise of global capital movement *across* nations states through force and violence (which we call external imperialism). This is not to ignore the latter but to connect *external imperialism* with internal imperialism, whose site of operation is domestic, deep inside the nation state and in need for a different interpretation than that flowing from the extant political theories of nation states and geography. The rest of this section is focused on accomplishing a connection between the mentioned triad and internal imperialism as a distinct policy of conquest carried out on behalf of global capital through force and violence.

Theorising internal imperialism, however, throws up the vexed problem of conceptualising world of the third as outside to the circuits of global capital. In so far as the study of imperialism is concerned, the clue to this line of thinking was present in Bukharin's invocation of 'colony'. The *colonial valve* that Bukharin refers to is literally sparse today if not non-existent, but the *idea* of 'colonial valve' is central in understanding contemporary imperialism. From our vantage point, colony must not be seen as geographical fix, pre-determined by conception of nation states, but as a name for the outside in geographical rotation. It refers to the outside of global capital(ism) – world of the third.

The rethinking of the idea of 'colony' is what makes us move from Bukharin to Aimé Césaire's *Discourse on Colonialism* in which the footprints of this idea of colony and its critique are pervasively present. An auto-critical conception of imperialism must not only confront the class question with reference to 'colony' but also the site of what Césaire called the problem of the 'Negroes', and that too do so by combining the two within a systemic presentation of imperialism. How do we bring Césaire's 'Negro' question and 'Negro' perspective into the framework? The clue to this is that while Bukharin's 'colony' entails a spatial reference, the inference to 'Negro' suggests a noun like existence, a body in living motion which has a perspective emanating from the 'colonial experience' or, in our terms, the experience of/from the outside.

In the specific context of imperialism, the outside needs to be theoretically dissected to give flesh to Bukharin-Césaire's insight from a class-focused angle. This produces in turn a class-imperialism connection. To begin with, the class-focused perspective entails a de-centred and disaggregated economy consisting of a variety of class processes of surplus labour (capitalist, feudal, slave, communitic, communist and independent);[13] 'capitalist' is a particular form in this diverse economy. Suppose for the sake of convenience we use capitalist class process and capital interchangeably as and when required; while they are not exactly the same, the point that capitalist class process harbours capital is enough for the above inference to be made. Following this cautionary note, accord 'global capital' the central privileged position in comparison to the diverse 'what are not capitalist' class process (feudal, slave, independent, communist, communitic forms). Once this privileged position of global capital is accepted, the new economic map that emerges can be construed in terms of circuits – camp of global capital and its outside – world of the third. We define 'circuits of global capital' as comprising all those processes that are directly or indirectly connected with the global capitalist enterprises, that is, all those processes that directly or indirectly affect or are affected by processes pertaining to global capital. Local capitalist enterprises and non-capitalist enterprises are intertwined with global capital through local-global markets via instances of outsourcing, subcontracting, off shoring, body shopping and so on. When we refer to the local-global markets with reference to a commodity, we mean the chain of local–local to global–global exchanges that make up the entire value sequence of a commodity. Through these, some enterprises (in production and in circulation including trading and financial enterprises) get directly and immediately connected to the global capitalist enterprises and together these clusters into what can be provisionally named as the *hub* of circuits of global capital. The rest in the chain who via the local–global markets are indirectly connected through outsourcing and subcontracting and are some distance away from the global capitalist enterprises comprise the *margins* of the circuits of global capital. The circuits of global capital – stretching from the margins to the hub to the centre of global capital – have been emerging from every pore of post-colonial economy such as India, including in the agricultural sector. In contrast, world of the third is a space that is outside of local–global market exchanges, hence, by default, it emerges as outside to the circuits of global capital. More specifically, the circuits of world of the third is a heterogeneously constituted spatial configuration containing the combined effects of class (with exploitative, non-exploitative and self-appropriative modes of appropriation) and non-class economic, political, cultural and natural processes that stands outside of the circuits of global capital, in a face-to-face encounter. World of the third does not signify any a priori value judgment (good, bad, indifferent) nor is it associated with any pre-determined sector or territory or state of socio-economy (such as rural or urban; it can be in Paris in France or in a village in the Indian state of Orissa; and both circuits can be present alongside one another, say in New Delhi). Rather, it is seen as a conceptually 'hollowed out void' that, depending upon the specific configuration of class and non-class effects that constitute it, concretely manifests itself in different forms across time and space; with overdetermined and contradictory processes working within and between, both the circuits of global capital and world of the third mutate and are in a state of flux, spatially as well as relation wise.

Our class-focused analysis clearly unmasks the political import of the centricity of global capital in contemporary imperialism and specifically in why and how it *forecloses* class process. The aspect of the language of class that brings to surface the conceptual place of economy as de-centred and disaggregated highlights the relevance of the class question as a critique of the capitalist form as unjust (which is true of all forms that are exploitative) and of class struggle in initiating a transformation of the exploitative class processes. It leaves no hiding place for capital's illegitimate assertion as a privileged centre (that it is an assertion is now made visible). As long as the class concept and its language are present, it becomes difficult, if not impossible for capital to impose its unchallenged rule over the disaggregated space of non-capitalist existences and the post-capitalist possibilities they open up. Politicisation of the seemingly apolitical rationale of its dominance and the opening of post-capitalist possibilities are dangerous propositions for its sustained existence and legitimacy. Normalisation of capitalist organisation of surplus or (global) capital as the privileged centre then is a political construct, a task that must be performed for it to become the rule of analysing, judging and transforming economies. To establish and secure the rule of capital, the category of class must be made discursively absent, foreclosed from the language of economy itself. What follows is the erasure of the heterogeneous and multi-faceted economy and with it the conceptual place of diverse non-capitalist existences. The conceptual division between economy as a diverse entity and capitalist class process as a particular form within it starts to blur. Following this, once capital(ist) is made into a naturalised centre, the rest of class processes gets clubbed into the homogeneous other of capital and non-capital. It is evident that if the language of class process was present, the homogeneous dual of capital, as undifferentiated non-capital would never arise, and the centricity of capital would become denaturalised. In the process of this hegemonic formation, in that opening where what is otherwise a *particular* of economy, that is, capital, gets re-presented and normalised as its *universal* projection, the category of class (as process of surplus labour) gets evacuated from the language of economy and from the discursive terrain. We call this hegemonic formation 'capitalism'. Evidently, without the foreclosure of class, there cannot be a formation of hegemony around the centricity of capital. Occulting the class question guarantees that the class-focused justice issues (such as exploitation, class inequality, class distribution, primitive accumulation, etc.) embodying capitalism are never invoked; these are never invoked because the category of class, and their effects can never be accessed. Instead, the hegemonic formation allows capitalism to present itself as a competitive market economy of contractual agents and in which there is no conceptual place for class as process of surplus labour and consequently, no place for class exploitation, class inequality and class domination in any explanation and action. Once class is evacuated from economic language and from representation of capitalism, imperialism as an instance of domination of global capitalist organisation of surplus in value form becomes discursively invisible. Sans class, imperialism appears as something else, in which the association of force and violence with the systemic functioning of global capitalism is disconnected and they appear as necessary instruments to fulfil a humanist mission summed up as 'democracy, anti-communism and free trade'.[14]

Once shorn of class concept and class language, (global) capital struts out as an un-problematical lens or perspective, which is in fact desired for the good of all. The outside qua world of the third is transmuted into a site of passive representation of a homogeneous non-capital; non-capital is now seen, dissected and managed through the lens of capital. Gibson-Graham[15] called this perspective 'capitalocentrism'. Occupying this perspective has enormous significance. Once class is foreclosed and with it the diverse non-capitalist class processes evacuated from the discursive terrain, there is no way to conceptually and ontologically locate non-capitalist class existences, actual and possible. Nor is it any longer possible to see anything of relevance of/in 'non-capital'. The economy as centred on global capital appears as already inevitable, made and inescapable, with no provisions to unmake and remake it. The articulation of perspective and spatial in the conceptualisation of economy and capitalism thus subjugate the working class since any challenge to the existence and power of capital (that is, to its presence as exploitative organisation of surplus in value form) is considered baseless, futile and utopian. If capitalism is formed by the foreclosure of class process, then the class question becomes a touchy counter-hegemonic entry point (the radical nature is precisely in excavating, and making, the foreclosed class process to return and hit the discursive terrain) since it not only unpacks the class character of imperialism but also does so in a way where the aspect of domination of working mass and of resistance through class and non-class struggles becomes palpable and important. That is why foregrounding class, as both Bukharin and Cesaire notes, is so essential in shaping an auto-critical understanding of imperialism. The above formulation though is not enough to complete the theorisation of outside, certainly not when the objective is to capture the dimension of internal imperialism. It is just the first step needed to theorise the outside and through that internal imperialism. The point is that, in a concrete setting, state – capital nexus does encounter world of the third, at times through force and violence and at other times through its management (for example, poverty alleviation programmes). The question is: what allows for a justifiable entry into the world of the third through force and violence? As it stands, this encounter per se does not have any legitimacy that would rationalise the intervention and make it socially acceptable. Capitalocentrism is not sufficient. It must be accompanied by a further perspectival displacement of world of the third into the *devalued other* of the third world so that the still horizontal face-to-face relation between circuits of global capital and world of the third becomes a hierarchical one. What was 'hollowed out void' manifesting in diverse concrete forms now gets re-presented as a pre-determined normalized space reflecting embodied deficiency in their knowledge systems, institutions and forms of life. Resultantly, world of the third is foreclosed through the foregrounding of third world. This second shift (that is akin to orientalism) is grounded in the *logic of lack* that indelibly stamps in certain ways the named societies over which this policy of conquest is supposed to work. In its most refined form, this logic of lack is integral to any policy of conquest and in fact must predate it. The lacking feature is presented/projected not in terms of what the outside is but in terms of what it is not, and that too in relation to the circuits of global capital. Once this orientalist perspective is married to capitalocentrism, the occultation of world of the third by third world is paralleled by a further displacement of the homogenous other of 'non-capital' into a homogenous *lacking other* named 'pre-capital', with pre-capital as a devalued space signalling backwardness and a temporality, that is, archaic and pre-historical; it symbolises pre-modernity, sometimes fondly called tradition. The specific formation of the lacking other is historically procured and in which colonialism played an important role. Putting this phenomenon in the context of colonialism, Cesaire noted, 'the great historical tragedy of Africa has been not so much that it was too late in making contact with the rest of the world, as the manner in which that contact was brought about'.[16] The terms and manner of contact are the issues and not contact per se. Once the two shifts secure the dual of circuits of global capital and the so-called traditional pre-capitalist formation (typified by the imageries of agriculture, forest, informal and household economy), it emerges logically that third world/pre-capital is not only dispensable but must be dispensed with for societies to progress.

The outside (colony–Negro couple) now emerges as a combination of perspectival and spatial construct (involving the foreclosures of class and world of the third), whose 'conquest' is not to be viewed as occupation or invasion but liberation from its own decrepit state. The force and violence that marks the process of imperialism is over world of the third but that moment gets grounded on a perspective that functions to substitute world of the third by third world by presenting it as inferior, servile, abnormal such that the intrusion is rendered justifiable. *Imperialism is defined then as a policy of conquest conducted on behalf of global capital through force and violence over the outside of world of the third in the name of uplifting of third world.*

In this context, world of the third can also serve as a platform which enables a reverse gaze of subjects towards global capital from the outside, the challenging look of the 'Negro' from a perspective taking off from the lived experience of the world of the third. This is in contrast to third world, which is a gaze through the lens of global capital and the imperial, reiterating what it cites and foregrounds. Invocation of third world appropriates the possibility of anti-imperialism (ensuring the devalued subjugation of the Negroes), while world of the third opens the possibility for the counter-hegemonic gaze of Negroes, hence, of anti-imperialism as a legitimate conduct of resistance. The aspect of force and violence that accompanies imperialism would be seen as liberation from a third world perspective, but the same appears as an instance of unnecessary intrusion, plunder and gross injustice from a world of the third perspective. Moreover, our class-focused approach ensures that, rather than being undifferentiated, world of the third is itself a heterogeneous space involving contestation and conflict emanating from various embedded injustices (for instance, class exploitation). This in turn directs attention to the necessity of class conflict and struggle from within the world of the third, especially when the process of imperialist expansion proceeds by grafting modern/class abuse onto ancient injustice including those residing inside the world of the third. The long-drawn history of recurrent alliance of various sorts between industrial/financial/mercantile capitalists with other kinds of non-capitalist exploiters and oppressors in world of the third are well documented across nations. In sum, our theoretical frame entails combining the two related axes of anti-imperialist struggles: class struggle to end exploitative organisation of surplus and class division including that within the world of the third and challenging the policy of conquest of world of the third carried out at the behest of global capital. Ours is then a methodological intervention that not only posits and explores the characteristics of contemporary imperialism but also accounts for, as Césaire demanded, comprehending resistances as 'anti-imperialist' moments. That is, we produce a theory of imperialism in the present historical stage such that imperialism comes out as both made and unmade.

Characteristics of imperialism under neoliberal globalisation and global capitalism

We begin by defining neoliberal globalisation as a new global order based on a proposed competitive market economy supposedly functioning through the mass of rational ability machines or homoeconomicus personifying the disposition of cost-benefit calculation in any decision-action. The unique character of competitive market economy in this phase lies precisely in the creation and normalization of local-global markets as a generalized form of trading, within and across nations. This is, of course, its idealised representation which manifests itself in different ways and forms, some nations having more of these features than others. While neoliberal globalisation, once it comes into existence, 'has a depressing inevitability about it and that is because it is configured as an unfolding of an economic logic',[17] the point is that its birthing and continual alterations require the tooth and claw approach of imperialism so as to bring its conditions of existence (for example, introduce and make local–global markets, competition, property rights, homoeconomicus subject-hood, etc.) to the surface and also secure their reproduction and modification. The supposed economic logic that nation states must (be made to) adjust to appear in sync with global capital, both productive and unproductive (see endnote 9). This though does not transpire due to any accident or embodied inherent logic of the economy but following an active intervention for the production of a historical conjecture that arises by virtue of implanting global capital as the centre/lens (which in turn involves, as already explained, the foreclosure of class process of surplus labour from the discursive domain). As we discussed earlier, the circuits of global capital require both the centrality of global capital and its normalized functioning in a commodified space that is locked into local–global markets backed by property rights and rational ability machines like subjects. This reformulation of economy into global capitalism entailing a global organization of surplus value (its production, appropriation, distribution and receipt) now takes place under a 'form' as conditioned by neoliberal globalisation, which allows capital to become and be global in its normal, functioning mode without any threat of expropriation or subversion. Imperialism secures the vital connection (albeit through force and violence shaping a global policy of conquest) between the *centrality of global capital* and the new global order based on *competitive market economy* without which global capitalism cannot be realized. This tooth and claw approach deployed to secure the subjugation of nation-states, regions and the working class to the dictate and principle of this vital connection can be described, for convenience sake, as 'external' imperialism. The name is appropriate for it refers to the policy of conquest in some connection to global capital or its interests that transpire at the hinge of the global order and nation states, a hinge that connects them, and through that connection makes and remakes both. Let me expand further.

The imperialist policy of conquest of national states (using visible and subtle force and at times even explicit violence) has characterised much of what is known as 'reforms'; 'reforms' is a name for a set of policies to alter the socio-economic structural conditions of existence of countries who are embracing or made to embrace capitalism in the mentioned direction. The role of international agencies such International Monetary Funds, World Bank and World Trade Organization, no doubt influenced and shaped by the United States and its partners, was vital in introducing this new global architecture. The last three decades have been witness to the combination of political, diplomatic and military strategies used by these global and regional powers to generate a situation which made it difficult and costly for smaller or weaker individual nation states to remain isolated; at times, outright occupation or intervention have directly played a role in integrating nation-states into the global order. The ruling disposition in some countries also saw this as an opportunity to take advantage of gains from trade, technology transfer and higher growth possibility. Whatever the reason of integration, the end result was neoliberal globalisation. A question though remains: what is the fundamental difference between this historical stage and colonial times? Instead of the humanist mission driven by the theme of 'Civilisation, Christianity and Commerce deployed in colonial times, today, for the imperial presidencies of Reagan, Bush I, Clinton, Bush II, the mission can be summed up as "Democracy, Anticommunism and Free Trade" ';[18] we may add to that Islamophobia. A repertoire of logics, modes of reasoning, strategies, techniques of imposing pressure and mechanisms of consent generation (including using military, aid, debt, oil, and fracking as a geopolitical device), occupation, war and others are combined to fulfil this humanist mission of the contemporary.

Moreover, the underlying principle of this global order, including competitive market economy and a suspicion towards protection, has also given rise to regional economic orders like NAFTA, ASEAN, the Trans-Pacific Partnership Free Trade Agreement, MERCUSOR and others alongside the European Union. This was unlike anything that existed during colonial times. The relation between the global and regional architecture intersect, compensate and reinforce one another; depending on the underlying objective of the nation states and regions, they also can be the ground of contradiction and conflict, as for example, between Greece and the European Union. Taken together, this reorganisation of global order, regional order and national policy paradigm can be described as the primary architecture of 'external imperialism' or of resistance to it at that level. That is one reason why some scholars consider imperialism less as a description and 'more as a project in (this) world; an attempt to make and remake that world'.[19]

Neoliberal globalisation has helped shape a new kind of capitalism that is global; it is the structure of circuits of global capital constitutive of the local–global markets through which surplus value is performed, appropriated, distributed and received. The circuits-camp of global capital or global capitalism appears from *within* nations that have embraced the 'reforms' pioneered by neoliberalism. While initially reluctant and resistant, some of the erstwhile 'developing' nations (such as India, China, etc.), after having absorbed the initial shock of the reform process (both in terms of what it means and its manifested forms), integrated the principle of new global order and are now serious competitors to house and produce global capital. Generally, once they have accepted the principle and provisions of competitive market economy, the nation states per se did have to adjust to the demands of global capital through a continual policy effort to create and re-create a 'place' for global capital, both productive and unproductive.[20] As personification of global enterprises, the dominant capitalists in a nation tend to be now global capitalists (industrial, financial, trading, etc.). In other words, the global order has a class character that has imploded within nations thereby changing their economic character and the subjects therein.

Not surprisingly, any 'crisis' that arises typically functions through this systemic relation between global order and capitalism by spreading the negative effects and news from nation to nation; thus, in the present, while the crisis is national, internal to the nation, its scope and effects are global.

(a) The conjunction of neoliberal globalisation and global capitalism has re-shaped the class configuration through both international division of labour and intra-national division of labour. These facilitated the reorganisation of the performance, appropriation, distribution and receipt of surplus value across a global value chain, a reorganisation in which the centrality of capitalist exploitation is created, maintained and expanded; this chain included the articulation of capitalist and non-capitalist class processes as well.[21] This shift in what Ruccio called 'imperial' economies was no doubt facilitated by mechanisms of off-shoring, out-sourcing, subcontracting and body shopping that facilitated the internationalisation of labour process. This was complemented by the 'flexibility' of labour market, workplace and work time imposed by the structure of competition and technological advancement in transport, IT, telecommunications and robotics that has been able to fragment activities across time zones, spaces, enterprises, and groups of workers as also enable the capitalists and their cohorts to control these activities across the globe. The global organisation of capitalist exploitation allowed productive capitalists to appropriate concentrated quantum of surplus value on a massive scale, an overwhelming part of which was reinvested in financial markets and property markets. Unproductive capitalists (bankers, shareholders and traders), in their capacity as recipients of the surplus value from productive capitalists for proving the latter's conditions of existence (advancing credit, advancing ownership capital, selling produce) and as independent players in the process of circulation also took positions in financial markets, property markets and for capital accumulation to reap surplus value in increasing concentrated amount. Often, these kinds of investments, markets and destinations got interlocked and at other times became substitutes, within and between which productive and unproductive capital can be swiftly moved; this created further instability in national economies which in turn enhanced the grip of (global) capital over the political institutions as also over their policy paradigms.

Concentration of capital could thus be combined with a host of dispersions and through this, a new uneven structure emerged that allowed for a small group of productive and unproductive capitalists and their cohorts to appropriate, distribute and receive surplus value on a global scale. With ever expanding income and wealth at their disposal, this group has acquired an unprecedented capacity to not just buy assets/property, education, healthcare, media and justice but also to use all power and security (repressive and ideological) to protect their privilege. On the other side, the abundance of labour power and competition between workers within and across the nation states that globalisation has made possible ensured that wages are kept low, workers are divided amongst themselves and thus easily disciplined, trade unions are demoted or dismantled and labour saving technologies and the reorganisation of the labour process are adopted without much opposition from workers. The combination of neoliberal globalisation and imperialism in the making of global capitalism has heavily tilted the balance of power in favour of global capital vis-à-vis the increasingly fragmented working masses, making it increasingly difficult for the workers to organise, bargain and resist in a collective way. The resultant growing income and wealth inequality is thus systemic, an endogenously produced outcome of contemporary global capitalism.

(b) A change is transpiring in the location of capitalism whose growth now is showing an indication of shifting from the developed countries to the BRICS, ASEAN and other nations. A snapshot view of the trend of changing location of global capitalism can be gleaned by the decadal shifts in the share of world GDP as presented in Figure 4.1.

In short, there seems to be an ongoing spatial reorganisation of capitalism driven in part by a pattern in the movement of global capital and the international and intra-national division of labour. No doubt induced by the low-wage regime, time–space compression, greater flexibility in the labour market and labour process and higher profit opportunities, global movement of capital away from developed nations is akin to what Bukharin had described as the 'world movement of capital'; an example of reorganisation of international

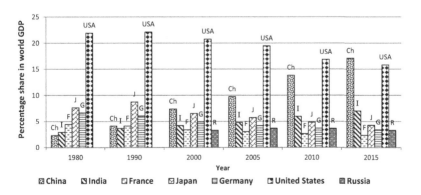

Figure 4.1 Changing share of world GDP
Source: Constructed from IMF WEO data, 2016.

division of labour is signified by the movement of manufacturing production from developed nations to BRICS, ASEAN, Mexico and other countries. Reorganisation of intra-national division of labour pertains to the shift to manufacturing and services (both formal and informal) away from agriculture as also the unprecedented process of urbanisation in the latter group of countries. These three aspects, while having a life of their own, seem to reinforce, compensate and intersect one another. By thus re-articulating and re-organising the global with the local, their combined effect creates a distinct historical conjecture and a reorganisation of the global economic map. Glossing over, for the time being, the nation-specific distinctions which do exist and are important, we can infer that this global reorganisation, in turn, has produced two kinds of distinct effects, one on the developed West (meaning United States and Europe broadly)[22] and the other on the developing world that have embraced neoliberal globalisation to facilitate capitalist-induced industrialisation and growth.

West: The opportunity for capitalists to move capital to BRICS and other nations has led to a process of de-industrialisation in the West. The pressure of deregulation and labour market competition across the globe that opened new profit opportunities for the capitalists led to labour market deregulation, real wage stagnation/decline, decline of secured job opportunity and employment uncertainty in the West. It has also led to the dismantling of social security, public service and the labour welfare regime that have been the hallmark of welfare policies of pre-1980 Europe/United States and have helped generations of working class families enjoy a higher standard of living under capitalism. Overall, a de facto austerity regime has thus been unfolding, sometimes slowly and other times rapidly, to attract global capital and also to prevent it from fleeing while keeping the state budget under stipulated restrictions. This is complemented in the way global capitalists (productive and unproductive or their cohorts) have been, wherever possible, convincing/blackmailing the political establishment in the developed nations into submission (Greece being a shining example). Even city authorities have been using gentrification to dispossess the working class by identifying parts of cities seen as attractive by financial and property dealers; the privatisation of public space and its obvious occupation by a well-off population (having purchasing power to buy highly priced privatized spaces) that follows is only one way in which the right to city is being handed over to the power of capital.[23] This process (by no means restricted to West but also encompassing centres of global capital in the developing nations) is not only reshaping the idea and content of cities and urbanism, but also sowing discontent amongst the population that lose out. A pattern has now emerged. While capitalists and their coterie in Western countries are able to maintain and expand their profit and income, the regime of stagnant income and wealth, falling social security and welfare provisions (for working people, poor, pensioners, students, etc.) along with declining quality employment opportunities for the greater mass of the population has led to a growing gap and contrast in the standard of living between these two sets of people. The contradictory effect of this scenario (some refer to it as crisis of global capitalism) on the socio-political front is all too evident, especially with the advent of Donald Trump, who was able to exploit the discontent to turn the table somewhat in favour of a variant of economic nationalism. This projected shift aspires not to demote capitalism in the United States but to give it a new direction by trying to reverse the outflow of capital (particularly productive capital) back in favour of investment in the United States.

Developing: Even after accepting the ongoing trend of capital movement, we ask whether there is a peculiar kind of spatialisation that is emerging in maturing capitalisms that are otherwise called developing/underdeveloped. In short, as global capital becomes the norm and functions from within nation states with the intent to expand the rate of exploitation, profit, investment and others, is there also a question of internally derived 'exception' that now emerges as a historically distinct phenomenon? To use a metaphor, is there another 'nation' within a nation? Is imperialism then related to how this 'exception' emerges in a perspective-wise and spatial sense, how is it to be represented and what happens or could happen to this 'other' space, this other 'nation'?

We make the following claim. Imperialism emerges from within, as a policy of conquest of this 'other' space, this exception, with the intent to secure, facilitate and expand global capitalism as part of domestic policy of formally free nation state. We have theorised this perspective-spatial 'other' ('nation') as world of the third, as the outside of circuits-camp of global capital. Taking the transition of the Indian economy into account, we claim that the churning of the Indian economic map into the circuits-camp of global capital and world of the third is what the combined effect of neoliberal globalisation and global capitalism have created. A host of measures such as primitive accumulation (in both its classical and non-classical forms), inclusive development, community reconstruction, war on internal terrorism and others have since been put in place to control/manage, subjugate and, when required, dismantle the world of the third.[24] In relation to this process of making and unmaking the world of the third, imperialism is both a defence of global capital(ism) as also an expression of its manifested form. Rather than being conducted externally, the path of imperialism is inward, where the protagonists – global capital, world of the third and the nation state – are internal to the national territory even as they are articulated to the global order. The defence of this conquest is to recast the idea of 'progress' in the imagery of developed capitalism and modernity, a recasting that is fundamentally based on the relocation of the 'nation' of world of the third as representative of the devalued *other* qua third world. Resultantly, third world is foregrounded, while world of the third is foreclosed. Global capitalism is thus constituted by the other qua third world, its constitutive/foregrounded inside and the other qua world of the third, its constitutive/foreclosed outside; the former is cited while the latter is not cited. Third world is (underdeveloped) location on a global map. World of the third is an existent in the human geography; it is a contingent experience of being outside. This move inherent in the epistemology of what constitutes development makes possible the hierarchy between global capitalism and its outside and, in the process, opens the path to legitimise the conquest of world of the third in the name of the liberating the 'third world' from its purportedly self-inflicted tragic abnormal state in the map. The concrete result of this conquest is the 'loss of concepts', a 'loss of events', a 'loss of mental states' and at least a 'threatened loss of identity' that world of the third has to endure.[25] It is not just an attack on the conception of what it *is* but, in one turn, also of what it is *to be*. Such a comprehensive policy of conquest, carried out at the combined axes of perspectival and spatial level, is what we refer to as the moment of 'internal' imperialism.

Imperialism is then the policy of conquest of world of the third at the behest of global capital where the source of the conquest – a political source – lies not in what is included but what must get excluded and declared an exception, a state of exclusion-exception that can only be defined and secured by force and violence backed by a host of ideological apparatuses to normalize it. It is this exclusion-exception that helps draw the (b)order of the inside (circuits of global capital and its referent body politic) and allows for capital to come, as Marx argued, 'dripping from head to foot, from every pore, with blood and dirt'.[26]

(c) Rather than inquire into whether nation states are subsumed in global capital or vice-versa, perhaps a different and better route is to look at the nature of the relationship between global capital and nation state without any a priori assumption concerning the structure or direction of their relation. Therefore, many kinds of possible relationship between nation state and global capital are possible. One amongst these is the kind that contemporary imperialism has been trying to bring to the fore. In this order, nation states can and do compete amongst themselves for global capital, to bring them home, to retain them and to expand them inwardly; hence, governments running the states do strive to incite and facilitate the constitution of global capitalism; they do and do so very actively. It, thus, is not just a matter of laying down structural conditions for capitalism to appear but also, following Althusser, for the state ideological apparatus to emerge as the missile head of imperialism. It is part of the discursive practices to construct the ideas of 'homoeconomicus' 'progress', global capitalism as progressive, 'world of the third' as devalued 'third world', third world's needed liberation from its self-inflicted decrepit state of existence and so on. The role of state (in connectivity with the social body harbouring norms, institutions, practices, etc.) in shaping the logical defence and trajectory of imperialism is thus a constitutive component of how imperialism as a process necessary for the existence and expansion of global capitalism may appear in the era of 'democracy', 'freedom' and 'equality'. And, that may, as we shall see later, mean even for maturing capitalisms like India combining 'internal imperialism' with that of facilitating the external expansion and aggression of global capital, that is, 'external imperialism'.

Coming back to internal imperialism per se, if colonialism is ruled out, then this conquest cannot be carried out without the consent (at least, formally) of the concerned nation-state or of a substantial part of the population because the theatre of this moment of imperialism is within. It is imperialism from the inside, in the inside that cannot transpire without the consent of state, without the deployment of its ideological apparatuses in conjunction with those funded and inspired by global capital (and that includes international agencies, NGOs, media, think tanks, academia and of course the political groups). Taken together, they form the ideological apparatuses *for* imperialism, putting forth a set of rationales and arguments that justifies the policy of conquest on behalf of global capital to materialise. Apparatuses, networks, norms and social dreaming combine in discursive practices to shape subjects for imperialism. In confronting the question of imperialism, Marxists and non-Marxist alike have in general looked *to* the external component, of how nation states wage war, occupy and plunder each other on behalf of capital or of how more powerful nations subjugate others. This is an important area of external imperialism that certainly continues to have relevance, but external imperialism without internal imperialism is no longer an adequate characterisation of imperialism. It is not a question of adding one to the other but that of telescoping the two into a theorisation of imperialism.

(d) Is the Indian form of global capitalism also characterised by imperialism? Is imperialism then becoming a pioneer of India's (global) capitalism? This question turns upside down the proposition of external imperialism that has been the hallmark of critical approach among Indian scholars, in which 'India' has been the object of imperialism and its policies (especially, US imperialism) but never its subject. This characterization points to another important facet. It reveals how fetters to the functioning of internal imperialism in maturing capitalism like India can, as part of an attempt to resolve this problem, induce, in turn, external imperialism. This shows that imperialism under the phase of global capitalism and neoliberalism can no longer be deemed as the exclusive property of developed/matured capitalisms like the United States.

Given the content of discussed internal imperialism, the state sponsored policy of conquest of world of the third is ongoing in connection with the restructuring of the Indian economy unfolding via the growing march of global capital that, in turn, is being facilitated by neoliberal 'reforms'.[27] Let us extend this discussion by suggesting one instance of India's 'external' imperialism as it starts to acquire its shape and see how it is related to the contradictions emerging from the evolution of internal imperialism.

There is presently an open policy encouragement for Indian global capitalist enterprises to hunt for raw materials abroad. It includes Indian enterprises grabbing 1.3 million hectares of land in Africa by 2013 by displacing millions. With China right at the top, India remains among the ten top land grabbers in that continent.[28] This is also true of state capitalist enterprises which are being exhorted to heavily invest abroad; the nature of this outward FDI is partly predatory, that is, extractive.[29] This external turn has especially become important in light of social resistance movements and judicial activism in India that has somewhat fettered, amongst others, the process of extraction of raw materials necessary for the process of capital accumulation. While attempts to subdue this domestic opposition are ongoing (dilution of environment and land acquisition laws as also social programs are indicative of this effort), extraction is also now being exported abroad to circumvent its slowdown in India's domestic front. The element of force and violence is now being deployed (with the help of rulers of home countries) over the world of the third inside Africa (using the same trope of uplifting of the third world therein) so as to enable the expansion of the circuits of global capital in India. It also shows that internal and external imperialisms are connected and shaped by their contradictory effects and desire/ability to adapt to them. It is perhaps an irony that the role of colonialism in the formation of Western European and US capitalism that Marx[30] had referred to is presently India's route to superpower status. What we are witness to is this growing effort to connect 'external' imperialism to that of 'internal' imperialism so as to shape a domestically produced policy of conquest of world of the third (home and abroad) on behalf of global capital, Indian and foreign.

(e) Imperialism as a 'necessity'! Imperialism as 'progressive'! Bukharin argued that the category of imperialism must be so defined and described that it will help unravel a critique in the form of underlying class divisions and the points of contradictions and crises that the category encapsulates. The latter is masked in the name of 'necessity' of imperialism, where the justification of the term 'necessity' is derived from the self-proclaimed 'progressive' content of the undertaken policy (of conquest) no matter what its consequences are. The auto-critique of imperialism seeks to unpack the otherwise repressed content encapsulated in the idea of 'progress' that, in turn, would open imperialism to questions of justice.

To begin with, as Bukharin[31] argued,

> For a consistent Marxist, the entire development of capitalism is nothing but a process of continuous reproduction of the contradictions of capitalism on an ever wider scale. The future of world economy, as far as it is a capitalist economy, will not overcome its inherent lack of adaption; on the contrary, it will keep on reproducing this lack of adaption on an ever wider scale.

Imperialism is a response to this set of contradictions and its policy an attempt to resolve capitalism's lack of adaption within the existing scheme of things. The relevance of Bukharin's insight becomes evident once we agree that the present form of imperialism is a continual process of managing the set of contradictions that capitalism is unable to solve.

For one, while technological and transportation innovations, globalisation and financialisation have opened new opportunities for global capital, the very opportunities, such as those enabling the exporting of plants, jobs and funds from the developed nations to the BRICS and other nations, in turn have introduced a new set of contradictions in the developed nations, epitomised by a period of sustained stagnating income, falling welfare and benefits, rising unemployment and poverty, instability in jobs and income, psychological disruption and, ultimately, an economic and social crisis. From a Marxist perspective, all these are not accidental events or plots by the 1 percent or by finance capital. Instead, they are a manifestation of a set of contradictions of capitalism introducing, in turn, a systemic socio-economic crisis on many fronts. The net result of these contradictory pulls and pushes is that while developed nations have been stagnating and some even declining, capital (productive and unproductive) has been rapidly shifting its base from there to the BRICS and other nations. However, and this is the point here, the mentioned resolution of the set of contradictions of global capitalism (that is, for the shift of base to transpire) must presuppose an alteration of policies within these 'developing' nations.

As we have explained, the alteration telescopes a domestic 'reform' policy of changing the socio-economic character of these nations, which is what we have captured with the term 'neoliberal globalisation'. It seeks to provide a 'place' for global capital as a systemic feature of the 'national economy'; once the place is granted, global capital is allowed, in turn, to function so as to re-signify and transform the 'space' in which it operates, thereby imposing, in turn, new kinds of demands and pressures on the state.[32] This includes the demand that a long-drawn 'domestic' policy of conquest of world of the third be ushered in, to secure for global capital greater access to resources, process of capital accumulation and an expansion of markets to sell its produce. Given the history and lesson of resistance from world of the third that denotes a contradictory movement to this tendency, there must also be a concurrent attempt on the part of the state to manage this space so as to control and subjugate it to its universal and abstract social dream of 'progress'. There is also a complementary attempt, if possible, to circumvent this fettering at home by shifting the occupation of world of the third abroad (see point e), a case of external imperialism; this is achieved by going into an alliance with the political/business establishment of other nation states where such events must be made to transpire. From the West to the BRICS/ASEAN to their own inside of world of the third to Africa and the corresponding world of the third and so on, the policy of conquest involving the repressive and ideological apparatuses of the ruling dispensation help tie global capital to all corners of the globe.

However, from the perspective of world of the third, this imperialist policy of conquest may not necessarily be seen as progress but rather as being unjust. It might subsequently, as it often does, invite resistance. The historical crisis of global capitalism (which impacts the working class and others connected to it) is thus ultimately displaced into a historical crisis of world of the third indicated by a new set of contradictions arising out of this domestic policy of conquest which in turn is perhaps laying the ground for another impending crisis of global capitalism. As global capitalism moves from contradiction to contradiction and crisis to crisis by shifting from one mode of adaption to another on an ever-widening scale, the forms of imperialism and anti-imperialism also keep mutating and polishing their swords.

Conclusion

Our analysis suggests the following: imperialism can only be ended by ending capitalism. Struggle to end capitalism and imperialism must be telescoped together, for which a critical gaze on global capitalism (to shore up the class question on behalf of the working mass) must be combined with a critical gaze on third world (to shore up the question of/from world of the third) so as to recast both. Anti-imperialism, thus, must be a work not only of the 'external' or the exteriorised but also in and of its *inside*, of the character of its insided-ness, or of the insided-ness of its character.

Notes

1 I am grateful to Satyaki Ray and Anup Dhar for challenging me to think through the arguments thoroughly and to Sayonee Majumdar for helping me to organize the paper. I am also thankful to Sunanda Sen and Byasdeb Dasgupta for their constant encouragement.

2 V. I. Lenin in the Preface to *Imperialism and World Economy*, New Delhi: Aakar Books (first published in 1915), 2010.

3 Nikolai Bukharin, *Imperialism and World Economy*, New Delhi: Aakar Books (first published in 1915), 2010.

4 The class-focused framework follows Stephen A. Resnick, and Richard D. Wolff, *Knowledge and Class: A Marxist Critique of Political Economy*, Chicago, London: University of Chicago Press, 1987; Stephen A. Resnick and Richard D. Wolff, *New Departures in Marxian Theory*, London, New York: Routledge, 2006; and J. K. Gibson-Graham, *The End of Capitalism (as We Knew It): A Feminist Critique of Political Economy*, Oxford, Cambridge: Wiley-Blackwell, 1996. This approach considers class as process of surplus labour. It can only appear in a social configuration. In any such social form, the class processes exists in overdetermined and contradictory relation with non-class processes.

5 Resnick and Wolff, *Knowledge and Class* and *New Departures in Marxian Theory*.

6 The theoretical structure underpinning this paper follows Anjan Chakrabarti and Stephen Cullenberg, *Transition and Development in India*, London, New York: Routledge, 2013; Anjan Chakrabarti, Anup Dhar and Stephan Cullenberg, *World of the Third and Global Capitalism*, New Delhi: World View Press, 2012; Anjan Chakrabarti, Anup Dhar

and Stephan Cullenberg, '(Ün)doing Marxism from Outside', *Rethinking Marxism*, 2016, 28(2): 276–94 ; and Anjan Chakrabarti, Anup Dhar and Byasdeb Dasgupta, *The Indian Economy in Transition: Globalization, Capitalism and Development*, New Delhi, London: Cambridge University Press, 2016, where the concepts, including that of the outside and world of the third, are detailed.

7 As Marx used England as the backdrop in *Capital*, in my treatment the theorisation of imperialism has India in the background.
8 Bukharin, *Imperialism and World Economy*.
9 This is never to say that seeds of the features that make up neo-liberalism today were not present in earlier stages. However, the congealed form that it has taken today, with a different degree of divergence across countries, is specific to the present post-globalisation era and hence is historically unique. I am thankful to David Ruccio for pointing this out to me in a personal conversation.
10 We follow Resnick and Wolff's interpretation of Marx in distinguishing between productive and unproductive capitalists/labourers. To begin with, productive capitalists are appropriators of surplus value/capital generated by workers in the capitalist class process in M–C–M' process. Unproductive capitalists personify the creation and possession of surplus value/capital in the process of circulation, that is, M–M'; therefore, banks/financiers, traders and shareholders (who advance M to receive more than M) personify capital and as such are (unproductive) capitalists. Like the 'capitalists', the 'working class' too is differentiated. At the least, productive labourers are those who create surplus value for the productive capitalists in the capitalist class process while the rest of the labourers can be delineated at various levels and, for convenience sake, in comparison to productive labourers, they can be referred to as unproductive labourers. Rather than see one as more important than the other, Marx was crystal clear about the overdetermined and contradictory relation amongst and between the differentiated groups of capitalists and workers. The rest of the chapter follows these definitions of capitalists and workers.
11 David F. Ruccio, *Development and Globalization: A Marxian Class Analysis*, London, New York: Routledge, 2011, p. 362.
12 For example, TATA Groups headquartered in India is a full-fledged global capitalist enterprise with operations across six continents.
13 Marx deploys the category of performance and appropriation of surplus labour to differentiate various economic forms of society: 'What distinguishes the various economic formations of society – the distinction between for example a society based on slave-labour and a society based on wage-labour is the form in which *this surplus labour is in each case extorted from the immediate producer*, the worker' (cited from Marx, *Capital*, Vol, 1, 1990, p. 325; italics author's; also see note 30).
Following Resnick and Wolff's definition of class as process of performance, appropriation, distribution and receipt of surplus labour, we use the above distinction of Marx to differentiate class processes in terms of self-appropriation (an individual performing and appropriating his own surplus), exploitation (collective of direct producers of surplus excluded from the process of appropriation of surplus conducted by non-performers – master, lord and capitalist) and non-exploitation (collective of workers not excluded from the collective appropriation of surplus they create). Upon

subsequent delineation, a further classification of class organisation of surplus emerges: self-appropriating class organisation of surplus is known as independent class process, non-exploitative class organisation of surplus is known as communist and AC communitic class process [performance of surplus individual (A) but appropriation collective (C) without excluding any performers] and exploitative class organisation of surplus are further classified into forms such as slave, feudal, capitalist and CA communitic [performance of surplus labour by a collective (C) but appropriation by an individual member (A) by excluding other members of the collective] (for details see, Chakrabarti, Dhar and Dasgupta, *The Indian Economy in Transition*). Evidently, the economy is de-centred and disaggregated and capitalist class existence is a component. The problem of hegemonic formation if it is to appear from within this de-centred and disaggregated economy is precisely this: how does the particular of capitalist class process emerge as a signpost of universal projection of what the economy *is* or appears as so?

14 Ruccio, *Development and Globalization*, p. 362.

15 Gibson-Graham, *The End of Capitalism*.

16 Aime Césaire, *Discourse on Colonialism*, Translated by Joan Pinkham, New Delhi: Aakar Books for South Asia (originally Monthly Review Press), 2010 (2000), p. 45.

17 Ruccio, *Development and Globalization*, p. 363.

18 Ruccio, *Development and Globalization*, p. 362.

19 Ruccio, *Development and Globalization*, p. 363.

20 See note 9.

21 Ruccio, *Development and Globalization*.

22 One can include East Asia here. However, despite sharing some common features with the United States/Europe, that region has some special features that I believe need careful consideration of its own.

23 David Harvey, *Rebel Cities: From the Right to the City to the Urban Revolution*, London: Verso, 2013.

24 Anjan Chakrabarti and Anup Dhar, *Dislocation and Resettlement in Development: From Third World to the World of the Third*, London, New York: Routledge, 2010.

25 Jonathan Lear, 'Working Through the End of Civilization', *International Journal of Psychoanalysis*, 2007, 88: 295–8.

26 Karl Marx, *Capital: A Critique of Political Economy*, Vol. 1, Translated by B. Fowkes and E. Mandel, London: Penguin Books, 1990, p. 926.

27 Chakrabarti, Dhar and Dasgupta, *The Indian Economy in Transition*.

28 Harry Madgoff, '21st Century Land Grab: Accumulation by Agricultural Dispossessions', *Monthly Review*, http://monthlyreview.org, 65(6), 2013, Land Matrix, http://landmatrix.org (accessed on 25 November 2014).

29 Reserve Bank of India, *Outward Indian FDI – Recent Trends & Emerging Issues*, Reserve Bank of India, 3 March 2012.

30 Karl Marx, *Capital: A Critique of Political Economy*, Vol. 1, Translated by B. Fowkes and E. Mandel, London: Penguin Books, 1990, Chapter 33.

31 Bukharin, *Imperialism and World Economy*, p. 143.

32 The place–space distinction follows J.K. Gibson-Graham, 'Place-Based Globalism: A New Imaginary of Revolution', *Rethinking Marxism*, 2008, 20(4): 659–64.

5 Is imperialism a relevant concept in today's world?

Subhanil Chowdhury[1]

Introduction

It can be argued, as has been done by many scholars, including Marxists, that imperialism as a concept of political economy and understanding the world that we live in, has become obsolete today. This assertion can be made on the basis of a set of (not necessarily mutually exclusive) arguments about the contemporary world. Let us first enumerate these arguments in no particular order of priority.

Spatial dimension

It can be argued that a division of the world into two clear segments, with one oppressing the other, is no longer valid. Hardt and Negri say that, 'we find the First World in the Third, the Third in the First, and the Second almost nowhere at all'.[2] In other words, a distinction of the kind that could have been talked about during the colonial era or even during the post-colonial era until the 1970s, of a world which can be distinctly divided into an advanced and a backward section is no longer valid. Moreover, the argument does not deny the existence of the third world per se, but it asserts that that existence is an inheritance from the past and currently, there is no section of the world oppressing the other.

Theories of imperialism ranging from Rosa Luxemburg to Lenin have emphasised imperialism as being a structure whereby the advanced capitalist countries oppress the poorer third world countries. In Rosa Luxemburg's theory,[3] capitalism cannot exist as an isolated system and needs a pre-capitalist sector for realising its surplus value. In order to do so, capitalism continuously attacks the pre-capitalist sector for its own growth and survival. Geographically, the bulk of this pre-capitalist sector is located in the third world countries. This oppression of the pre-capitalist sector by the capitalist sector, or the oppression of the third world countries by the advanced countries is what constitutes imperialism in Luxemburg's theory.[4] Lenin too talked about the oppression of the majority of the people of the colonies by the advanced countries.[5] Therefore, if it is no longer the case that there is a spatial distinction between a set of countries who oppress another set of countries, then imperialism as a category loses its significance.

Decolonisation

The process of decolonisation of the erstwhile colonies has been completed. Clearly, today, the colonies or today's developing countries are politically independent. Lenin was talking about a time when the capitalist countries in aid of their respective nation state-based monopoly capital were marking out territories for exploitation. This entire architecture, at least at the political level, does not exist anymore. This marks an important departure from the world conjuncture in Lenin's time.

Capitalist development in developing countries

There has been a set of arguments in various strands of Marxist thought which talked about imperialism retarding the development of capitalism in developing countries. Paul Baran argues that because a significant part of the surplus of the developing countries has been siphoned off by the advanced countries through imperialism, the capitalist development in the first set of countries has been adversely affected.[6] The entire dependency school[7] essentially argues that the underdevelopment in the periphery is a direct result of the development in the metropolis.

It can be argued that this entire theoretical structure of imperialism has become invalid. There is significant capitalist development in the developing countries of today. For example, in China there has been massive capitalist development, with the country now having the second largest economy and being highest exporter in the world. Even in India, there has been significant capitalist development.[8] This can be further buttressed by the fact that, according to the billionaires list published by *Forbes* magazine in 2016, China currently has 251 dollar billionaires which is the second highest in the world, after the United States. India is placed at number four in the list, with 84 billionaires.[9] However, according to another list on dollar billionaires published by the China-based Hurun Report, China tops the list of dollar billionaires with 568 members, while United States comes second with 535 and India third with 111 in 2016.[10] In the list of Fortune 500 companies of 2015, there were 98 companies from China, again ranking second only after the United States. India had eight companies in the list.[11] The cities of countries like India, China, Brazil and others are comparable to mega cities located in advanced capitalist countries. The economies of these countries are located within the overall circuit of global capital, through globalisation. As a result, these economies have access to global finance, markets and technology. Therefore, imperialism thwarting capitalist development of developing countries is no longer true in today's world, at least for a set of significantly large countries.

International division of labour

It was argued by many theories of Marxist and other persuasions that imperialism essentially imposed an international division of labour whereby the world economy could be envisaged as being divided into two segments – the developing countries producing primary commodities and the developed countries producing manufactured commodities.

This idea of international division of labour has also become irrelevant in the current era. Currently, we are witnessing countries like China, or other countries of East Asia, emerging as major manufacturing hub in the world. If we consider developing countries as a whole, then it is seen that the share of manufactured goods in the total exports of developing countries has increased from 5.1 percent in 1960 to 34.2 percent in 2006.[12] Therefore, it can be concluded that the earlier notion of developing countries exporting only primary commodities is no longer true.

Issue of capital flows and FDI

Earlier, it was the case that capital investors from developed countries were wary of investing in developing countries because of a number of factors.[13] But now, with globalisation, there is a free flow of capital across the world and developing countries have become a preferred destination for capital inflows. According to the World Investment Report 2012, in 2011, China was the most preferred destination for inward FDI, followed by the United States and India. Other developing countries like Indonesia, Brazil, Thailand and Vietnam figure within the top 15 preferred FDI destinations in the world. According to the World Investment Report, in 2014, developing and transition economies accounted for 55 percent of the total FDI inflows. Moreover, developing economies now account for almost 35 percent of the total FDI outflows. Therefore, the earlier idea that FDI does not flow in easily to developing countries is no longer valid. This inflow of FDI in developing countries also helps in the development of capitalism in these economies. At the same time, capital from developing countries is also getting invested in other countries, as the share of outward FDI from these countries is increasing.

Role of the third world bourgeoisie

With the coming into dominance of capitalism in third world countries, the big bourgeoisie of these countries have become major players in the international market. As has been already noted, within the richest bourgeoisie in the world, China and India have a very high number. These companies have global ambitions and are operating across the globe both in the financial and industrial sectors. For example, a company like Tata Motors from India has bought Jaguar, one of the leading automobile companies in the world, located in the United Kingdom.[14] The Indian company Reliance has a worldwide reach and is engaged in oil and gas exploration all across the globe. There are even reports that the Indian and Chinese companies are buying huge tracts of land in African countries, like Ethiopia, for business purposes.[15] If the bourgeoisie of the third world has indeed risen up to the level of metropolitan bourgeoisie then again this argument about imperialism thwarting the capitalist development in the third world becomes problematic.

Intra-imperialist rivalry

One of the basic arguments made by Lenin in his classic text *Imperialism* was that imperialism gives rise to intra-imperialist rivalry. Lenin argued that as capitalism progresses, monopoly capital develops. This monopoly finance capital was significantly tied with the nation states of their origin. In order to earn profit, this nation state-backed finance capital tried to repartition the world into their respective areas of intervention and exploitation. But as the entire world slowly came under the dominance of monopoly capital, there were no more areas which the capital backed by nation state could exploit. At that point, conflicts and rivalry between the different blocks of nation state backed finance capital must arise to realign their areas of influence. In such a situation, war becomes inevitable.[16]

The experiences of the First and Second World Wars show the correctness of Lenin's prognosis about imperialism at that particular juncture. But currently, there is hardly any conflict within the advanced capitalist or imperialist countries. Most of the policies they adopt are in unison, decided through global forums like the G7, G8 and after the 2008 crisis, the G20. Most importantly, since the Second World War, there has not been any case of military conflict within the advanced capitalist bloc. Therefore, one of the fundamental characteristics of imperialism, namely, intra-imperialist rivalry, is not of much relevance in today's world.

Making sense of the changes in developing countries

In the last section, we have discussed the stylised facts of the contemporary world conjuncture. On the basis of the above, it has been claimed that as a result of globalisation, the world has become flat, and theories of imperialism that posit a division of the world between the advanced capitalist countries and the third world are wrong. If the current world conjuncture is fundamentally different from the times of Lenin, then of course the theory of imperialism has to be reformulated. But before doing that, we need to articulate whether the world has indeed become flat or not. To do this, we put forward three sets of arguments.

Firstly, we have noted that there has been rapid capitalist development in the developing countries. This has resulted in a situation where the share of the developing and emerging countries in world GDP has increased significantly (see Figure 5.1).

From Figure 5.1, it is evident that the share of advanced capitalist countries has been declining consistently. It was above 60 percent in 1992, declining to 51 percent in 2011. At the same time, the share of developing and emerging economies has increased from around 35 percent in 1992 to 49 percent in 2011. On the basis of this, it can be concluded that there has been significant growth in the developing countries to increase its share in world GDP. However, this does not reveal the complete picture. If we look at the share of developing and emerging economies without including BRIC countries – Brazil, Russia, India and China – then it is seen that the share of the remaining developing countries actually has not increased much. It was 20.5 percent in 1992 and marginally increased to 22.5 percent in 2011. In other words, the rise of the share of the developing countries in world GDP is mainly propelled by the BRIC countries whose share in world GDP increased from around 15 percent in 1992 to 26.3 percent in 2011.

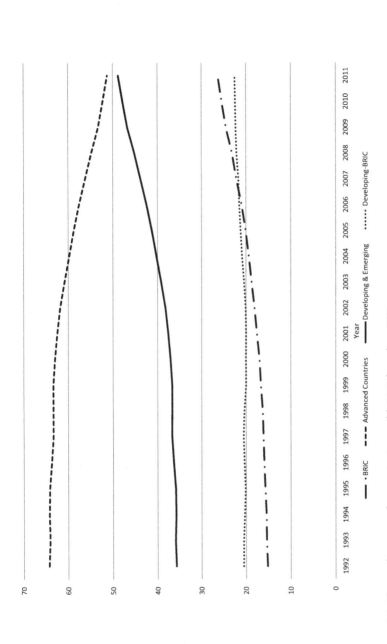

Figure 5.1 Share of groups of countries in world GDP based on PPP

Source: World Economic Outlook (WEO) database, IMF.

Note: Developing-BRIC represents the share of developing countries excluding the BRIC countries.

Therefore, what seems to be a rapid rise in the share of developing countries in world GDP is basically because of the rise in the share of the BRIC countries. Moreover, if we look at the individual share of the BRIC countries in world GDP, then another picture emerges (see Figure 5.2).

From Figure 5.2, it is evident that while there has indeed been a rapid increase in the share of the BRIC in world GDP, it is in turn mainly propelled by China, whose share increased from 4.3 percent of world GDP to 14 percent, and India, whose share increased from 3 percent to 5.7 percent of world GDP. Therefore, it is clear that the increase in the share of world GDP for developing countries is because of rapid growth in a small set of countries. Thus, the story of the last 20 years in terms of a shifting of economic weight in the world economy from the developed to the developing countries is the story of the rise of the BRIC. We will come back to the question of BRIC and China in detail later.

We have noted that there has been significant increase in the number of companies from countries like China, India and Brazil in the Fortune 500 list of companies. But a detailed look at the list reveals that the number of Fortune 500 companies has decreased from above 350 to under 300 for the G-7 countries, while the number of these companies in BRIC has increased from 35 in 2006 to 117 in 2015.[17] Thus, again it is seen that G-7 countries still has the maximum number of representatives in the biggest companies in the world. But the weight of the BRIC has increased primarily because of a rise in the number of such companies in China.

Hence, it is evident that there has been significant growth and capitalist development in the developing countries, led primarily by the BRIC. This growth has been so phenomenal that there are discussions about a change in the engine of growth of the world economy from the developed countries to the BRIC. But does this mean that the problem of underdevelopment has been solved in these countries? Does it mean that these countries have successfully made the transition from developing to advanced capitalist countries? In order to answer these questions we look at how the workers in these countries have fared with respect to those living in the advanced capitalist countries.

Figure 5.3 shows the average monthly wage of workers in BRIC countries with the monthly average wage of workers in United States indexed at 100.

From Figure 5.3, it is clear that in spite of the fact that the BRIC countries have managed to significantly increase their share in global GDP, the workers in this countries are way behind those of the United

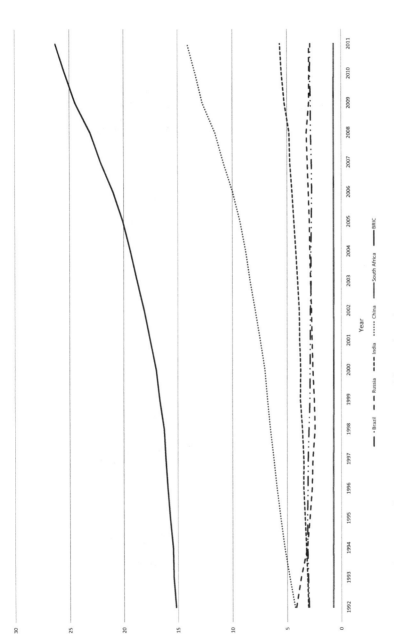

Figure 5.2 Share of BRICS and its constituents in world GDP based on PPP

Source: World Economic Outlook (WEO) database, IMF.

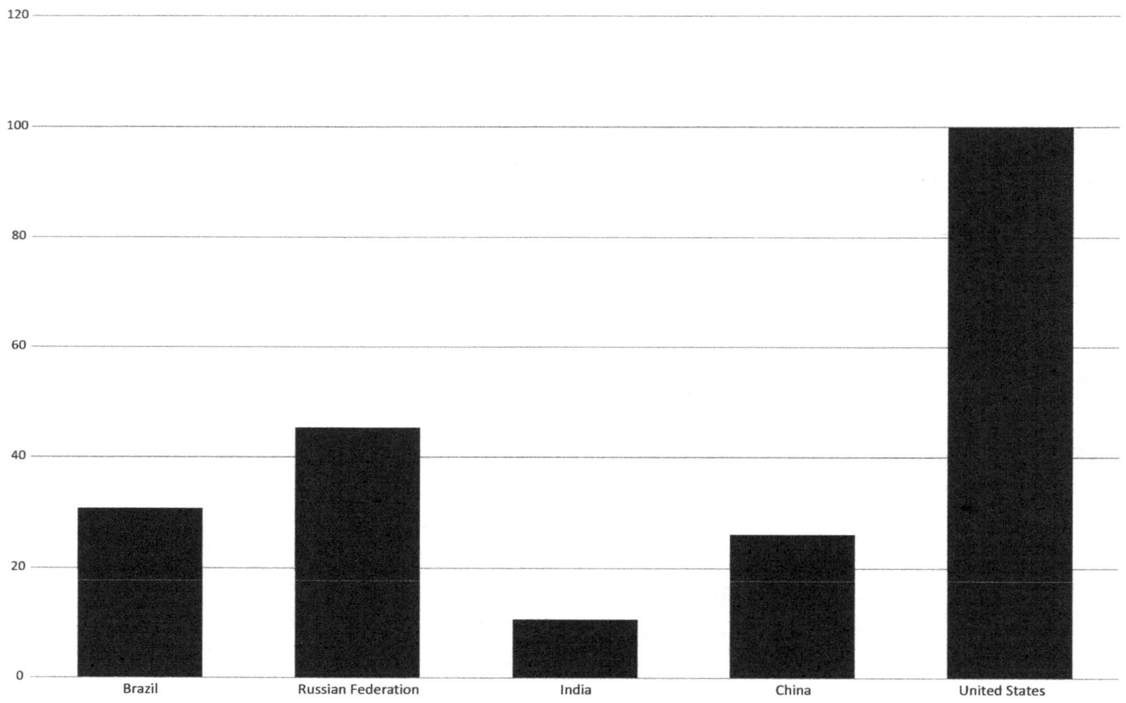

Figure 5.3 Index of average wage of BRIC with respect to United States for 2010

Source: Average wage taken from ILO Global wage data base. Converted to PPP on the basis of PPP conversion factor for individual countries provided by the World Bank.

States in terms of their wages. Thus it is seen that while the big capitalists of the countries of BRIC are trying to become a part of the global capitalist high table, the workers of these countries are way behind their brethren in advanced capitalist countries like the United States. In other words, for vast masses of the people in these countries who are workers, their lives are not at par with those of the workers in developed countries. Clearly, the world has not become flat, and there are areas of underdevelopment in the world. Thus, to argue that the third world has vanished or that the entire globe has been uniformly drawn into a global capitalist development path is not correct.

The discussion so far has pointed towards the fact that the tilt in the global balance of economic power towards the developing countries is mainly because of the rise of the BRIC. The capitalists of these countries have amassed huge wealth, and some of their companies are the largest in the world. But the workers of these countries have not gained much in comparison to their brethren in the advanced capitalist world order. What this signifies is not the assertion that the world has become flat. Rather it signifies a world conjuncture where new aspiring capitalists based in these countries are staking their claim in the global capitalist order. How this is affecting the global balance of forces in the context of imperialism is a question to which we will return shortly. Before that we need to look deeper into the functioning of the world economy in the current era.

Economic growth in the global economy and dollar hegemony

Figure 5.4 shows the growth rate of GDP in advanced capitalist countries.

From Figure 5.4 it is clear that the growth rate of all the major developed countries/blocks has been decreasing since the 1970s. This decrease in the growth rate of GDP of the capitalist core is related to three interrelated developments within capitalism itself. Firstly, as Kalecki had argued, for sustained growth under capitalism, there must be some exogenous stimulus.[18] Three kinds of exogenous stimulus have been discussed in the literature, namely, external markets or colonies, innovations and government expenditure. By the 1970s, the major exogenous stimulus in terms of colonies or external markets was exhausted with the process of decolonisation coming to an end. Secondly, the high growth rates observed in the capitalist core in the 1960s was largely a result of the Keynesian demand management policies adopted in these countries after the Second World War.

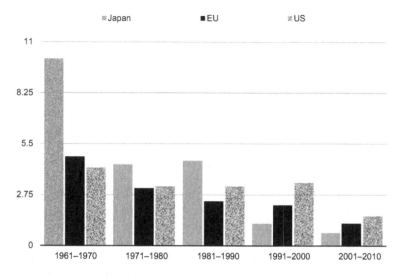

Figure 5.4 GDP growth rates in developed countries

Source: Thomas I. Palley, *Financialization: The Economics of Finance Capital Domination*, New York: Palgrave Macmillan, 2014.

Thirdly, with the rising dominance of international finance capital in the 1970s, there was a regression in economic policy making with the pre-Keynesian ideas coming back under the garb of monetarism, which advocated that government expenditure should be curtailed. This hegemony of global finance capital, with the boom period of state-led demand boom coming to an end, the virtues of free market under the new ideology of neoliberalism were asserted again. This resulted in the demand management policies, since the Second World War was coming to an end and, with it, the end of the state-led boom.[19]

While it is indeed true that there has been decline in the growth rates of GDP across the developed world, a close look at the growth rate of world GDP along with other countries reveals a more detailed picture. This is shown in Figure 5.5.

Figure 5.5 shows that, since around 2000, there has been a period of significant economic growth in the world as a whole which ended only with the global financial crisis of 2008. The growth rates in the emerging countries were the highest during the period followed by the advanced capitalist countries. Remarkably, this is also the period when the current account deficit of the United States as a share of GDP started to increase and reached almost 6 percent of GDP.

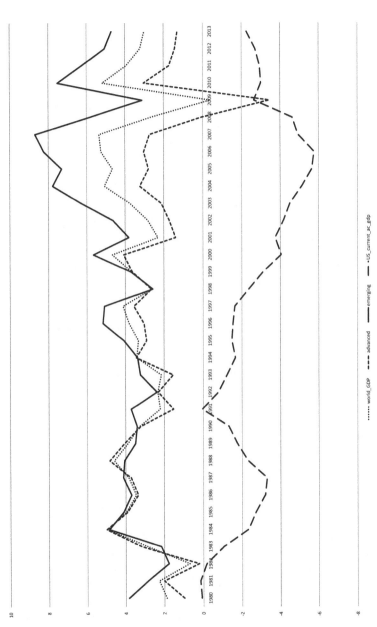

Figure 5.5 US current account and growth rates of GDP across countries

Source: WEO Database, IMF.

This current account deficit of the United States is the highest for any single country.

Thus, at a time when the world economy was growing rapidly, the United States, by expanding its current account deficit, provided markets for other economies, on the basis of which the overall growth rate of the world economy itself increased. This becomes clearer if we look at the data on current account deficit of various countries and the global imbalance. As the World Economic Situation and Prospects Report, 2014 of the United Nations shows, between 1997 and 2007, the United States had the highest current account deficit in the world, which was matched by current account surpluses by countries like China, Germany, Japan, oil exporters and others.

Now, if any country runs a current account deficit persistently, then the country must face problems in terms of financing the deficit through loans from the world market. If the current account deficit becomes too high, then there can be pressure on domestic currency to depreciate. But still the United States has been maintaining a huge current account deficit for a long period of time. The question is how?

The United States could maintain its current account deficit because the US dollar is the reserve currency in the world. Everybody wants to hold on to the dollar because people believe that the dollar is as good as gold. The countries across the world hold on to the dollar and ensure that the United States never lacks debt to finance its current account deficit. This is corroborated by the fact that the foreign exchange reserves of all countries are mostly denominated in terms of dollar. This is shown in Figure 5.6.

It is seen from Figure 5.6 that within the allocated reserves, claims in dollars are the most important component, comprising of more than 60 percent of the world's total foreign exchange reserves over the last two to three decades. The Euro, after its inception, comes a distant second in this regard. This signifies that most of the world foreign exchange reserve is actually held in dollar-denominated assets. This helps the United States to attract huge amount of resources from across the globe. This has resulted in a situation where the foreign ownership of US assets is greater than US ownership of foreign assets.[20] The importance of the dollar as the reserve currency of the world can also be gauged from the fact that in 2010, 84.9 percent of all foreign exchange transactions had dollar on one side of the deal, which increased to 87 percent in 2013.[21]

According to the Council on Foreign Affairs in the United States, there has been a significant increase in foreign ownership of US assets which became greater than the US ownership of foreign assets in

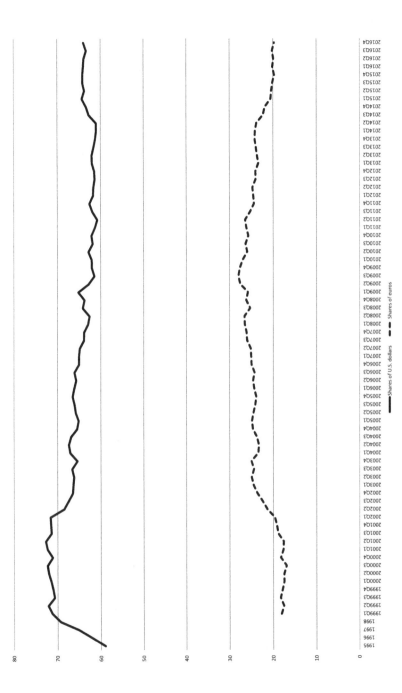

Figure 5.6 Share of US dollars and Euro in world foreign exchange reserves
Source: COFER Database, IMF.

1985. Since then, the former has remained above the latter.[22] This process of foreign ownership of US assets has been possible because of the free flow of capital regime instituted since 1973, which gathered momentum in the 1980s and 1990s with the globalisation policies being adopted across the world. Thus, in a world of free flow of capital flows, the United States has been able to maintain confidence in investors about the stability of the value of dollar. Investors across the world have held on to dollars and invested in the United States. Two important issues arise from the above discussion – one is the issue of stability of the value of dollar and second is the question of the free flow of capital across international borders. Let us first discuss the stability of the value of dollar or the dollar hegemony.

Maintaining the stability of the dollar

If world-wide wealth holders want to hold their wealth in dollar denominated assets, then the value of the dollar must be relatively stable compared to other currencies. In normal circumstances, a country running a huge current account deficit will find it difficult to maintain the stability of the currency's value. But in the case of the United States, as we have discussed above, it has been running a huge current account deficit but is still able to attract wealth holders towards dollar-denominated assets. This is possible because, in spite of the huge current account deficit, wealth holders across the world perceive dollar to be a stable currency. What explains this phenomenon?

There are two crucial factors which ensure that the value of dollar remains stable. The ultimate guarantor of the stability of the dollar is United States huge military machinery. Table 5.1 shows the military expenditure and its share in world's military expenditure of the top 15 countries.

This huge military expenditure of the United States enables it to not only maintain the world's most sophisticated army, navy and air force, but also operate through military bases strewn across the globe. It is difficult to get the exact number of military bases of the United States across the globe, since many of them are secret bases. But according to the Base Structure Report, FY 2012 Baseline of the Department of Defense of the United States, the Department of Defense has 666 overseas locations which it owns or leases for military purposes. This huge network of the US military enables it to attack any country it wishes in a matter of minutes. This network forms, as it were, the spokes of the wheel of US imperialism through which it has managed to exert its hegemony.[23] The military dominance of the world by the

Table 5.1 Military expenditure of the top 15 countries in the world along with their share in total military expenditure

Country	Military expenditure ($ bn)	Share of world total (in %)
USA	640	36.6
China	188	10.8
Russia	87.8	5.03
Saudi Arabia	67	3.84
France	61.2	3.5
UK	57.9	3.31
Germany	48.8	2.79
Japan	48.6	2.78
India	47.4	2.71
South Korea	33.9	1.94
Italy	32.7	1.87
Brazil	31.5	1.8
Australia	24	1.37
Turkey	19.1	1.09
UAE	19	1.09
Total 15 States	1408	80.6
Total World	1747	100

Source: Trends in Military Expenditure 2013, Stockholm International Peace Research Institute.

United States does not end merely with its huge military expenditure and global bases. The United States is also the top exporter of arms in the world. Between 2011 and 2015, the United States accounted for 33 percent of the total arms exports in the world.[24] According to the SIPRI data, out of the top 100 arms producing and military services companies, 44 are from the United States, accounting for 54.4 percent of total revenue from arms sales.[25] The fact that the United States is the leading arms exporter and manufacturer in the world serves US interests in two alternative ways. Firstly, as has already been noted, the huge military might of the United States gets further buttressed by its arms exports, since governments who are buying arms have to fall in line with US global ambitions. Secondly, the fact that the United States is the largest supplier of arms means that in a world of conflict, the demand for arms will rise, which will create a market for United States.

The most important commodity in the world today is oil. The price of oil in global trade is denominated in terms of dollar. This gives a huge advantage to the United States in terms of having its control over the strategic commodity. Moreover, the stability of the dollar is intertwined with the stability of the value of oil in terms of dollars.[26]

If the value of oil increases greatly in terms of dollars, then the stability of dollar as a reserve currency will also fall, because its purchasing power of buying one barrel of oil will come down. So, the United States has to maintain a grip over oil-producing regions in the world to ensure that there are no supply shocks to oil or that some oil producing country arbitrarily increases the price of oil substantially. This is again ensured through the global bases of the US military. The military intervention of the United States in Iraq, Libya and the entire Persian Gulf region is a result of the pursuit of United States to maintain its control over world oil reserves.[27]

It is this military might of the United States and its control over oil reserves in the world that provides a guarantee to the wealth holders that the stability of the dollar will not be jeopardised. If at all there is any challenge to the dollar, then the ultimate solution will be a military one. The network of US military bases, its ultra-modern and sophisticated arms and ammunition pushes it way ahead of any other rival military power. The wealth holders across the world know that their ultimate guarantor is the US military. Thus, the dollar continues to maintain its hegemony, even though the United States has a huge current account deficit. This is one of the most important pillars of modern imperialism.

Imperialism: old and new

Until now, we have discussed the changes in the structure of the world economy with the coming into being of the powerful bloc of the BRIC countries. We have also discussed how the United States maintains its hegemony through its currency, which is ultimately backed by its military power. Now, we discuss how the current world conjuncture differs from the one during Lenin's time to understand the uniqueness of our times in the context of imperialism.

Lenin's theory of imperialism explained remarkably well the First and Second World Wars, resulting from what he called 'intra-imperialist rivalry'. But as has been noted earlier, this intra-imperialist rivalry has become muted, and there has not been any major war between the advanced capitalist countries since the Second World War.

Lenin talked about centralisation of capital leading to monopoly capital. But after Lenin's time, this centralisation of capital increased even further. With the oil price hike of 1973, the OPEC countries deposited their bonanza in European and US banks. Thus, a huge stock of finance capital was piled up within the banking sector of Europe and United States, which wanted profitable investment. This huge finance capital, searching for profitable investment, was allowed to go global. On the other hand, deflationary policies were introduced in the advanced and developing countries. This was because finance capital abhors state intervention which might result in inflationary pressure, since rentiers are adversely affected by inflation as the real rate of interest falls. Therefore, once a country is opened up to finance capital, it has to go for deflationary policies, fearing a capital flight which can cripple the economy. These deflationary policies adversely affected the workers. Thus, on the one hand, finance was made mobile, and on the other hand, workers were weakened. This marked the era of neoliberal capitalism.

The character of this finance capital is different from that of Lenin's conception in three fundamental ways. Firstly, while Lenin emphasised finance capital as capital 'controlled by banks and employed in industry', the new finance capital is not necessarily tied to industry in any special sense.[28] Rather, it moves around the world in the quest for quick speculative gains. This finance capital largely constitutes what is referred to as 'hot money'. Secondly, finance capital in Lenin's time had its base within a particular nation, and its international operations were linked to the expansion of national 'economic territory'. But the finance capital of today, though it has its origins in particular nations, is not necessarily tied to any national interest. It moves around globally, and its objectives are no different from the finance capital that has its origins in some other nation. In other words, the distinctions between national finance capitals have become meaningless today with finance capital taking an international dimension. This international finance capital is detached from any particular national interest and has the world as its arena of operations. Thirdly, in order to ensure such uninhibited global operation, the world should not be split up into separate blocs or into economic territories which are the preserves of particular nations and out of bounds for others.[29]

A number of conclusions follow from the above. Firstly, since finance capital has been transformed into international finance capital which is highly mobile, the role of the nation-state has witnessed a transformation. If it is profitable for international finance capital to move freely from one place to another without hindrance, then the role of any nation state in controlling this flow of capital is curtailed. Precisely this has been sought to be achieved with the introduction of the policies of neoliberal globalisation across the globe, which is essentially nothing but a policy of allowing free movement of finance capital. Thus, states of the developing countries also witness a transformation from undertaking policies for the benefit of the people towards implementing policies aimed at satisfying international finance. Secondly, since international finance capital needs the entire globe for its operations and does not want the world to be split up into separate blocs, intra-imperialist rivalry remains muted. Thirdly, finance capital opposes government intervention, which is against its interests. As a result, states across the globe have cut back on their expenditures, particularly those earmarked for development. With the rise of dominance of international finance capital, therefore, the role of state intervention as an exogenous stimulus for growth gets severely constrained if not totally absent. Fourthly, speculative activities take the centre stage of the global economy rather than industrial activities, because the role of the international finance capital is essentially to reap rapid speculative profits from one part of the world to another. This in turn brings in a stagnationary tendency on the world economy as a whole.

Thus, the absence of intra-imperialist rivalry is a direct result of the dominance of international finance capital. But the absence of intra-imperialist rivalry of the kind witnessed during Lenin's time does not mean either (a) wars have become a thing of the past or (b) contradictions within the global geo-politics has ended. What it means is that the nature and geography of these have changed fundamentally.

Let us first take the case of wars. It is true that after the Second World War, there has not been any major armed conflict between the advanced capitalist countries. However, there have been very serious military interventions in countries like Yugoslavia, Afghanistan, Iraq and Libya to name just a few. Wikipedia lists more than 40 armed conflicts in which the US army participated since the Second World War.[30] In all these military aggressions, the entire advanced capitalist countries have acted as a single block under the leadership of the United States. In all these cases, the attack was against a developing country. This essentially shows that the muting of intra-imperialist rivalry of Lenin's time has brought in an alliance of the imperialist bloc under the leadership of the United States.

The alliance between the advanced capitalist countries does not end there. International multi-lateral bodies like the World Bank, IMF, WTO or the UNPCCC have witnessed how developed countries act as a block and try and out-manoeuvre developing countries to maintain their advantageous position in the world economy. These continuing wars waged against the third world countries and the economic bargaining against the developing countries in different forums, essentially show how, even today, there exists conflict in the world arena; but the geography of that conflict has changed from being intra-imperialist to being conflict between the advanced capitalist countries and the developing countries.

Theorising global conflicts today

In an earlier era, within the premise of Marxist theories, there was this idea that the bourgeoisie of the erstwhile colonies were nationalist in nature or compradors. By nationalist bourgeoisie, it was meant that the ruling classes of these countries were in conflict with imperialism and wanted capitalist development in the domestic economy which imperialism thwarted. The other idea was that in some countries the ruling classes were completely subservient to global metropolitan capital and acted as agents of imperialism. Therefore, the earlier theories predicted a conflict between nationalist bourgeoisie and imperialism and collaboration between comprador bourgeoisie and imperialism. Our point is that both these characterisations have become irrelevant and cannot explain the conflicts of the current era.

There is no doubt that the bourgeoisie in the third world countries, particularly in BRIC, have become immensely powerful since the policies of globalisation have been adopted. All indicators in terms of the total assets, wealth, profits and so on of the big companies in these countries suggest their increasing strength. It is also the case that some of these companies have become global players in the world market.

There exists a complex relationship between the bourgeoisie of these countries and imperialism. On the one hand, we have certain bourgeoisie coming into the ranks of the global players. This is happening through a process of enrichment of the ruling classes through the policies of reforms and globalisation itself, or through its alliance with global finance capital. However, as has been argued above, the vast masses of people remain detached from these capitalist processes and remain impoverished. This co-option of the bourgeoisie of the third world as junior partners of imperialism is a feature of today's world conjuncture.

But in fulfilling the global aspirations of these ruling classes, conflicts arise between metropolitan capital and these bourgeoisies. These conflicts are fundamentally different from the times of colonialism. During colonialism, the big bourgeoisie was essentially fighting to implement capitalism under its own leadership in countries like India. However, in order to mobilise the masses for independence, certain demands of the people, like land reforms, were incorporated into the demands of the freedom struggle and implemented to some degree after independence. Moreover, the bourgeoisie of the newly independent countries tried to pursue a developmental path autonomous to imperialism by following a planning process in the domestic economy. This anti-imperialist stance of the bourgeoisie was hailed as being nationalist, and indeed, the processes of decolonisation helped improve the lives of the people to some extent.

But today's conflicts with imperialism have got no such pro-people content. It is aimed simply at maintaining the global reach of the bourgeoisie. That global reach has not resulted in any improvement of the working people, as has been enumerated above. Hence, the bourgeoisie cannot be termed as nationalistic any more, in the sense that class interests are not aligned with the interests of workers, farmers or common people in its nation-state. This does not mean that the bourgeoisie of these countries have become compradors. Comprador bourgeoisie do not have any production base and essentially live off commissions from the sales of the metropolitan bourgeoisie. But as has been repeatedly argued, today's third world bourgeoisie, particularly BRIC, are very powerful and have a global production base. In other words, in order to characterise the current conjuncture, we need to do away with these terms which were applicable for a conjuncture which is long past.

Therefore, we come back to the earlier assertion that while it is true that the intra-imperialist rivalry of Lenin's period has come to an end, contradictions in the realm of global political or geo-political economy has not become a thing of the past. Currently, the contradiction between BRIC and US-led advanced capitalist countries are coming to the fore. We have seen repeatedly how BRIC, as a block, has taken contrary positions to those of the United States or G7 in international forums like the UN or UNPCCC. Moreover, India and particularly China, because of its growth, is exerting a tremendous demand on the energy resources of the world. China's forays into Latin America and Africa are manifestations of that. Here, conflict between the United States or advanced capitalist countries with China is bound to arise. The conflict in Syria and recently in Ukraine show that this conflict is moving into the domain of military or strategic conflicts, beyond purely economic contradictions between the upcoming bourgeoisie of BRIC and that of advanced capitalism.

Conclusion

Let us try and pull the threads of the arguments together. In this essay, we have tried to argue that imperialism, in its essence, must be looked at in a conjunctural manner. In other words, there cannot be 'one' theory of imperialism but many theories depending upon the changing nature of the global capitalist development. During the nascent phase of capitalism, when capital had not penetrated the entire globe geographically, colonialism was the main means of imperialism aimed at primitive accumulation of capital. With this process, centralisation of capital took place, resulting in the formation of nation state-based monopoly capital which tried to re-draw the map of the world in order to chalk out individual areas of control and influence. As a result, conflicts between these powers necessarily arose, leading to the World War. This was the theory of imperialism as proposed by Lenin.

However, it must be acknowledged that the current world conjuncture is significantly different from the time of Lenin. We argue that the current world conjuncture is characterised by three important developments. Firstly, a group of countries, the BRIC, has successfully managed to increase its share in world GDP, so much so that the share of developing countries as a whole has significantly increased. Secondly, in spite of the changes that has taken place in the world economy and a historically high current account deficit of the United States, the dollar is still functioning as a reserve currency. We argue that this is so because the value of the dollar is guaranteed by the military might of the United States. Thirdly, the intra-imperialist rivalry of Lenin's period is basically absent, and now the contour and geography of the conflict has shifted towards one where the conflict is essentially between the advanced capitalist world and the countries. This does not imply that the ruling classes of developing countries and BRIC have become anti-capitalists. Rather, the conflict is a manifestation of their rapid capitalist accumulation within a world where resources are limited. Today, this conflict has not blown out into war. But in the case of Syria and Ukraine, it is clear that the countries like Russia are even ready to put in their weight behind military-strategic global issues.

Thus, to answer the question as to whether imperialism is a relevant concept in today's world or not, our answer is, yes it is indeed relevant. Imperialism of our times gets manifested essentially in the maintenance of dollar hegemony through the military might of the United States, the persistence of underdevelopment in the developing countries, including BRIC and the military attack on strategic third world countries by the combined bloc of advanced capitalist countries under the leadership of the United States. But this conjuncture is also one of a growing dominance of upcoming capitalist emerging economies who are coming into conflict with the erstwhile global architecture of dominance. This conflict is still unfolding. Therefore, we need to look at imperialism today from a perspective which considers all the characteristics of the present conjuncture. It is still a relevant concept and provides important perspectives about global balance of forces. But it needs to be continuously updated to capture the particular conjuncture.

Notes

1 The author would like to acknowledge a research grant from the Indian Council of Social Science Research (ICSSR), for working on the theme, 'Imperialism in the Current Era'. A special thanks to Prasenjit Bose for providing key insights for writing the paper.
2 Michael Hardt and Antonio Negri, *Empire*, Cambridge, MA: Harvard University Press, 2000.
3 Rosa Luxemburg, *The Accumulation of Capital*, London: Palgrave Macmillan, 2013.
4 For a detailed discussion on Rosa Luxemburg's theory of imperialism, see Prabhat Patnaik, *The Value of Money*, New Delhi: Tulika Press, 2008.
5 V.I. Lenin, *Imperialism: The Highest Stage of Capitalism*, New Delhi: Leftword Books, 2000.
6 Paul Baran, *The Political Economy of Growth*, New York: Monthly Review Press, 1957.
7 For a detailed discussion and critique of the dependency school, see, Jose Gabriel Palma, 'Theories of Dependency', in Amitava Krishna Dutta and Jaime Ros (eds.), *International Handbook of Development Economics: Volume 1*, Cheltenham, UK: Edward Elgar, 2008.
8 For a detailed discussion on the recent debates on developments in India and China, see Amiya Kumar Bagchi and Anthony P. D'Costa (eds.), *Transformation and Development: The Political Economy of Transition in India and China*, New Delhi: Oxford University Press, 2012. For a critique of the Chinese growth process, see Martin Hart-Landsberg and Paul Burkett, *China and Socialism: Market Reforms and Class Struggle*, New Delhi: Aakar, 2006.
9 List of Dollar Billionaires, *Forbes*, www.forbes.com/sites/nickdesantis/2016/03/01/forbes-billionaires-list-map-2016-billionaire-population-by-country/#4bf7270e30af (accessed on 8 July 2016).
10 Hurun Global Rich List, 2016, www.hurun.net/en/ArticleShow.aspx?nid=15703 (accessed on 8 July 2016).
11 Calculated from the Fortune 500 list, http://fortune.com/global500/ (accessed on 20 July 2016).
12 Deepak Nayyar, 'Developing Countries in the World Economy: The Future in the Past?' WIDER Annual Lecture 12, 23 February 2009.
13 For a discussion on this argument, see Prabhat Patnaik, *Accumulation and Stability Under Capitalism*, Oxford: Clarendon Press, 1997.
14 'TATA Buys Jaguar in 1.15 billion Pounds Deal', *BBC News*, 26 March 2008, http://news.bbc.co.uk/2/hi/business/7313380.stm (accessed on 8 July 2016).

15 Anuradha Mittal, 'Indian Land Grabs in Ethiopia Show Dark Side of South – South Co-Operation', *The Guardian*, 25 February 2013, www.theguardian.com/global-development/poverty-matters/2013/feb/25/indian-land-grabs-ethiopia (accessed on 8 July 2016).

16 For an alternative articulation of the theory of Imperialism, see Nikolai Bukharin, *Imperialism and World Economy*, New Delhi: Aakar, 2010.

17 Data retrieved from http://money.cnn.com/magazines/fortune/global500/index.html (accessed on 20 July 2016).

18 Michael Kalecki, 'Observations on the Theory of Growth', *Economic Journal*, 1962, 72(285): 134–53.

19 For a detailed discussion on this theme see, Prasenjit Bose, 'Capital Accumulation and Crisis: A Theoretical Study', unpublished Ph.D dissertation submitted to Jawaharlal Nehru University, 2003.

20 Dinah Walker, 'Quarterly Update: Foreign Ownership of US Assets', Council on Foreign Relations, www.cfr.org/united-states/quarterly-update-foreign-ownership-us-assets/p25685 (accessed on 20 July 2016).

21 'Triennial Central Bank Survey, Foreign Exchange Turnover in April 2013: Preliminary Global Results', Bank for International Settlements, September 2013, www.bis.org/publ/rpfx13fx.pdf (accessed on 20 July 2016).

22 Walker, 'Quarterly Update'.

23 For a discussion on the military might of the USA being used for strategic purposes, see Noam Chomsky, *Hegemony or Survival: America's Quest for Global Dominance*, Allen & Unwin, 2007.

24 'Trends in International Arms Transfers', SIPRI, 2015, http://books.sipri.org/files/FS/SIPRIFS1602.pdf (accessed on 20 July 2016).

25 http://books.sipri.org/files/FS/SIPRIFS1512.pdf (accessed on 20 July 2016).

26 See Patnaik, *The Value of Money*, for a discussion on the value of oil tied with dollar.

27 For a detailed account of USA's efforts to control oil through military means, see Michael Klare, *Blood and Oil: The Dangers and Consequences of America's Growing Dependency on Imported Petroleum*, New York: Holt Paperbacks, 2005.

28 Lenin, *Imperialism*.

29 Prabhat Patnaik, 'Notes on Contemporary Imperialism', *MRZine*, http://mrzine.monthlyreview.org/2010/patnaik201210.html (accessed on 20 July 2016).

30 http://en.wikipedia.org/wiki/List_of_wars_involving_the_United_States (accessed on 20 July 2016).

Part II

Patterns of contemporary imperialism

6 Latin America in the new international order

New forms of economic organisations and old forms of surplus appropriation

Noemi Levy Orlik

New forms of imperialist dominance emerged as a result of recessions in the industrialised countries in the late 1960s.[1] The unprecedented combination of inflation and economic stagnation (stagflation) opened up an era of deregulation and globalisation in the productive, financial and commercial structures that imposed financial capital as the 'master' of economic decisions.[2] In this changing environment, economic theory underwent a profound revolution, expelling the theory of effective demand from mainstream US and European universities and, more importantly, economic policy objectives went through a reversal. The goal of full employment was replaced by inflation controls and economic growth was subjected to price stability, with the emergence of concepts such as Non-Accelerating Inflation Rate of Unemployment (NAIRU) to highlight the fact that economic activity ought to be limited to objectives of monetary stability.[3]

Under this framework, the organisation of economic production was modified at various levels. The relation among and within social classes changed, the appropriation of profits took place through financial instruments and financial gains were seized by rentiers, while workers' income shrank, especially for those directly related to production, and the international division of labour changed. The new features of the economic order can be summarised under three headings. Firstly, the dominance of financial capital combined with deep income concentration. Secondly, in international organisations, demand was decoupled from supply and investment from savings. Thirdly, the new economic order was based on structural disequilibria in which the imperialistic country, the United States, operated under current account deficits and capital account surplus, mobilising financial surplus into its financial system; while other economies had current account surpluses and capital account deficits, with the exception of Latin American and Caribbean (LAC) economies.

The manufacturing processes of production (including high value-added divisions) moved away from the United States towards developed and developing economies, giving rise to structural imbalances: the US economy turned into the world's engine of demand as well as the global borrower, sustained by the ability of the US financial system to retain its power of issuing the international unit of account, with almost unlimited liquidity at low cost that, taken together, converted the US financial system into the liquidity sink of the world.

This new imperialist order set off a process of financialisation along with neomercantilism, which become two parts of the same process. The United States imposed a new international division of labour in which its main function was to provide international liquidity (financial services), operating on the basis of wide and deep financial markets, while the rest of the world (developed and developing economies) were to become producers. The LAC region increased its exports while not reaching a current account surplus, the counterpart to which was higher external financial capital dependence. These economies were obliged not only to reduce their labour costs but also to raise their financial margins, which were coupled with deindustrialisation processes. For the first time in history, foreign direct and portfolio investment dominated the LAC region and financial markets deepened and enlarged but, instead of increasing domestic financial savings via recirculation to the productive sector, appropriation of surpluses by the United States expanded.

The globalised and financialised economic order became more complicated than the previous centre–periphery relation,[4] colonial (external markets)[5] or imperialistic domination.[6] LAC underdeveloped economies continued to require external capital inflows to equate their balance of payments; hence, on top of reducing their labour costs, they had to part with increased interests and financial payments, signifying the reappearance of former colonial external resource appropriation under new forms.

This essay is organised into five sections. Following this introduction, the second section discusses the concepts of financialisation and neomercantilism as a part of a unique process within the current dominant international order. The third section analyses the financial and external market structures of Latin American countries, based on a sample of six economies. The fourth section is devoted to the analyses of the external financial channel, looking into the primary balance of the current account, to show that dividends paid to external capital further expand the current account deficit, followed by a discussion of income distribution that shows increased inequality for the countries analysed. Lastly, some conclusions are put forward.

Financialisation and neomercantilism: two sides of one coin

In this section, we discuss three issues. Firstly, income concentration within and between countries based on surplus extraction in financial-led economies, followed by a discussion of the meaning of financialisation and neomercantilism.

New trends in the capitalist system: income concentration and surplus appropriation

Financial capital became the leading actor in capitalist decisions in which rentiers acquired strength over the business bureaucracy (entrepreneurs), who subjugated their interests to the former leading capitalist group, giving way to a conflation of relations among the ruling class, against the expectations of classical economists.[7]

On the side of workers, the salary–income share of those directly related to production diminished (blue and white collar workers), especially in stagnant periods, without reducing the overall share of salaried income in GDP, since business bureaucracy payments partly took the form of salaries, giving rise to what has been named income segmentation. In this process, the gap widened between upper and middle-ranking managerial labour, whose income is associated with overhead or fixed labour and rank-and-file workers (including lower-ranking managers), who are linked to direct labour.[8] According to Lavoie (2009), in vertically integrated sectors, all direct costs can be transformed into variable labour,[9] while overhead costs are related to mark-ups and prices, from which it follows that higher direct costs diminished workers' real wages as well as their share in income (white and blue collar workers).[10] The striking result was that in stagnating economies,[11] higher managerial costs have positive effects on the economy, since the additional purchasing power granted to high and medium-rank managers overtakes the negative effects induced by the rise in prices and the fall in the real purchasing power of direct labour,[12] while effective demand expands and drives up the actual rate of capacity utilisation.

The principal outcome of this economic organisation is the extreme concentration of the distribution of income, in which top management employees' salaries (based on increased compensations and options) and rentiers' financial wealth increased, making up the notorious richest 0.1 percent segment of the economy.[13] Therefore, the surplus extraction between social classes rocketed, favouring especially those not directly related to the production process (managers, accountants and administrators, among others).

At the international level, the US appropriation of surplus from neomercantilists developed and developing countries increased, by pushing down US import prices (neomercantilist countries export prices) and increasing the prices of financial instruments (guaranteeing capital market financial inflation). The less benefited economies were those unable to reach trade surplus positions, forced to reduce their labour costs (which became their sole competitive advantage) and part with higher financial payments (interests and dividends) that increased even further their current account deficit position.

Since the end of the Second World War, and more clearly from the late 1960s, when the second period of financial capital domination commenced, the manufacturing industry moved from the United States to other developed and developing countries; and these economies turned into worldwide suppliers, while the United States specialised in financial services. De Cecco[14] argues that in this process, the United States retained the 'privilege' to dictate the rules of surplus creation and distribution, along with a process of capital centralisation, which determines the way in which surplus should be distributed among classes, countries and regions. In this context, the US economy turned into the main international borrower, a condition shared with LAC countries that, however, did not issue international units of account, compelling them to part with increased capital payments (the LAC region did not get close to the US capitalisation value, as will be discussed later).

The characteristics of the second era of financial capital domination were: firstly, that the United States became the sole provider of the international unit of account, with no liquidity limitations from gold or other commodities or currencies, and maintained power over the determining the rate of interest and, thereby, the floor prices of financial instruments, which gave them control over attracting or deterring financial capital flows and, more importantly, financial savings concentrated in their financial market, accruing capital market gains. Secondly, the extraction of surplus from the rest of the world changed. It was based on financial flows,[15] increasing US foreign ownership of real and especially financial assets. Unlike the previous imperialist power (Great Britain) and the first period of US international domination, in this second era of financial capital domination, the United States ceased to be the global producer of manufactured goods and the supplier of advanced technological innovations, de-industrialising its economy; foreign capital flows poured into its financial system, without losing its privilege of determining the main prices of accumulation.

What is financialisation and how does it operate?

Although a consensus has not reached on the meaning of the concept of financialisation, the most-cited definition of Epstein that 'financialisation means the increasing role of financial motives, financial markets, financial actors and financial institutions in the operation of domestic and international economies'[16] laid the ground for certain specific aspects of the operation of the financial system under the dominance of financial capital.

Following the above argument, one measurement of financialisation in the United States (from the 1950s) is the increasing participation of the finance, insurance and real estate (FIRE) sector in total financial operations, in terms of corporate profits and in terms of gross domestic product (GDP).[17] In this line of reasoning, Pollin and Heintz provide extensive evidence on how the US financial system broadened and diversified, from 1980s onwards, in which the financial system moved their operations from credit creation to financial trading, creating shadow banks, composed of mutual and pension funds, finance companies, real estate investment trusts, hedge funds and others.[18]

This financial organisation spread worldwide and the US system turned into the major 'nerve centre within a global system that has been integrating at a rapid rate since the early 1980s',[19] modifying the US debt composition and quadrupling foreign ownership under the form of corporate debts and treasury bonds.[20] From this it may be concluded that financialisation created new channels of profit creation, defined as (a) pattern of accumulation in which profit primarily accrues through financial channels rather than through commerce or commodity production. Financial here refers to activities related to the provision (or transfer) of liquid capital in expectations of future interest dividends or capital gains.[21]

This altogether strengthened the 'portfolio income' (interest, dividends and capital gains), which increased in relation to cash flows of the entire non-financial sector and within the manufacturing sector.[22] Following the financialisation literature, there is no doubt that the financial sector financial gains turned into an important source of profit appropriation for the United States and the big transnationals that widened and deepened financial markets.

A forerunner to the increased financial flows can be found in the second half of the nineteenth century, when capitalism underwent a process of oligopolisation, and non-financial firms started to issue 'equity or common stocks in excess of what is required for the productive and commercial activities of a firm',[23] which diminished capital market efficiency[24] (this process has also been named overcapitalisation; see the discussion of Marshall, Lavingstone, Hobson, Veblen). Overcapitalisation has been dominant in two historical periods, first, before 1929, and it was 'associated with the "watering down" of a company's shares when a company promoter, responsible for the sale of new shares, would sell shares in excess in order to obtain a higher commission for managing the share issue'.[25] Secondly, it reappeared in the 1970s with the rise of institutional investors (pension funds, insurance companies and intermediaries to which they sometimes allocate the more speculative parts of their portfolios, hedge funds and equity funds), which led to a process of capital market inflation and increase of capital gains from holding stocks, the peculiarity being that capital gains accrue on sale of a security and are paid for by the buyer of the security rather than by the company that originally issued the security. . . . This made shares a very cheap form of finance for companies.[26]

From here it follows that 'in a period of capital market inflation, (corporations) could rely on the market to pay a considerable part of the return on shares that were issued'.[27]

Another prominent characteristic of financialisation is the reduction of labour costs, as argued above, which has been an outcome of the new organisation of non-financial institutions that switched from 'create and retain' to 'downsize and distribute'.[28] In this context, the retention of money and people employed and the reinvestment in physical capital and complementary resources[29] have been substituted by a process of downsizing the labour force, which meant reducing the labour income of workers directly related to production and the security of jobs (based on contracts), along with a process of labour pauperisation and precarisation,[30] whose main outcome has been wage stagnation.

As noted above, new types of employees (business bureaucracy) appeared on the basis that part of their income was paid in the form of salaries, but their objective was unrelated to upgrading the production sector; their main concern was to maximise returns on equity, because another important source of their income was options. Under this condition, shareholders were the principals and managers (business bureaucracy) were their operators. For the latter, 'the rate of return on corporate stock was their measure of superior performance, and the shareholder value their creed'.[31] This process emerged together with income differentiation. In 1965, the pay packages of the CEOs of US corporations, in comparison to the factory workers, were 44 times higher; in 1998, these had risen to 419 times higher.[32]

Considering the above discussion, there can be no question that financialisation modified financial market operations, imposing the 'Anglo-Saxon' model of financial organisation worldwide, which moved away from a credit creation to a security model of trading. This process attracted foreign capital inflows into the US financial system, leading to financial inflation that provided financial gains and almost limitless liquidity to the imperialistic economy.

How does neomercantilism operate?

This term has been defined as

> the pursuit of economic policies and institutional arraignments that considers net external surplus as a crucial source of profits. The solution to the problem of effective demand is seen as lying above all in a position trade balance. Moreover, the current account surplus is seen as increasing the private sector's ability to operate on international market.[33]

Following the above definition, neomercantilism situates net exports as the driving force of economic growth, and the external market its leading objective, coupled with reduced internal markets, competitive (undervalued) exchange rates and low salaried income. Demand and supply decouple and a new division of labour is imposed, in which the imperialistic country acquires the role of triggering (international) effective demand, while other developed and developing economies become the global producers. This process was directed by a political order that set a pecking order in which the central economy benefited most from international financial inflation and reduced price imports (especially wage commodities); followed by developed economies that retained complex production processes, and developing countries that produced manufactured goods at the lower levels of the global chain; last in the list are developing economies that did not acquire a net surplus in their trade balance and specialised in raw materials or in the final part of the manufacturing process, also known as the assembly or maquila processes.

Specifically, the European countries defeated in the Second World War (and Japan) became producers of manufactured goods and net surplus exporters in the early post-war period, a role that switched to developing countries in the 1980s and 1990s; with different positions in the global chain of production and within the financial system. The first group of producer countries (Germany and to a lesser extent Japan) supplied the technological know-how and tool and machine designs, and the financial sector was the main share buyers (in US domination currency) that swelled stock and share prices of the main financial centres. The second group was the producer countries composed by developing net manufacture export economies on the lower levels of the production process that, in the financial market, became the main buyers (particularly China) of US bonds, giving rise to what Bernanke (2005)[34] calls the 'saving glut'. The third group was composed of raw material export and maquila manufacture producers, mainly the LAC economies, which remain net importers, thereby retaining their positions as net borrowers and parting with increased financial payments (interests) to attract foreign capital inflows.

The US economy developed its financial service sector centred on financial innovations, initially based on information and, afterwards, on knowledge-based developments (Boyer 2000);[35] it was headed by small social groups and sustained by highly educated elites; their manufacturing sector shrank significantly, together with the labour force income and job stability, converting the US economy into a net importer of intermediate and final goods. The US manufacturing industry underwent offshoring processes and operated on the basis of global supply chains and global value chains.

The main characteristic of the global supply value chain was the detachment of centralisation from concentration of capital,[36] which weakened production backward linkages, downsizing workers' income independently of their geographical location. A process of global production was imposed, creating worldwide networks in different geographical locations. Specifically, the backward linkages of the US manufacturing sector of the first half of the twentieth century were dispersed across different geographical locations, giving way to a process of 'slicing up the chain value', that set a 'vertical disintegration' or the 'globalisation of production', defined as the 'tendency by firms to break up the process of producing goods and services and locating different parts in different locations depending on costs, markets, logistic or politics'.[37] In this process, the oligopolistic industrial market structure continued, with the peculiarity that this process was disseminated worldwide, extracting the highest possible return in each production process, establishing a global market of semi-finished goods, under the control of non-financial corporation headquarters. On this account, non-financial corporation became oligopolies controlling the demand and prices of semi-finished and final commodities.

Principal disequilibria in Latin America

The LAC region underwent a neomercantilist process without achieving a lasting external trade surplus and, consequently, remained net borrowers; although their financial markets expanded, they did not attain positions near to the level of the US financial market. The following analysis is based on the available data for the Latin America and Caribbean region, highlighting the performance of six economies: Argentina, Brazil, Colombia, Chile, Mexico and Peru. These countries were chosen because of their different sizes and distinct economic specialisations that, however, did not make remarkable difference in the process of financialisation and neomercantilism.

Financialisation in LAC economies

The discussion of LAC financial market development is based on market capitalisation of listed countries in relation to their GDP (stock traded in millions of dollars and number of listed firms) backed by the turnover ratio, price to earnings relation, price to book value and the annual change of local market price indexes.

The international trend of increased market capitalisation was replicated in LAC economies. The value of listed firms' market capitalisation in terms of GDP expanded notoriously between 1988 and 2012 (see Table 6.1), but it continued to be relatively small in relation to the US figures (US market capitalisation value in relation to GDP, on average, was four times bigger than LA economies) and more unstable (see coefficient of variation, Table 6.1). Thereby, the US capital market set the pace of LAC financial markets that comparatively remained relatively small and shallow.

These differences are much more notorious when analysing the trend of stock traded (in millions of US dollars), in which the United States was 50 times bigger (between 1988 and 2012) and four times larger in terms of the listed companies (Table 6.1). The Chilean market capitalisation value in terms of their GDP is the biggest, followed by Brazil, Mexico, Peru, Colombia and Argentina, which are also more unstable (Table 6.1). The LAC market where the most stocks are traded is Brazil (87 percent LAC), followed by Mexico in a distant second place

Table 6.1 Financial market evolution in Latin America

	LA&C (all income levels)	Argentina	Brazil	Chile	Colombia	Peru	México	United States
Market capitalization of listed companies (% of GDP) (1988–2012)								
mean	31.35	24.73	36.97	90.87	25.08	31.25	26.59	105.92
CV	0.48	0.93	0.64	0.34	0.83	0.73	0.40	0.32
Stock traded, total value, current US million dollars (1988–2012)								
mean	341599	7194	252202	16329	5725	2541	55909	19309544
CV	1.09	0.86	1.24	1.13	1.49	0.77	0.63	0.85
Listed domestic companies, total (1988–2012)								
mean	1767	131	470	248	113	227	169	6302
CV	0.14	0.25	0.18	0.10	0.32	0.15	0.18	0.23
Stocks traded, turnover ratio (%) (1989–2012)								
mean	36.13	21.09	53.43	12.71	9.84	15.90	32.70	146.42
CV	0.30	1.00	0.34	0.42	0.52	0.82	0.24	0.61
Price/earnings ratio * (1995–2007) simple mean								
mean		20.72	14.63	20.89	18.77		17.36	22.87
CV		0.61	0.54	0.35	0.35		0.26	0.18
Price/book value (1994–2007)								
mean		1.86	1.48	1.84	1.16	2.51	1.16	3.35
CV		0.54	0.56	0.25	0.47	0.54	0.47	0.22
Local market price indices, annual % change (1994–2012)								
mean		18.67	24.29	11.66	21.53	27.91	19.51	7.91
CV		2.28	2.06	2.03	1.89	1.88	1.50	2.42

Source: "Base de Datos de América Latina, Proyecto PAPIIT IN303314" based on World Bank and Emerging Stock Markets Factbook data.

* Omitted extreme values in Argentina, 2000: 293.3; Colombia, 2002: -52

(16.4 percent), Chile (4.8 percent), Argentina (2.1 percent), Colombia (1.7 percent) and Peru (0.7 percent).

The turnover ratio (number of stocks traded in terms of market capitalisation) in LAC economies is extremely low compared with the US market (36 percent versus 146 percent; Table 6.1). Brazil and Mexico top the list for the LAC region; Chile (with the highest market capitalisation value of the region) occupies the last place with Colombia, meaning they lack a robust financial system.

Another important measure of capital market robustness is the price earnings ratio, which is clearly below the US, with higher levels of variation coefficients, resembling the ups and downs of the financial markets (gains and losses are bigger; see Table 6.1). The relation of corporation price shares and book values is more evident: the US value is twice as big in relation to six Latin American countries analysed (1.67 versus 3.35); the price movements of Latin American stock indexes are much more volatile (see Table 6.1).

Even though the stock market increased and financial instruments diversified in the six LAC economies analysed and the non-banking financial institutions expanded, their financial system did not turn into an Anglo-Saxon model with capital-based organisation. The banking sector remained the leader in financial activities, while the US banking sector remained relatively constant. The region's bond market remained shallow and small, without approaching the size of the US bond sector. The capital market operations (stock trade in terms of GDP) were also small in relation to the US market, although they expanded significantly during the period (see Table 6.2). Therefore, economies with less developed financial centres were not able to accrue financial gains from financial instruments operations, particularly those that remained net borrowers.

Neomercantilism in Latin America

The economic structure of LAC countries and their external balance also reveals significant changes. The first thing to note is that the region did not benefit from stable and robust economic growth, with major drawbacks in the second part of the 1990s (see Table 6.3), revealed by the different crises that took place in developing economies (1994 Mexican crisis; the East Asian, Brazil, Turkey and Russian crises of the late 1990s and early 2000s). The second and most import feature of this period was the rise of the export share in terms of GDP, acquiring the leading role in economic growth, well above the ratio of investment to GDP (see Table 6.3). The third characteristic is that private

Table 6.2 Financial sector size in term of country's GDP (%)

	1989	1993	1997	2001	2005	2007	2008	2010	2012	1989–2008	
										Mean	CV
Bank credits to GDP^a											
Argentina	69.8	23.6	28.8	31.4	30.4	24.2	21.5	24.8	26.7	30.5	0.4
Brazil	131.6	108.5	35.7	51.2	52.8	43.1	50.4			55.3	0.4
Chile	49.5	49.5	57.3	64.4	68.6	74.7	81.1	69.9	78.0	59.0	0.2
Colombia		20.4	27.9	30.1	35.1	50.9	43.3	41.9	50.1	27.8	0.4
México	20.0	41.4	44.7	34.0	39.7	45.9	36.8			36.6	0.2
Peru	13.5	14.5	26.0	27.8	22.1	22.4	26.4	26.2	28.9	21.6	0.3
US					59.2	67.5	70.0	61.5	59.6	63.6	0.1
Total bonds /GDP^b											
Argentina	20.3	9.1	11.8	13.9	39.9	29.1	20.4	4.9	3.4	19.0	0.6
Brazil		17.7	40.1	58.0	62.2	69.7	51.8	93.6	94.7	45.2	0.4
Chile	23.1	36.4	43.1	48.7	34.9	24.7	22.8	48.6	50.1	38.0	0.2
Colombia	2.5	4.2	8.7	20.0	27.7	24.8	21.6	25.3	24.5	13.6	0.7
México	19.9	9.5	8.2	22.9	31.1	33.8	29.0	40.9	45.8	19.2	0.5
Peru		3.0	3.9	13.3	14.3	20.6	15.1	16.8	15.9	10.1	0.6
US	120.4	130.4	134.8	137.2	150.9	160.9	167.3	218.9	209.2	138.9	0.1
Stock market to GDP^c											
Argentina	5.5	18.6	20.2	71.6	33.6	33.2	16.0	17.3	7.2	28.3	0.9
Brazil	10.4	22.7	29.3	33.6	53.8	100.3	35.6	72.1	54.6	33.3	0.7
Chile	33.8	93.5	87.0	77.8	109.7	123.0	73.7	157.0	116.1	87.1	0.3

										Mean	CV
Colombia	2.9	16.6	18.3	13.5	31.4	49.1	35.7	72.6	70.9	18.2	0.6
México	10.1	39.4	32.2	17.2	27.5	38.1	21.2	43.4	44.6	24.8	0.4
Peru	4.5	14.7	29.7	20.6	45.3	98.6	42.9	63.3	47.5	27.1	0.8
US	62.0	74.7	131.4	130.4	129.6	137.8	79.7	114.6	114.9	108.0	0.3

Financial market size to GDP[d]

										Mean	CV
Argentina	95.6	51.3	60.7	116.9	103.8	86.5	57.9	47.0	37.3	77.9	0.5
Brazil		148.8	105.1	142.8	168.9	213.0	137.8			127.0	0.3
Chile	106.3	179.4	187.4	191.0	213.2	222.4	177.6	275.5	244.3	184.1	0.2
Colombia		41.2	54.9	63.5	94.2	124.8	100.5	139.8	145.5	59.6	0.5
México	50.0	90.2	85.2	74.1	98.3	117.8	87.0			80.6	0.2
Peru	18.0	32.2	59.6	81.7	81.7	141.6	84.5	106.3	92.3	56.7	0.5
US					339.7	366.2	317.0	395.0	383.8	344.1	0.1

a **Bank credits:** include central bank credits, local governments and municipalities, non-financial public entities, private sector and non-bank financial entities.

b **Total bonds:** includes bonds of the federal government, financial sector and non-financial corporations.

c **Market:** capitalization value of listed enterprises in terms of GDP.

d sum of the three sectors.

Source: Author calculations based on data from International Financial Statistics, IMF (CD-Room, Jan 2014). BIS Quarterly Review. March 2014. Table 16A: Domestic debt securities and World banks for stock markets.

Table 6.3 GDP main components of the Latin American and Caribbean region and economic growth rates

	LA&C				Argentina				Brazil				Colombia			
	1990–2012	1990–1999	2000–2012	2000–2007	1990–2012	1990–1999	2000–2012	2000–2007	1990–2012	1990–1999	2000–2012	2000–2007	1990–1912	1990–1999	2000–12	2000–07
GDP growth*	3.2	3.1	3.2	3.4	4.2	5.2	4.0	3.7	3.0	2.3	3.3	3.4	3.5	2.5	4.3	4.5
Priv. Consum.	63.9	66.5	63.0	64.1	64.9	69.2	61.9	67.9	61.6	63.8	60.8	61.1	66.5	71.9	64.4	67.2
GFI	19.7	19.3	19.9	19.2	20.0	18.3	21.2	19.9	17.8	17.2	18.0	16.5	21.7	21.6	21.4	19.1
Exports	20.3	15.6	22.1	23.0	14.7	10.5	17.7	16.8	11.4	7.9	12.7	13.9	15.7	12.2	17.1	16.5
Net trade	-0.2	-1.3	0.2	0.9	0.1	0.1	-0.1	-0.4	0.0	-0.7	0.3	1.8	-2.9	-4.7	-2.1	-2.7
CO	40.9	32.6	44.0	45.1	29.7	19.8	36.7	38.7	22.8	16.5	25.1	25.9	34.2	29.1	36.3	35.6

	Chile				Mexico				Peru			
	1990–2012	1990–1999	2000–2012	2000–2007	1990–2012	1990–1999	2000–2012	2000–2007	1990–2012	1990–1999	2000–2012	2000–2007
GDP growth	5.2	6.6	4.1	4.4	2.8	3.4	2.2	2.3	4.9	4.0	5.7	5.3
Priv. Consum	62.0	66.2	60.7	60.6	67.3	67.6	67.1	67.3	65.8	72.5	63.5	67.0
GFI	22.2	23.4	21.6	20.0	21.7	21.2	21.9	21.7	22.8	21.2	23.3	19.1
Exports	34.8	26.6	37.6	37.7	26.3	22.2	28.0	26.3	21.9	13.6	24.7	22.6
Net Trade	3.7	-0.6	5.1	7.1	-1.6	-1.7	-1.5	-1.6	1.5	-3.6	3.2	3.6
C O	65.9	53.7	70.1	68.4	54.1	46.2	57.5	54.2	42.3	30.8	46.3	41.6

Source: "Base de Datos de America Latina, Proyecto PAPIIT IN303314", based on Economic Commission for Latin America and the Caribbean (CEPALSTAT) data.

consumption, in terms of GDP decreased, and the relation between investment and GDP stagnated, which together led to a shrinkage of internal LAC markets.

If we look at the different experiences of the countries analysed, the rise in exports in terms of GDP applies to all countries, especially in Chile and Mexico, less so in Peru, with the export coefficient above the average in the LAC region (see Table 6.3), with commercial openness of these economies being the highest in the region. On the other hand, Brazil, Colombia and Argentina showed the smallest share of exports, and their commercial openness was also the lowest. During the 2000s (before the international recession), the peak of the countries' export coefficients was achieved, and external demand became the key variable of economic growth, a condition that remained until 2013, despite the international recession (see Table 6.3).

The investment to GDP ratio remained relatively stable through the region, with figures below the export share, which resembles the de-industrialisation process that took place in this period. Higher investment spending took place in Argentina, Brazil and Colombia, while Chile, Mexico and Peru showed relatively stagnant, or even declining figures. Therefore, countries' export specialisation was not related to investment spending.

Finally, the share of private consumption in terms of GDP was downward in the entire LAC region, slightly increasing in the 1990s (with the exception of Mexico); therefore, a higher share of export in term of GDP did not expand internal markets.

A deeper analysis of the external trade composition indicates that the region failed to adopt a successful neomercantilist model. During the 1980s, when structural reforms were initiated, on average, the region was on a trade surplus, within a context of low economic growth (these years are known as the 'lost decade'). In the 1990s, this trend reversed and a net trade deficit dominated, igniting different crises in developing economies (see above). The main feature of the 2000s was the external trade surplus centred on raw materials and manufactured goods based on raw materials, while manufacturing exports unrelated to raw materials continued to be in the deficit (see Table 6.4).

The sub-sector of manufactured goods categorised as low-tech and the most typical manufacturing sector of the import substitution industrialisation model (ISI), based on medium-level technology, reached the highest trade deficit between 1983 and 2012, while the trade balance of high-tech manufactured goods remained in deficit throughout the period, increasing from the middle of the 2000s.

Table 6.4 Latin American and Caribbean trade balance by technological intensities

Country's composition of exports by technological intensities

	% of total	Total	Argentina	Brazil	Colombia	Chile	Mexico	Peru
Mean	100.0	82.0	8.2	22.2	4.4	7.0	37.0	3.1
CV	0.8	0.8	0.8	0.8	1.0	0.8	1.1	1.1
Raw material exports								
Mean	35.1	66.8	10.7	22.1	2.8	7.2	19.0	3.8
CV	0.9	0.9	0.7	1.1	0.4	1.0	0.7	1.2
Manufacture exports based on raw material								
Mean	19.8	86.6	10.3	27.0	10.9	18.8	15.1	4.5
CV	0.8	0.8	0.8	0.8	1.1	1.0	0.8	0.9
Low technological manufacture exports (1983–2001)								
Mean	9.3	87.5	6.0	23.5	5.4	1.5	48.0	3.0
CV	0.6	0.6	0.4	0.4	0.7	0.7	0.7	0.8
Medium technological manufacture exports (1983–2001)								
Mean	22.3	94.3	6.6	23.5	2.2	1.5	60.2	0.3
CV	0.8	0.8	1.0	0.7	0.9	0.9	0.8	1.0
High technological manufactures exports (1983–2001)								
Mean	11.3	95.1	1.8	12.4	0.7	0.3	79.8	0.1
CV	0.9	0.9	0.9	0.9	1.1	0.9	0.9	0.9
Exports: other transactions (1983–2011)								
Mean	2.2	85.4	6.5	12.4	7.7	12.9	21.4	24.4
CV	1.2	1.2	1.4	0.8	1.4	1.0	1.6	1.4

Country's composition of imports by technological intensities

	% of total	Total	Argentina	Brazil	Colombia	Chile	Mexico	Peru
Mean	100.0	82.0	7.4	20.9	5.1	6.3	42.1	3.2
CV	0.8	0.8	0.8	0.9	0.8	0.9	0.8	1.0
Raw material imports								
Mean	12.3	84.0	4.3	32.5	3.6	10.7	25.3	5.0
CV	0.8	0.7	0.7	0.7	1.0	0.8	1.0	1.0
Manufacture imports based on raw material								
Mean	18.2	78.2	6.8	21.7	5.7	5.8	35.1	3.1
CV	0.9	0.9	0.8	0.9	0.8	1.1	0.9	0.9
Low technological manufacture imports (1983–2001)								
Mean	13.4	82.2	6.4	12.3	4.5	6.5	49.5	3.0
CV	0.8	0.8	0.8	1.1	0.9	0.8	0.8	1.1
Medium technological manufacture imports (1983–2001)								
Mean	35.4	87.9	9.2	20.4	5.6	6.4	43.0	3.3
CV	0.8	0.8	0.8	1.0	0.8	0.8	0.8	1.0
High technological manufactures imports (1983–2001)								
Mean	19.2	90.5	7.1	21.0	5.3	3.9	51.2	2.1
CV	0.9	0.9	0.8	0.9	0.9	0.8	0.9	0.9
Imports: other transactions (1983–2011)								
Mean	1.5	84.4	7.0	4.5	3.8	4.4	63.4	1.2
CV	1.4	0.7	0.9	0.6	0.4	0.4	0.9	0.5

Country's trade balance to GDP and composition

	Argentina	Brazil	Colombia	Chile	Mexico	Peru
Mean	2.4	1.5	-0.7	5.4	-0.6	1.5
Net trade of raw material						
Mean	5.2	1.8	1.7	5.4	2.3	4.3
Net trade of manufacture based on raw material						
Mean	1.5	0.8	3.6	11.2	-1.7	2.0
Net trade of low technological manufacture						
Mean	-0.3	0.3	-0.1	-2.6	-0.9	-0.5
Net trade of medium technological manufacture						
Mean	-2.3	-0.6	-3.7	-6.9	-0.2	-5.3
Net trade of high technological manufactures						
Mean	-1.6	-1.0	-2.4	-2.6	0.1	-1.9
Net balance of other transactions						
Mean	0.1	0.1	0.3	0.9	-0.2	2.9

Source: "Base de Datos de América Latina, Proyecto PAPIIT IN303314", based on Foreign Trade Statistics Database CEPAL (BADECEL) and World Bank.

Therefore, the region as a whole did not benefit from the new international division of labour, which shifted the manufacturing industry from the United States to developing economies. In this context, it can be argued that the industrialisation achievements of the import substitution industrialisation period (ISI) reversed, leading to a process of de-industrialisation, irrespective of their export specialisation.

Specifically, the export side of the trade balance, between 1983 and 2011, in the raw material and the manufacturing based on raw materials averaged 54.9 percent of the total exports; while the import side in these sectors reached 30.9 percent, attaining a significant trade surplus (see Table 6.4). The countries which exported most of the raw materials were Brazil and Mexico, and manufacturing exports based on raw materials were also led by Brazil and closely followed by Chile. However, Chile, Argentina and Peru achieved the highest share of net exports of manufactured goods based on raw materials in terms of GDP, relating to their economic specialisation.

Exports not related to raw materials, between 1983 and 2011, on average, reached 45.1 percent of total exports, while imports of these divisions reached 69.5 percent, meaning their trade balance was negative. Brazil and Mexico specialised in these exports, with Brazil taking an outstanding position in manufactured exports based on low and medium technology, reaching a 0.3 percent surplus and 0.6 percent net deficit in terms of GDP, respectively. Mexico specialised in exports of high-tech manufactured goods, with a net deficit of 0.2 percent in terms of GDP (see Table 6.4).

An important element that explains the regional trade balance of raw materials, especially in the 2000s, needs to be understood in terms of the higher commodity prices that increased the terms of trade (see Figure 6.1). However, since the region did not attain trade surpluses, it was obliged to further liberalise the countries' financial markets. Capital flows poured into the region, dominating foreign portfolio and direct investment, reducing capital entries under the form of credits.

From the above analysis, it can be argued that the region's economic structure liberalised with unfavourable results, because they either specialised in raw materials or maquila manufacturing exports; in neither of the countries analysed did investment spending play an important role in export specialisation, with the Mexican economy being the most puzzling example because of the specialisation in high-tech manufactured goods.

Therefore, we found that history repeats itself in the LAC region, since export-based models (irrespective of this specialisation) are highly unstable because of their high-import dependence, with low wages becoming the main competitive advantage, as discussed below.

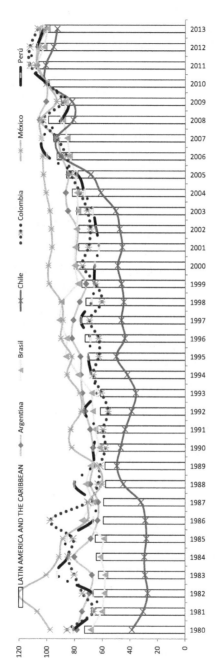

Figure 6.1 Terms of trade of the Latin America region and specific countries

Source: "Base de Datos de América Latina, Proyecto PAPIIT IN303314", based on Economic Commission for Latin America and the Caribbean (CEPALSTAT) data.

The external financial channel

The variables discussed in this section are the current account trends and compositions, differentiation of the primary income account, composed by net income employees' compensation and, more importantly, financial assets (direct, portfolio and other investment) from the secondary income account (income between residents and non-residents, particularly workers' remittances), and net income resulting from net trade.

As noted earlier, the balance of goods and services after the 1980s was in deficit with the exception of Chile, and Peru and Argentina, which achieved surpluses in the 2000s, while the US goods and services balance showed the highest negative results. The primary income[38] account was the second important source of current account deficit, showing the reversal in the US economy; explained mainly in terms of workers' remittances, in which the US showed an important net income deficit because most of the remittances originated in that economy. This means external capital inflows (under the form of direct and portfolio investment) required to balance the trade account provoked additional income leakages in the LAC economies, which shaped the external financial channel (see Figure 6.2).

Looking more closely at the primary account, in the 1980s, it was dominated by 'other investments', which switched to 'portfolio investment' in the 1990s, and 'direct investment' in the 2000s, especially in Chile, Peru and Colombia. It is interesting to note that Argentina also showed high participation in foreign portfolios and direct investments, despite the weak and shallow capital market; Brazil's net primary income deficit from portfolio investment was as big as the FDI net primary income deficit. Mexico more closely resembled the Chilean model, while the US primary income surplus was merely based on FDI (see Figure 6.3). These results show that LAC backward economies had to part with increasing financial payments, which meant higher surplus appropriation of US and other economies' exporting capital.

The net income composition from foreign portfolio and direct investment shows that in LAC countries dividends were the main source of income outflows, followed by reinvested utilities and interests from portfolio investment, which formed the smallest source of income outflows, with the exception of Argentina, in which interests took the lead of capital outflows. The US current account was an important receiver of those flows (see Figure 6.4).

The interest differentials between LAC and the United States, calculated on the basis of 10-year maturity sovereign bonds, were extremely

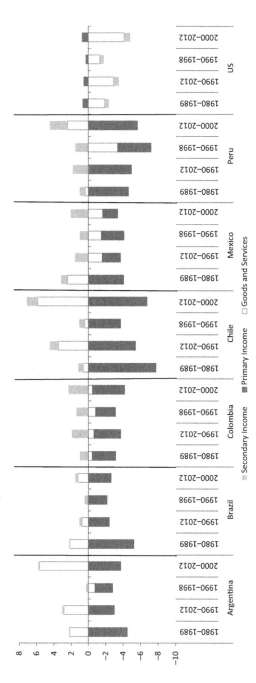

Figure 6.2 Main components of the financial account of specific Latin American countries and the United States

Source: "Base de Datos de América Latina, Proyecto PAPIIT IN 303314", based on Balance of Payments International Monetary Fund, CD Room January 2014 and World Bank data.

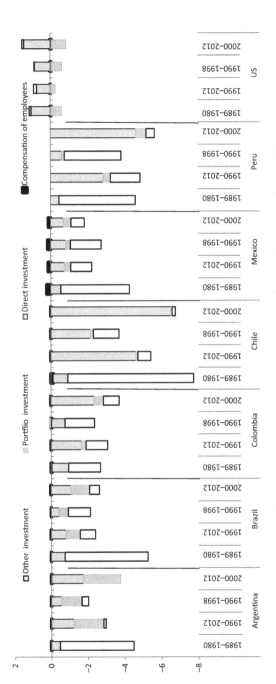

Figure 6.3 Main components of the primary account of specific countries of Latin America and United States

Source: Author's own elaboration based on Economic Commission for Latin America and the Caribbean (CEPALSTAT) data.

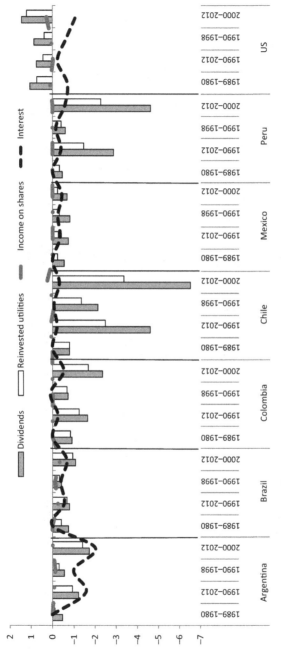

Figure 6.4 Net income composition from direct and portfolio investment of specific countries in Latin America and the United States

Source: "Base de Datos de América Latina, Proyecto PAPIIT IN 303314", based on Balance of Payments International Monetary Fund, CD Room January 2014 and World Bank data.

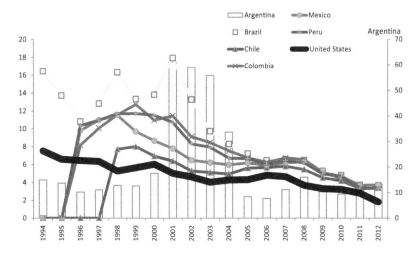

Figure 6.5 Interest rate and sovereign bonds in different countries of Latin
America and the United States

Source: "Base de Datos de América Latina, Proyecto PAPIIT IN303314", based on
World Bank, Global Economic Monitor (GEM) data.

significant (see Figure 6.5). This shows big interest rate margins that
attracted foreign capital inflows into the region, and more importantly,
it served as a means to restrict economic growth, especially in periods
of economic stagnation. The other important variable is the exchange
rate, which has to remain steady for the purchasing power of financial
flows to not lose value. Chile, Mexico and Colombia had relatively
stable overvalued exchange rates, while Brazil, Peru and Argentina
show undervalued exchange rates (Figure 6.6), which partly explains
the relatively high interest margins of Argentina and Brazil.

An important outcome from the outflows of income depicted by the
current account, which resembles the surplus appropriation of the US
economy, is the income distribution concentration. The lowest decile
(first) throughout the region averaged 1.4 percent of national income,
with a coefficient of variation of 0.3; while the highest decile (tenth)
average was 40 percent of the total income, depicting a highly unequal distribution of income. The most unequal economy in the lowest
decile is Brazil. The poorest 10 percent of the population capture less
than 1 percent of the total income, while Peru's first decile got 2 percent of the total income. In terms of income concentration, the upper

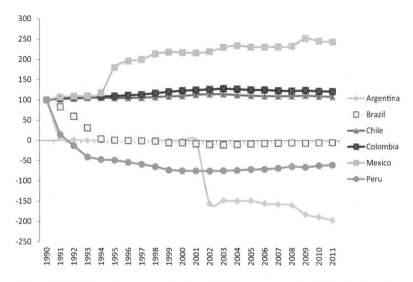

Figure 6.6 Real exchange rate index of different countries in Latin America (1990 = 100)

Source: "Base de Datos de América Latina, Proyecto PAPIIT IN303314", based on International Financial Statistics, International Monetary Fund data.

decile (tenth) appropriates over 40 percent of the total income in all the regional economies surveyed (see Table 6.5).

Finally, if grouped by deciles, the 2nd and 3rd accrue 7.7 percent of the total income; the 4th and 5th capture 11.7, while the 6th and 7th gain 16.8 percent of the total income, the 8th and 9th capture 26.8 percent, and the 10th decile alone receives 40 percent of the national income. This means that the population of these countries, on average, is relatively poor, with an insignificant middle class, while the upper 10 percent of the population (10th decile) alone captures most of the income produced in their economies. Therefore, this neoliberal model changed the LAC region, deregulating and globalising the productive, finance and commercial structures and imposed an export-led growth model that concentrated, even further, the distribution of income and reduced internal markets.

Conclusions

Financialisation and neomercantilism are the new faces of surplus appropriation in the modern neoliberal period led by financial capital.

Table 6.5 Income distribution by deciles (% of total income)

Income distribution by deciles (% of total income)

	1990–2012 Argentina		1990–2012 Brazil		1990–2012 Chile		1991–2012 Colombia		1989–2012 Mexico		1997–2012 Peru		Simple average Six economies	
	Mean	CV	Mean	CV	Mean	CV	Mean	CV	Mean	CV	Mean	CV	Mean	CV
Decil 1	1.1	0.3	0.9	0.1	1.3	0.1	1.2	0.2	1.9	0.1	2.0	0.1	1.4	0.3
Decil 2	2.3	0.1	1.9	0.1	2.4	0.1	2.3	0.1	2.9	0.1	3.4	0.1	2.6	0.2
Decil 3	3.2	0.1	2.8	0.1	3.3	0.1	3.2	0.1	3.8	0.1	4.4	0.1	3.5	0.2
Decil 4	4.3	0.1	3.6	0.1	4.1	0.0	4.1	0.1	4.6	0.1	5.3	0.1	4.4	0.1
Decil 5	5.3	0.1	4.6	0.1	5.1	0.0	5.1	0.1	5.6	0.0	6.4	0.1	5.5	0.1
Decil 6	6.7	0.1	5.8	0.1	6.2	0.0	6.4	0.0	6.8	0.0	7.6	0.1	6.7	0.1
Decil 7	8.5	0.1	7.4	0.1	7.9	0.0	8.1	0.0	8.4	0.0	9.2	0.1	8.4	0.1
Decil 8	11.1	0.0	9.9	0.0	10.4	0.0	10.7	0.0	10.8	0.0	11.4	0.0	10.8	0.1
Decil 9	15.9	0.0	14.7	0.0	15.5	0.0	15.6	0.0	15.3	0.0	15.4	0.0	15.5	0.0
Decil 10	41.4	0.1	42.6	0.1	43.8	0.0	43.2	0.1	40.1	0.1	35.1	0.1	40.2	0.1

Source: "Base de Datos de América Latina, Proyecto PAPIIT IN 303314", based on CEPALSTAT data.

In this context, imperialism has been able to not only reduce wages throughout capitalist economies and increase their profit share but also to extract surplus from the circulation sphere through strengthening financial markets, in which financial capital became the main vehicle of US surplus global appropriation, particularly through foreign direct and portfolio investment.

The international division of labour, dominant from the end of the Second World War and more clearly since the demise of the Bretton Woods system, enabled the US economy to mobilise external current account surpluses into their financial system, create conditions of financial inflation and extract financial gains and mobilise dividends, utilities and interest from Latin American economies.

Beginning in the 1970s, the most powerful country in the world de-industrialised its economy and sustained its economic growth on the basis of worldwide surplus appropriation, in which the financial market played an outstanding role, on the basis of the dollar being the international unit of account that could set financial instrument floor prices.

Other developed and developing countries that did not possess the 'privilege' of issuing international units of accounts became world producers, adopting a neomercantilist regime. In that context, the reduced wages did not impact the process of realisation of their production, and the multinational corporations dominated production and could access financial gains.

In this international order is it interesting to highlight the pecking order of surplus appropriation? First of the list was the United States, whose ruling class could benefit most from the financial gains generated in their financial markets. Second were developed countries that controlled know-how and technology and were able to seize the largest share within the global value chains of production. Developing countries with external current account surpluses combined with high investment spending were able to grow at high rates and consolidate their manufacturing sector, coming third in the pecking order of the global value chains of production. In last place are the LAC economies that adopted neomercantilist regimes but failed to attain external surpluses and were forced to almost completely liberalise their financial market and part with increased dividends, utilities and interest.

These countries' exports were based either on raw materials or assembly of manufactured goods and, regardless of their export strategies, none of them achieved long-lasting surplus conditions. In addition, all these economies shared the peculiarity of constant and stagnant investment coefficients that de-industrialised the region, going back to the primary export model, dominant in the pre-Second World War era, highly unstable because of their dependence on external terms of trade. Therefore, a major shortcoming of the increased raw materials activities was that they did not spark robust economic growth, in spite of the fact that prices rocketed in the 2000s.

Therefore, the international order dominant from the 1970s was able to strengthen the surplus appropriation of the United States on the basis of reduced workers' salaries and, more importantly, increased surplus appropriation in the financial market.

Notes

1 This essay was written as part of the research project PAPIIT IN-303314 sponsored by DGAPA-UNAM.
2 See Ellen Russell, *New Deal Banking Reforms and Keynesian Welfare Capitalism*, New York: Routledge, 2008.
3 Franco Modigliani and Lucas Papademos, 'Targets for Monetary Policy in the Coming Year#', in *Brookings Papers on Economic Activity*, 1975.
4 Raul Prebisch, 'El desarrollo económico en América Latina y algunos de sus principales problemas' (The economic development in Latin American and some of its principal problems), in *Cincuenta años pensamiento en la CEPAL, Texto seleccionados*, 1949/1998, ECLAC Thinking, Selected Texts (1948–98), Vol. 1.
5 Rosa Luxemburg, 'International Loans', in *The Accumulation of Capital*, www.marxists.org/archive/luxemburg/1913/accumulation-capital/index. htm, 1913 (accessed on April 2015).
6 Viadimir Lenin, *El imperialismo, fase superior del capitalismo* (Imperialism, the Highest Stage of Capitalism) Moscú, Russia: Progreso, 1917 [1936].
7 Marx, in the discussions between interest bearing capital and industrial capital, assumes that there is a conflict between those two segments of the ruling class, see Jan Toporowski, *Crédito y Crisis de Marx a Minsky* (Credit and Crisis: From Marx to Minsky) Facultad de Economía, UNAM Mexico: Miguel Angel Porrua editors, 2016; Keynes also assumed conflicting interests between speculative investors and entrepreneurs, see John M. Keynes, 'The State of Long-Term Expectations', in *The General Theory of Employment, Interest, and Money*, First Harvest, Harcout Inc., 1936. For further discussion, see James Crotty, 'Owner-Management Conflict and Financial Theories of Investment Instability: A Critical Assessment of Keynes, Tobin, and Minsky', *Journal of Post Keynesian Economics*, 1990, 12.
8 Marc Lavoie, 'Cadrisme Within a Post-Keynesian Model of Growth and Distribution', *Review of Political Economy*, July 2009, 21(3): 369–91.
9 Lavoie, 'Cadrisme Within a Post-Keynesian Model of Growth and Distribution', p. 373.
10 Lavoie, 'Cadrisme Within a Post-Keynesian Model of Growth and Distribution', p. 376.
11 This occurs when the actual rate of capacity utilisation is below its standard level; when the actual profit is below its normal level, see Lavoie, 'Cadrisme Within a Post-Keynesian Model of Growth and Distribution'.

12 Lavoie, 'Cadrisme Within a Post-Keynesian Model of Growth and Distribution', 380.
13 Basak Kus, 'Financialisation and Income Inequality in OECD Nations: 1995–2007', *The Economic and Social Review*, 2012, 43(4): 477–95.
14 Marcello de Cecco, 'Global Imbalances: Past, Present, and Future', *Contributions to Political Economy*, 2012, 31.
15 Joseph Halevi, 'Imperialism Today', in Riccardo Bellofiore (ed.), *Rosa Luxemburg and the Critique of Political Economy*, London: Routledge, 2009.
16 Gerald Epstein, 'Introduction: *Financialisation* and the World Economy', *Financialisation and the World Economy*, Cheltenham, UK, Northampton, MA: Edward Elgar Publishing Limited, 2005, p. 4.
17 Greta Krippner, 'The Financialization of the American Economy', *Socio-Economic Review*, 3: 179.
18 Robert Pollin and James Heintz, 'Study of U.S. Financial System', Working Paper, 10, 2013, *Financialisation, Economy, Society and Sustainable Development* (FESSUD).
19 Pollin and Heintz, 'Study of U.S. Financial System', p. 21.
20 Pollin and Heintz, 'Study of U.S. Financial System', p. 22.
21 Krippner, 'The Financialization of the American Economy', 3: 174–5.
22 Krippner, 'The Financialization of the American Economy', 3: 185–6.
23 Jan Toporowski, 'Overcapitalisation', in Jan Toporowski and Jo Michell (eds.), *Handbook of Critical Issues in Finance*, Cheltenham: Edward Elgar, 2012, p. 270.
24 According to Toporowski, 'Overcapitalisation', the capital market become less efficient because firms do not reallocate through the capital market to other firms where it may obtain a higher return and, additionally, companies that are overcapitalised are under less internal financial pressure to allocate their capital to the most efficient uses.
25 Toporowski, 'Overcapitalisation', p. 271.
26 Toporowski, 'Overcapitalisation', p. 271.
27 Toporowski, 'Overcapitalisation', p. 271. Following the overcapitalisation argument, it is argued that the distribution of dividends among shareholders decreases (instead of increasing, as argued by William Lazonick and Mary O'Sullivan, 'Maximizing Shareholder Value: A New Ideology for Corporate Governance', *Economy and Society*, 2000, 29(1): 6, undermining their claim of higher pay-out ratios (even when the rate of profit decreased) and stock repurchases as a means of shareholder maximisation strategy.
28 Lazonick and O'Sullivan, 'Maximizing Shareholder Value'.
29 Lazonick and O'Sullivan, 'Maximizing Shareholder Value', 14.
30 R. Bellofiore and J. Halevi, 'The Great Recession and the Third Crisis in Economic', in E. Brancaccio and G. Fontana (eds.), *The Global Economic Crisis: New Perspectives on the Critique of Economic Theory and Policy*, USA and Canada: Routledge, 2011.
31 Lazonick and O'Sullivan, 'Maximizing Shareholder Value', 16.
32 Lazonick and O'Sullivan, 'Maximizing Shareholder Value', 35.
33 Riccardo Bellofiore, Francesco Garibaldo and Joseph Halevi, 'The Global Crisis and the Crisis of European Neomercantilism', *Socialist Register*, 2010, 47: 120.

34 Ben S. Bernanke, 'The Global Saving Glut and the U.S. Current Account Deficit', At the Sandridge Lecture, Virginia Association of Economists, Richmond, Virginia, 2005.

35 See Table 6.1 in Robert Boyer, 'Is a Finance-Led Growth Regime a Viable Alternative to Fordism? A Preliminary Analysis', *Economy and Society*, 2000, 29(1).

36 Riccardo Bellofiore, 'Financial Keynesianism', in Jan Toporowski and Jo Michell (eds.), *Handbook of Critical Issues in Finance*, Cheltenham, UK: Edward Elgar, 2012.

37 William Milberg, 'Shifting Sources and Uses of Profits: Sustaining US Financialisation With Global Value Chains', *Economy and Society*, 2008, 37(3): 424.

38 Primary income payments refer to employee compensation paid to non-resident workers and investment income (payments on direct investment, portfolio investment and other investments).

7 Latin America and imperialism

Amiya Kumar Bagchi

Introduction: Latin America, a continent of hope and fear

Latin America is a continent of both hope and fear. It is a continent of hope because in 1959 under the leadership of Fidel Castro, Cuba carried out a revolution against tremendous odds, kept that revolution alive despite the illegal embargo and aggression carried out by the United States and kept the beacon of an egalitarian society burning even after the fall of the Soviet Union. It is a continent of hope also because between 1998 and 2009, 15 Latin American countries elected left-leaning presidents in multi-party elections. They were Venezuela, Chile, Brazil, Argentina, Dominican Republic, Suriname, Nicaragua, Peru, Bolivia, Ecuador, Uruguay, Paraguay, El Salvador, Honduras and Costa Rica. In 2005, the BBC reported that out of 350 million people in South America, three out of four of them lived in countries ruled by left-leaning president selected during the preceding six years.[1] According to the BBC, another common element of the left-wing turn is a clean break with what was known at the outset of the 1990s as the 'Washington consensus', 'the mixture of open markets and privatisation pushed by the United States'.[2]

This was a unique development not only in Latin America but throughout the world as well. Before 1998, from the time of its liberation from Spanish and Portuguese rule, Latin America had been ruled by dictators. Even those people who were elected in multi-party elections represented only the *criollo* elite, people who claimed descent from the Spaniards or Portuguese.[3] Those elite ruled by collaborating with imperialist powers and refusing to carry out pro-peasant land reforms. It is well-known that even capitalism cannot develop in a country which has not abolished landlordism. The histories of France, the Scandinavian countries, the United States, Taiwan and South Korea are eloquent testimonies to this proposition.[4]

In Latin America, genuinely left-leaning and democratically elected presidents, such as Gustavo Arbenz of Guatemala, Salvador Allende of Chile and Daniel Ortega of Nicaragua (the first time he came to power) were removed by CIA machinations, killing thousands of innocent people in the process. Chile had its own 9/11 in 1973, the day Allende was assassinated on the orders of General Augusto Pinochet. There was a bloody coup d'état on 11 April 2002 in Venezuela.[5] Similar to the overthrow of the Allende government in Chile nearly 30 years prior, an unlikely bond between labour unions, business associations and the elite military command had been formed with a common goal: to remove President Hugo Chávez Frías from his elected office. In a stark contrast to Chilean history, the coup in Venezuela failed, and two days later, President Chávez was reinstated.

Fears for Latin America

But the fear of CIA machinations, in collaboration with local big business, military leaders and corrupt labour leaders for removing duly elected presidents of the country lingers. Neither the United States nor its local right-wing collaborators, including military bosses, have given up trying to topple left-leaning regimes. When the elected president of Honduras, Manuel Zelaya, was dragged from his bed and flown out of the country in his pajamas in 2009, it was no surprise to find that this classic coup was led by a graduate of the School of the Americas, the notorious army training school in Fort Benning, Georgia. But General Vasquez was simply following a well-trodden path for autocrats in Honduras – after all, two of the country's most hated past dictators, Juan Melgar Castro and Policarpo Paz Garcia, had also attended the school.

More than 60,000 Latin American soldiers have been trained at the School of the Americas – among them, some of the region's most notorious human rights abusers, such as Salvadoran death-squad leader Roberto D'Aubuisson. In all, 11 dictators have attended its courses: men such as Argentine junta leader, Leopoldo Galtieri, infamously responsible for the 'disappeared' – that is, for killing anybody suspected of opposing the regime by dropping them from planes, torturing and killing them in prisons or using undercover agents to kill them[6] and Guatemala's Efraín Ríos Montt, whose scorched earth campaign against indigenous villages, was classified as 'genocide' by a UN-sponsored commission.[7]

Founded in the Panama Canal Zone in 1948, it was originally named the Army Caribbean School. It was renamed the School of the Americas in 1963, and a new curriculum was introduced, offering courses in counter-insurgency, military intelligence and psychological warfare. The school was moved to Fort Benning in 1984 and, in 2001, in an attempt to improve its image, its name was changed again to the Western Hemisphere Institute for Cooperation.[8]

That, however, is not the only fear. There is also the fear of the corruption of the ideals of the parties which had inspired the people to vote for them. There are two kinds of corruption here. The first kind is corruption in the conventional sense, that is, making money illegally by using public office or misusing its facilities. There is, however, a more insidious kind of corruption, namely, betraying the ideals without realizing that such betrayals are taking place. Again, imperialist machinations are at work here. The World Bank may offer aid or loans apparently without any strings. But the strings are hidden. Before you know it, the whole government has become infected by the mercantile ideology of neo-liberalism. This danger is more apparent in centre–left regimes than in regimes strongly committed to egalitarian values such as those of Cuba and Venezuela. In Brazil, President Dilma Rouseff was impeached on charges of corruption after being re-elected in 2014 with a comfortable margin. What was that corruption? She had shown the state of the economy to be better than it was and had used funds of public enterprises to finance social welfare projects. Normally this would have only required just a revision of figures of the state budget and budgets of state enterprises. But the right wing of her government used the anger of the people, fuelled by economic woes following a drop in prices for Brazilian commodities such as oil, iron ore and soya.[9]

The manipulation of the national budget could be considered unorthodox; however, the funds were mostly used on covering the costs of popular social programmes. Acting President Michel Temer is simultaneously being investigated for bribery and corruption; however, he is a great friend to Wall Street and is a US intelligence informant, which arguably puts him beyond reproach when considering impeachment or indictment.[10]

An example of the threat of incorporation of the capitalist–imperialist system of globalization has loomed in Bolivia.

> Bolivia's relations with the monetary fund and the World Bank, both based in Washington, are a sharp contrast to those of some of its leftist allies. Venezuela, Ecuador and Argentina refuse to take part in annual economic reviews by the monetary fund. . . . 'The World Bank does not blackmail, or impose conditions, not

anymore,' Mr Morales said, according to a publication on the bank's website. To celebrate, he played a friendly soccer game with the bank's president, Jim Yong Kim.[11]

Hope for countries sticking to ideals

Now let us look at the contrast with Cuba. Cuba went through very difficult times after the collapse of the Soviet bloc. It was already suffering from the US embargo. Now the former countries of the Soviet bloc were also refusing to trade with it. But Cuba did not give in. Trading with the Soviet bloc, it had become specialized in the production of sugar and citrus fruits. Most of the land was occupied by big state farms, using modern machinery. When during the troubled times, fuel and spare parts could not be bought to service the state farms, land was distributed to workers and they began using oxen. With a nationwide breeding programme, the number of oxen rose from 100,000 to 600,000 by the end of the 1990s. But Cuba did much more than that. From chemical fertilisers it turned to biofertilisers, from industrial pesticides it turned to entomophages, that is, insects that eat pests. It also increased biodiversity by turning from monoculture of sugar to a diversified mix of crops.

By 2002, 35,000 acres of urban gardens produced 3.4 million tons of food. In Havana, 90 percent of the city's fresh produce came from local urban farms and gardens, all organic.

> In 2003, more than 200,000 Cubans worked in the expanding urban agriculture sector. In 2003, the Cuban Ministry of Agriculture was using less than 50 percent of the diesel fuel it used in 1989, less than 10 percent of the chemical fertilisers and less than 7 percent of the synthetic insecticides.[12]

Thus it is contributing to the fight against global warming when the advanced capitalist countries are heedlessly aggravating it by continuing on the path of unlimited use of non-renewable resources. Cuba also utilised its excellent biotechnological research by selling its medicines and vaccines. Its vaccine against hepatitis B, for example, was considered more effective than the Belgian vaccine. But in marketing, it faced both commercial and political obstacles in the shape of the stringent and illegal US embargo.[13] But eventually, between 2015 and 2016, the United States took the initiative to normalise diplomatic relations with Cuba.

But there is a more general hope for Latin America. According to Birdsall, Lustig and McLeod,

> Latin America is known to have income inequality among the highest in the world. That inequality has been invoked to explain low growth, poor education, macroeconomic volatility and political instability. But new research shows that inequality in the region is falling.[14]

There are other reasons for hope for Latin America as well. In Bolivia and Venezuela, Morales and Chavez have tried to build a participatory democracy, which mitigates racist discrimination against American Indians who constitute the majority of the population.[15] Ecuador is the first country in the world to have recognized, in 2008, the rights of nature. Nature is not to be treated as property to be exploited indefinitely but to be conserved for the sake of the future of humanity.[16] Even those countries which are not fervently socialist like Cuba have rejected the Washington Consensus, that is, neoliberalism. The people of Latin America experienced neo-liberalism from the 1980s to 1990s and found it wanting. Two examples should suffice here. In 1985, President Paz Estenssoro of the Revolutionary Nationalist Movement (MNR) in Bolivia carried out extensive economic reforms, fulfilling all the conditions of what later came to be known as the Washington Consensus. But Bolivia continued to stagnate, and the Bolivian people remained among the poorest and most illiterate people in Latin America. Things changed after the election of Evo Morales, the first American Indian as president of Bolivia in 2005.

> Bolivia's economic growth in the last four years has been higher than at any time in the last 30 years, averaging 5.2 percent annually since the current administration took office in 2006. Projected GDP growth for 2009 is the highest in the hemisphere. It is worth noting that Bolivia's growth for 2009 follows its peak growth rate in 2008.[17]

With proper attention paid to the American Indians, human development also went up.

In the past six years, Bolivia has become one of the Latin American countries most successful at improving its citizens' standard of living. Economic indicators such as low unemployment and decreased poverty, as well as better public healthcare and education, are outstanding.

Between 2005 and 2010, the proportion of those in moderate poverty went down from 60 percent to 49.6 percent, while extreme poverty fell from 38 percent to 25 percent. Likewise, the unemployment rate decreased from 8.4 percent to 4 percent. The United Nations Development Programme (UNDP) points out that Bolivia is the top country in Latin America in terms of transferring resources to its most vulnerable population – 2.5 percent of its gross national product (GNP).[18]

The second example is that of Argentina. Under the Peronista administration of Carlos Menem in the 1990s, Domingo Cavallo, a poster-boy of the World Bank, became finance minister and introduced neoliberal reforms with a vengeance. The economy was dollarised, and most state enterprises were privatised and handed over to foreign companies. The result was that by 2001, Argentina had become a basket case, with one of the highest levels of foreign debt in the world, and per capita income rapidly falling to half of what it was in 1999. In 2003, after a rapid change of several presidents, Néstor Kirchner became president of Argentina and declared that his first priority was social policy, not the repayment of foreign debt. He renegotiated $84 billion of the debt on his own terms, refusing to accept the conditions of the IMF. In December 2005, following Brazil's initiative, Kirchner announced the cancellation of Argentina's debt to the IMF in full and offered a single payment, in a historic decision that generated controversy at the time. The Argentine example shows that with proper determination, the diktats of IMF and the US lobby can be defied to the benefit of ordinary people.[19]

Policy changes as above also explain how left-wing presidents are elected in Latin America. Ethnicity, class, ideology, beliefs about neo-liberalism and retrospective economic evaluations are important determinants of vote choice in Latin America. Across the region, most non-whites seem to prefer leftist candidates.[20] Furthermore, supporters of Latin America's left do not appear to be significantly less supportive of democracy, though they do seem more likely to hold beliefs that reject the basic tenets of neoliberalism.[21]

US imperialism under Obama

Despite US President Obama's protestations about the need to build new relationships with Latin American countries, US imperialism continued to support coups by military leaders and did not raise a finger as local leaders of left-wing movements were killed by the local elite. During the Obama administration, the first coup took place in Honduras in 2009, when the then-president Manuel Zelaya was kidnapped by the military and flown out of the country. In protest, most Latin American nations and the entire European Union severed ambassadorial ties with the Central American country. The Spanish prime minister branded the move 'illegal', while Argentina's President Cristina Kirchner called it a reminder of 'the worst years in Latin America's history'. International groups, including the Organization of American States and the United Nations General Assembly, called for Zelaya's immediate return.

Although Obama did call for Zelaya's return, the United States was one of the few countries to retain its ambassador in Tegucigalpa. Furthermore, the White House and State Department strenuously avoided labelling the events in Honduras a coup. Such a designation would have barred the administration from sending military aid to the coup government.[22]

Now, thanks to Wikileaks, a cable from the US embassy in Honduras has been released showing that the State Department indeed believed Zelaya's removal clearly constituted a coup. 'Subsequent revelations showed that several of the coup's supporters had ties to then Secretary of State Hillary Clinton's inner circle'.[23]

The second coup took place in 2012 in Paraguay, when ex-bishop Fernando Lugo was ousted in what has since been described a parliamentary coup. Lugo was impeached by his opponents and given 24 hours to defend himself following a land dispute that resulted in the death of six police officers and 11 farmers.[24] Highly reminiscent of the fallout after the Honduran coup, Latin American leaders from all political walks of life protested the events. In March 2015, Obama slapped sanctions on Venezuela, calling it a security threat and expressing concerns about human rights violations by Venezuelan officials; barred visas for seven top-ranking Chavezistas; and froze their US assets.[25] His approach was similar to that of President Ronald Reagan in 1985, when he made a similar declaration in order to impose sanctions – including an economic embargo – on Nicaragua. Like the White House today, he was trying to topple an elected government that Washington did not like. He was able to use paramilitary and terrorist violence, as well as an embargo, in a successful effort to destroy the Nicaraguan economy and ultimately overturn its government.[26]

If Obama is concerned about human rights, why does he not condemn human rights violations in Colombia, which has about 5 million displaced people, the highest number in the world?[27] Colombia also tops the list in respect of the number of trade unionists routinely killed.

Human Rights Watch Report 2012 reports that trade union deaths in Colombia are greater than in any other country in the world. According to the National Labor School (ENS), Colombia's leading NGO monitoring labour rights, 51 trade unionists were murdered in 2008, 47 in 2009, 51 in 2010, and 26 from January to 15 November 2011.[28]

In the name of war on drugs, the United States has continued the militarization of Latin America. For instance, taking the total of military, police and economic aid to Colombia for 2010–2015, the United States has given nearly US$3 billion in the form of 'aid' to fight the so-called 'War on Drugs'. Similar military and economic aid has been given to many Central American countries, including Honduras and El Salvador.[29] As in Colombia, the militarisation and brutalisation of the administration continue with the local elite. In Mexico, for example, the police and paramilitary forces shoot to kill. In the case of elite forces, there are from 20 to 30 persons killed for one person wounded.[30]

Barring Cuba, the horizon of even left-wing governments in Latin America is that of state-guided capitalism and social democratic welfare measures. Hence, the resistance of some of the most vulnerable groups of population is often curbed by the local elite with violence. For instance, in Brazil, the elite portray the Movement of Landless Rural Workers (Movimento dos Trabalhadores Rurais Sem Terra; MST), the largest popular movement in Brazil, as a threat to democracy. In fact, the MST demands that the state play an active part in reducing the nation's stark social inequities through the institution of an inclusive model of development.[31] More than 1,150 rural activists associated with MST have been killed in Brazil in the last 20 years – an average of between four and five deaths every month.[32]

Conclusion

The United States will not easily give up trying to dominate its backyard of Latin America, however, isolated it may become from the majority of the Latin American and Caribbean states from time to time. Apart from strategic and military reasons, the region is rich in natural resources. Venezuela is supposed to have the second largest reserves of oil in the world and ranks seventh as supplier of oil to the USA. Bolivia and Ecuador are rich in natural gas and oil. Many of the left-wing regimes, including Chavez's Venezuela, Rafael Correa's Ecuador and Morales's Bolivia are (or were) dependent on the revenues from these resources for maintaining their social democratic programmes. When the prices of oil, gas or other commodities like copper go down, US and right-wing elements can exploit the disaffection of the people and destabilise the left-wing regimes, as they have done in Nicolás Maduro's Venezuela and Dilma Rousseff's Brazil. The Bank of the South, established by Argentina, Brazil, Venezuela and other left-wing regimes with a projected capital of $20 billion, still exists only as a legal entity and cannot act as a counter-weight to the IMF or World Bank. China emerged as a rival of the Western countries as a buyer of Latin American commodities, but it is now caught up in global recession, and its economic challenge to the Western powers has faded. So long as the Latin American countries remain wedded to a basically capitalist system and contain an elite deeply complicit with imperialism, the threat of coups orchestrated by Washington persists. If the left-wing regimes seek to establish themselves as an effective buffer against imperialism, they will have to try and become real knowledge economies like Cuba and seek to become less dependent on non-renewable resources. But that prospect is still a long way off.

Notes

1 James Painter, 'South America's Leftward Sweep', *BBC News*, 2 March 2005, http://news.bbc.co.uk/2/hi/americas/4311957.stm (accessed on 29 March 2017).

2 John Williamson, 'AShort History of Washington Consensus', paper commissioned by Fondación CIDOB for a conference 'From the Washington Consensus towards a new Global Governance', Barcelona, 24–25 September 2004, https://piie.com/publications/papers/williamson0904-2.pdf (accessed on 3 April 2017).

3 Amiya K. Bagchi, 'Underdevelopment in Latin America: Historical Roots', in *The Political Economy of Underdevelopment*, Cambridge: Cambridge University Press, 1982.

4 See, in this connection, C.T. Morris, 'Politics, Development and Society in Five Land-Rich Countries in Later Nineteenth Century', *Research in Economic History*, 1992, 14: 1–68; Stanley L. Engerman and Kenneth L. Sokoloff, 'Factor Endowments, Institutions, and Differential Paths of Growth Among New World Economies: A View From Economic Historians of the United States', December 1994, NBER Historical Working Paper No. 66; Stanley L. Engerman and Kenneth L. Sokoloff, 'Factor Endowments, Inequality, and Paths of Development Among New World Economies', *Economia*, 2002, 3(1).

5 Eva Golinger, *The Adaptable US Intervention Machine in Venezuela*, Caracas: The Communication and Information Ministry, Government of Venezuela, 2004.

6 'General Leopoldo Galtieri', *The Guardian*, 13 January 2003, www.the guardian.com/news/2003/jan/13/guardianobituaries.argentina (accessed on 30 March 2017).

7 'Efrain Rios Montt and Mauricio Rodriguez Sanchez', *International Justice Monitor*, www.ijmonitor.org/efrain-rios-montt-and-mauricio-rodriguez-sanchez-background/ (accessed on 30 March 2017).

8 Grace Livingstone, 'The School of Latin America's Dictators', *The Guardian*, 20 November 2010, www.theguardian.com/commentisfree/cifamerica/2010/nov/18/us-military-usa (accessed on 9 May 2016); 'Close the School of the Americas', SOA Watch, 2016, www.soaw.org/about-the-soawhinsec/what-is-the-soawhinsec (accessed on 12 June 2016).

9 Conn Hallinan, 'A Very Brazilian Coup', www.counterpunch.org/2016/06/03/a-very-brazilian-coup/ (accessed on 31 March 2016).

10 José L. Flores, 'Wall Street's New Man in Brazil: The Forces behind Dilma Rousseff's Impeachment', *CounterPunch*, 26 May 2016, www.counterpunch.org/2016/05/26/wall-streets-new-man-in-brazil-the-forces-behind-dilma-rousseffs-impeachment/ (accessed on 31 May 2016).

11 William Neuman, 'Turnabout in Bolivia as Economy Rises from Instability', *New York Times*, 16 February 2014.

12 Gladys Hernández Pedraza, 'The Evolution of Agrarian Relations in the Global Crisis: The Updating of Cuban Agrarian Relations', paper presented at the 10th Anniversary Conference of the Foundation for Agrarian Studies, Kochi, 9–12 January 2014.

13 Tom Fawthrop, 'Cuba Sells its Medical Expertise', *BBC News*, 21 November 2003.

14 Nancy Birdsall, Nora Lustig and Darryl McLeod, 'Declining Inequality in Latin America: Some Economics, Some Politics', Center for Global Development, Working Paper 1120, May 2011, http://citeseerx.ist.psu.edu/viewdoc/download?doi=10.1.1.899.7239&rep=rep1&type=pdf (accessed on 30 March 2017).

15 Nancy Postero, 'The Struggle to Create a Radical Democracy in Bolivia', *Latin American Research Review*, Special Issue, 2010, 59–78; Marta Harnecker, 'Chávez's Chief Legacy: Building, With People, an Alternative Society to Capitalism', *Monthly Review Magazine*, 6 March 2013.

16 'Ecuador Adopts Rights of Nature in Constitution', *The Rights of Nature*, 2008, http://therightsofnature.org/ecuador-rights/ (accessed on 27 June 2016).

17 Mark Weisbrot, Rebecca Ray and Jake Johnston, 'Bolivia: the Economy During the Morales Administration', Center for Economic Policy Research, December 2009.

18 Luis Hernández Navarro, 'Bolivia has Transformed Itself by Ignoring the Washington Consensus', *The Guardian*, 22 March 2012.

19 Mark Weisbrot, 'Economic Policy Changes With New Latin American Leaders', *International Herald Tribune*, 28 December 2006.

20 Noam Lupu, 'Electoral Bases of Leftist Presidents in Latin America', August 2009, www.udesa.edu.ar/files/UAHumanidades/EVENTOS/Paper NoamLupu100809.pdf (accessed on 6 April 2014).

21 Lupu, 'Electoral Bases of Leftist Presidents in Latin America', 2009.

22 Karen Attiah, 'Hillary Clinton Needs to Answer for Her Actions in Honduras and Haiti', *Washington Post*, 10 March 2016.

23 Rohan Chatterjee, 'Even After the Cuba Deal, Latin America Is Still Leery of Obama. Here's Why', *Foreign Policy in Focus*, 11 August 2015, http://fpif.org/even-after-the-cuba-deal-latin-america-is-still-leery-of-obama-heres-why/ (accessed on 28 May 2016).

24 Saul Landau, 'A Coup in Paraguay? Is That in Africa?' *CounterPunch*, 6 July 2012, www.counterpunch.org/2012/07/06/a-coup-in-paraguay-

is-that-in-africa/ (accessed on 31 March 2017); Benjamin Dangl, 'A Coup Over Land: The Resource War Behind Paraguay's Crisis', *Upside Down World*, 17 July 2012, http://upsidedownworld.org/archives/paraguay/a-coup-over-land-the-resource-war-behind-paraguays-crisis/ (accessed on 3 April 2017).

25 '"Deeply Concerned" Obama Imposes Sanctions on Venezuelan Officials', *The Guardian*, 9 March 2015, www.theguardian.com/world/2015/mar/09/obama-venezuela-security-threat-sanctions (accessed on 27 May 2016).

26 Mark Weisbrot, 'Obama Absurdly Declares Venezuela a Security Threat', *Al Zazzera*, 10 March 2015, http://america.aljazeera.com/opinions/2015/3/obama-absurdly-declares-venezuela-a-national-security-threat.html (accessed on 27 May 2016).

27 Conn Hallinan, 'Militarizing Latin America: Four More Years', *Counter-Punch*, 16 January 2013, www.counterpunch.org/2013/01/16/militarizing-latin-america/ (accessed on 26 May 2016).

28 Melissa Moskowitz, 'Free Trade Agreement Ignores Colombian History of Violence Against Trade Unions', Foreign Policy in Focus, 22 May 2012.

29 Eric Draitser, 'The US and the Militarization of Latin America', *Counter-Punch*, 11 September 2015, www.counterpunch.org/2015/09/11/the-us-and-the-militarization-of-latin-america/ (accessed on 26 May 2016).

30 Adam Ahmed and Eric Schmitt, 'Mexican Military Runs Up Body Count in Drug War', *New York Times*, 26 May 2016.

31 Miguel Carter, 'The Landless Workers Movement and Democracy in Brazil', *Latin American Research Review*, Special Issue, 2010, 186–217.

32 Sarah de Sainte Croix, 'Amazon MST Leader Killed in Pará, Brazil', *The Rio Times*, 2011, http://riotimesonline.com/brazil-news/rio-politics/amazon-mst-leader-killed-in-para-brazil/# (accessed on 26 May 2016); see also Cândido Grzybowski, 'Rural Workers and Democratisation in Brazil', *The Journal of Development Studies* (JDS), 1990, 24(4): 19–43.

8 Did US workers gain from US imperialism (1985–2000)?

Gerald Epstein[1]

A framework for assessing the impact of US imperialism on US workers

This essay attempts to answer the following question: did US workers gain from US imperialism during the period 1985–2000? This period is of interest because it is during this period that neoliberalism emerged and Iraq had not been invaded. Very little economics literature has considered the costs and benefits of US imperialism to the United States, much less the distributional consequences of that imperialism. Lebergott and Zevin focus on the motivations of particular businesses and financiers and their interests in US military intervention abroad, particularly in Central and Latin America.[2] Lebergott focused on imperialism at the turn of the century; Zevin covers a larger sweep of history. They both conclude that imperialism is neither necessary for the prosperity of the US economy as a whole, nor, indeed, is it necessarily good for the US economy. While they do not consider explicitly the effect on US workers, there is an implicit message in their essays. If imperialism costs workers anything, for example, if they have to pay taxes to finance the military, then, since they receive no benefits, workers are necessarily harmed by imperialism. The answer to the question in any particular historical period becomes an empirical question.

A framework for estimating the distributional impact of US imperialism

First I must define what I mean by imperialism. Even in the case of eighteenth and nineteenth-century Britain, a period of intense historical scrutiny there has been no universally agreed-upon definition. For example, there has been a large degree of ambiguity and debate about the nature of the 'formal' versus the 'informal' empire, with the estimates of benefits and costs only referring to the formal empire. In the case of the United States, this obviously will not work since in the latter part of the twentieth century, the time period of our study, the United States has had very little or no 'formal empire' so the focus must be on an informal US empire.

First for a definition of imperialism:

> Empires are relationships of political control imposed by some political societies over the effective sovereignty of other political societies. They include more than just formally annexed territories, but they encompass less than the sum of all forms of international inequality. Imperialism is the process of establishing and maintaining an empire.[3]

While there are many definitions available, this captures pretty well what I have in mind.

Next we must distinguish between two types of imperialism. To do this I recall the old saying that capitalism works not like an invisible hand, but like an 'iron fist wrapped in a velvet glove'. So here I distinguish between these two:

> *Illiberal or iron fist imperialism:* imperialism that makes use of military force or explicit threats of force to maintain or expand empire.
>
> *Neoliberal or velvet glove imperialism:* all the policies associated with neoliberalism and the Washington Consensus which have served to integrate countries into a web of neoliberal-dominated sets of policies and institutions. A key aspect of this 'velvet glove' imperialism is the use by the United States of various non-military instruments of power, including power in the IMF and World Bank and other international institutions, the legal system that enforces creditor relationships, such as we saw in the recent Argentina case, and economic sticks and carrots in a diplomatic sense to spread the neoliberal policies and institutions and to extract gains from them.

The US has used both of these types of imperialism in the late twentieth and early twenty-first centuries. Before discussing how to estimate the impacts of these mechanisms, I first need to develop an estimating or accounting framework.[4]

An estimating framework

The following simple accounting framework will be used to organise my estimates of the impact of imperialism on the well-being of American workers. I initially define well-being simply as workers' real consumption.

The accounting framework is represented in Equation (1):

$$(1) \quad C^w/P^w = (W/Y) \times (W^{AT}/W) \times (C^w/W^{AT}) \times (P/P^w) \times (Y/P)$$

where:

C^w = worker's nominal consumption

P^w = price index for worker's consumption which reflects the price of imports (among other factors)

$C^w/P^w = c^w$ = workers' real consumption

W = workers' total nominal income (primarily wages + non-wage compensation)

Y = nominal GNP

$W/Y = w$ = wage share in national income

W^{AT} = workers' after-tax nominal income (after-tax nominal wages)

$W^{AT}/W = tf$ = tax factor (higher ratio means lower tax rate for workers)

$C^w/W^{AT} = c$ = workers' nominal consumption relative to after tax wages.

P = price deflator for GNP

$P/P^w = \rho$ = terms of trade

$Y/P = y$ = real GNP

According to Eq. (1), workers' real consumption can be decomposed into the following factors: the wage share in national income, the taxes paid by workers, workers' consumption relative to their after-tax incomes, terms of trade and the level of real gross national product (GNP).

We can gain insight into some key factors by further decomposing the third term, C^w/W^{AT}, workers' nominal consumption relative to their after-tax nominal income. How can workers' consumption differ from their after-tax income? There are two main ways: first they can borrow and, therefore, spend more than their incomes; on the other hand, they can save, and thereby spend less than their income. The second is that their consumption can consist of other components, most importantly for our purposes, public services and goods provided by government, including national defence, education and infrastructure.

It is well known that American workers as a whole save relatively little. They do, however, borrow a lot. Most relevant for our purposes is the amount that they borrow from abroad, an amount that can be represented by the current account deficit. Implicitly, I assume that internal borrowing is from other members of the working class so that they net out. This is obviously a simplification but not an important one for the purpose of this essay. Using functional notation we have Eq. (2):

$$(2) \quad C^w / W^{AT} = c = c \left(S^w / W^{AT}, CAD / W^{AT}, PS / W^{AT} \right)$$

where:

S^w = workers' savings
CAD = current account deficit
PS = public services (such as public spending on education, national security, infrastructure used by the working class)
$S^w / W^{AT} = s$
$CAD / W^{AT} = cad$
$PS / W^{AT} = ps$

One can differentiate Eq. (2) to obtain the impacts of these factors on workers' nominal consumption relative to their after-tax consumption where the signs of the partial derivatives are given by:

$$c_s < 0, \ c_{cad} > 0, \ c_{ps} > 0$$

We can see how workers' real consumption changes depending on changes in these factors by taking natural logs and totally differentiating Eq. (1) and taking Eq. (2) into account,

where $\hat{x}$ = proportional rate of change of x, to generate Eq. (3):

$$(3) \quad \hat{cw} = \hat{w} + \hat{tf} + \hat{c} + \hat{p} + \hat{y}$$

Note that, from Eq. (2), the proportional change in nominal consumption relative to after-tax income is given by:

$$(4) \quad \hat{c} = c_s \hat{s} + c_{cad} \hat{cad} + c_{ps} \hat{ps}$$

assuming $\hat{s} = 0$, then Eq. (4) reduces to:

(4) $\hat{c} = c_{cad}\, c\hat{a}d + c_{ps}\, \hat{p}s$

so that the change in nominal consumption relative to after-tax income depends positively on the change in the current account deficit and change in public services provided to workers. Substituting Eq. (4) into Eq. (3) yields:

(5) $c\hat{w} = \hat{w} + \hat{tf} + \hat{p} + \hat{y} + c_{cad}\, c\hat{a}d + c_{ps}\, \hat{p}s$

Equation (5) states that the change in worker's real consumption depends on the change in the wage share, tax rates, terms of trade, economy-wide real income (that is, economic growth), current account deficit weighted by the workers' share of current account borrowing and change in public services weighted by workers' consumption of these services.

Equation (5) is very useful, but it leaves out some important Keynesian effects (for example, the role of effective demand) on employment and wages. To incorporate those impacts, on occasion, it will be useful to decompose the wage share, W/Y, in the following way:

(6) $W/Y = W/L \times L/L^* \times L^*/Y^* \times Y^*/Y$

where:
- W/Y = labour share
- L = employed labour force
- W/L = the wage rate
- L^* = available labour force
- L/L^* = employment rate (under assumptions of this essay, a measure of the unemployment rate)
- Y^* = full capacity rate of nominal output
- L^*/Y^* = the inverse of the output–labour ratio at full capacity utilisation (a measure of technical labour-intensity of production)
- Y^*/Y = the inverse of the capacity utilisation rate

As Eq. (6) indicates, changes in the wage share can be decomposed into changes in the wage rate, unemployment factor, capacity utilisation rate and technical relations of production.[5]

Impact of imperialism on workers' welfare

The next step is to make conjectures about the impacts of imperialism on worker's welfare as represented by Eqs. (1), (2), (5) and (6). Here, it is crucial to distinguish between what we have called *illiberal imperialism* (the iron fist) and *velvet glove imperialism* (neoliberalism).

Illiberal imperialism

(1) $C^w/P^w = W/Y \times W^{AT}/W \times C^w/W^{AT} \times P/P^w \times Y/P$

(2) $C^w/W^{AT} = c = c\left(S^w/W^{AT}, CAD/W^{AT}, PS/W^{AT}\right)$

(5) $\hat{cw} = \hat{w} + \hat{tf} + \hat{p} + \hat{y} + c_{cad}\,\hat{cad} + c_{ps}\,\hat{ps}$

(6) $W/Y = W/L \times L/L^* \times L^*/Y^* \times Y^*/Y$

Illiberal imperialism is that aspect of US foreign economic policy most directly connected to US foreign military action, both threatened and actual. What are the economic channels through which this type of imperialism affects workers? Using the framework of Eqs. (1)–(6) (reproduced above) and as we describe in more detail below, the main hypothesised channels are the following: on the 'positive side' (from the material perspective of US workers), US military might protects the availability of raw materials, and especially oil, thereby improving the terms of trade (ρ); US military power also helps to underpin the reserve currency role of the US dollar, and, as a related matter, strengthens the political security of US financial markets; it thereby helps the United States run a large current account deficit (CAD); military expenditure for domestic use and export also expands aggregate demand, and through Eq. (6), it may increase employment and capacity utilisation (though some have argued that it makes production less labour intensive).

On the negative side, for US workers, military spending costs tax money; therefore, either the taxes that workers must pay are raised (reducing tf in Eq. [5]), expenditures on public services of use to workers reduced (reduce ps in Eq. [5]) or both.[6]

Velvet glove (neoliberal) imperialism

The impacts of *illiberal imperialism* are difficult to measure, and the 'imperial accounting' for neoliberal imperialism may be even more difficult.[7] On the possible benefits side, neoliberalism plausibly leads to more exports for US firms, thereby increasing aggregate demand and leading to more employment (a lower CAD); neoliberal imperialism, by increasing the supply of inexpensive imports for the United States, might improve the US terms of trade.[8] On the negative side, making the world safe for US foreign investment might increase outsourcing, jobs costing foreign investment and threat effects;[9] this might reduce the wage rate, employment rate and, therefore, labour share accruing to workers. Moreover, there are additional expenditures in terms of military spending, diplomacy and foreign aid tied to the neoliberal project. These add costs to workers to the extent that they lead to higher taxes or cut-backs in social spending.

In the rest of the essay, I study the cost and benefits to workers of the iron fist (illiberal imperialism). In a subsequent essay, I plan to present evidence on liberal imperialism and US workers.

Illiberal imperialism: the net benefits of the iron fist

Costs of military power

For the period under consideration, it was safe to say that the United States was the world's only superpower.[10] A few numbers make it clear just how superior the United States was, at least in terms of its *military expenditures* (see Figure 8.1). The US military budget request for 2002 was 343.1 billion dollars. The total military expenditure of the so-called rogue states for around the same period was roughly 14.4 billion dollars.[11] Russia, China, India, Taiwan and Pakistan all add to another 115 billion dollars or so. So, US expenditure in 2002 was roughly three times of all the potential enemies combined. If one adds the expenditures of US 'allies' in NATO and the Far East, the US plus allies' expenditures was 555.8 billion dollars or so, meaning that the US and its 'allies' spent more than five times as much as all likely enemies combined.

Of course, there have been ups and downs in the US military expenditures. Figure 8.1 shows the trend of US military expenditures since the end of the Second World War. The ups and downs are obvious: the build-up during the Vietnam War of the late 60s, the decline thereafter, the Reagan build-up in the 1980s, and then the decline in the 1990s. Another expansion occurred as a result of the wars in Iraq and Afghanistan following the 9/11 attacks.

But what is equally obvious is that, despite the fluctuations, the average level had stayed remarkably high, war or no war. Even though

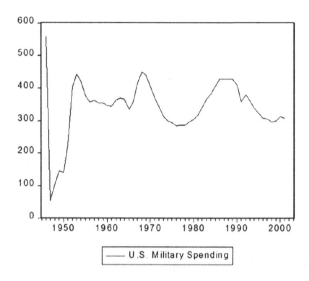

Figure 8.1 Real military spending in the United States
Source: Center for Defense Information, 2001.

there was a decline after the fall of the Berlin Wall, the huge disarmament and peace dividend that many predicted never materialised. Moreover, these data are actually 'under-estimates' of the true military budget. Table 8.1 presents data on military expenditures that are often hidden in other categories.

Table 8.1 presents data on military and military-related spending in the fiscal years 2001 and 2002. They show the number of categories left out; more importantly, they show that when more of the costs are included, the real military budget goes up by almost 60 percent.

Even these numbers may be an underestimate, because they almost certainly leave out the various intelligence services. The 518.9 billion dollar figure above is not trivial. It represented about 5 percent of GDP in 2002.

The difficult, but crucially important, question is: how much of this spending was used to support 'iron fist' (illiberal) imperialism? This is of course virtually impossible to know, but we must come up with a way of allocating expenditures to defence and other 'legitimate' uses, on the one hand, and to 'imperialism' on the other.[12]

Scholars on military strategy could undoubtedly undertake a more nuanced approach. But here I will basically follow two crude strategies: first, I will compare the US expenditure with expenditures by countries

Table 8.1 Military and military-related expenditure, 2001 and 2002, billions of US dollars

Military expenditures

	2001 budget	*2002 budget*
Department of Defense	284.9	313.0
Department of Energy (Military)	13.4	14.3
misc.	3.1	1.4
Total national defence	299.1	328.7
Military-related		
Foreign military aid	7.1	7.1
International peace keeping	1.1	.9
Space (military)	2.6	2.7
Military retirement pay	34.2	35.3
Veterans' benefits	45.4	51.6
Subtotal	90.4	97.6
Interest attributable to past military spending	94.8	92.6
Military and military-related grand total	**484.3**	**518.9**

Source: Center for Defense Information, 2001, p. 34.

that most experts would agree are non-imperialist. I will take the difference between what the US spends and what other countries spend as a measure of the 'iron fist budget'; second, I will consider in a crude fashion, what part of the military budget might be for imperialistic purposes, focusing on controlling oil in the Middle-East (see below).[13]

Method one: if the United States were Sweden

Table 8.2 presents data on military expenditure as a share of GDP for a sample of countries from 1986 to 2000.

There may be some surprises here: 'peace loving' Sweden has a share of military expenditures comparable to that of United Kingdom; and, for some years, France's expenditures, as a share of their GDP, are comparable to the figures for the United States in the recent period. During the 1980s, however, the United States spent far more as a share of GDP than did any of the other countries.

When comparing these data, it is important to remember the hidden US military expenditures noted above. The true military expenditures of the United States are likely to be as much as 60 percent higher than those listed here.[14] On the other hand, some would argue that the other countries are able to spend so 'little' because they get a 'free ride'

Table 8.2 Military expenditure in a sample of countries, 1985–2000

	Australia	Canada	Denmark	France
1985	2.73	2.10	NA	3.95
1986	2.67	2.19	NA	3.88
1987	2.69	2.10	NA	3.89
1988	2.35	2.00	2.05	3.79
1989	2.19	1.99	2.04	3.68
1990	2.21	1.99	1.94	3.57
1991	2.43	1.90	2.04	3.56
1992	2.47	1.89	1.95	3.38
1993	2.58	1.80	1.96	3.39
1994	2.47	1.70	1.77	3.38
1995	2.41	1.51	1.68	3.08
1996	2.28	1.42	1.68	3.00
1997	2.20	1.23	1.67	3.00
1998	2.19	1.29	1.66	0.28
1999	2.04	1.27	1.62	2.76
2000	1.95	1.16	1.52	2.64

	Sweden	United Kingdom	United States
1985	2.93	NA.	6.06
1986	2.84	NA	6.20
1987	2.74	4.56	6.06
1988	2.73	4.07	5.72
1989	2.51	4.05	5.45
1990	2.60	4.03	5.15
1991	2.71	4.23	4.66
1992	2.50	3.75	4.74
1993	2.68	3.56	4.43
1994	2.63	3.40	4.04
1995	2.53	3.08	3.76
1996	2.34	2.99	3.47
1997	2.33	2.71	3.27
1998	2.30	2.66	3.08
1999	2.29	2.54	2.98
2000	2.25	2.51	3.02

Source: See Appendix.

with the US. By this reasoning, some of the US expenditures are not for imperialism but to help 'protect' its allies.

While this argument might have had some plausibility during the 'Cold War', there was very little justification for such spending in the period under consideration, when it seemed that the Cold War was over. It therefore seems plausible to assume that the US defensive (that is, non-imperialist) share should be something closer to the figures for

Table 8.3 Average military expenditure shares and the military cost of US imperialism 1985–2000 (share of GDP and in billions of 1996 US dollars)

	Australia	Canada	Denmark	France	Sweden	UK	US (lower estimate)	US (higher estimate)
Average military share 1985–2000	2.3	1.5	1.9	3.4	2.5	3.8	4.5	7.2

Memo: Non-US average: 2.6 percent of GDP.

US average: standard estimate: 4.5 percent of GDP.

US average: higher estimate: 7.2 percent of GDP (60 percent higher).

Difference: US standard estimate – non-US share: **1.9 percent of GDP (military cost as GDP share).**

Difference: US high estimate – non-US share: **4.6 percent of GDP (military cost as GDP share)**

Military (economic) cost of imperialism, 1985–2000: low estimate: **2.193 trillion (1996 dollars)**

Military (economic) cost of imperialism, 1985–2000: **higher estimate: 5.311 trillion(1996 dollars).**

Source: Appendix, and Economic Report of the President, 2003, tables, B-1, B-3, B-25 (and earlier years).

Canada, Sweden, Denmark and Norway, than what it spent in the 80s and 90s. So I assume here that the non-imperialist expenditure is the average of those countries' shares, and that the real expenditure of the United States is 60 percent higher than that shown in these figures. Table 8.3 calculates these numbers.

The non-US average share between 1985 and 2000, including Britain and France, which are still (very small) imperial powers, is 2.6 percent of GDP (see Table 8.2 above). This compares with a low estimate of 4.5 percent share for the US and a high estimate of 7.2 percent, based on the higher figures cited in Table 8.1.

What do these differences translate into in terms of US dollar costs of imperialist military expenditures? As calculated at the bottom of Table 8.3, these numbers imply the following low and high estimates of the accumulated US military expenditures in support of imperialism between the period 1985 and 2000: a low estimate of $2193.63 billion of 1996 dollars and a high estimate of $5310.89 billion of 1996 dollars.

*Method two: how much does it cost to protect the supply of
oil and other obvious imperialist adventures?*

Another method to estimate the military costs of imperialism would
be to calculate how much of the military budget was used to engage in
'obviously' imperialist activities during this period, such as protecting
the supply of oil (see Table 8.4).

According to Michael Klare, Five-College Professor of Peace and
World Security Studies, experts generally estimate that in the 1980s
and 1990s, the US military spent about 15 percent of its budget in the
Middle East and 25 percent in Asia and the Pacific. Focusing on oil,
then, I make a very low estimate of the military budget attributed to
imperialism and estimate that it is about 15 percent. Of course, this
is quite arbitrary, but given the nature of this study, it is better to aim
low than to aim high.

How much tax does the working class pay?[15]

How much of these military costs do the working class pay? Here,
I must decide whether to use an estimate of the share of taxes paid
out of labour income or the share paid by income groups that we
would normally think of as 'working class'. Since there is no consensus
on precisely how this concept maps into the income distribution, any
decision I make here will be somewhat arbitrary.

There have been a number of studies done on the distributional
characteristics of the US federal, state and local taxes, at least since the
mid-1960s and for the period under consideration.[16]

Table 8.5 shows the most recent data available,[17] and the share of
federal taxes paid by the bottom 60 and 80 percent of households is
slightly less than their share of income, whereas the shares paid by the
top 5 and 1 percent are somewhat higher than their shares of income.
Table 8.5 also shows that while the tax shares of the bottom groups

Table 8.4 Approximate distribution of US military budget (percent)

Function/area	Percent of budget
Nuclear arms, and general global defence	25
Small wars and activities, including Latin America	10
Europe	25
Asia and the Pacific	25
Middle East	15

Source: Professor Michael Klare, personal correspondence.

Table 8.5 Share of total income and total federal taxes by income quintiles of households 1979, 1985 and 1997

		1979	1985	1997
Bottom 60%				
	income share	32.2	29.6	26.9
	tax share	21.7	22.1	17.2
Bottom 80%				
	income share	54.3	51.4	47.1
	tax share	42.7	43.4	35.3
Top 5%				
	income share	20.8	23.6	28.9
	tax share	30.0	28.5	39.1
Top 1%				
	income share	9.3	11.3	15.8
	tax share	15.5	14.2	23.0

Source: See Appendix.

Table 8.6 Tax costs to 'working class' of US imperialist military expenditure 1985–2000, billions of US dollars (1996 dollars)

	Low estimate of costs: 2193.63	*High estimate of costs:* 5310.99
Bottom 60% Tax share: 19.65%	431.05	1043.61
Bottom 80% Tax share: 39.35	863.19	2089.9

Source: See Tables 8.6 and 8.8.

went up between 1979 and 1985, they went down between 1985 and 1997. Of course, as Table 8.5 shows, inequality of income went up significantly during this period.

So, how should we define the working class for purposes of this essay? Does it make up the bottom 80 percent or the bottom 60 percent? For purposes of the essay, we will look at it both ways. Using these data, and averaging the tax shares between 1985 and 1997, Table 8.6 gives the amount of the military expenditure paid by the working class.

Table 8.6 shows that the low estimate of the military cost to the bottom 60 percent is between 431 billion and 1 trillion dollars, and for the bottom 80 percent, the military budget cost is between 863 billion and 2 trillion dollars between 1985 and 2000.

US working class benefits from iron fist imperialism

What possible benefits could the 'working class' receive from this rather large expenditure of funds? Remember that we are using only a portion of the military expenditures during this period (1985–2000), the portion that we are estimating to be the military costs of imperialism; so by construction, workers are not getting 'national defence' from these expenditures.

Many authors have suggested that one of the major reasons for US imperialism is to protect access to raw materials, including oil, and to keep their prices low. Hence, according to this view, not only will oil companies and other large multinational corporations receive access to commodities that they can sell at large profits, but working class Americans can also receive cheaper commodities.[18]

Military power might yet play a further role in supporting the consumption of working class Americans: it might underpin the international key currency role of the dollar.[19] The international role of the dollar, in turn, may be a key factor underpinning both the high valuation of the dollar, which helps support high terms of trade, as well as the ability of the United States to run a large current account deficit, thereby augmenting the consumption of US workers.

Below, we consider these possible benefits to US workers.

Military power, the dollar and the current account deficit

In the run-up to the Iraq war, stories circulated around the internet that the *real* reason for the US invasion of Iraq was that Iraq was pricing its oil in Euros and that this threatened the reserve (or key) currency role of the dollar which, in turn, was crucial to the ability of the United States to run a large current account deficit. While clearly ludicrous as the explanation for the Bush administration's invasion, the claims, nonetheless, may have had a kernel of truth in the following sense: the reserve currency role of the dollar is an important determinant of the ability of the United States to run a current account deficit and, furthermore, US military power is an important determinant of the reserve currency role. Finally, there is some evidence that in the past, at least, in particular during the OPEC price increases of the 1970s, the United States went to some effort to make sure that oil continued to be priced in dollars, rather than special drawing rights (SDRs).[20]

Economists have hypothesised the importance of military power for maintaining the reserve currency role of currencies.[21] But there have been very few serious theoretical and econometric investigation of the

role of military power in the determinants of reserve currency status. In an excellent paper, Roohi Prem undertakes a time series and
cross sectional econometric analysis of the reserve currency roles of
various currencies.[22] She shows that the standard determinants such
as inflation, interest rates and other monetary variables are unimpor-
tant. What *is* important are what Prem calls the 'enforcement' variables, and in particular, military expenditure: the greater the military
expenditure, the larger the reserve currency role.[23]

Of course, one has to go several steps further to establish the relationship between reserve currency role and ability to run current
account deficits, but this connection is fairly widely accepted.

US current account deficits

The US has certainly taken advantage of its ability to run current
account deficits. At the turn of the twenty-first century, the US net
international investment position was over 20 percent of GDP, quite
large by historical standards. But how much of the US current account
deficit can be explained by US military expenditure? Again, we need a
standard of comparison. One way is to look at other countries that do
not have a reserve currency or large military.

Table 8.7 presents data on the US current account balance as a share
of GNP compared with those of other countries.

The striking thing about these data is that the United States does not
seem off the scale, relative to other developed countries, in its ability
to run current account deficits. Moreover, even its large negative net
investment position is not without precedent. According to Lane and
Milesi-Ferretti, nine developed countries had negative net foreign asset
positions of 20 percent or greater.[24]

Table 8.7 Current account balance as share of GDP, average and minimum over the period 1970–2000

	Aust	Can.	Den	France	Germ	Italy	Japan	Swed	UK	US
Current account balance as share of GDP	–3.7	–2.2	–.88	.27	.72	–.11	1.56	–.34	–.59	–1.2
Minimum		–7.3	–4.8	–5.3	–2.1	–2.4	–4.4	–1.0	–3.4	–4.5	–5.4

Source: World Bank, *World Development Indicators* http://data.worldbank.org/data-catalog/world-development-indicators.

What are we to surmise from this? Perhaps the impact of the US military role on the ability to run a larger current account balance had not been fully exploited by the early twenty-first century. And indeed, it has gone up substantially since that time. Perhaps, the subsidy works in another way, for example, through lower real interest rates. Still, what if we did assume that the total cumulative dollar costs of the current account deficit were a 'benefit' of imperialism? The total between 1986 and 2000 is –1918.5 billion in 1996 dollars; 1985–2000 = –1918.5 billion in 1996 dollars. Let us say the bottom 80 percent benefited from this according to their share of income, which, from Table 8.5 was an average of 49.2 percent between 1987 and 1997. Then, their benefit from the current account deficit would be roughly 944 billion dollars. This would cover the low estimate of the bottom 80 percent tax cost of military expenditure, but it is far below the high estimate of over 2 trillion dollars. Moreover, it seems rather unlikely that all of the current account deficit, or even most of it, can be attributed to the US imperialistic military expenditure.

Military power, oil and the terms of trade

Another mechanism by which military spending might help workers is through its impact on the terms of trade. Riddell and Bowles, Gordon and Weisskopf find that military spending improves the terms of trade.[25] But they look at the impact on the profit rate and not on workers' consumption. Moreover, there is evidence that the major factor driving US terms of trade are oil prices. Partly for that reason, we focus on oil prices here.

At one level, the role of oil in US foreign and military policy in the Persian Gulf is undisputable. The Carter doctrine, for example, is an explicit presidential statement that speaks for itself:

> An attempt by any outside force to gain control of the Persian Gulf region would be regarded as an assault on the vital interest of the United States of America and such an assault will be repelled by any means necessary, including military force.[26]

The role of oil in US military strategy as far back as the early twentieth century and during the Second World War, up to the present time has been well documented.[27] The motivations for this key role of oil are myriad: economic, business profits and campaign contributions from the oil companies, and geo-strategic interests as well. The control of oil is undoubtedly one of the fundamental pillars of empire.

At another level, however, it is very difficult to assess the returns that the US economy as a whole and the workers in it, get from this focus on controlling oil. Do US workers get a lower price of oil? Do they get a more stable price of oil, with the same average price as they would get were there no US military control of the Persian Gulf? Or do they get nothing at all, with the rents going entirely to the big oil companies? All of these hypotheses have been suggested somewhere in the voluminous literature on oil and the economy.[28]

Where is the role for politics and military force in all of this? Certainly in the last case, political factors come into play in an important way. How Saudi Arabia chooses to set the price of oil undoubtedly is strongly affected by the Saudi family's military and political relationship with the United States.[29]

Experts seem to agree that both the low level and the stability of oil prices in the 1950s and 1960s had everything to do with the role of the major oil companies, and, therefore, with the military and political role of the US and Great Britain.[30] Most experts also agree that the oil price increases of the 1970s were unsustainably large, but, nonetheless, were partly a correction of the early low price of oil. What there seems to be much less agreement about is whether the real price of oil at the turn of the twenty-first century was due to competition, or US military and political influence, through its influence over the Saudi government. In other words, little seems known about what the average real price of oil would be if the US influence no longer were in play. However, there does seem to be a consensus that without US military power projections in the Persian Gulf, there may be more instability in oil production and prices.[31]

There has been a great deal of economic analysis on the impact of oil price 'shocks' on the US economy.[32] Most of this literature suggests that these oil price spikes have a significant effect on US output and employment. In view of the lack of agreement about the impact of US policy on the average price of oil, at least after the 1960s, I will focus here on the relationship between US military power, the stability of oil prices and US workers.[33]

Clearly, these trends are volatile and due, at least in part, to political events. Table 8.8 below lists some important political events and their estimated impacts on the quantity of oil produced.

Such events, and the prospects of more, are what I have in mind when I suggest that US military power might reduce the incidence of severity of shocks in oil prices. If this is true, what might be the impact on the US economy in general and US workers in particular?

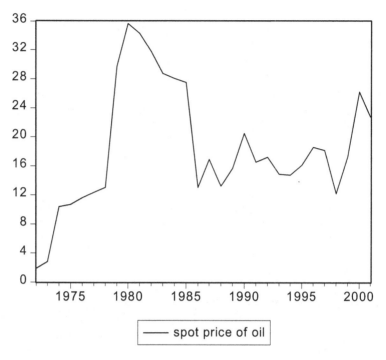

Figure 8.2 Spot price of oil
Source: Appendix.

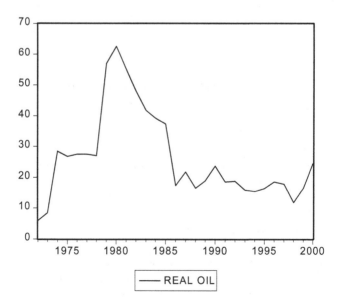

Figure 8.3 Real price of oil
Source: Appendix.

Table 8.8 Disruptions in world petroleum supply

Date	Event	Drop in world production	Percentage increase in oil prices
Nov. 1956	Suez Crisis	10.1%	NA
Nov.1973	Arab–Israeli War	7.8	400%
Dec. 1978	Iranian Revolution	8.9%	200%
Oct. 1980	Iran–Iraq War	7.2%	20%
Aug. 1990	Persian Gulf War	8.8%	33%
Memo: average Price increase major disruption			300%
Minor disruption			26.5

Source: Hamilton (2000), p. 39.

Rotemberg and Woodford present estimates of the impact of oil price increases on output, wages and employment in the US.[34] They find that a 1 percent increase in the price of oil leads to a 0.25 percent decline in output after 5–7 quarters and to a decline of real wages of 0.5 percent after 10 quarters. Davis and Haltiwanger further found that there were a loss of 260,000 production jobs after two years, based on data for 1972–1988.[35]

There is, furthermore, evidence of asymmetry in these relationships: oil price increases have much larger impacts than oil price declines.[36] Table 8.9 shows that these disruptions have significant impacts on oil prices. The average percentage increase from major disruptions is 300 percent and from minor disruptions, 26.5 percent.

Over the 15-year period we are dealing with, how much disruption would there have been had the United States not exerted military control over the Persian Gulf? Of course, this is impossible to answer with precision. Table 8.10 gives several relevant scenarios, however.

These estimated gains to US workers of US imperialism in the Persian Gulf are, of course, highly speculative. They amount to somewhere between 155 and 540 billion dollars (see Table 8.10).

Military expenditure, employment and growth

There is a large literature on the impacts of military expenditure on employment and growth. There are a number of issues involved: what is the impact in the short run on employment? What is the impact in the long run on growth? Again, the results depend on the counterfactual.[37] Spending surely has myriad effects on the economy. Large amounts

Table 8.9 Cost of oil price hikes due to political disruption

	GNP (%)	Annual cost billions of 1996 dollars	Workers' share	Real wages annual billions of 1996 dollars
Major disruption (300% increase)	7.5%	586	Bottom 60% 115.15 billion Bottom 80% 230.billion	264
Minor disruption (26.5% increase)	.66	51	Bottom 60% 10 billion Bottom 80% 20 billion	23.2

Source: Author's calculations from tables above.

Table 8.10 Counter-factual cost to worker of no US military action in Persian Gulf, 1985–2000, based on GNP estimates, billions of 1996 dollars

	Bottom 60%	Bottom 80%
one large disruption and two small	155.15	310
two large disruptions and two small	270.30	540

Source: Author's calculations. See text.

of spending can increase output through traditional multiplier effects, and inflation, as it did during the Vietnam War. There is a large debate, going back at least as far as Baran and Sweezy as to whether military spending is necessary to full employment. There seems to be little economic reason why this should be so.

As for the literature on economic growth and military spending, there is a pretty large consensus that military spending does not lead to higher economic growth in the long run.[38] In terms of our calculation, we have already assumed that our military budget includes money to protect the United States from threats. So there are no added benefits to be accounted for. As for short run benefits of large military spending, they are undeniable from the perspective of aggregate demand creation. But, as for counterfactuals, there are better ways to generate employment.[39]

Summary: benefits and costs

So, what is the bottom line? Do US workers benefit from the iron fist? Table 8.11 presents our first tentative 'bottom line' answer to the

Table 8.11 Do US workers gain from the iron fist? 1985–2000, billions of 1996 dollars

	Low estimate of costs: $2193.63	Benefits from oil price stability		High estimate of costs: 5310.99	Benefits from oil price stability	
		Small disrupt	Large disrupt		Small disrupt	Large disrupt
Bottom 60% tax share: 19.65%	$431.05	155.1	310	$1043.61	155.1	310
NET COSTS		275.95	121.05		888.5	733.61
Bottom 80% tax share: 39.35	$863.19	270.3	540	$2089.9	270.3	540
NET COSTS		592.9	323.19		1819.6	1549.9

Source: Author's calculations from tables above.

Tax shares are averages of 1985 and 1997 rates, as shown in Table 8.8.

Source: See Tables 8.6 and 8.8.

question posed by the essay. The answer for the period 1985–2000 is *no*; the US working class does not gain from the iron fist of US imperialism. It loses anywhere from 121 billion over that 15-year period to 1.8 trillion dollars. This, comes on top, of course, of the enormous loss of life and sustained injuries of soldiers that have devastated them and their families as a result of imperialistic military adventures.

Conclusion

Obviously, there is much remaining to be done to fully answer this question. The tentative conclusion is that US workers do not, on balance, gain from US imperialism, at least since 1985. I suspect the situation was probably different in the 1950s, 1960s and 1970s. At that time, US workers had much more power to extract rents from US capitalists. Therefore, they had much more power to get a piece of the imperialist pie. Oil prices were extremely low and very stable. Taxes were more progressive. Trade competition was not as intense. Future research should include 'liberal imperialism' and then add the earlier period to the analysis. As for the costs to US workers of the US imperialist disasters in Iraq and Afghanistan in the 2000s, the costs to US workers seem enormous and self-evident. For a full accounting, those costs of US imperialism too will have to be added to the tab in future research.

Appendix
Data sources and methods

Main series

Output is defined as GDP from the IMF World Economic Outlook (WEO) Database April 2003 www.imf.org/external/pubs/ft/weo/2003/01/data/index.htm. World output is defined as the sum of GDP over all countries. These data were available in current US$ and converted to constant 2000 US$ using the CPI.[40]

Current account balance data were taken from the World Bank World Development Indicators 2001 (1960–1999) and from WRI Earth trends online database http://earthtrends.wri.org (2000–2001). These data were available in current US$ and were converted to constant 2000 US$ using the CPI.

Military expenditures data were taken from the World Bank World Development Indicators 2001 (1985–1999) and the SIPRI Military Expenditure Online Database[41] (2000–2001). These data were available in current LCU and were converted to constant 2000 US$ using historical exchange rate data[42] and the CPI.

Official Development Assistance/Official Assistance (ODA/OA) data were taken from the British Government Department for International Development (DFID)[43] tables (1996–2000) and from the OECD Development Assistance Committee (DAC)[44] (2001). ODA is defined by the OECD DAC as 'flows to developing countries and multilateral institutions provided by official agencies . . . [with the intention to promote] economic development . . . [that contain] a grant element of at least 25 percent'.[45] Official assistance is defined as flows of the same nature going to countries not defined as developing, such as the 'former centrally planned economies'.[46] These data were available in current LCU and converted to constant 2000 US$ using historical exchange rate data and the CPI.

Contributions to international organisations data were taken from Birdsall and Roodman.[47] These contributions are defined as financial contributions to UN peacekeeping operations plus a dollar value 'equivalent' of personnel contributions to UN and non-UN operations. Data are taken directly from Table 8.12; see source for detailed explanation. These data were available in current US$ and converted to constant 2000 US$ using historical exchange rate data.

Terms of trade adjustment data were taken from the World Bank World Development Indicators 2001. The terms of trade adjustment is a dollar-value adjustment based on the terms of trade, rather than a ratio of price indices. These data were available in constant 1995 US$ and not converted.

United States assistance abroad data were taken from US Overseas Grants and Loans Online database.[48] Data on Economic Assistance, Military Assistance and their sum, Total Assistance were taken from this database. Economic Assistance includes all contributions to international organisations. Military Assistance includes all sales and gifts of weapons and other machinery, costs of training, etc. These data include loans and grants. These data were available in current US$ and converted to constant 2000 US$ using historical exchange rate data.[49]

Conversion series

Historical Exchange Rate Data were taken from the World Bank World Development Indicators 2001 (1960–1999) and the Antweiler Exchange Rate dataset (2000–2003).[50]

Consumer Price Index data were taken from the Bureau of Labor Statistics.[51]

Population data were taken from the IMF International Financial Statistics 2002.[52]

Notes

1 I thank Sunanda Sen and Cristina Marcuzzo for very helpful editing suggestions. In addition, I want to thank without implicating Anita Dancs, Carol Heim, Michael Klare, William Hartung, Stanley Malinowitz, Seymour Melman and Michael Remer for providing important materials and/or helpful discussion on aspects of this project. I also thank Dorothy Power, Mariam Majd and Devika Dutt for excellent research assistance.

2 Stanley Lebergott, 'The Returns to US Imperialism, 1890–1929', *Journal of Economic History*, 1980, 40(2): 229–52; Robert Zevin, 'An Interpretation of American Imperialism', *The Journal of Economic History*, 1972, 32(1): 316–60.

3 Michael W. Doyle, *Empires*, Ithaca: Cornell University Press, 1986, p. 19.

4 In this essay, I have space just to discuss 'iron-fist' imperialism.

5 See, for example, Thomas Weisskopf, 'Marxian Crisis Theory and the Rate of Profit in the Postwar US Economy', *Cambridge Journal of Economics*,

1979, 3(4), December, who developed a useful related framework on which I have built.

6 Remember, I am leaving out for now the significant direct costs borne by soldiers and their families.

7 Note that in the accounting exercises for the British Empire, no one attempted to calculate the net benefits of informal imperialism.

8 Illiberal imperialism can also secure export markets. See Daniel Berger, William Easterly, Nathan Nunn and Shanker Satyanath, 'Commercial Imperialism? Political Influence and Trade During the Cold War', *American Economic Review*, 2013, 103(2): 863–96 for evidence that CIA interventions overseas increased export markets for US companies.

9 For example, Kate Bronfenbrenner, 'Uneasy Terrain: The Impact of Capital Mobility on Workers, Wages and Union Organizing', Report to the U.S. Trade Deficit Review Commission. mimeo. Cornell University, 2000; Gerald Epstein and James Burke, 'Threat Effects and the Internationalization of Production', PERI Working Paper, 2001; Minsik Choi, 'Threat Effect of Foreign Direct Investment on Labor Union Wage Premium', PERI Working Paper, 2001.

10 By 2016, the threats to US military hegemony had become greater, particularly from Russia and China, but according to most experts, US military power remains, still, overwhelming.

11 All these numbers are taken from the invaluable 2001–2002 Military Almanac, published by the Center for Defense Information, www.cdi.org. The rogues include Iran, Syria, Iraq, North Korea, Libya, Cuba, and Sudan.

12 This was the common approach taken in the vast literature on analysing British imperialism.

13 A third method, not attempted here, would be to consult experts who have attempted to develop non-imperialist military budgets. Many of these were done many years ago, but they still might be relevant today, assuming they are upgraded to today's prices. Then the imperialist military expense budget would be the difference between what the US spends and what a purely defensive military budget would cost.

14 William D. Hartung in 'Military – Industrial Complex Revisited: How Shaping Weapons Makers Are Shaping US Foreign and Military Policies', in Martha Honey and Tom Barry (eds.), *Global Focus: U.S. Foreign Policy at the Turn of the Millennium*, New York: St. Martin's Press, 2000, pp. 22–43 estimates that expenditures on intelligence agencies plus other agencies doing military work throughout the government in 1998 cost more than 27 billion dollars. On top of that, he argues that the military gives large subsidies to defense contractors, adding up to almost 8 billion dollars during the same period.

15 This section draws heavily on Joseph A. Pechman and Benjamin Okner, *Who Bears the Tax Burden?* Washington, DC: Brookings Institution, 1973; Joseph A. Pechman, *Who Paid the Taxes, 1966–1985*, Washington, DC: Brookings Institution, 1985; Joseph A. Pechman, *Tax Reform, The Rich and the Poor*, Washington, DC: Brookings Institution, 1989; Richard Kasten, Frank Sammartino and Eric Toder, 'Trends in Federal Tax Progressivity, 1980–93', in Joel Slemrod (ed.), *Tax Progressivity and Income Inequality*, Cambridge: Cambridge University Press, 1994, pp. 9–50; Joel

Slemrod and Jon Bakija, *Taxing Ourselves*, Cambridge, MA: MIT Press, 1996; and research from Citizens for Tax Justice www.ctj.org and the joint Brookings Institution-Urban Institute Tax Center, www.taxpolicycenter. org/ (accessed on 5 March 2003); Center on Budget Priorities, www.cbp. org (accessed on 5 March 2003).

16 Pechman and Okner, *Who Bears the Tax Burden*; Pechman, *Who Paid the Taxes*; Kasten, Sammartino and Toder, 'Trends in Federal Tax Progressivity, 1980–93'.

17 Congressional Budget Office, 'Effective Federal Tax Rates, 1979–1997', www.cbo.gov/publication/42875 (accessed on 5 March 2003).

18 Many have written about the role of oil in US foreign policy, including Thomas L. McNaugher, *Arms and Oil: U.S. Military Strategy and the Persian Gulf*, Washington, DC: Brookings Institution, 1985; David Painter, *Oil and the American Century: The Political Economy of U.S. Foreign Oil Policy, 1941–1954*, Baltimore: Johns Hopkins University Press, 1986; Daniel Yergin, *The Prize: The Epic Quest for Oil, Money and Power*, New York: Touchstone Books, 1991; David E. Spiro, *The Hidden Hand of American Hegemony*, Ithaca: Cornell University Press, 1999; Michael Klare, *Resource Wars*, New York: Metropolitan Books, 2001.

19 Fred Bergsten, *The Dilemmas of the Dollar*, New York: New York University Press, 1975; Roohi Prem, *International Currencies and Endogenous Enforcement: An Empirical Analysis*, mimeo IMF, African Department, January 1997.

20 Spiro, *The Hidden Hand of American Hegemony*, p. 124.

21 See Bergsten, *The Dilemmas of the Dollar* for a comprehensive survey; also see Gerald Epstein, 'Domestic Stagflation and Monetary Policy: The Federal Reserve and the Hidden Election', in Thomas Ferguson and Joel Rogers (eds.), *The Hidden Election*, New York: Pantheon Press, 1981.

22 Prem, *International Currencies and Endogenous Enforcement*.

23 Prem, *International Currencies and Endogenous Enforcement*.

24 Philip R. Lane and Gian Maria Milesi-Ferretti, 'Long-Term Capital Movements', IMF Working Paper, WP/01/107, August 2001.

25 Samuel Bowles, David M. Gordon and Thomas Weisskopf, *After the Wasteland*, Armonk, New York: M.E. Sharpe, 1990.

26 McNaugher, *Arms and Oil*, p. 3, fn. 3.

27 Painter, *Oil and the American Century*; Yergin, *The Prize*; Klare, *Resource Wars*.

28 See for example, Steven A. Schneider, *The Oil Price Revolution*, Baltimore: Johns Hopkins University Press, 1983; Morris A. Adelman, *The Genie Out of the Bottle: World Oil Since 1970*, Cambridge, MA: MIT Press, 1995; Michael Tanzer and Stephen Zorn, *Energy Update: Oil in the Late 20th Century*, New York: Monthly Review Press, 1985; Djavad Salehi-Isfahani, 'Models of the Oil Market Revisited', *The Journal of Energy Literature*, 1995, 1(1): 1–21 and the references cited in note 16.

29 Painter, *Oil and the American Century*; Yergin, *The Prize*; Klare, *Resource Wars*.

30 Personal communication with oil expert Michael Renner.

31 For example, Schneider, *The Oil Price Revolution*.

32 Michael Bruno and Jeffrey Sachs, *Economics of Worldwide Stagflation*, Cambridge, MA: Harvard University Press, 1985; James D. Hamilton,

'What Is an Oil Shock?', NBER Working Paper, 7755, 2000, www.nber. org (accessed on 5 March 2003).

33 There is another important factor and literature that has become important since 2008, namely, the role of financial speculation. Excellent work in this area has been undertaken by Jayati Ghosh, Robert Pollin, James Heintz and others. See, for example, Jayati Ghosh, James Heintz and Robert Pollin, 'Speculation on Commodities Futures Markets and Destabilization of Global Food Prices: Exploring the Connections', PERI Working Paper, 2011.

34 Julio J. Rotemberg, and Michael Woodford, 'Imperfect Competition and the Effects of Energy Price Increases on Economic Activity', NBER Working Paper No. 5634, 1996.

35 Steven J. Davis and John Haltiwanger, 'Sectoral Job Creation and Destruction Responses to Oil Price Changes', NBER Paper 7095, 1999.

36 James D. Hamilton, 'What Is an Oil Shock?' NBER Working Paper, 7755, 2000, www.nber.org (accessed on 5 March 2003).

37 This section draws on Robert W. Jr. DeGrasse, *Military Expansion, Economic Decline: The Impact of Military Spending on U.S. Economic Performance*, Armonk, New York: M.E. Sharpe, 1983.

38 Joshua Aizenman and Reuven Glick, 'Military Expenditure, Threats and Growth', NBER Paper 9618, 2003.

39 For example, Pollin and colleagues have shown that investments in 'green energy' generate far more jobs than expenditures on the military. Robert Pollin, Heidi Garrett-Peltier, James Heintz and Bracken Hendricks, 'Green Growth: A U.S. Program for Controlling Climate Change and Expanding Job Opportunities', Center for American Progress and Political Economy Research Institute (PERI), 2014.

40 See the section on CPI.

41 See www.sipri.com (accessed on 5 March 2003).

42 See the section on exchange rates.

43 'International Comparison Table 17: World Aid Flows: Net Official Development Assistance to Developing Countries and Official Aid to Other Countries', see www.dfid.gov.uk/SID/index.htm (accessed on 5 March 2003).

44 OECD DAC, 'Net Official Development Assistance Flows in 2001', www. oecd.org/pdf/M00037000/M00037871.pdf (accessed on 5 March 2003).

45 Helmut Fuhrer, 'The Story of Official Development Assistance', Paris: OECD, 1996, www.oecd.org/pdf/M00003000/M00003431.pdf, p. 24 (accessed on 5 March 2003).

46 Tatyana P. Soubbotina and Katherine Sheram, *Beyond Economic Growth: Meeting the Challenges of Global Development*, Washington, DC: World Bank, 2000, www.worldbank.org/depweb/beyond/global/chapter13.html (accessed on 5 March 2003).

47 Nancy Birdsall and David Roodman, 'The Commitment to Development Index: A Scorecard of Rich-Country Policies', Center for Global Development, April 2003, www.foreignpolicy.com (accessed on 5 March 2003).

48 USAID, 'US Overseas Grants and Loans Online [Greenbook]', 2000, http://qesdb.cdie.org/gbk/overview.html (accessed on 5 March 2003).

49 Oil Prices taken from British Petroleum website: www.bp.com/en/global/ corporate/energy-economics/statistical-review-of-world-energy/down loads.html

50 Werner Antweiler, University of British Columbia, Vancouver, BC, Canada, 2003, http://pacific.commerce.ubc.ca/xr/data.html (accessed on 5 March 2003).
51 Bureau of Labor Statistics (All Urban Consumers) Series No. CUUR0000SA0, http://data.bls.gov/cgi-bin/surveymost?cu (accessed on 5 March 2003).
52 IMF IFS Series No. 99Z.ZF.

Part III

Imperialism and the colonial context

9 India's global trade and Britain's international dominance

Utsa Patnaik

The increasing production of export crops was the theme of B.B. Chaudhuri's pioneering work titled *The Growth of Commercial Agriculture in Bengal 1777–1900*, which traced the conditions under which indigo and opium were grown and sold during the eighteenth and nineteenth centuries in Bengal presidency.[1] This significant work detailed through meticulous research the coercive conditions under which the East India Company secured a supply for export of these crops from the peasantry of Bengal. In principle, the term 'commercial agriculture' can refer to producing for the domestic market as well and can take place under the stimulus of expanding domestic demand. It was taken for granted by scholars of this period that the driving force behind the expansion of commercial crops was external metropolitan demand and not internal demand. The external demand, in turn, was qualitatively different depending on the purpose of growing the crop concerned: as a dye used in the new cotton textile industry, indigo was exported to northern industrialising countries (to Britain first, and thence a part was re-exported elsewhere), while opium was thrust on an unwilling imperial China to pay for Britain's increasing trade deficit with that country.

As a large tropical country endowed with biodiversity, especially exceptional botanic diversity, India, in common with other tropical regions colonised by the West European countries, was a valuable source of manufactures like cotton and silk textiles, of a variety of foodstuffs and tropical raw materials including fibres, dyes and hardwoods, none of which could be produced at all in the latter countries owing to their cold climate. The products of these tropical countries were in great demand by northern populations for improving and diversifying their consumption basket, which was rather poor as long as they depended on their limited domestic productive capacity alone; B.H. Slicher van Bath has documented this in his magisterial *Agrarian*

History of Western Europe AD 500 to 1850.[2] Acquiring political control meant the right of tax collection over a large tropical region, and this for a European nation, was rather like enjoying monopoly control over gold and diamond mines with unlimited yield since these tropical products were in high demand in cold temperate lands. A large part of the taxes raised by the English and Netherlands East India Companies from colonially subjugated peasant and artisan populations in Asia were used to purchase export goods ranging from cotton textiles to foodstuffs and raw materials. This 'purchase', therefore, was not normal purchase by a trading company, which always entails advancing its *own* funds for buying goods and realising a profit by selling the goods for a higher amount. It was qualitatively quite different because it meant acquiring the export goods completely free, as the commodity equivalent of locally raised taxes.[3]

The metropolitan country benefited greatly as it did not have to pay for the import of these goods (in excess of its exports if any to the colony) and, thus, incurred no external liability at all for its trade deficit. European countries without direct access to tropical regions bought their requirements of the tropical goods from the leading colonising countries. This is the reason that Britain and the Netherlands, for example, always imported a much larger volume of tropical products from their colonies than they could absorb within their own countries. They wished to re-export tropical goods to their temperate land neighbours to obtain the goods they needed, since their own domestic exports were in inelastic demand. The Netherlands re-exported a larger value of its tropical goods than its own domestic exports.[4] The temperate land goods, in which Britain was deficient, included foodgrains, timber, iron and naval supplies that were obtained from Continental Europe by substantially re-exporting tropical goods in addition to its own domestic products. The Navigation Acts in England of the 1650s, which were not seriously modified until the run-up to the Industrial Revolution, were designed precisely to ensure a monopoly of trade from the colonies.[5] No matter how distant the country of final destination might be, all important goods from the colonies had to be carried in English bottoms, routed through English ports, warehoused and then re-exported. The only exceptions were enslaved humans, who were directly shipped from West Africa across the Atlantic.[6]

There is little knowledge to this day in the extant scholarly literature on the rise of industrial capitalism of the exceptionally large magnitude of India's export earnings which were appropriated by Britain, hence, the tremendously important role that its largest colony was made to play in providing a substantial part of the real and financial resources for sustaining the growth of the international capitalist system in the era of imperialism and the gold standard. This lack of knowledge extends to developing country scholars too, despite the fact that India has a larger literature on metropolis–colony trade and the 'drain of wealth' than any other colonised country, literature which dates back over a century with the penetrating analyses by Dadabhai Naoroji[7] and later by Romesh Chandra Dutt.[8]

This author has argued that without explicitly cognising the prolonged protective policies against the manufactures of the colonies, especially cotton textiles,[9] and the very large tax-financed resource transfers from colonies to the leading metropoles, in particular to Britain, the country which emerged as the world capitalist leader, it is impossible to explain why the first Industrial Revolution took place at all. The transfers were sustained over an immensely long period of nearly two centuries, they provided free goods which the metropolis could not produce, and roughly doubled the investment rate during the first Revolution of the eighteenth to nineteenth century, compared to what would have otherwise prevailed. Sayera Habib[10] and Utsa Patnaik[11] have estimated the contribution of colonial transfers to capital formation in Britain during the period of Industrial Revolution.

Scholarly work on the patterns of global trade and investment in the nineteenth to twentieth century by S.B. Saul[12] and Marcello de Cecco[13] has recognised the 'balancing role' of India's export earnings in Britain's international payments but has ignored the question of tax-financed transfers in this role, since apparently they were not aware of the use of colonial budgetary resources for this purpose. The actual mechanism of resource transfer in India always operated through the foreign ruler raising taxes and using a large part of these taxes to 'purchase' and export goods to the world, in excess of imports into the colony.

After the English Crown took over from the East India Company, the global export surplus earnings of India, in financial gold and foreign exchange, were pre-empted and absorbed by the metropolis under a remarkably effective system. The Secretary of State for India in Council, based in London, offered rupee bills (termed Council Bills) to an equivalent value against deposit with him by foreign importers of Indian goods, of financial gold and foreign exchange as their payment, up to the entire value of India's global commodity export surplus earnings. The exchange rate (of rupees against sterling, the latter being fixed with respect to gold) was carefully calibrated down to the last farthing to ensure that foreign importers would always find it less paying to ship gold directly to India as opposed to taking the Council

Bill route, where they sent the bills by post or telegraph to the Indian exporters. While India's total financial gold and forex earnings were thus completely swallowed up in London, the middlemen exporters in India, tendering the Council Bills they received through exchange banks, were issued rupees by the Indian Treasury *out of the budgetary revenues*. After taking their cut, the exporters, in turn, paid the actual producers of these earnings – the peasants and workers – who had been obliged to contribute the bulk of the tax revenues in the first place, as land revenue and indirect taxes. Thus, colonised producers were not even issued the local currency equivalent of their forex earnings as additional liquidity but were 'paid' out of their own tax contribution. The cleverness lay here in their not being actually paid – all that happened, albeit in a more circuitous manner than before, was that the relevant part of their taxes changed its form, from cash to export goods, just as had been the case earlier under the Company's rule. Naoroji and Dutt were quite correct to term this 'unrequited export surplus'.[14]

Historical data compiled by the United Nations (1942[15] and 1962)[16] on the network of international trade from the late nineteenth century shows that the Indian sub-continent's export surplus earnings from the world were the second largest globally of any country for decades, second only to that of the United States. Despite this, India was never permitted to post an overall current account balance leave alone surplus, since Britain appropriated these exchange earnings by imposing, at will, offsetting invisible liabilities *to a greater extent* than India's global exchange earnings, forcing India to borrow and incur increasing interest burdens. Britain used these very large exchange earnings it appropriated from India, to meet its own external deficits, and to export capital to developing areas. The invisible liabilities imposed on India included, but were often far in excess of the usual items mentioned in the 'drain of wealth' literature and included munificent 'gifts' to Britain that no Indian knew about.

Studying the evidence leads to the conclusion that colonial transfers were crucial to the very existence and working of the international payments system based on the gold standard and centred on Britain during the half century starting from the 1870s, marking the age of high imperialism. These facts do not find any mention in the history of capital emanating from northern universities. A case in point is Thomas Piketty's *Capital in the 21st Century*[17] in which there is no mention at all of the economic reasons for centuries of West European colonisation or the slightest awareness that the mechanism of systematic transfers played a vital role in sustaining accumulation within the global capitalist system.

The reasons for this neglect are manifold. One important reason is the entire tradition of theorising in economics in the north over the last two centuries that has privileged and developed David Ricardo's logically incorrect theory of trade (the theory of comparative advantage) over all alternative expositions by the classical economists. Ricardo had argued using a two-country, two-good model (England and Portugal, both assumed to produce woollen cloth and wine) that specialisation according to relative cost of production would benefit both countries engaged in the trade.[18] The crucial assumption was that 'both countries produce both goods', for without this assumption, comparative cost or comparative advantage, could not even be defined. Ricardo's contempt for material reality is shown in the fact that the example he gave contradicted his own assumption, since England could not produce grapes for commercial wine production, particularly at that time when genetic modification of plants was unknown. Incorrect statement of fact constitutes material fallacy, which renders incorrect the concerned theory. The assumption that both countries produce both goods, and by extension all countries can produce all goods, was not true for over half of the world trade, which was in tropical products, that could never be produced in temperate lands.

For example, since India could produce both raw cotton and cotton textiles, the relative cost could be defined for India, namely, the number of units of cotton cloth producible by redirecting it to the labour released by reducing raw cotton output by one unit. But Britain could never produce raw cotton, so no cost of production was definable, leave alone the possibility of computing relative cost. One cannot reduce the output of a non-existent, non-producible good by one unit to see how much extra of the other good can be produced. This author has pointed out[19] that the particular fallacy in Ricardo's theory was what logicians, beginning from Aristotle, have termed the 'converse theory of accident', namely, from a restricted, highly specific premise – 'both countries produce both goods' – a general conclusion of mutual benefit from trade is improperly drawn and said to hold universally, even where the premise is not satisfied. The fact that for two centuries, leading economists have glossed over the patent absurdity of the premise and propounded this incorrect theory only underscores the deeply ideological nature of the discipline. They found the theory convenient and chose to ignore its illogic, because observed trade patterns which were actually the outcome of the exercise of naval might and military subjugation of peoples could be interpreted to say that the happy Ricardian reason of perceived 'mutual benefit' underlay all specialisation and exchange at the international level. 'Capitalism's blustering violence', to use Rosa Luxemburg's[20] lapidary phrase, was neatly sanitised by Ricardo's theory as incidental, as something to be safely ignored because only relative cost mattered: and never mind, if cost could not be defined at all.

Far from being of benefit to the colony, such trade in which they were obliged to specialise in exporting more primary products demanded abroad led to decline in production of foodgrains. Tropical land is virtually fixed in supply, and diversion of area and resources to exports always led to declining basic staples supply needed by the local population, while on the demand side, their purchasing power was restricted by imposing heavy tax or rent extraction. The inverse relation between more exports and less basic food for the local population is a trend common to every colonised country and has re-surfaced again in developing countries in present times, as free trade is revived using the fallacious Ricardian argument of mutual benefit. For example, India, after achieving rising foodgrains output per capita during four decades of protection from Independence up to the early 1990s, has once again seen steeply declining per capita grain output and availability in the last quarter century of export thrust from trade-liberalised agriculture. Given the hegemony exercised by the self-serving theoretical traditions emanating from northern universities, intellectuals in the developing world continue to teach and propagate these theories uncritically even though they are fallacious, and their inferences are at complete variance with the actual experience of their own countries.

Another important reason for the neglect of colonial transfers is that the leading economic historians of the metropolitan countries have been quite careful to understate in their empirical work, either knowingly or owing to conceptual confusion, the importance of colonies to their own trade. For example, Deane and Cole[21] in their widely quoted book *British Economic Growth 1688–1959, Trends and Structure*, applied a definition of special trade which is not found in any macroeconomics textbook dealing with an open economy such as Krugman and Obstfeld[22] and not used by any international organisation presenting country-wise trade to GDP ratios, such as United Nations, the World Bank or the International Monetary Fund. These organisations define and present always the *total* trade of each country, namely, all imports, whether retained within the country or re-exported, plus all export: not the domestically produced goods export alone but also the re-exported part if any, of imports; this is called *general trade*. In their definition of 'the volume of Britain's trade', however, Deane and Cole simply added up imports retained within Britain and domestic exports. Thus, they omitted entirely the re-exports from both the import and the export side without any discussion of why they did so. Re-exports of tropical goods imported by Britain were very large, allowing it to obtain imports from temperate lands which entered as wage goods (corn) and raw materials (cotton, iron) into its domestic production and without which a large part of its domestic output and exports, especially cotton cloth, would not have been possible. Excluding re-exports from trade is incorrect and is not a practice followed by economists or by any international organisation, which always present trade data for all countries according to the concept of general trade. The British government made available to the United Nations its official general trade series for the late nineteenth century onwards while separately providing the re-exports series.

Using the same basic data series that Deane and Cole themselves used from Mitchell and Deane,[23] we had shown earlier that re-exports amounted to 11 percent of Britain's GDP by 1800. By excluding them from both imports and exports, these historians were actually excluding trade amounting to 22 percent of GDP.[24] By 1800–1804, the actual annual trade figure with the correct definition was £82.7 million, whereas the Deane-Cole figure, widely quoted by many others, was only £50.8 million (see Table 9.1). The correct figure is nearly 63 percent higher. When they fail to calculate their own trade series, one can hardly expect the concerned academics or those who use their misleading figures, to have any idea of the importance of trade with their colonies for their own industrialisation and for the subsequent rise of their country to global dominance.

This chapter presents calculations of regional trade balances which have not been compiled or presented before, for the late eighteenth to the mid-nineteenth century, using basic data series prepared by the economic historians of Britain. The objective is to ascertain the share of colonial imports in total British imports, the commodity structure of trade and to shed light on the special nature of Britain's trade deficits with the colonies compared to its trade balances with sovereign areas. This discussion will enable us to understand the late nineteenth to early twentieth-century period of high imperialism when Britain, the world capitalist leader at the centre of the global payments system, was crucially dependent on the rising export earnings of India in particular to sustain the system.

Table 9.1 Britain's trade volumes 1750–1754 to 1800–1804: special trade and general trade

	Special trade Dom. X + Retd. M (DX+RM)	General trade Total X + Total M (TX+TM)	Difference (TX +TM) minus (DX+RM) = 2RXM	Percent of difference	
				to Special trade %	to General trade %
1750–1754	16.343	23.27	6.928	42.4	29.8
1755–1759	17.67	24.757	7.087	40.1	28.6
1760–1764	20.118	28.92	8.802	43.8	30.4
1765–1769	21.241	30.4	9.159	43.1	30.1
1770–1774	22.225	33.48	11.255	50.6	33.6
1775–1779	20.994	31.166	10.172	48.5	32.6
1780–1784	22.452	30.672	8.22	36.6	26.8
1785–1789	30.847	40.747	9.9	32.1	24.3
1790–1794	36.621	50.306	13.684	37.4	27.2
1795–1799	41.157	65.174	24.017	58.4	36.9
1800–1804	50.848	82.708	31.86	62.7	38.5
Average	*27.32*	*40.145*	*12.826*	*46.9*	*31.9*
Total	*1502.6*	*2208*	*705.42*	*46.9*	*31.9*

Sub-period

1750 to 1764	18.044	25.65	7.606	42.2	29.7
1765 to 1784	21.728	31.43	9.702	44.7	30.9
1785 to 1804	39.868	59.733	19.865	49.8	33.3

Source: Basic data series from Mitchell and Deane (1962) and Deane and Cole (1969).

Values are constant official values at early eighteenth century prices. Imports are c.i.f. values.

Note: Total exports TX = Domestic exports DX + Re-exported imports RXM.

Total imports TM = Retained imports RM + Re-exported imports RXM.

Re-exported imports appear in both Exports and Imports, hence twice the value of re-exports (shown under *Difference*) is excluded by Deane and Cole who apply the special trade concept.

This table reproduced from U. Patnaik (2000).

Pattern of trade with colonised regions including Asia, 1784–1826

The English customs-house records have been used by Ralph Davis to present the commodity structure and the source as well as destination of Britain's exports and imports over the period 1784–1856 in the appendix to his book *The Industrial Revolution and British*

Overseas Trade.[25] Painstakingly summarising the data related to hundreds of items from the original records was very time-consuming in the absence of modern computational aids at that time, so a continuous time series was not attempted. Davis gave three years' figures of current value trade centred on mid-decades, and from these data, this author has re-arranged and obtained three-year averages for the values presented in the tables. Asian trade excludes trade with China which was not a full-fledged colony of a single power.

The overall commodity composition of Britain's total trade, and how it changed as the industrial revolution proceeded, is shown in Table 9.2. Manufactured goods, mainly textiles but also naval supplies and iron, comprised 14 percent of all imports in the initial period 1784–1786, which declined to 6 percent by 1824–1826 as import-substitution took place in textiles. Foodstuffs comprised 42 percent of the total imports in the initial period and declined a little to 40 percent

Table 9.2 Britain's imports by commodity groups, 1784–1786 to 1824–1826, three year averages in £ million

	Manufactures MF	Foodstuffs FS	Raw materials RM	TOTAL imports M
1784–1786	3.235	9.609	9.917	22.761
1794–1796	4.05	18.212	15.655	37.917
1804–1806	3.796	23.953	27.809	55.558
1814–1816	2.762	32.018	37.016	71.796
1824–1826	3.889	26.37	36.13	66.389
Percentage share				
1784–1786	14.2	42.2	43.6	100
1794–1796	10.7	48	41.3	100
1804–1806	6.8	43.1	50.1	100
1814–1816	3.8	44.6	51.6	100
1824–1826	5.9	39.7	54.4	100
Index 1784–1786 = 100				
1784–1786	100	100	100	100
1794–1796	125	190	158	166.6
1804–1806	117	249	280	244.1
1814–1816	85	333	373	315.4
1824–1826	120	274	364	291.7

Source: Calculated from Davis (1979), appendix tables.
Values are in current prices.

four decades later, while raw materials rose from 44 percent to 54 percent. The value of manufactured goods imports rose by one-fifth over the period, while foodstuff imports rose 2.74 times and raw materials rose 3.64 times.

In this period of transition when the share of all workers engaged in manufacturing was rising, Britain became food deficit and resorted to importing more corn and animal products to make good its domestic output shortfall, in which rent-financed imports from Ireland were made to play a major role. It has been established through recent detailed empirical research into foodgrains production that the period of eighteenth century enclosures and capitalist transformation which is supposed to have raised productivity, in fact, saw actual *decline in per capita corn (wheat) output* and increasing reliance on imports. The five-decade-long agitation, the most prolonged in European history on a political economy issue, for more grain imports and against the Corn Laws, underscores the increasing food deficiency from domestic sources that Britain experienced. There was no 'agricultural revolution' in the sense of adequate rise in domestic productivity, as this author has argued elsewhere.[26] This is why foodstuffs imports remained so important. By the 1850s, the value of imported primary products far exceeded Britain's own domestic primary sector output.

The commodity structure of imports from the two major tropical colonised areas – Asia and the West Indies – is brought out in Table 9.3. Foodstuffs made up two-thirds of the total imports from these regions at the end of the eighteenth century with raw materials amounting to just over one-fifth. The share of foodstuffs actually rose between the triennia centred on 1785 and 1815, from 63 percent to 73 percent, before declining to just over half by the mid-1850s. The most important items of the foodstuffs accounting for not less than 88 percent of the total were sugar, coffee and tea, while the remainder comprised mainly tropical cereals and spices.

More than half of Britain's imports came from Asia, West Indies and Ireland during the last two periods of the eighteenth century (Table 9.4), and in the next three decades, the share never fell below 44 percent. Foodstuffs were especially important, averaging as much as 32 percent of the total of *all* imports into Britain during the two triennia 1784–1786 and 1794–1796. The consumption basket of the population was already changing fast as early as the first decades of the Industrial Revolution. The period 1785–1815, saw a trebling of the current value imports taking both the tropical colonies and Ireland, growing at 3.73 percent annually, while volumes continued to rise even after the post-Waterloo price deflation. The share

Table 9.3 Commodity structure of Britain's imports from Asia and West Indies, 1784–1786 to 1854–1856

	Asia and West Indies combined			
	Manufactures MF %	*Foodstuffs* FS %	*Raw materials* RM %	*All imports* M %
1784–1786	14.4	63.3	22.3	100
1794–1796	10.7	66.4	22.9	100
1804–1806	4	70.2	25.8	100
1814–1816	1.8	72.7	24.5	100
1824–1826	2	65.7	32.2	100
1834–1836	2.3	62.8	35	100
1844–1846	3.2	56.1	40.7	100
1854–1856	1.9	51.8	46.4	100

	Foodstuffs imports			*Raw materials*
	Sugar %	*Tea & coffee* %	*Both* %	*Raw cotton* %
1784–1786	27.4	28.8	56.2	6
1794–1796	36	23.6	59.6	2.9
1804–1806	33.4	31.2	64.6	2.6
1814–1816	38.2	25.5	63.7	3
1824–1826	33	25.7	58.7	5.9
1834–1836	31.4	23.7	55.1	11.1
1844–1846	32	17.5	49.5	11.2
1854–1856	22.1	18	40.1	15.9

Source: Calculated from Davis (1979) appendix tables.

Values are in current prices.

of manufactures in imports from Asia and West Indies declined from over 14 percent to below 2 percent over the seven decades from the mid-1780s to the mid-1850s while the share of raw materials rose the most, from 22.3 percent to 46.4 percent of the total imports, with raw cotton accounting for its largest component.

Britain carried out the bulk of its trade with Continental Europe according to the historians of this period. This is true of Britain's total exports, but as regards imports, the data show otherwise, that imports from its three colonised regions – Asia, West Indies and Ireland combined – considerably exceeded Britain's imports from the whole of

Table 9.4 Britain's imports from Asia, West Indies and Ireland by commodities, 1784–1786 to 1824–1826, £ million

	Manufactures MF	Foodstuffs FS	Raw materials RM	Total imports M
1784–1786	3.23	9.61	9.92	22.76
1794–1796	4.05	18.21	15.66	37.92
1804–1806	3.8	23.95	27.81	55.56
1814–1816	2.76	32.02	37.02	71.8
1824–1826	3.89	26.37	36.13	66.39

Share of Asia, West Indies and Ireland in Britain's

imports	of Manufactures MF	of foodstuffs FS	of raw materials RM	Total of all imports M
1784–1786	76	72.7	24.38	52.3
1794–1796	81.7	67.4	25.2	51.5
1804–1806	76.2	70.3	31.6	45.6
1814–1816	92.4	78.4	21.2	49.5
1824–1826	87.4	70.9	19.2	43.7

Source: Calculated from Davis (1979) appendix table.

Values are in current prices.

MF, FS and RM are manufactures, foodstuffs and raw materials, respectively.

Europe in every period up to 1825. Even excluding Ireland, the combined imports from Asia and West Indies exceeded the imports from Europe (Table 9.5). After 1825, the trade data are no longer separately available for Ireland, and the imports from Asia started falling a decade earlier, as textiles imports from India into Britain declined, substituted by Lancashire factory goods in European and other markets. This reduced Indian textile exports, hence, production, even before the new factory-made yarn and cloth started to be dumped into India itself. The demand for ending the East India Company's monopoly started from 1813 when its charter came up for renewal, and the process was completed by 1833.

There was a vital connection between Britain's trade with its tropical colonies and its trade with Europe. A substantial part of its imports from Europe could not have been financed at all without re-exporting tropical goods. Interestingly, Phyllis Deane had pointed this out in her sole-authored book *The First Industrial Revolution*, where she

Table 9.5 Britain's imports from Europe and from its colonies 1784–1786 to 1854–1856, three year average, £ million

	Europe	Asia & West Indies	Ireland	Colonies combined	GDP Britain
1784–1786	8.9	9.5	2.4	11.9	106
1794–1796	15	15.9	3.6	19.5	156
1804–1806	23.2	20.4	4.9	25.3	250
1814–1816	22.7	28.5	7	35.5	288
1824–1826	23.1	19.6	9.4	29	300
1834–1836	26.3	19.5	n.a.	n.a.	370
1844–1846	30.2	20.1	n.a.	n.a.	465
1854–1856	55.1	34.4	n.a.	n.a.	558

Source: Calculated from Davis (1979) appendix tables.

Mid-decade GDP interpolated from estimates in W.A.Cole (1981) and C. Feinstein and S. Pollard (1988).

showed that four-fifths of re-exports went to Europe, because while Britain's own domestic products faced inelastic demand, the tropical goods were in great demand on the continent, enabling Britain to purchase vital goods like bar-iron, timber and naval supplies like pitch and tar.[27] Yet, in her jointly authored book with W.A. Cole published only two years later, *British Economic Growth, Trends and Structure 1688 to 1959* (first printing 1967) not only was this important discussion omitted completely, but re-exports were actually wrongly eliminated from the trade series they presented, as we have seen.

As the factory system got under way from the 1780s, annual re-exports volumes to Europe trebled over the next decade, from £1.8 million during 1784–1786 to £5.5 million by 1794–1796 (Table 9.6). This rise is explained in part by the increased import of slave-produced goods from West Indies and partly by the quantum jump in land revenue collection in Bengal after the 1792 Permanent Settlement. About a third of the net Bengal revenues was used for purchasing and shipping out export goods, thus creating no external payment liability with India.[28] It did not matter that its own domestic exports to Europe grew only by 3 percent over the decade, the massive growth by 300 percent of re-exports meant that by 1794–1796 the ratio of re-exports to domestic exports reached an astonishing 99.3 percent, namely, the purchasing power of Britain's domestic exports was doubled.

In Table 9.6, Britain's trade deficit with Europe and the United States is shown both without taking re-exports into account (total imports TM from Europe minus exports of domestically produced

Table 9.6 Britain's trade balance with Europe and the United States, 1784–1786 to 1854–1856, three year average, £ million

	Domestic exports DX	Re-exports RXM	Total exports TX	Total imports TM	Trade Balance B1 = DX – TM	Trade Balance B2 = TX – TM
Europe						
1784–1786	5.35	1.86	7.21	8.93	–3.58	–1.72
1794–1796	5.53	5.5	11.03	15.04	–9.51	–4.01
1804–1806	13.72	6.55	20.27	23.19	–9.47	–2.92
1814–1816	21.14	14.19	35.33	22.72	–1.58	12.61
1824–1826	13.9	6.13	20.03	23.12	–9.22	–3.09
1834–1836	17.61	7.27	24.88	26.34	–8.73	–1.46
1844–1846	23.25	7.44	30.69	30.19	-6.94	0.5
1854–1856	32.99	16.54	49.53	55.08	–22.09	–5.55
United States						
1784–1786	2.84	0.21	3.05	1.16	1.68	1.89
1794–1796	6.4	0.24	6.64	1.94	4.46	4.7
1804–1806	10.14	0.27	10.42	4.17	5.97	6.25
1814–1816	7.35	0.25	7.59	3.98	3.37	3.61
1824–1826	5.69	0.31	6	6.06	–0.37	–0.6
1834–1836	9.44	0.78	10.22	13.22	–3.78	–3
1844–1846	7.16	0.55	7.71	14.06	–6.9	–6.35
1854–1856	20.08	0.81	20.89	30.28	–10.2	–9.39
Europe and the United States						
1784–1786	8.19	2.07	10.26	10.09	–1.9	0.17
1794–1796	11.93	5.74	17.67	16.98	–5.05	0.69
1804–1806	23.86	6.82	30.69	27.36	–3.5	3.33
1814–1816	28.49	14.44	42.92	26.7	1.79	16.22
1824–1826	19.6	6.44	26.03	29.18	–9.59	–3.69
1834–1836	27.05	8.05	35.1	39.56	–12.51	–4.46
1844–1846	30.41	7.99	38.4	44.25	–13.84	–5.85
1854–1856	53.07	17.35	70.42	85.36	–32.29	–14.94

Source: Calculated from Davis (1979) appendix tables.

Values are in current prices.

goods DX) as well as the deficit after factoring in re-exports. Had Britain imported what it did from Europe against its domestic exports alone, it would have run up an unsustainable trade deficit of over 6 percent of GDP by 1794–1796. Owing to re-exports, which equalled the value of its domestic exports, the actual deficit was reduced to a manageable 2.6 percent of GDP. There was another large spurt of re-exports, more than double between the triennia centred on 1805 and 1815 when the country was deeply embroiled in the continuing Napoleonic wars. This re-exports spurt turned the deficit which Britain had with Europe considering its domestic exports alone, into a substantial surplus by 1814–1816. Ever since 1700, the consumption of Asian cotton textiles had been banned in Britain, and the East India Company had imported Asian cloth wholly for re-export, mainly to European countries. Later, as exports from Britain's new factory sector grew at the expense of India's textile exports to the continent, the re-exports as percentage of domestic exports to Europe dropped, but they still remained a substantial 32 percent or more, right up to the middle of the nineteenth century.

Britain had enforced a positive trade balance with the United States until its war of independence by mercantilist laws that prevented the American colonists from manufacturing a range of goods and obliging them to rely on imports from Britain and by banning import directly from third countries: but the impact of these policies ended before 1814–1816. Up to that point, Britain's positive trade balance with the United States compensated for its negative balance with Europe, but thereafter, the balance with the United States turned into a deficit as increasing volumes of raw cotton, tobacco and foodgrains were imported. The combined deficit with the Europe and the United States taking domestic exports alone, rose fast after 1815 to reach a massive £32 million or nearly 6 percent of GDP by 1854–1856: only re-exports halved the deficit to 2.8 percent.

The combined deficit with Asia and the West Indies ranged between 4 percent and 6 percent of Britain's GDP up to 1814–1816 which saw a sudden price deflation following the end of the Napoleonic wars. While in volume terms total trade continued to grow, in value terms it declined during the next two decades and spurted thereafter to reach £54 million by 1854–1856, entailing a deficit of £16 million for Britain. This deficit would have been much larger if India had not been kept compulsorily trade-liberalised to absorb increasing volumes of British textiles, entailing substantial de-industrialisation.

The historians of growth and trade in Britain have never conceptually linked any part of its trade with the property systems that Britain established in its colonies. They never referred to the increased tax collections in India and exports using taxes or the expanding slave-based plantation system generating slave rents taken in commodity form and imported from the West Indies, so they have always felt very uneasy about the tremendous growth of trade in tropical commodities and of re-exports, since they were unable to explain it.

Imports from Europe, the United States, Asia and the West Indies, detailed by Tables 9.4–9.8, made up 87 percent of all Britain's imports taking the five periods 1785–1825. Imports from Ireland contributed another 10.7 percent of Britain's total imports; Britain systematically ran a trade deficit with Ireland too after 1810, which reached

Table 9.7 Britain's trade with Asia and the West Indies and trade balance as share of GDP, 1784–1786 to 1854–1856, three year averages in £ million

	Domestic exports DX	Re- exports RXM	Total exports TX	Total imports TM	Trade balance		As share of GDP	
					B1 = (DX – TM)	B2 = (TX – TM)	B1/ GDP %	B2/ GDP %
ASIA								
1784–1786	1.81	0.07	1.88	4.95	–3.14	–2.07	–3	–2.9
1794–1796	3.54	0.09	3.63	7.34	–3.8	–3.71	–2.4	–2.4
1804–1806	2.7	0.29	2.99	8.01	–5.31	–5.02	–2.1	–2
1814–1816	2.76	0.44	3.2	11.8	–9.04	–8.6	–3.1	–3
1824–1826	3.68	•0.66	4.34	11.02	–7.34	–6.68	–2.4	–2.2
1834–1836	4.85	0.73	5.58	11.54	–6.68	–5.96	–1.8	–1.6
1844–1846	9.64	0.82	10.46	14.12	–4.48	–3.66	–1	–0.8
1854–1856	13.46	0.6	14.06	25.7	–12.24	–11.64	–2.2	–2.1
WEST INDIES								
1784–1786	1.43	0.14	1.57	4.57	–3.14	–3	–3	–2.8
1794–1796	4.49	0.55	5.04	8.59	–4.1	–3.55	–2.6	–2.3
1804–1806	7.26	0.57	7.83	12.4	–5.14	–4.57	–2.1	–1.8
1814–1816	6.91	0.37	7.28	16.66	–9.75	–9.38	–3.4	–3.3
1824–1826	4.12	0.28	4.4	8.58	–4.46	–4.18	–1.5	–1.4
1834–1836	4.12	0.39	4.51	7.95	–3.83	–3.44	–1	–0.9
1844–1846	3.87	0.38	4.25	5.94	–2.07	–1.69	–0.4	–0.4
1854–1856	3.95	0.25	4.2	8.71	–4.76	–4.51	–0.9	–0.8
ASIA + WEST INDIES								
1784–1886	3.24	0.21	3.45	9.52	–6.28	–6.07	–6	–5.7
1794–1896	8.03	0.64	8.67	15.93	–7.9	–7.26	–5	–4.7
1804–1806	9.96	0.86	10.82	20.41	–10.45	–9.59	–4.2	–3.8
1814–1816	9.67	0.81	10.48	28.45	–18.79	–17.98	–6.5	–6.3
1824–1826	7.8	0.94	8.74	19.6	–11.8	–10.86	–3.9	–3.6
1834–1836	8.97	1.12	9.83	19.49	–10.51	–9.4	–2.8	–2.5
1844–1846	13.61	1.19	14.71	20.06	–6.55	–5.35	–1.4	–1.2
1854–1856	17.41	0.85	18.26	34.41	–17	–16.15	–3.1	–2.9

Source: Calculated from Davis (1979) appendix tables. Values are in current prices. For GDP estimates, see Table 9.5.

Table 9.8 Britain's trade balance with Ireland 1784–1786 to 1824–1826

	Domestic export DX	Re-export of import RXM	Total export TX	Total import TM	Trade Balance B1 = DX – TM	B2 = TX – TM
1784–1786	0.92	0.93	1.85	2.38	–1.46	–0.53
1794–1796	2.26	1.4	3.66	3.59	–1.33	0.07
1804–1806	3.71	1.52	5.23	4.94	–1.23	0.29
1814–1816	3.53	1.66	5.19	7.06	–3.53	–1.87
1824–1826	4.61	1.52	6.13	9.41	–4.8	–3.28

Source: Calculated from Davis (1979) Appendix tables. Values are in current prices.

£3.3 million by 1824–1826. We are thus talking of regions accounting for 97.7 percent of Britain's imports, where imports exceeded exports and the country incurred large deficits, totalling one-tenth of its GDP. In addition, Britain also ran a rising trade deficit with China for most of the period before the forcible opening of China's ports in the 1840s to opium exports from India. The question then arises, if Britain incurred deficits with every country and region with which it traded, how did the country pay for these deficits and balance its payments? Legitimate invisible incomes were small during this period and do not provide the answer.

Financing deficits with sovereign regions using transfers from colonies

All English official data for imports in this period, whether constant value or current, are for imports at port of origin and are not the landed cost, namely, they are imports *f.o.b.* and not imports *c.i.f.* To obtain the landed cost, about one-third by way of combined invisible charges of freight, insurance and commission – or 'freight' for short – had to be added to the official total import figures according to Deane and Cole, which they did to obtain a series for total imports *c.i.f.* But we have deliberately not attempted to obtain landed cost from Davis' imports *f.o.b.* figures. First, since these invisible payments for 'freight' went as income entirely to British firms, by deducting imports *f.o.b.* from exports *f.o.b.*, the 'trade balance' we obtain is close to Britain's current account balance, entailing higher surpluses and lower deficits for Britain. Second, we have stayed with the Davis official imports *f.o.b.* figures because the average one-third mark-up applicable to total imports from all parts of the world to obtain landed cost, will not do. The tropical areas were much more distant, and the mark-up was at least 50 percent, while for Europe it was only about 15 percent. Merchandise trade deficits of Britain using the imports *c.i.f.* concept would be relatively larger for trade with the colonies than for trade with nearby areas.

Not one of the historians of British trade and industrialisation has constructed Tables 9.6–9.8, showing Britain's trade balances with different regions, even though the basic data series were available. Had they done so, they would have faced the awkward question of how Britain could possibly have attained external balance. While Davis compiled the primary data series we have worked with, he did not concern himself with the question of trade balance. No writer seems to have noticed an apparently insuperable inconsistency – that Britain had trade deficits even after including a large part of invisibles, with *every* part of the world, especially after 1814–1816, when the surplus with Ireland and the United States turned into a deficit in both cases. Britain could not possibly have paid for such large global deficits. By 1835, its own domestic exports fell short of its imports from the continent plus the United States, to the extent of £ 12.5 million, amounting to 3.4 percent of its GDP, and by 1855, the figure had ballooned to £32 million deficit, a massive 5.8 percent of GDP. Only the re-exports of mainly tropical products reduced its deficit to 2.7 percent of GDP. But it had very large deficits with the colonised areas: the excess of Britain's imports from Asia and the West Indies over its total exports to these regions, by 1815, had reached a high of £19 million, amounting to 6.2 percent of Britain's GDP.

If we treat the trade with colonies formally on par with the trade with sovereign areas, as the historians of Britain have always done, then the rising combined deficit with the temperate plus tropical areas (but excluding Ireland) by 1835 amounted to 8.6 percent of Britain's GDP. Using the alternative trade balance by deducting imports *c.i.f.* from exports, the deficit would have been even higher, 4.8 percent with Europe and USA plus 5.2 percent with Asia and West Indies totalling 10 percent of GDP. This is an unsustainable order of trade deficit even by modern standards when international lending institutions exist to tide countries over balance of payments difficulties, which was not the case then. Britain either needed to earn invisible incomes to the same enormous extent as its trade deficits so as to attain current account balance, or if invisible earnings fell short, it needed to either send out specie (monetary silver and gold) in payment, or borrow from its creditors in order to balance its external payments.

However, Britain's invisible earnings from overseas at this date were insignificant, since the capital invested abroad was small. Feinstein and Pollard,[29] in their definitive work on capital formation (see Table 9.9), estimate the cumulated holdings abroad by Britain between 1761 and 1800 to have reached at most £4 million by the latter date. Britain was a small maritime country with a population of barely 9 million persons in 1801,[30] quite developed by the standards of the time but very far from being an economic giant. Even if we assume an unrealistically high 20 percent rate of return on its foreign capital holdings, only £0.8 million could have been the invisibles dividends inflow – a trivial sum compared to the £6.3 million total deficit with Europe, the United States, Ireland, Asia and the West Indies combined; the actual deficit is larger once the trade with China is factored in. By 1835, the total holdings abroad were £14.6 million giving at the most £2.9 annual return, far below the total £14 million trade deficit for this period.

Table 9.9 Investment: Great Britain 1761–1860 and United Kingdom 1851–1860 (£ million)

	Gross domestic fixed capital formation	Increase in stocks and work in progress	Total	Net investment abroad	GNP at 1851–1860 prices
Great Britain at 1851–1860 prices					
1761–1770	7.4	1.1	8.5	0.7	93
1771–1780	9.4	1.9	11.3	0.7	98
1781–1790	11.2	2	13.2	1.3	111
1791–1800	13.7	3	16.7	1.3	134
1801–1810	16	1.4	17.4	−2	161
1811–1820	19.2	3.1	22.3	5.6	203
1821–1830	25.1	5.7	30.8	7.8	–
1831–1840	35.1	1.6	36.7	4.4	–
1841–1850	46.9	4.8	51.7	7.3	–
1851–1860	53.3	4.7	58	18.9	–
UK at 1851–1860 prices					
1851–1860	55.7	4.7	60.4	18.9	–
UK at 1900 prices					
1851–1860	60	4	64	19	–

Source: Feinstein and Pollard (1988, Appendix Table XX, p. 466) and Feinstein 1981, p. 136 for GNP at 1851–1860 prices.

Earnings from freight, insurance and commission are already taken into account since Davis's import figures relate to current value imports at the port of origin (imports *f.o.b.*), as explained earlier, and so total import values are on average around 33 percent lower than if the landed cost had been taken. In effect, the deficits documented in these data are not just merchandise trade deficits which would be much larger, but they approximate the current account deficits Britain incurred. The country did not have a fraction of the gold and silver required to meet the deficit through specie outflow, nor did any European country have the resources to lend such a sum to it. Moreover, far from borrowing, according to the Feinstein and Pollard estimates, Britain was a net exporter of capital throughout the period except one decade, 1800–1810 (see Table 9.10). So the question remains – how did the country not only meet its huge trade deficits with every region in the world, but actually invest abroad, apart from undertaking the rising internal investment required for making the transition to factory production which took place in this period. This is a question which has not been posed, let alone answered by the economic historians.

We have provided the answer already: the data make no sense at all if the deficits on colonial trade are treated conceptually on par with deficits with sovereign regions. But the fact was that Britain's trade with its tropical colonies and with Ireland was qualitatively quite different from its trade with sovereign regions like Europe and the United States. Trade deficits with sovereign countries created an external liability for Britain, which had to be settled through outflow of specie, or by borrowing, or a combination of the two. But the trade deficit with the colonised areas where Britain had established tax collection rights or extracted land rent or slave rent, was a pure transfer. It created no liability for Britain because the import surplus was simply the commodity form of taxes or rents wrung from peasants and tenants or slave rents in product form. (Slave rent is the surplus of slave produced net output over the cost of slave subsistence.)

When we add up the import surplus from Asia, the West Indies and Ireland and remove the negative sign from the total recognising that Britain's deficits with its colonies were not the result of normal trade but, being tax or rent-financed, represented transfer, we see that it averaged over 5 percent of GDP for the first five triennia, up to 1825 and declined thereafter. With the addition of transfers, Britain's overall negative balance becomes a positive one for every period up to 1824–1826, but after this it remains negative. However, this is because the transfer from Ireland can no longer be estimated after 1825, since

Table 9.10 Britain's trade deficit with Europe and the United States compared with transfer from Asia, the West Indies and Ireland (1784–1786 to 1854–1856, £ million)

	1	2	3	4	5
	Europe and the United States	Ireland	Asia and The West Indies	Combined nominal deficit	GDP
1784–1786	−1.9	−1.46	−6.1	−9.46	106
1794–1796	−5.1	−1.33	−7.3	−13.73	156
1804–1806	−3.5	−1.23	−9.6	−14.33	250
1814–1816	1.8	−3.53	−18	−19.73	288
1824–1826	−9.6	−4.8	−10.9	−25.3	300
1834–1836	−12.5	*n.a.*	−9.6	−22.1	370
1844–1846	−12.8	*n.a.*	−5.4	−18.2	465
1854–1856	−32.3	*n.a.*	−16.1	−48.4	558

	6	7	8	9	10
	Combined nominal deficit / GDP, %	Transfer from Ireland	Transfer from Asia and West Indies	Total transfer (7 + 8)	Net balance (9–1)
1784–1786	−8.9	1.46	6.1	6.56	4.66
1794–1796	−8.8	1.33	7.3	8.63	3.53
1804–1806	−5.7	1.23	9.6	10.83	7.33
1814–1816	−6.9	3.53	18	21.53	23.33
1824–1826	−8.4	4.8	10.9	15.7	6.1
1834–1836	−6	*n.a.*	9.6	9.6	−2.9
1844–1846	−3.9	*n.a.*	5.4	5.4	−7.4
1854–1856	−8.7	*n.a.*	16.1	16.1	−16.2

Source: Trade data calculated from Davis (1979) appendix tables. For GDP estimates, see Table 9.5.

its trade data were merged with those of Britain. The exploitation of Irish tenants, if anything, intensified after this with larger costless rent-financed imports of wheat and livestock products into Britain. This culminated in the great famine of 1846–1847, when one million Irish starved to death because they had to continue to export wheat even while their cheap staple, the potato crop failed. This early Victorian holocaust still remains inadequately documented and analysed.

Academics sometimes object to the term 'costless' imports because they say that nationals in the metropolis paid fully for the goods imported from colonies and indeed paid prices which were high owing to the distance the goods travelled, and high traders' margins – so the only people who benefited were the traders making profits. This, however, misses the fact that individual agents and the macro-economy are different entities. Individuals clearly must have been willing to pay the price, however high, for the tropical goods, otherwise the trade would not have existed in the first place. (No one forced David Ricardo to consume imported coffee sweetened with imported sugar, to drink imported wine, to wear a shirt made with imported raw cotton while writing at a desk made of imported mahogany – all goods which could never be produced in England – while formulating his fallacious theory which assumed that 'all countries produce all goods'.)

The relevant point is that for the country as a whole, if its nationals have such a high propensity to consume imported goods that the country's imports exceed its exports, namely, there is a deficit on current account, then this under normal conditions always creates an external liability for that country which has to be settled, either through outflow of specie, namely, financial silver and gold to the required extent, or by allowing foreign nations to hold claims against it namely, by borrowing, or a combination of the two. The large deficit on trade with the colonies created no such external liability for Britain and so for that country, the goods were costless, representing the transfer in commodity form, of taxes and rents wrung from subjugated populations. But mainstream economic and historical studies have never recognised either the special nature of total export surplus from the colonies or the very high degree of dependence of the rise of capitalist industrialisation on these transfers.

Conclusion

In view of the analysis presented here, it will not surprise the reader that Britain continued to follow the same pattern of using the exchange earnings of its colonies, in particular the largest and most lucrative colony India, in an even more heightened and intensified form during the period of high imperialism from 1870 to the end of First World War. Britain ran rising deficits on current account (merchandise plus invisibles) with the continent, North America and the regions of recent settlement, while also lending to these regions, thus, running up very large balance of payments deficits. It would have been impossible for it to do so without access to the rising foreign exchange earnings of its colonies, which were entirely appropriated by Britain to settle its own deficits and to export capital.

The capitalist industrialisation of the European countries, North America and the regions of recent European settlement generated rising demand for tropical goods for use as raw materials and directly for consumption. India's export surplus with the world, and hence, exchange earnings, rose extremely fast, even while its own per capita income hardly grew. From the 1890s right up to 1928, India posted the second largest merchandise export surplus in the world, second only to that by the United States. The basic data from the United Nations (1960) matrix of world trade showing this, have been presented earlier by this author.[31] Suffice it to say that by 1911–1913, the Indian subcontinent's export earnings from the world reached $765 million, while export surplus earnings were $175 million, serving to finance 40 percent of Britain's global deficits. By 1928, the Indian sub-continent's global export earnings, despite already falling prices, reached a peak of $1392 million, and export surplus earnings, excluding UK trade, were nearly half a billion dollars at $497 million, not surpassed by any country except the United States and entirely appropriated by Britain, as always. The subsequent precipitous decline of India's exchange earnings with the sharp fall of global primary product prices (there was a 80 percent drop in earnings between 1925 and 1931), meant that the major source of support for Britain's balance of payments disappeared, marking its final demise as word capitalist leader.

For the last quarter century, the United States has been running continuous current account deficits with the world, and this could only be sustained, since it does not have colonies or access to transfers in the old form, by borrowing explicitly from its creditors, making it the world's largest debtor. Britain with direct political control was in a stronger position and could ensure that the pound sterling would be considered 'as good as gold', as long as it could appropriate its colonies' global exchange earnings and so maintain the fiction that it was meeting its international payments and exporting capital solely out of its own resources.

Notes

1 Binay Bhushan Chaudhuri, *The Growth of Commercial Agriculture in Bengal 1777–1900*, Calcutta: Bengal Past and Present, 1964.
2 Bernald Bernard H. Slicher van Bath *The Agrarian History of Western Europe A.D. 500 to 1850*, London: Mathew Arnold, 1963.
3 Utsa Patnaik, 'Tribute Transfer and the Balance of Payments in the *Cambridge Economic History of India, Vol.11*', *Social Scientist*, 12(12); reprinted in Utsa Patnaik, *The Long Transition: Essays on Political Economy*, New Delhi: Tulika Books, 1999, pp. 305–22.

4 Angus Maddison, *The World Economy, Volume 1: A Millennial Perspective, Volume 2: Historical Statistics*, OECD Development Centre, 2003.
5 Christopher Hill, *Reformation to Industrial Revolution: The Making of Modern English Society, 1530–1780*, New York: Pantheon Books, 1967.
6 Seymour Drescher and Stanley L. Engerman, *A Historical Guide to World Slavery*, New York: Oxford University Press, 1998.
7 Dadabhai Naoroji, *Poverty and Un-British Rule in India*, New Delhi: Govt. of India, Reprint, 1962. (First published in 1901).
8 Romesh C. Dutt, *The Economic History of India Vol. 1: Under Early British Rule 1757–1837; Vol. 2: In the Victorian Age, 1837–1900*. First published in 1903 and 1905, New Delhi: Govt. of India.Second reprint by arrangement with Routledge & Kegan Paul, London, 1970.
9 Paul Mantoux, *The Industrial Revolution in the 18th Century*, London: Methuen, 1928.
10 Sayera Habib, 'Colonial Exploitation and Capital Formation in England in the Early Stages of Industrial Revolution', Proceedings of the Indian History Congress, Aligarh, 1975.
11 Utsa Patnaik, 'The Free Lunch: Transfers From the Tropical Colonies and Their Role in Capital Formation in Britain During the Industrial Revolution', in K.S. Jomo (ed.), *Globalization under Hegemony – The Changing World Economy*, New Delhi: Oxford University Press, 2006, pp. 30–70.
12 S.B. Saul, *Studies in British Overseas Trade, 1870–1914*, Liverpool: Liverpool University Press, 1960.
13 Marcello De Cecco, *The International Gold Standard: Money and Empire*, London: F. Pinter, 1984.
14 For a brief discussion of the mechanism of transfer, see Utsa Patnaik and Prabhat Patnaik, *A Theory of Imperialism*, New York/New Delhi: Columbia University/Tulika Books, 2016.
15 League of Nations, *The Network of World Trade*, Economic Intelligence Service, League of Nations, Geneva: Princeton University Press, 1942.
16 United Nations, 'International Trade Statistics 1900–1960', 1962, www.unstats.un.org/unsd/trade/imts/Historicaldata1900-1960.pdf (accessed on 15 June 2012).
17 Thomas Piketty, *Capital in the 21st Century*, Translated by A. Goldhammer, Cambridge, MA: Harvard University Press, 2014.
18 David Ricardo, *Principles of Political Economy and Taxation*, Volume 1, Piero Sraffa (ed.) and Maurice Dobb (editorial assistance), *The Works and Correspondence of David Ricardo*, Cambridge: Cambridge University Press, 1970.
19 Utsa Patnaik, 'Ricardo's Fallacy – Mutual Benefit From Trade Based on Comparative Costs and Specialisation?' in K.S. Jomo (ed.), *The Pioneers of Development Economics*, New Delhi: Tulika Books, 2005, pp. 31–41.
20 Rosa Luxemburg, *The Accumulation of Capital*, London: Routledge, 1963.
21 Phyllis Deane and W.A. Cole, *British Economic Growth, 1688–1959 – Trends and Structure*, 2nd edition, Cambridge: Cambridge University Press, 1969.
22 Paul R. Krugman and Maurice Obstfeld, *International Economics: Theory and Policy*, New York: Harper Collins, 1994.

23 B.R. Mitchell and Phyllis Deane, *Abstract of British Historical Statistics*, Cambridge: Cambridge University Press, 1962.
24 Utsa Patnaik, 'New Estimates of 18th Century British Trade and Their Relation to Transfers from the Colonies', in T.J. Byres, K.N. Panikkar and U. Patnaik (eds.), *The Making of History – Essays Presented to IrfanHabib*, New Delhi: Tulika, 2000, pp. 359–402.
25 Ralph Davis, *The Industrial Revolution and British Overseas Trade*, Leicester: Leicester University Press, 1979.
26 Utsa Patnaik, 'The "Agricultural Revolution" in England: Its Cost for the English Working Class and the Colonies', in Shireen Moosvi (ed.), *Capitalism, Colonialism and Globalisaton*, New Delhi: Aligarh Historians Society and Tulika Books, 2011, pp. 17–27.
27 Phyllis Deane, *The First Industrial Revolution*, Cambridge: Cambridge University Press, 1965.
28 Dutt, *Economic History of India Vol.1*.
29 Charles Feinstein and Sidney Pollard, *Studies in Capital Formation in the United Kingdom, 1750–1920*, Cambridge: Cambridge University Press, 1988.
30 R.D. Lee and R.S. Schofield, 'British Population in the Eighteenth Century', in Roderick Floud and D.N. McCloskey (eds.), *The Economic History of Britain Since 1700, Vol.1 1700–1860*, Cambridge: Cambridge University Press, 1981, pp. 17–35.
31 Utsa Patnaik, 'India in the World Economy 1900–1950: The Inter-War Depression and Britain's Demise as World Capitalist Leader', *Social Scientist*, January–February 2014, 42(1–2): 13–35.

10 Unrequited exports of labour from India in late-nineteenth and early-twentieth centuries

Britain's financial interest in plantation colonies

Sunanda Sen[1]

Background

One can observe, by the end of the nineteenth century, a noticeable change in the mode of expropriation of colonies within the British empire, moving from piracy and robbery on part of merchants in the high seas to settled cultivation in the plantation islands.

Slavery, however, ended in the plantation islands in successive stages, often backed by attempts of 'abolitionists' in England who started voicing protests as early as 1796. A formal end to slavery, announced for the British colonies on 28 August 1833, with the passing of the Slavery Abolition Act[2] in British Parliament, was followed by a withdrawal of slave trade in the British-owned plantation and other colonies. The Act effectively outlawed British participation in the slave trade from Africa, thus terminating two-thirds of such trade by British citizens. While such trade in the non-British colonies was to continue on an informal basis for some more time, the slave population in overseas colonies started declining as fresh supplies were turned off. Between 1807 and 1834, the number of enslaved people in the British Caribbean, as a whole, had already decreased by 14 percent, with similar shrinkages in the slave population in the British colony of Mauritius in the Indian Ocean. The decline was most marked in the relatively new sugar-producing colonies of British Guiana and Trinidad, which had already received the highest proportion of African-born slaves.[3]

Slavery, coming to an end in British colonies by the 1830s, did put the plantation islands under Britain in a fix due to shortages of labour. While slaves were freed in terms of the 1833 Act, they could voluntarily remain attached to their past owners in terms of an apprenticeship system which, too, came to an end by August 1840.[4] Incidentally, an initiative was taken by the British government to set aside £20 million as compensation to the plantation owners for losses in their 'property' due to end of slave labour.[5] Such measures were clearly indicative of British financial stakes in the fortunes of those plantations.

With planters failing to turn labour power into a commodity, as they previously could under slavery, attempts were made by the planters as well as by British commercial and financial agencies to seek 'an alternative and politically acceptable form of unfree labour', which was finally found by indenturing labour from British colonies like India.[6] Changes as above brought in the new category of labour, who faced 'restrictions on freedom of movement, penalties for negligence', and 'absence of work' considered 'criminal offence'. Thus, labour as above was 'in practice near bondage due to dispossession and fear of vagabonding which was punishable'.[7]

Faced with shortage of labourers, at end of slavery, the planters started pressuring the British government to help out their fortunes, which was in a state of disarray. Given the arduousness of the work and the low wages the planters were ready to pay, it soon became apparent that it was only those who were too poor to pay their own passage to the islands would accept such terms of employment. Though labour from around the Atlantic was tapped in the first instance for plantations in the West Indies, the search for an adequate supply of recruits soon targeted the denser populations of Asia which included those in the poverty and famine-stricken India. One recalls at this point the severe famines in India around 1897 and later in 1907–1908.[8]

Helping out sugar plantations with fortunes often close to those of the London city, the British government started organizing large-scale emigration of indentured labourers from India to the plantation colonies. Thus began indenturing as a major form of labour transport, from large Asian economies like India and China to the overseas plantations.

The indenturing of labour from the British colonies like India, which continued until the 1920s, was a quick solution to redress the problems faced by the plantation islands. As pointed out by the Royal Commission of Labour in 1892, 'importation of East Indian Coolies did much to rescue the sugar industry from bankruptcy'.[9]

It may be recalled here that by the second half of the nineteenth century, Britain had already taken possession of several older colonies that soon were major importers of indentured labour needed for plantation. These included the islands of Trinidad, acquired from Spain in 1797, Mauritius/Isle de France taken from France in 1810 and British

Guiana, annexed from Holland in 1814.[10] As for India, which was under the direct administration of the British Crown since 1858, these island plantation colonies of Britain turned out as a major destination for the indentured labour from the country. In effect, Britain was enabled to use her colonies both as source as well as destinations of indentured labour.

Operating in alliance with the colonial office in Britain and in league with the Indian government, shipments of indentured labour proved effective in ensuring steady supplies to the plantations. In this the state power, as well as finance, in Britain had a significant role to 'replace free workers (erstwhile slaves) with unfree equivalents' under indenturing. By this, as has been observed, 'legal, political and economic systems . . . served to limit worker rights and incomes'; in effect this provided a basis for the creation of unfree labour which could be coerced through 'threat or physical violence or (state administered) legal compulsion'.[11]

The new form of labour movements took place across the high seas till 1920, when the practice of indenturing ended. Such movements relied as much on the West's 'informal' empire of financial and commercial networks as it did on the 'formal' empire of colonies. In general, as the cost of ocean travel was going down and its speed was higher than in the nineteenth century, distant parts of the world became accessible to the Western imperial powers. By one calculation, the volume of world trade rose ten-fold between 1850 and 1913.[12] Trade in labour across the seas was one aspect of the above.

Transactions involving India, the plantation islands and Britain in this period, present a web of triangular trade. Above encompassed the indentured labour flows to plantations, exports of raw sugar from plantations to Britain, exports of white sugar from Britain to other destinations and, simultaneously, investments by British plantation owners in plantation estates. In addition trade, as above, considerably aided the shipping lines owned by British merchants.

Fortunes of sugar plantations determined the changing flows of indentured labour

The large flow of indentured labour from India and China which moved to the plantation islands in the late nineteenth and the early twentieth centuries was comparable in numerical terms to the number of slaves from Africa who arrived in the Americas during late eighteenth and early nineteenth centuries. Of those indentured labourers, two-thirds came from India.[13]

Details relating to the timing as well as the direction in above labour flows indicate that those movements were subject to conditions prevailing in both the originating and the receiving areas, thus confirming the relevance of both push and the pull factors which are often used to explain migration in the literature. An explanation of the migrant flows from India in terms of the 'push factors' has to dwell on the socio-economic conditions relating to the domestic economy, relying, in particular, on conditions in the eastern and northern part of India, from where most of the immigration took place. The peak flow, between the eight years 1856–1865, reached 36,145 persons per year on an average. The period also witnessed the political and economic dislocations of the 1857 Sepoy Mutiny in North India and, in later years, distress for people connected with famine and the related destitutions through the 1890s. Both famines and the political disruptions did have an impact on the flow of migration from the country over the subsequent decades, with the flow rising to 74,100 in 1891/1892 and 95,616 in 1900/1901. On the whole, the causal links between migration and the political as well as economic disturbances in India during the nineteenth century were close enough to be interpreted as a push factor to explain the indentured labour flows.

However, from an alternate perspective, which in literature has been described as a 'pull factor', the changing flows of migration from India can also be explained by variations in the demand for such labour in the individual plantations. Immigration can thus be linked to the changing scale of cultivation in those islands. As can be observed, growth in sugar cultivation in the plantations continued to provide a major link to actual flows of immigrant labour from India during the period. The three major factors which determined the scale of cultivation in sugar plantations, include: (a) exports of raw sugar from these islands to Britain, (b) the duty structure on imports of sugar (raw and processed) in Britain and (c) the financial state of plantation estates.

Flows of indentured labour from India, initially reaching out both Mauritius and West Indies during the earlier years of indenturing, declined sharply for Mauritius by the quinquennium 1886–1870.[14] It can be observed that the peak level of sugar output which was produced in Mauritius by the 1860s overlapped with the flow of immigrant labour reaching a peak during 1831–1860. In percentage terms, the proportion of migrant labourers which moved to Mauritius was also the highest between 1851 and 1860 (see Figures 10.1 and 10.2).

230   *Sunanda Sen*

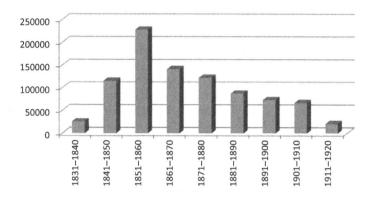

Figure 10.1 Emigration to Mauritius and British Caribbean

Source: David Northrup, *Indentured Labour in the Age of Imperialism*, Cambridge University Press, 1955: Appendix.

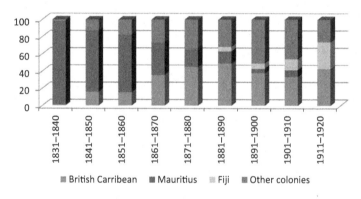

Figure 10.2 Destination of emigration in shares

Source: David Northrup, *Indentured Labour in the Age of Imperialism*, Cambridge University Press, 1955: Appendix.

The decade, as above, also recorded the highest level of immigration from India if one combines the flows to Mauritius and the British Caribbean (see Figure 10.1).

As is evident from the pattern and scale of cultivation in the plantation colonies, raw sugar provided the mainstay of these plantations, while simultaneously instituting the major plank in forging the economic and political links of Britain and those islands.

For Mauritius, the output of raw sugar hit a peak by the 1860s and then remained at around the same average until further declines. Sugar

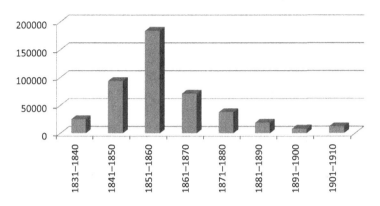

Figure 10.3 Emigration to Mauritius

Source: David Northrup, *Indentured Labour in the Age of Imperialism,* Cambridge University Press, 1955: Appendix.

output in Mauritius shot up, from 11,000 tons in 1825 to 21,000 tons in 1828 and then to 100,000 tons in 1854. However, since the 1860s, sugar production in Mauritius started declining, due to the availability of sugar from other countries (primarily Brazil), the production of beet sugar in Europe, the opening of Suez canal in 1869 which diverted traffic from the Indian ocean and finally, with the drop in sugar prices.[15] This was matched by a slowing down in the rate of population growth for Mauritius.[16]

As for plantations in the British Caribbean, their share in the flows of indentured labour from India rose after 1865, while reaching a peak during 1881–1890, a decade which also coincided with rising levels of sugar production in those islands. Earlier than that, the end of slavery in 1833 and of apprenticeship in 1840 had caused a drop in the share of British West Indian islands in Indian emigration during 1831–1860. On the whole, flows of immigrants and the scale of sugarcane production moved together in British Caribbean, as in Mauritius. The region turned out to be the dominant world producer of cane sugar by the last quarter of nineteenth century, with the British Caribbean as the largest supplier of raw sugar output.

British tariff structure to determine fortunes of plantations

As mentioned above, the tariff structure in Britain had a bearing on imports of sugar from different sources. The variations included differential rates of duties, both on different categories as well as from different sources. As for the different varieties, rates on refined sugar, usually imported from non-British colonies, had been higher than those on raw sugar till 1874, while thereafter, all duties on sugar were completely removed in Britain. Rates of duties on unrefined sugar (Muscovado), mostly imported from British-owned colonies (West Indies and Mauritius), remained till 1874 as the lowest. However, rates also varied between sources, with higher rates of duties levied on imports from Mauritius (as compared to those from West Indies) till 1846, when the rates were equalised across plantation islands; thus ending the preferential rates so far enjoyed by the West Indies. The preferential duties enjoyed by the West Indies colonies on their exports of sugar to Britain till 1846 enabled the West Indies to get a larger share in British imports as compared to the share of the eastern island, Mauritius. The pattern continued even after the rates were equalised in 1846 or even when abolished in 1874 (see Figure 10.4).

Imports of raw sugar from the plantation colonies at little or no duty in terms of the differential duty structure enabled Britain to retain its monopoly power in the processing of brown (raw) into white sugar for domestic consumption as well as for exports. Benefits for Britain, as pointed out, were based on the fact that white sugar was durable and capable of preservation, and could be easily handled and distributed all over the world.[17] In addition, exports to her older colonies in Asia were facilitated by practicing what has been described as 'free

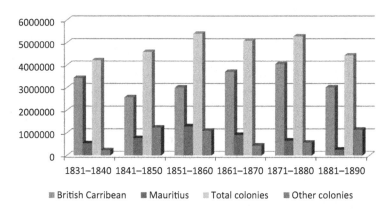

Figure 10.4 Import of raw sugar from various colonies

Source: Robert Montgomery Martin, *Statistics of the Colonies of the British Empire*, RareBooksClub.com (accessed on 14 May 2012).

Note: Imports in every decade is the average sterling value of imports in that decade. Decade 1881–1890 excludes the years 1888, 1889 and 1890.

trade imperialism', where protection in the home land is coupled to the opening of markets in colonies.[18]

We draw attention here to the fact that Britain always maintained a virtual ban on imports of processed sugar. Thus, even during the earlier centuries, duties imposed on the processed varieties were nearly four times those on brown sugar. The aim obviously was the protection of the upcoming sugar processing industry in Britain. Protection as above in the metropolis also included further restrictions, including a ban on sugar processing in the plantation islands, which obviously suited the interests of the British manufacturers in the sugar industry.[19]

Interestingly, the restrictions on processing did not affect the processing of molasses, a by-product of raw sugar. Instead, those were always processed within the islands to turn into rum which was then exported to England. As pointed out, 'rum was indispensable (with) its connection with the triangular trade. . . . Rum was an essential part of the cargo of the slave ship.'[20] While we deal later in this essay the relevance, in the above context, of what we have described as 'triangular trade', we just want to draw attention at this point as to how Britain's discretionary tariff structure was of significance to Britain's industry as well as maritime commerce. Thus, the plantation islands seem to be providing not only raw sugar for the processing industries of Britain but even rum to be consumed by the sailors for whom it turned out as essential.

Tariff policies pursued by Britain vis-à-vis the plantation colonies were, in large measure, subject to the influence of the absentee plantation owners of England, who had a lot of clout in the British Parliament. Thus, as raw sugar prices started declining in world markets due to new supplies from Brazil and Cuba, the strategy for the British planters was to somehow maintain profitability in the plantations by exercising their monopoly rights over production and prices. At the same time, advantage was taken of the differentiated tariff structure which made imports of raw sugar from British-owned plantations cheaper than those from other sources. The end result was to make the processed stuff more competitive compared to those produced in other countries.

Interestingly, the interests of British plantation owners in maintaining the financial viability of the estates were often opposed to those for the sugar processing industry in Britain. While the latter relied almost exclusively on imports of raw sugar procured at lower duties from the plantation colonies, the planters with their monopoly power over their estates wanted to restrain production in order to maintain high prices of raw sugar, thus rendering it costly for the processing industry to procure raw material. The rift between the rentier absentee owners of plantations and domestic sugar processing industry provides an example of the emerging conflicts between the rentiers as property owners and the nascent industry in England. As pointed out,

> Under the mercantile system the sugar planters had a monopoly of the home market (the British isles), and foreign imports were prohibited. It was therefore the policy of the planters to restrict production in order to maintain a high price. Their legal monopoly of the home market was a powerful weapon in their hands, and they used it mercilessly, at the expense of the whole population of England.[21]

Thus, the non-resident planter community in Britain posed a dilemma in this transition from merchant to industrial capital, by creating hurdles for the nascent sugar industry of Britain with the high price policies for raw sugar from the plantations.

Planters from West Indies were ranked high in England as wealthy persons since the beginning of the mercantilist era. As held by Adam Smith, 'Our tobacco colonies send us home no such wealthy planters as we see frequently arrive from our sugar islands.'[22] For Smith, the sugar planters in the mercantilist epoch were among the richest capitalists in Britain during the period. By mid-nineteenth century, as the century of trade was changing hands to one of production, and manufacturing was coming up under the fold of the industrial revolution, foundations were laid for industrial capital to emerge as a powerful lobby. As pointed out, 'The seventeenth and eighteenth centuries were the centuries of trade, as the nineteenth century was the century of production.'[23] However, plantation estates overseas were not authorised to process their wares into white sugar, given the restrictions imposed by the ruling country, Britain.

Plantation owners of the West Indies emerged as an influential lobby in Britain which had the ability to impact economic policies in the country. Their group included John Gladstone of Liverpool who not only owned estates in the plantation islands but also was engaged in shipping and trade, dealing with transportation, of labourers from India as well as raw produce from his own estates in West Indies.[24] An earlier protagonist of slaves, Gladstone, as a planter, had received a large sum of £86.7 thousand out of the total compensation of £20 million paid by Britain to the planters in terms of the Emancipation Act passed in 1833.[25] We will discuss aspects of the compensation doled out to plantation owners in the West Indies later in this chapter.

However, in England there also had emerged, by early nineteenth century, an alternate lobby, backed by the upcoming industrialists in Britain which included those engaged in sugar processing. The group was quite influential in championing the case for 'free trade' which brought in, first, an equalisation of duties in 1846 on sugar imported from plantations in both the east and the west and, later, the complete removal of such duties in 1874. Removal of duties in Britain on imports of raw sugar made for their processing in the country at prices even lower than what prevailed then. The wave of free trade and laissez faire which ended the era of preferential rates so far enjoyed by the West Indies on their exports of raw sugar to Britain, was matched by an end to duties on corn in terms of the repeal of corn laws in 1846.[26] The moves for free trade as above finally culminated in an end to all import duties in Britain by 1874.

It can be pointed out here that while industry in England was opposed to protection by the mid-nineteenth century, the surpluses Britain reaped during earlier centuries from what we described above as a pattern of 'triangular trade' in sugar and slaves had mostly been used in setting up British industries under protection with mercantilism.[27] One can interpret the sequence as a turn to 'Free Trade Imperialism'[28] practiced by Britain at the end of industrial revolution in the country.

The end to tariff protection which took place in Britain by 1874 did not, however, mean a rising value of sugar imports from the plantations. The latter had more to do with declining sugar prices from 1884 (see Figures 10.4 and 10.5). The above affected the sugar estates, whose earnings as well as the influx of immigrant labourers therein declined proportionately. One can here reaffirm the conclusion that a considerable part of the waves in immigrant flows were related to the fortunes of sugar plantations which, in turn, were invariably linked to demand for raw sugar from Britain, the chief source of demand for the products from the plantations.

To continue with the plantation estates in the British Caribbean, which already were affected by the equalisation of import duties on sugar imports in 1846, further economic stress came up for those islands when such duties were altogether abolished in 1874. This was because raw sugar imported from the islands was now exposed to global competition from other sources in British markets. The stress was particularly due to the competition from the non-British plantations of Cuba and Brazil, which were still relying on cheap slave labour. The competition was even more as Europe started producing beet sugar as an alternative to cane sugar by 1830s.[29] Related shifts in

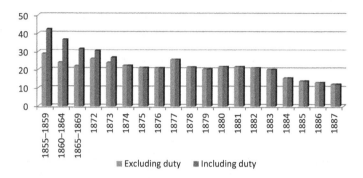

Figure 10.5 Average import price of sugar in shillings per cwt.

Source: Robert Montgomery Martin, *Statistics of the Colonies of the British Empire*, RareBooksClub.com (accessed on 14 May 2012).

sugar production as took place were visible by the second half of the nineteenth century and also by end of the nineteenth century. Thus, one could see some dramatic changes in the world sugar market and in the technology of sugar production all over. Between changes in technology in the production of white sugar (by using mechanised processing), with alternate sources of production, especially of beet sugar and with changes in tariff rates of Britain, the production of raw sugar and its location were considerably affected in the nineteenth century.

However, despite all the competition it faced, the British Caribbean continued to produce and export increasing quantities of sugar all through the 1860s and 1870s (see Figure 10.4). But for a few exceptions like Jamaica, and for years following the initial declines in production at the end of slavery in 1833, raw sugar output in the British West Indies, as a whole, increased consistently throughout the nineteenth century.

Incidentally, one can point out that that despite the ban on slavery, dependence on coerced plantation labour for sugar production in plantation islands persisted throughout most of the nineteenth century. Thus, till the 1880s, nearly two-thirds of cane production was from locations where production was dependent on either slave or contract labour, using slaves in the non-British owned plantations.[30] After the emancipation of slave labour, sugar production picked up in colonies where Britain possessed her plantations, which, of course, was based on imports of indentured labour from elsewhere, for which the British colony of India was most suited.

British finance in the plantation colonies

It may be recalled here that the problems experienced in the plantations of West Indies did generate concerns both for the planters and
the colonial office in London. By the 1840s, this led to the initiation
of two large-scale parliamentary committees in Britain to inquire into
the West Indian distress.[31] The reports stressed the point that while
the planters wished to continue with the plantations, they were facing 'shortages of labour', especially at wages they could afford to pay,
given the declining prices for sugar between 1860 and 1870. Moreover, the fact that the former slaves were unwilling to offer more than
a few hours of labour at the end of the apprentice programme often
created further shortages of labour in terms of the needs of sugarcane
cultivation. One can notice here that the price of raw sugar in the London market was fluctuating throughout the early nineteenth century.
Thus, the year-to-year fluctuations in sugar prices between 1839 and
1841, for example, varied between £39 a ton in 1839 and £49 in 1840
before falling back again to £40 in 1841. Aspects as the above were
clearly not conducive for the financial health of the plantations.[32]

As the use of slave labour was stopped with the passing of the
Emancipation Act in the British Parliament in 1833, both financiers in
the city and colonial planters were pleading with the government that
abolition affected the viability of the plantations. To this the administrators and members of Parliament conceded, often by using the data
reported in Parliamentary Papers.

Commenting on the rather ambiguous intent of those official
reports, it was pointed out that

> Dozens of government officers and Parliamentary Committees
> were appointed between 1837 and 1915 to investigate aspects of
> indentured migration from India, or conditions of the sugar colo-
> nies . . . which in effect were synthetic political projects. . . . Indian
> indentured labour was a site where hierarchies of empire were
> enunciated, contested and inscribed.[33]

However, with details documented in these reports becoming accessible to the wealthy and influential planters of the West Indies like John
Gladstone, in effect those also provided a valuable opportunity for the
planters 'to shape the opinion of imperial policymakers and legislators, and of the reading public as well'.[34]

Responses by the British government to enable the plantations
(which included the shippers as well as the planters) to continue along

with the related agents in India included, as mentioned earlier, an outright cash compensation of £20 million to planters and opening the facilities for continuing the use of the ex-slaves as 'apprentices' over an interim period.

As for the effectiveness of such gestures, it was pointed out that

> the vast sum of £20 million, paid from the British exchequer was not only to cover the loss of slaves but also to reduce the high debt burden of planters and to enable them compete with colonies outside the British empire which were still using slave labour. Amounting to just under half the market value of the freed slaves, the compensation payments did reduce the planters massive indebtedness but this increase in their individual creditworthiness failed in most cases to attract new investment because of well-justified doubts about the ability of British sugar plantations to turn out a profit without slavery.[35]

As for the interests of British merchants, financiers and investors in sugar estates of the plantations, their perusal of official policies relating to sugar plantations continued. This was especially apparent in the moves mentioned above for the £20 million grant as compensation to slave owners along with a sanction of the 'apprentice' scheme.[36] Evidently, interests of merchant creditors prevailed in the £20 million compensation to slave owners for the loss of slaves. Such payments clearly enabled the financiers to recuperate the loans made to planters. Interested parties in British Guiana, Mauritius and London, while vocal in urging a revocation of all barriers to trade in 'the name of free labour movements',[37] were equally keen to be compensated for the change from slavery to indenturing in the plantation colonies. Naturally, many of the payments were offered in the interest of continuity in the plantations, in turn, providing a crucial link in the process of expropriations.

Further moves in British official policies can also be witnessed to ease the finances of the plantations. One was the temporary suspension of the so-called 'coolie trade' (of indentures) in 1839 and its quick re-opening in 1842. The short-lived lull in immigrations as resulted was followed by a large influx of labour to the plantations, which was financed by an annual sum of £25 thousand from the colonial revenues. Known as the 'Bounty scheme', it contributed to the planters an additional £6–£7 per adult transported on this basis. Additional costs, if any, were to be met by planters while the colonial government in Mauritius was allowed to impose a consumption duty on all spirits (like rum) manufactured or consumed in Mauritius to meet the additional costs as already covered under the bounty scheme.[38]

As for facilitating borrowings by plantation owners, especially with the expanding production of raw sugar in Mauritius, the heavy borrowings by plantation owners in the earlier part of nineteenth century met little resistance from the British bankers. In this the metropolitan bankers of England had little reluctance to lend further, especially during the initial stages of those lendings. However, between 1844 and 1848, five such British financial houses as had already lent to Mauritius, along with the bank of Mauritius collapsed. This was followed by the bankruptcy of several sugar estates in Mauritius. Problems faced by the plantation estates also led to a crisis in Britain's financial sector. Thus, with British financial houses having close links with the plantation estates in terms of their investments in plantations, there took place in Britain as well a series of bank crises during 1840s. As a consequence, the British financiers, having no further interest in their investments with the sugar plantations of Mauritius, pulled out their investment from Mauritius between 1839 and 1848. Such acts were also related to some economic, linguistic and legal problems which had already erupted in the island.[39] In Mauritius, the British bank, Barclays and Blyth already held, between 1811 and 1850, three-fourths of the sugar estates in the island, having invested a sum which was approximately 1162 thousand British pounds.[40] British investors had already pulled out their investment from Mauritius by 1832, expressing a lack of interest in further investments in the sugar industry due to the prevailing economic, linguistic and legal problems which were continuing in the island.[41]

Links between British financial interests and the plantations were particularly close with West Indies, which had received large investments from Britain, involving the British government, planters and banks. Britain's financial system was thus closely linked to investments in West Indies. In 1844, the colonial government in the Caribbean passed an ordinance to raise money which ostensibly was for promoting 'Immigration of Agricultural Labourers from the British Dominion in India and elsewhere'. In terms of this ordinance, the agents responsible for importing indentured labour were given an authority to borrow money up to 500,000 sterling pounds from Britain by issuing bonds on the security of the revenue of the colony. The loan with interest was to be paid back by the agents within a stipulated period.[42]

Arrangements, as above, reflect the stake of the British plantation owners, mostly residing in Britain, as well as of the city and of British finance as a whole. The pattern speaks for the close connections

between British finance and the fortunes of the British-owned plantation colonies.

A new web of triangular trade and finance: Britain and colonies between late nineteenth and early twentieth centuries

Triangular trade, as defined earlier in the context of such trade
between countries in the seventeenth and eighteenth centuries, spelt
out a network of trade which involved countries like 'England, France
and Colonial America equally (supplying) the exports and the ships;
Africa the human merchandise; (and) the plantations the colonial raw
materials.' Further,

> The slave ship sailed from the home country with a cargo of man-
> ufactured goods. These were exchanged *at a profit* on the coast
> of Africa for Negroes, who were traded on the plantations, *at
> another profit*, in exchange for a cargo of colonial produce to be
> taken back to the home country.
>
> (italics added)[43]

Here 'home' refers to countries in the northern hemisphere (France,
Britain, North America), which were capable of producing and exporting manufactures.

As pointed out, the triangular trade as above (see Figure 10.6) gave
'a triple stimulus' to 'home' industry of Britain, first, by using the British wares to buy slaves; second, by using those slaves to grow raw
materials in the plantation colonies; and third, by selling manufactures
in the markets in the latter.

Looking closely at the network of transactions as analysed in the
present chapter for late nineteenth and early twentieth centuries, one
can identify a similar pattern of a triangular network involving labour
(indentured), commodities (both raw materials and processed) and
British finance. By the mid-nineteenth century, Britain was in control
of the colonies in Asia (especially, the Indian subcontinent) which
could be used to procure labour on an indentured basis and to ship
those to the British-owned plantation colonies across the oceans. The
flow of such labour aimed to ameliorate the scarcity of labour in the
plantations, especially at the end of the emancipation of slave labour
by 1833. Indentured labour, as procured, was lifted by British ships to
plantations owned by Britain, thus providing further avenues of profit
for the British-owned shipping industry. Labour in those plantation

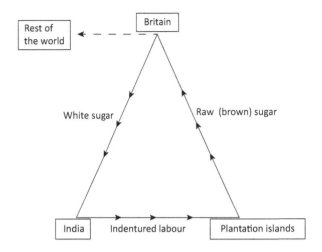

Figure 10.6 Triangular trade – Britain and plantation colonies
Source: Author.

islands was used to cultivate raw sugar, to be transferred to Britain to process as white sugar, both for home consumption and for exports.

As in the earlier centuries, trade, as described above, entailed a triangular pattern, operating across Britain's colonies and the metropolis. Triangular trade, in this case, also provided a triple stimulus to Britain. While slaves were earlier procured from Africa in exchange of British manufactures sold in Africa, a somewhat similar pattern prevailed this time with British ships transporting indentured labour from the Indian soil (at nominal cost) to plantations which produced sugar and other tropical products, including cotton, indigo, molasses and others. It may be mentioned here that under the prevailing Navigation Law of Britain, which was in force till its repeal in 1849, no foreign ship was allowed to carry wares from British colonies. Thus, indenturing was also facilitating the British shipping industry by a very large extent.[44] As for the raw material produced in the plantations, much of those were carried back and processed in the upcoming sugar processing industries of England. While a similar pattern of trade, as took place during seventeenth and eighteenth centuries, provided profits as one of the major streams of primitive accumulation of capital in England which financed the Industrial Revolution, the new pattern of triangular trade in late nineteenth and the early twentieth centuries equally arranged for the ongoing appropriation of surpluses by Britain from the colonies, relying, as in earlier centuries, on movements of commodities as well as labour. However, in this period, finance from the city of London played a major supplementary role, with plantations providing profitable avenues of investments in estates owned by the British planters. The triangular trade, as above, thus supported both flows of labour to the plantations and of raw materials therefrom, both facilitated by British business houses and the government.

As contrasted to the earlier pattern, triangular trade, in this period was relying on high finance rather than on maritime commerce alone. The pattern was clearly one which conformed to the escalated role of finance in this period of finance capital. Thus, the story of triangular trade in the nineteenth century, as above, remains incomplete in absence of a reference to the active interest of the British finance in sugar plantations. While a large number of absentee plantation owners were influential enough in London, even to the extent of influencing parliamentary affairs, the banking industry had big stakes in the financial performance of those estates, with loans advanced to the plantation owners or the colonial governments which managed the islands.

Investments by British financial interests in the plantation islands proved rewarding for British capital, not only in fetching high returns on the financial flows, and to some extent in making use of its shipping lines at high profits; but also in stimulating production and exports by British industry. In effect, indenturing of labour from within the British empire and transporting those to the plantation islands controlled by Britain proved a lucrative source of earning surpluses which were appropriated by the commercial and financial interests of imperial Britain.

Conclusion

The use of indentured labour from colonies like India to promote Britain's commercial and financial interests in the late nineteenth and early twentieth centuries unfolds a story of uneven power relations, between labour in the colonies and capital in the ruling country under state patronage. Labour procured by indenturing from old colonies like India provided additional opportunities of extracting surpluses as those were deployed in the plantations where they had a near-slave status. With the recruitment of indentured labour at terms which hardly compensated them for the hard and arduous work at the plantations, the flow of labour could be treated as the source of one more 'drain' (or unrequited transfers) from colonial India, in addition to the disputed transfers against the 'Home Charges'.[45] We have documented in this essay the multiple channels through which such surpluses were appropriated by those who were in power, including the ruling state of Britain and British capital deployed in industry and finance.

British capital, which had invested in industry as well as finance, seemed to have an upper hand in moulding the country's plantations policies in general. Examples include the use of concessional tariff duties (as compared to the rates on similar imports from other sources) on imports of raw produce from plantations in Britain. One also notices the prohibitory orders on processing of raw sugar in the plantation islands and similar prohibition on the use of ships other than those owned by Britain as means of transport, for labour to plantations and raw material therefrom to Britain. Measures as above were clearly in the interest of the sugar processing industry in Britain as well as of its shipping industry. The measures were also evidently beneficial for British capital deployed in industry and the shipping lines.

With finance taking a lead over industry by late nineteenth century, Britain's financial hubs were active in influencing state policies. Instances can be found with the plantation owners of Britain wanting to maintain profitability by exercising their rights to fix prices and output by virtue of having monopoly power there. Incidentally, such policies to keep prices high by plantation owners often conflicted with the interest of the processing industry in Britain, which needed the raw produce at lower prices. In this the interests of the financial community, having a stake in the plantations, often prevailed over concerns of the sugar processing industry with its demand for cheaper sources of raw produce from the plantations and at relatively lower tariff rates.

The predominance of finance in the plantation policies in Britain was also evident in the concerted efforts made by the British government to protect the viability of the plantations at end of slavery in 1833, with generous compensations to the planters. The stakes of British finance, in terms of investments in plantations, provided sufficient reasons for alerting its financial community in times of stress which threatened the sustainability of the estates. It was thus natural, for British capital, both industrial and financial, as well as the state, to be active in terms of their involvement in the affairs of the plantations.

The engagement of Britain in the running of the plantations comes out in the triangular pattern of trade across Britain and the two wings of her colonies, which included India and the plantation islands. The nexus of trade as described above, where labour from India was shipped, treated as commodities to plantations for forwarding raw materials to Britain, opened the possibilities in Britain of further rounds of trade; this time with exports of processed sugar to the rest of the world. As we mentioned above, the triangular trade of the late nineteenth and early twentieth centuries, supplemented by flows of finance, was a bit different from what prevailed in earlier centuries. The former had its origin in the rise of finance by this time, running parallel to flows of trade with investments, subsidies and others, to the plantation estates which in the aggregate was providing opportunities of earning surpluses at different levels.

We end this chapter with a commentary on the changing forms of institutions. The changes over time, which include the transformation of colonial states to nations politically independent, have a continued pattern in terms of the unequal relations, between those wielding economic power and others who do not, which include labour. Our analysis of labour in times of indenture helps to throw light on this continuum, both in the developing as well as in recession-prone advanced regions. The distance in time, nearly a century since indentured labour recruitments stopped in British colonies by 1920, has not altered the pattern of coercion and expropriation of workers, a growing proportion of whom are today employed as casual and temporary workers, engaged by the employers with an informal arrangement. Power here continues to vest with those who own capital, leaving a shrinking space for labour in its capacity to resist.

Notes

1 Thanks are offered to Zico Dasgupta for his help in collection of material for this chapter.
2 www.saylor.org/site/wp-content/uploads/2011/05/Slavery-Abolition-Act-1833.pdf (accessed on 20 December 2015).
3 David Northrup, *Indentured Labour in the Age of Imperialism*, Cambridge: Cambridge University Press, 1955, pp. 18–19.
4 Peaceful protests in Port of Spain, Trinidad, continued until the government passed a resolution to abolish apprenticeship and the slaves gained de facto freedom. Full emancipation for all slaves was legally granted on 1 August 1838, ahead of schedule, making Trinidad the first British slave society to end slavery. For details see: http://en.wikipedia.org/wiki/Abolitionism_in_the_United_Kingdom#Slavery_Abolition_Act_1833 (accessed on 20 December 2014).
5 For details see: http://en.wikipedia.org/wiki/Abolitionism_in_the_United_Kingdom#Slavery_Abolition_Act_1833 (accessed on 20 December 2014)
6 Robert Miles, *Capitalism and Unfree Labor*, London: Tavistock Publications, 1981, p. 89.
7 Miles, *Capitalism and Unfree Labor*, pp. 76, 91. Also Hugh Tinker, *New System of Slavery: Export of Indian Labour Overseas, 1830–1920*,

Hartford, UK: Paperback Hansib Publishing, Ltd; 2nd edition (October 17, 1993), pp. 191–2.
8 See Sunanda Sen, *Colonies and Empire 1870–1914*, Calcutta: Orient Longmans, 1992, pp. 146–83.
9 Royal Commission of Labor, Foreign Reports Vol. 2, Parliamentary Papers 11892, *The Colonies and the Indian Empire*, @ Proquest 2005, p. 99.
10 Northrup, *Indentured Labour in the Age of Imperialism*, p. 29.
11 Robert J. Steinfield and Stanley J. Engerman, 'Labor – Free or Coerced? A Historical Reassessment of Differences and Similarities', in Tom Brass and Marcel van der Linden (eds.), *Free and Unfree Labor: The Debate Continues*, Peter Lang Pub Inc., 1967.
12 http//:sharresearch.files.wordpress.com/2011/07/Indian-indenturedlabor.pdf (accessed on 20 December 2014).
13 Stanley L. Engerman, 'Contract Labour, Sugar and Technology in the Nineteenth Century', *The Journal of Economic History*, 1983, 43(3) September: 642.
14 Imre Ferenczi and Walter F. Willcox, *International Migrations*, Vol.1, pp. 904–5; cited in Engerman, 'Contract Labour, Sugar and Technology in the Nineteenth Century', p. 646.
15 www.country-data.com/cgi-bin/query/r-8613.html (accessed on 20 December 2014).
16 Engerman, 'Contract Labour, Sugar and Technology in the Nineteenth Century', p. 648; also Noel Deerr, *The History of Sugar*, London: Chapman and Hall Ltd., 1949, pp. 203–4; and R.R. Kuczynski, *Demographic Survey of the British Colonial Empire*, Vol. 2, London, 1949, pp. 779 and 796, cited in Engerman, 'Contract Labour, Sugar and Technology in the Nineteenth Century', p. 649.
17 Eric Williams, *Capitalism and Slavery*, (paperback) Charlotte: University of North Carolina, 1994, pp. 75–6.
18 Sunanda Sen, 'Free Trade Imperialism in South East Asia', *Studies in History*, 1981.
19 Williams, *Capitalism and Slavery*, pp. 75–6, 78.
20 Williams, *Capitalism and Slavery*, p. 78.
21 Williams, *Capitalism and Slavery*, p. 76.
22 Adam Smith, *Wealth of Nations*, Cannan edition, 1937, p. 185, cited in Williams *Capitalism and Slavery*, p. 85.
23 Williams, *Capitalism and Slavery*, p. 51.
24 See Sunanda Sen, 'Indentured Labour from India in the Age of Empire', *Social Scientist*, January–February 2016, 44(1–2).
25 Williams, *Capitalism and Slavery*, p. 90.
26 David Eastwood, 'The Corn Laws and their Repeal', www.historytoday.com/david-eastwood/corn-laws-and-their-repeal-1815-1846 (accessed on 20 December 2014).
27 Eastwood, 'The Corn Laws and their Repeal', p. 110.
28 John Gallaghar and Robinson, 'The Imperialism of Free Trade', *The Economic History Review*, New Series, 1953, 6(1): 1–15. See for a critique of the above, Sen, 'Free Trade Imperialism in Asia'.
29 Northrup, *Indentured Labour in the Age of Imperialism*, p. 31.

30 Engerman, 'Contract Labour, Sugar and Technology in the Nineteenth Century', p. 650–51.
31 Reports and Testimony in the *Select Committee on the West Indian Colonies* (1842) and in the *Report from the Select Committee on Sugar and Coffee Planting* (1847–1848). Also cited in Engerman 'Contract Labour, Sugar and Technology in the Nineteenth Century', p. 652.
32 Reports and Testimony in the *Select Committee on the West Indian Colonies* (1842) and *Report from the Select Committee on Sugar and Coffee Planting* (1847–1848).
33 Madhavi Kale, *Fragments of Empire: Capital, Slavery, and Indian Indentured Labor in the British Caribbean*, Critical Histories series, Philadelphia: University of Pennsylvania Press, 1998, pp. 7, 10.
34 Kale, *Fragments of Empire*, p. 31.
35 Northrup, *Indentured Labour in the Age of Imperialism*, p. 19.
36 Kale, *Fragments of Empire*, p. 35.
37 Kale, *Fragments of Empire*, p. 54.
38 Kale, *Fragments of Empire*, p. 54.
39 Kale, *Fragments of Empire*, p. 54.
40 Noorjahan Dauhoo, 'The History of Sugar With Reference to 19th Century Mauritius', http://dutchguyana.wordpress.com/2013/12/14/mauritius-history-the-sugar-and-enslaved/ (accessed on 20 December 2014).
41 Noorjahan Dauhoo, 'The History of Sugar With Reference to 19th Century Mauritius', p. 22.
42 British Parliamentary Papers 1846.
43 Williams, *Capitalism and Slavery*, pp. 50–2.
44 'Navigation Acts were a series of laws that restricted the use of foreign ships for trade between Britain and its colonies. They began in 1651 and ended 200 years later. They reflected the policy of mercantilism, which sought to keep all the benefits of trade inside the Empire, and minimise the loss of gold and silver to foreigners', http://en.wikipedia.org/wiki/Navigation_Acts.
45 See for an interpretation of the notion of the 'drain' in the context of colonial India, Sen, *Colonies and the Empire*, pp. 15–70.

11 Labour laws and the global economy

The discourse of labour control and welfare in India, 1919–1947

Sabyasachi Bhattacharya

The relationship between the discourse of labour control and welfare through legislation in colonial India and the global economy is a somewhat neglected subject of study. That is surprising, because the disempowerment of labour through legislation, or lack thereof, seems to be a systemic feature of the regime of globalisation and instances of that are being provided today in India by proponents of neoliberalism and 'good governance'. At the same time, the approaching centenary of the International Labour Organisation (ILO) has brought it from the margins to the centre of attention in some scholarly work on its global impact in the past. The end of the First World War and the beginning of a new wave of labour welfare legislation under pressure from the ILO, according to the generally accepted version of history, marked the commencement of a new era in many parts of the world. Connected themes have been briefly touched upon in some recent writings, for example, in a special number of the *Economic and Political Weekly*, edited by Gerry Rodgers, J. Krishnamurthy and Sabyasachi Bhattacharya and in a collection of essays edited by Jasmien van Daele et al., as well as the writings of Steve Hughes and Nicola Countouris.[1]

In this essay, I will look at the early years of the interaction between the ILO and the discourse of labour welfare and labour control in colonial India, chiefly focusing on the period between the foundation of the ILO in 1919 and the commencement of the global depression in 1929. The conventional view is that international initiative, led by the ILO, had persuaded or compelled the colonial government in India to undertake labour legislation; hence, there was a wave of welfare measures. The approach in the following pages is different, since it is driven by the following argument: while there was a reformist trend in a drive towards welfare legislation, there was another element in

248 Sabyasachi Bhattacharya

the discourse that was often neglected. Arguably, the ILO was also *a consensus-making body serving a global agenda of economically advanced countries* and was anxious to remove impediments to the development of an economic system transcending national boundaries; therefore, it demanded member states' legislation in accordance with global norms. Some contemporary observers pointed out that it was to the advantage of the countries, which were most advanced in the regulation of conditions of industrial employment, to ensure similar conditions *wherever a level and fair field of competition needed to be established*. In other words, the developed countries needed to ensure that the higher level of wages in their own countries did not become an impediment in competing with the less developed countries with a lower wage cost burden on industries. This means that the welfare legislation in India, since 1919, may be understood in a manner quite different from the received version of history of 'welfare thinking'. Further, that trend of thinking worked alongside a rigorous labour control policy in Indian labour legislation. Thus, it may be argued that some features of the present-day situation, in the interface between the global economy and the legal regime governing the lives of the labouring masses, were foreshadowed in the history of the pre-independence era.

If that is our argument, re-thinking the historiography of the legal regime under the impact of the ILO is necessary. The labour laws in India enacted in the early decades of the twentieth century have been conventionally viewed in the context of 'policy studies' with focus on the British bureaucracy reacting to the recommendations of the International Labour Office at Geneva and to the pressures emanating from labour movements and industrial unrest in India. Insofar as the political economy of law is explored at all, the guiding assumption has been that there was a trend towards approximation (with due regard to the peculiarities of India) to the normative or mandatory codes, in respect of labour, developed in the West, more particularly in England since the nineteenth century.[2] In examining the adequacy of this approach, we have to raise the question, why in the post-First World War period the ILO and an international legal regime began to try to review and reorder labour–capital relations and conditions of labour? Was this in some way concerned with the growth of transnational capital and increasing internationalisation of the labour market in the emerging global economic system? We shall consider one possible approach to the question, though that cannot claim to provide a decisive answer (see Section I). A second set of questions relates to the global links of the national/local labour movements. How real and effective was 'proletarian internationalism and was legal protection of labour one of its achievements?' (See Section II.) Finally, how was the need for the legitimation of norms and codes regarding labour met by the representation of labour interests in the legislative forums? This question is important because the international labour conventions could not be a sufficient source of legitimacy and the Government of British India, perfectly aware of that fact, gave a lot of attention to the need for representation of labour and capital in the law-making bodies (Section III).

Labour laws and the global economy

First, a bare outline of the course of labour legislation in this period, a subject that need not detain us, since it has been chronicled by many authors.[3] The first Factory Act of the twentieth century was based on the deliberations of the Indian Factory Labour Committee (1908) which had been appointed as a result of 'vigorous agitation carried on by Lancashire and Dundee trade interests'.[4] The Factories Act of 1911 prohibited night work by women labourers, reduced children's working hours to six, and limited working hours for men and women to a maximum of 12. The Act was almost infructuous for want of monitoring by inspectors and within three years of the First World War, exigencies led to the suspension of its application.

Thus, it was only after the formation of the ILO in 1919 and the International Labour Convention of Washington that labour legislation seriously commenced. Thereafter, the following major Acts were passed in rapid succession: (a) The Factories Act of 1922 prohibited employment of children below 12, and restricted work for children aged 12–15 years to 6 hours and for others to 11 hours per day; (b) the Mining Act of 1923 prohibited employment of children below 13, and by the amendments of 1928, restricted hours of work to 12 hours per day; (c) the Workmen's Compensation Act of 1923 legally provided compensation in cases of injury by accident or specified industrial diseases; (d) the Factory Act of 1934 reduced hours of work to 11 per day and 54 per week in factories; (e) the Mines Act of 1935 increased minimum employment age to 15 and in general reduced hours to 10 above ground and 9 below the ground; (f) the Payment of Wages Act, 1936, ensures payment within specified maximum periods and in cash in factories; and (g) finally, the Indian Emigration Acts of 1922 and 1938 empowered the government to prohibit emigration outside India if the government felt the need to do so. It is important to note that there was no legislative protection of the right to strike; indeed, it seems that there was no consensus in the ILO with respect of right to strike.[5] On the contrary, in 1928 India witnessed rigorous legislation against strike action by factory workers, in the face of resistance from trade unions, as well as nationalist leader like Jawaharlal Nehru.

Leaving aside the issue of limited success in the enforcement of laws, like those against child labour or for workmen's compensation, an issue established beyond debate by the researchers cited earlier, let us turn to the question of international pressures which were avowedly behind this spate of law making. It is clear from the statements of purpose in the Legislative Assembly Debates that the ILO norms in conventions, signed by India, were an important factor. The ILO adopted not less than 16 conventions in the years 1919–1921 on hours of work, night work for women, minimum age for employment, workmen's compensation, emigration and others.[6] Signatories of the Treaty of Peace of Versailles were expected to implement these norms, though they were not legally bound to do so. The ILO conventions were some of the earliest of those international instruments which, though not in the nature of binding treaties, were declarative statements expected to be followed in state practice; in later times, the UN Declaration of the New International, Economic Order is of a like nature.[7]

Why did the world's leading powers promote an agenda of devising an international normative or proto-legal regime through the agency of the ILO in the post-First World War period? A hypothesis worth exploring would be whether a partial answer to the question lies in the emerging global economic system, growth of transnational capital and internationalisation of the labour market. The very notion of an International Labour Organisation seems to have originated in the appreciation by the developed countries of the need to set up international standards in the labour market; after the War, 'once free competition had been restored', it was necessary that 'similar standards were applied to all competing markets'.[8] Right from the day E. J. Phelan, the British civil servant who later headed the ILO, authored a memorandum in 1918 proposing such an organisation; it was felt that it was to the advantage of the countries that were most advanced in the regulation of conditions of industrial employment to ensure similar conditions wherever a level and fair field of competition needed to be established.[9] In other words, there was a need felt by the developed countries to ensure that 'the higher level of wage and benefits in their own counties do not become an impediment' in competing with less developed countries with a lower wage cost burden on industries. This is not unexpected. What is surprising is the extent to which the same approach was internalised by spokesmen of labour interests.

The lobby organised in the form of Workers' Welfare League of India (WWLI) pushed the argument that cheapness of labour in India was a threat to British industry and hence to British industrial workers. The same point about self-interest, rather than altruism, was made by Neil Maclaren, a member of Parliament, who spoke on the issues raised by WWLI in the Commons.[10] At the other end of the pole, M. N. Roy in the Comintern journal *In. Pre. Cor.* put forward the same argument to persuade the British trade union to support measures in India to hike wages and other benefits of Indian workers; the lower the rate at wages in India, the worse are the prospects of British commodities in the Indian market. For example, given the prevailing low wages in Bombay, 'not only Japanese but Lancashire fabrics will be driven out of the Indian market.'[11] Thus, the Comintern ideologue, the British trade union lobby, and the big powers promoting the ILO agree on one point: the consideration of the condition of the workers in countries such as India could not be de-linked from the global industrial interests.

There have been some theoretical discussions on the internationalisation of capital and how it impinges on the function of the nation-states and on the conduct of business.[12] While in the sphere of business the most visible actors in that process are the transnational corporations, in setting the policy-making agenda for the state, the nation-state or the colonial state, the inter-governmental organisations (IGO hereafter) were the main actors. As the first IGO of this kind, the ILO performed transnational functions of the kind that were later assumed by other IGOs in recent decades.

That is not to say that the ILO was merely a tool in the hands of advanced industrialised countries or transnational capital; a 'conspiracy theory' of collusive transactions at Geneva is not being suggested. In point of fact, the ILO was the successor to a very useful body known as the International Association for the Legal Protection of Workers, which drafted the first labour conventions in 1905–1906, and the ILO was the repository of a strong philanthropic humanist tradition which continued to inspire in the inter-war period labour leadership in many countries.[13] Moreover, the ILO was, compared to other IGOs (intergovernment organisations), relatively free to make decisions which one or more member governments wished to reject. The ILO included representatives of workers as individuals with a legal right to vote independently of the government of the country they belonged to; this was and remains very unusual in an IGO.[14] The Indian delegation to ILO provides some examples of independent action by the labour representatives; for example, in 1935, complaint regarding infraction by the Indian Railways of the ILO convention in respect of hours of work led to a virtual censure on the British Indian Government; or again, the British Indian Government's proposal to allow placement of convicts with private business corporations for labour was rejected at the instance of the Indian labour delegate.[15] Having conceded all that, it needs to be recognised that the ILO was sometimes perceived as a consensus-making body serving a global agenda of economically advanced countries which were anxious to remove impediments to the development of an economic system transcending national boundaries, and therefore, demanding of the members' states legislation in accordance with global norms.

An obvious manifestation of the internationalisation of the labour market was labour migration. According to Kingsley Davis's estimate, net migration, that is, after deduction of number of immigrants, was about 4,161,000 from India to other countries in 1891–1930; it is equally significant that in the period of the Great Depression migration was reversed, so that 1931–1935 displays a negative rate – evidence of the close link between migration from India and the cyclical pattern in the global economy.[16] A better index than the numbers would be the earnings from this source as compared to the GNP but unfortunately, we do not have estimates for the early twentieth century.[17] Needless to say, the emergence of a world market of labour is manifested not only in the form of migration but also in other forms like location of labour-intensive industries in less developed countries with lower wage costs by way of sub-contracting and other arrangements. As far as metropolitan industrial interests are concerned, the factor that loomed large in their perception was the possibility of losing their market in countries such as India on account of the cost advantage to indigenous industries due to lower wage costs. This apprehension was shared by metropolitan countries' labour interests that shrinkage of world market would reduce employment, a factor that assumed special importance in critical periods like the Great Depression from 1929.

It is interesting to note that the Indian labour delegates to the ILO, in their interventions in that forum or in discussions at home, did not, as a rule, frame their arguments in terms of a Marxian theory although some labour leaders in India, for example, S. A. Dange and B. T. Ranadive, among their contemporaries, did fleetingly refer to Marx on occasions. It is true that Marx's observations on the international labour market were not widely known at that time. His remarks on 'the tendency to create world market . . . given in the concept of capital itself' in *Grundrisse* remained untranslated.[18] In the chapter, 'National Difference of Wages', Marx addressed the question of 'the law of value in its international application', comparing the variations in labour 'intensity' and productivity according to the degree of development of capitalist production in different countries. Marx put forward the idea that there is an 'international level' of labour intensity/productivity in the 'world market', and he posited the notion of the 'relative price of labour' which is P/PV, that is, wages as a ratio of the product value. Apart from this and observations on immigrant labour, Chapter 33 of *Capital* does not offer any extended treatment of the international labour market. The theoretical literature on labour, in this aspect, was undoubtedly sparse compared to the literature on internationalisation of capital. In any event, the Indian delegates to the ILO were nominees of the Government of India from among Indian labour leaders, and it is not surprising that they eschewed reference to the authority of Karl Marx.

International affiliations of the trade union movement

'The working-class in its struggle against capitalism is obliged to unite industrially, nationally and internationally.' That was how S. A. Dange characterized the international affiliation of the Indian labour movement; it was part of the statement of the communist leaders in 1932 at their trial, generally known as the Meerut Conspiracy Trial.[19] Dange went on to say that while the All India Trade Union Congress (hereafter AITUC) should have been such a national unity movement of the working class, actually it began as a means of finding a representative of trade unions whom the government could send to the International Labour Office. Thus, command from above, on account of this 'immediate incentive', led to the formation of AITUC. 'In India, there was no body that could make any recommendation' regarding a trade union representative and this need was met by the AITUC. This statement of Dange has been challenged by later authors as excessively simplistic.[20] Be that as it may, in the conjuncture at the time of the foundation of ILO and the AITUC in 1919–1920, the 'international' task on the agenda underlined by Dange was significant.

Irrespective of the ILO, international links were developing in the labour movement. Not to take that into account is to leave out of our purview a major factor which influenced the discourse of labour legislation in most countries. As far as India was concerned, a very important event was the submission of a memorandum signed by leaders of major trade unions of Britain to Secretary of State for India, Montague, in January 1919. 'Industries in modern times have a close international connection', the British trade nations said: 'vast differences in labour conditions of two countries within one and the same empire should be generally known and intelligently dealt with'.[21] Specifically, the memorandum demanded legislation and representation in legislative bodies. On 'condition of labour' the views were unclear. But it was the general line of the lobby in England interested in Indian labour to push forward wage increase for the Indian worker. The Workers Welfare League of India, founded in London in 1917, emphasised on their propaganda, lobbying activities on the danger of cheap labour in India: 'the threat to English Labour from the cheap unorganised Indian Labour' was a major theme, according to Intelligence Department reports received by the Government of India.[22] The Indians associated with this League were Saklatvala, B. P. Wadia, Satyamurti, Madhav Rao and others who became prominent labour leaders later. The League planned 'to promote in India an All-India Labour Union'; it was reported just six months before the AITUC was founded.[23] Between the British and Indian trade union leadership, the contact was alive from 1919, though the 'Bolshevik' contacts of Indian trade unions, although extensively speculated upon by British intelligence sources, were feeble or almost non-existent till the Red International Labour Union came on the scene in the late 1920s.[24]

One may also note that many of these international links were transitory and no more than symbolic gestures. Such a gesture was the raising of subscriptions by the AITUC to help British workers at the time of the famous General Strike they launched in 1926. Or again, correspondence between the Bombay labour leader Baptista and Lansbury or B. G. Tilak's letters from Britain, intercepted by the Indian government, reveal nothing more than a shared concern for the Indian labourers – operationally of no significance in the labour movement.[25] International links beyond Britain were even more tenuous. For example, the Indian immigrant workers in Canada were highly unionised, with union literature in the Gurumukhi script of Punjab and possible Bolshevik links, but the British Indian government reports no contact between them and the workers' organisations in India.[26] Finally, it is also notable that at the factory level, the selection of representatives to the International Labour Conference was not always perceived by the workers themselves as a matter of any importance. The Police Commissioner of Bombay reports in 1919 that a series of meetings were called and dissolved for want of attendances: at one meeting 20 turned up, at another 50, and at a third 'the speakers all attended but no mill-hands'![27]

In the late 1920s, the international links of Indian labour organisations began to assume importance, since the external organisations tried to claim contact with and influence over Indian organisations. The Red International Labour Union, or RILU, competed with the International Federation of Trade Unions (Amsterdam) and gained considerable mileage from its propaganda against the 'reformist' rival because of its association with the League against imperialism (hereafter LAI). The latter was a sister organisation and, like RILU, controlled by the Comintern. But the LAI, since its first two conferences in Brussels and Amsterdam in 1927, attracted from colonial countries, including India, many leaders who would not have joined an explicitly communist organisation like the RILU.[28] The resistance to RILU was reduced in nationalist ranks due to its association with the LAI which was welcomed as an international forum against imperialism.

As regards to the left leadership, Dange's was possibly a representative stance: there was, he said, 'an organised offensive of the Second International, the British labour imperialists, and the IFTU (Amsterdam) to prevent the working class in India, not from joining the RILU or the Comintern only (sic), but from joining the movement of political emancipation'.[29] This was also the view of M. N. Roy, till his expulsion from the Comintern. The world communist leadership, of course, strongly endorsed such views, most notably in a message to the Indian working class from 13 communist party leaders, including Thalmann, Thorez and Dimitrov, on 16 May 1929, from Brussels. Thus, in the last half of the decade of the 1920s, the major issue in the Indian working class movement was the international affiliation they would choose. The general trend of the post-world war scene was that the global links of the Indian labour movement moved to the centre stage. The director of intelligence of the Indian Government put it in these words: 'India was no longer isolated from world movements. If so, it is well to recognise the present economic currents in the World. It is that the day of unrestricted capitalism has passed'.[30] In looking upon the process in this light, in expecting 'restrictions' on capitalism, there was an element of naiveté. Things were a little more complicated than that.

Class representation in legislature

Labour legislation, unless accompanied by the state's endeavour to ensure legitimation of the normative and/or mandatory code, could not be effective. The representation of the economic actors, the employees and the employer and labour and capital as legislative actors was a part of the legitimation process. This question of representation of capital and labour was answered in different ways all over the globe in the late nineteenth and early nineteenth centuries within the rubric of national or local constitutional law and the theory inherent in it. We will now examine how the colonial state in India met this question. First, what was the answer in theory?

Although the language of class (to use Asa Brigg's suggestive phrase) was not explicitly employed, the bureaucracy and the makers of constitutional laws relating to representation in legislative bodies used 'interests' as a surrogate for 'class'.[31] The concept was useful in articulating and rationalising a policy of securing representation of particular classes (for example, landed interests and European commerce to begin with, and Indian business interests at a later stage) in the provincial and central legislatures. The ideational framework underlying the British Indian government's approach to the issue of representation of social strata or classes was probably consonant with nationalist thinking till at least the 1920s. The idea of separate representation of 'interests', however, was mainly the outcome of the efforts of the colonial bureaucracy to structure a system of representation that would have legitimacy and credibility. The legislative translation of this in the constitutional laws, that is, the Government of Acts of 1892, 1919 and 1935, was facilitated by the absence of universal franchise and the ability of the state to discriminatingly confer franchise on special electorates.

The shades of Jeremy Bentham and his Anglo-Indian disciples are not too far in the background even at the turn of the century.[32] It is, however, increasingly in the late nineteenth and early twentieth centuries in the *timber* of bureaucratic thinking rather than the digits of discourse where one continues to see its influence. Bentham developed a contrastive dichotomy between the legislator and the politician. The former is an outsider from afar – disinterested and free of connections with the people he legislates for. The politician is concerned with the parliamentary process of law making – one whose action is based on the principle of self-preference. He attends to what people want, while the legislator prescribes what is good for the people.[33] This dichotomy in Bentham seems relevant to the British bureaucracy's general stance on the question of building a legal regime. Bentham's legislator corresponds to the self-image of the Anglo-Indian bureaucrat – the disinterested outsider, free of connections – while the necessity of finding out what the people want (rather than what is good for them) leads to the induction into the legislature of others who act on the principle of self-preference; hence, the policy of representing interests.

The Government of India Act of 1919 which, as Governor-General Chelmsford put it, instituted, 'the first electoral system set up in India' and spawned a large number of policy documents of historic importance. Of these the report of the Franchise Committee was a crucially important one. The Committee, headed by Lord Southborough, included top-ranking civil servants like F. G. Sly and W. M. Hailey, as well as Indian spokesmen, for example, Surendranath Banerjea and V. S. Srinivasan. The inclusion of Banerjea was significant: he was the author of the 1886 resolution of the Congress on the inadequate representation of 'all the great interests' in the British Indian legislature. The terms of reference of this committee were the following: 'to advise how far representation can be adequately and effectively secured by territorial electorates, or where circumstances seems to require it . . . to secure adequate representation of minorities, of special interests . . . etc.'[34] The representation of special interests was to be secured by (a) special electorates, (b) reservation of elective seats in plural constituencies and (c) nomination. The Southborough Committee used the last expedient in the case of labour constituencies which it created for the first time in 1919; for the representation of the interest of landholders' business classes, universities and others, the special electorate was the preferred solution. The Southborough Committee on franchise recognised that under the 1909 dispensation, representation of the 'special interests' of commerce had meant 'in the main, though not exclusively, representation of European commercial interests' and Bombay's was the only Legislative Council where 'the special interests of Indian commerce are at present [i.e., before the 1919 reforms] represented'. The Franchise Committee brought into existence 'special representation of this interest in seven out of eight provinces'. However, the Franchise Committee of 1919 rejected the idea of labour electorate. One labour seat was conceded in the provincial legislative council of Bombay (likewise in Bengal, Bihar and Orissa, and Central Provinces) in 1919, but this single labour seat was to be filled by nomination by the governor. Labour, it was argued, could not be expected to obtain representation by any practicable system of election.[35]

It is interesting to note that Viceroy Chelmsford and his council were fully aware that the 'interest' theory had developed a peculiar system of representation. They admitted that it was 'not desirable to stereotype the representation of the different interests in fixed proportions; the longer the separate classes and communal constituencies remain set in a rigid mould, the harder it may become to progress towards normal methods of representation'.[36] But the government was unable to devise means towards changing the mould of 'interest representation'. So integral was this idea to the constitutional thinking of the British Raj that the removal of that foundation stone would have jeopardised the whole structure of representation not only of special interests (that is, business, labour, landholders, university graduates, etc.) but also that of the communal blocks (Muslim, depressed classes, Anglo-Indians, Indian Christians, etc.). During the 1920s, the working of the 1919 constitution solidified the two types of constituencies the 'interest' theory had spawned – what Chelmsford (in the despatch cited above) called the 'class constituencies' and the communal constituencies.[37]

The other major development of the 1920s was a push towards the extension of the principle of *election* as opposed to *nomination* by the government. The European and Indian 'Commerce Constituencies' were, of course, from the beginning represented, both at the provincial and central legislatures, by members elected by chambers of commerce and trade bodies, as mentioned earlier. The labour constituencies, however, were not allowed to hold elections on the grounds that no trade union bodies existed that were fit to be regarded as generally representative of urban workers. With the development of the All-India Trade Union Congress – the founding session in Bombay in 1920 was attended by top national leaders including Motilal Nehru, Lala Lajpat Rai (president), Vitthalbhai Patel, Annie Besant, M.A. Jinnah, C.F. Andrews and others – pressure mounted on the government to recognise the possibilities of making labour seats elective. The Reforms Enquiry Committee of 1924 (known as the Muddiman Committee) in fact made a recommendation to this effect. Further, the committee observed regarding 'depressed classes' and 'labour' constituencies that 'both these interests should receive further representation'. While accepting the recommendation regarding an increase in labour representation in the legislature, the Government of India rejected the idea of filling them up by means of election, for they preferred nomination by the government.

At the end of the decade, the question was revived by the Simon Commission, celebrated mainly as the object of nationalist boycott. The Commission suggested that the government should use elections as a mechanism for choosing labour representatives, and, should that be impossible, nomination may be made after consultation with labour organisations. The government's response was somewhat disingenuous: 'we would prefer that their representation should where possible be by election; but are bound to admit that the possibility of this still seems remote'.[38]

This statement is possibly disingenuous because it was no longer the non-existence of labour organisations that made election impossible: elections could be impolitic because there were by now organisations which were of the wrong kind. The foundation of the Workers' and Peasants' Party and the Communist Girni Kamgar Union in Bombay, the almost continuous strike for one year in the textile industry, the spread of socialist influence in the trade union movement, and others were factors which probably weighed with the British Indian government.[39]

As for the labour constituencies, the majority of this new Franchise Committee of 1932 underlined the need to represent capital in legislature as a corollary to the representation of capital. 'We found substantial support throughout India for the principle that if special representation is to be granted to capital through the reservation at seats in the legislatures for commerce and industry, representation should also be accorded to labour'.[40] This was also the position taken in the report of the Royal Commission on Indian Labour of 1931. 'If special constituencies are retained, it should be recognised that labour has no less claim to representation than capital . . . there is hardly any class with so strong a claim to representation by this method as industrial labour.'[41]

Meanwhile, the machinery erected on the basis of interest representation was becoming obsolete. It was no longer an adequate response to the political situation, since the national leadership began to break away from that theory and demanded adult franchise. The neat grid scheme of separate interests became increasingly irrelevant as the nationalist leaders acquired a hegemonic position. This is evident in the analysis of Irwin's government in 1930, when it talks of various interests or classes in Indian society – the 'commercial classes', 'industrial labour' and others – and then the logic of the language of interest theory leads the government to postulate a 'political class'. 'It is in the larger town that are to be found those elements which give direction or support to the political force of the day . . . what we may call the political classes.'[42] This so-called 'political class' had broken away from the scheme of things, which the Acts of 1892, 1909 and 1919 took for granted. Whereas the Congress had earlier spoken the language of 'interest representation' and had demanded separate special constituencies from the All Parties Convention of 1921, universal adult franchise became a part of the Congress political programme. When a national political party, the Congress began to acquire a wider base of social support, circumventing the 'interests' established in the legislatures, the rules of the game began to change; hence, the obsolescence of the interest representation mechanism. The elections of 1937 and of 1946 all over India under the Government of India Act of 1935 included election of legislators from 'Labour Constituencies'. Almost all the labour seats were captured by the Indian National Congress in both the elections. The sole labour constituency member of the Communist Party of India, who was elected in the last election held by the British Indian government in 1946, was Mr. Jyoti Basu of Bengal; he became the leader of a communist government in West Bengal for over three decades.

Conclusion

The colonial state in India put on the statute books an impressive number of labour laws, avowedly following the ILO norms; the ineffective application of these laws is well established in published works cited above. In the legislative discourse, we have looked at an important question – to what extent was legislation a consequence of pressure of the international labour movement, the ILO and labour opinion in England? We have considered the growing international links of the Indian labour leadership. A lobby in England promoting labour legislation in India seems to be active from 1917; a major motivation seems to be that cheapness of Indian labour was perceived as a threat. Proletarian internationalism as an ideology was more consciously propagated by the Comintern agencies but, locked in battle with the 'reformism' they derived in the International Federations of Trade Unions, the RILU spent most of its limited powers in India in intra-TU struggles. The papers of the All India Trade Union Congress (AITUC), now collected in the Nehru Museum archives, contain many examples of the consolidation of labour's international links in the 1930s. Even earlier, the AITUC had made gestures in that direction, for example, N. M. Joshi's statement on 'international solidarity of labour' on the occasion of the General Strike in England in 1926; letters also began to be exchanged between the General Federation of Japanese Labour and All-China Labour Federation and the AITUC about this time.[43] Nevertheless, labour laws of the post-war period could be scarcely construed as achievements of a proletarian international movement.

The need for the legitimation of prescriptive codes devised by the colonial state in British India in respect of industrial labour, in line with the norms laid down by the ILO since 1919, was partially met by the representation of labour and capital in the legislative forums. It was only partially met because the representation of labour was till 1937 through a system of nomination by the government and not by election, and their representation was numerically insignificant; in these respects, business interest representation was far better secured. In the theory behind colonial state practice, 'interest representation' was a surrogate for class representation; the rubrics developed on these lines came in handy to include interests of other kinds, for example, religious communities and depressed castes. The paradigm became increasingly obsolete in the 1930s, not only because the system of representation was perceived to be inadequate in the case of labour representation but also because the paradigm of adult franchise replaced that of 'interest representation' in the minds of the supposed beneficiaries of the representation system. As the nationalist movement acquired a hegemonic position, the question was no longer one of legitimation of state actions in respect of particular interests, such as labour; what was in question was the legitimacy of the colonial state itself.

This central question is what drove the creation of new labour laws. The search for the roots of the legal regime in respect of labour, leads us to the market, a primary, though not the exclusive, determinant of distribution and also the object of normative or mandatory prescriptions and proscriptions. Insofar as the market is nationally bounded, the latter are locally determined; when it is not so, global factors enter the process. Internationally, the most visible form of operating capital in the twentieth century is the multi-national corporation but, of course, internationalisation of the labour market cannot be ignored. Even prior to large-scale employment of immigrant labour in the advanced countries, the factor of wage cost differential and the resultant disadvantage to the countries with higher wages and labour regulations loomed large in the calculations of metropolitan industrial interests. *Standardization of labour regulations through an international legal/normative regime was one of the means of reducing this disadvantage.* Some countries like Japan retained their cost advantage by using low-paid labour and free of regulations.[44] In India, the colonial government legislated with great promptitude, but the laws were of marginal importance not only due to ineffective implementation but also the limits of their applicability. One must bear in mind the fact that Factory Laws were applicable to a small section of the industrial workforce – to about 1,045,200 persons in 1925 – while the total industrial workforce numbered 10.65 million, according to the Census of India of 1921; labour in the unorganised sector and small industrial establishments were disregarded. Thus, for a very limited section of the Indian labour force, laws were elaborated by the government following norms laid down by the ILO. It will be difficult to answer the question, why this happened, unless we view the new legal regime in the context of the agenda of transnational capitalist interests.

Notes

1 Gerry Rogers, J. Krishnamurthy and Sabyasachi Bhattacharya, 'India and the ILO in Historical Perspective', *Economic and Political Weekly*, 46(10) 5 March 2011; J. van Daele et al. (eds.), *ILO Histories: Essays on the International Labour Organisation and Its Impact on the World during the Twentieth Century*, Amsterdam: Peter Lang, 2010; J. van Daele et al. (eds.), *ILO Histories: Essays on the International Labour Organisation and Its Impact on the World During the Twentieth Century*, Amsredam: Peter Lang, 2010; Steve Hughes and Nigel Haworth, *The International Labour Organisation, Coming in From the Cold*, New York: Routledge, 2013; Nicole Countouris, *The Changing Law of Employment Relationship*, Aldershot: Kobo, 2013; also see an earlier work, N. Vaidyanathan, *ILO Conventions and India*, Calcutta: Minerva Associates 1975.

2 The best exposition of this view was in Vera Anstey, *The Economic Development of India*, 1929, 1952, 1957, London: Amo Press, p. 295. There was, of course, a contrary view emphasizing the interests of capital as the driving force. Aditya Sarkar in his recent research has proposed a rethinking of that view as well as the general historiographic approach to labour legislation which ignored the historically contingent and contested nature of labour laws in the late nineteenth century; his work, in progress, promises a counter-narrative of which a portion has been published in: Aditya Sarkar, 'The Work of Law: Three Factory Narratives from Bombay Presidency, 1881–4', in Marcel van der Linden and Prabhu P. Mohapatra (eds.), *Labour Matters: Towards Global Histories*, New Delhi: Tulika, 2009.

3 Vera Anstey, *The Economic Development of India*, is a bland but comprehensive narrative; also see R.K. Das, *History of Indian Labour Legislation*, Calcutta: R.K. Das, 1941; H.M. Trivedi, *Labour and Factory Legislation in India*, Bombay: Law Publishers, 1945; A.K. Sen, *Indian Labour Legislation*, Calcutta: Minerva Associates, 1961. The limitations of approaches to labour in the Indian context have been critically examined by Prabhu Mohapatra in his research on labour law and more generally in Prabhu P. Mohapatra, 'Situating the Renewal: Reflections on Labour Studies in India', *Labour and Development*, Noida: National Labour Institute, 1999.

4 Anstey, *The Economic Development of India*, p. 299.

5 Bernard Gerignon et al., *ILO Principles Concerning the Right to Strike*, ILO, 2000. It may be noted that Indian nationalist leaders were far from being unanimous about the right to strike; Nehru, unlike Mahatma Gandhi, recognised workers' right to strike; Sabyasachi Bhattacharya, 'Swaraj and the Kamgar: The Indian National Congress and the Bombay Working Class, 1919–31', in Richard Sisson and Stanley Wolpert (eds.), *Congress and Indian Nationalism*, Berkeley: University of California Press, 1988.

6 P.J.G. Kapteyn, R.H. Lauwaars, et al., *International Organization and Integration: Annotated Basic Documents*, vol. 1, B, The Hague: Martinus Nijhoff Publishers, 1982.

7 Oscar Schachter, 'The Evolving International Law of Development', *Columbia Journal of Transnational Law*, 1976, 15.

8 A. Alcock, *History of the ILO*, London: Palgrave Macmillan, 1971, p. 90.

9 J.T. Shotwell, *The Origins of the ILO*, New York: Columbia University Press, 1934.
10 Govt. of India, Home Department, Political Branch, February 1920, File no. 52, National Archives of India, New Delhi, hereafter cited as Home. Pol., NAI. All references hereafter to the correspondence and files of the government of India are to the archived unpublished documents of the Indian government in the National Archives of India, New Delhi, hereafter NAI.
11 M.N. Roy, in *International Press Correspondence*, 1925, p. 231.
12 Kees van der Pijl, in Hans Overbeek (ed.), *Restructuring Hegemony in the Global Political Economy*, London: Routledge, 1993; R. Murray, 'The Internationalization of Capital and the Nation State', *New Left Review*, May 1967, 67; H. Gunter, *Transnational Industrial Relations the Impact of the MNC and Economic Regionalism on Industrial Relations*, London: Palgrave Macmillan, 1972.
13 Kapteyn, Lauwaars, *International Organization and Integration*.
14 G.A. Johnston, *The ILO*, London: Europa Publishers, 1970.
15 Kapteyn, Lauwaars, *International Organization and Integration*, op. cit. Document 2C.
16 Kinglsey Davis, *Population of India and Pakistan*, Princeton, NJ: Princeton University Press, 1951, p. 99.
17 According to one estimate, in 1980–1981 remittances from labour migrants were 8.8 percent of GNP in Pakistan, 3.4 percent in Bangladesh and 1.1 percent in India; the remittances home were respectively 69.9 percent, 53 percent and 19.9 percent of merchandise exports, ref. R.T. Appleyard, *International Migration Today: Trends and Prospects*, Paris: UNESCO, 1988, Vol. 1, Table 5, p. 104.
18 Karl Marx, *Grundrisee, Foundations of the Critique of Political Economy*, Translated by Martin Nicolaus, Penguin, 1973, p. 408, in Marx, *Capital*, Chapter 22, Vol.1.
19 Meerut Conspiracy Case Documents, Depositions, 4.1.32, p. 2573, National Archives of India, hereafter cited as MCC Documents.
20 For example, Sukomal Sen, *Working Class in India*, Calcutta: K P Bagchi & Co, 1977, 1979. p. 163.
21 GOI, Home Pol., File no. 92, Apr. 1919, NAI.
22 Director, Central Intelligence, 12.1.20, Home Pol.. February 1920, No. 52, NAI.
23 Weekly Report, Central Intelligence, 16.2.20, Home Pol. February 1920, no. 75, NAI.
24 India Office, Pol. Secret, File. no. 1229, 1920; Dange, MCC Documents, NAI, p. 2579.
25 Home Pol. File nos. 181–184, February 1919, NAI.
26 Home Pol. No. 13, July 1920, NAI.
27 Central Intelligence Report, 15.9.19, Home Pol. B, no. 456, September 1919, National Archives of India.
28 Govt of India, Home Pol. F. 152, 1929, NAI.
29 S.A. Dange, MCC Documents, NAI, p. 2580.
30 GOI, Home Pol. March 1920, no. 89, NAI.
31 Asa Briggs, 'The Language of Class' in Asa Briggs (ed.), *Essays in Labour History*, London, 1960.

32 Eric Stokes, *English Utilitarians and India*, Oxford: Oxford University Press, 1959.
33 N.L. Rosenblum, *Bentham's Theory of the Modern State*, Cambridge, MA: Harvard University Press, 1978.
34 Southborough, Chairman, *Franchise Committee*, 1919.
35 *Report of Franchise Committee*, Chairman: Lord Southborough, Govt. of India, Calcutta, 1919.
36 Despatch of Govt. of India, i.e. Governor-General in Council, India, to Secretary of State for Indian Affairs, England, 23.4.1919, hereafter cited as dispatch of GOI, NAI.
37 Govt of India to Secretary of State for India, 23.4.1919, NAI
38 GOI to Secretary of State, 20.9.1930.
39 Sabyasachi Bhattacharya, 'The Colonial State, Capital and Labour in Bombay City, 1919–31', in Romila Thapar and S. Bhattacharya (eds.), *Situating Indian History*, New Delhi: Oxford University Press, 1986.
40 *Report of Franchise Committee*, 1932 (Lord Lothian, Chairman), Govt. of India, Calcutta, 1932.
41 *Report of the Royal Commission on Labour in India*, Calcutta, 1931, p. 436.
42 GOI to Secretary of State, 20.9.1930.
43 AITUC Papers, Manuscripts collection F. 1926–35, New Delhi: Nehru Memorial Museum.
44 Ehud Herari, *The Politics of Labour Legislation in Japan: National International Interaction*, Berkeley: University of California Press, 1973.

Part IV
Contemporary capitalism and the Indian economy

12 Financialisation in contemporary capitalism

An inter-sectoral approach to trace sources of instability in finance, real estate and business services in India

Sukanya Bose and Abhishek Kumar

Pattern of present growth under financialisation

Financialisation creates space for transactions in the financial sector of economies and, in doing so, helps to raise the share of activities in finance, insurance, real estate and business services (FINREBS) in an economy. Largely driven by deregulation, the process works to make assets in those sectors, especially in finance and real estate (or even commodity trade), relatively attractive as compared to other assets, by offering both better returns and potential capital gains.

From the 1980s, the United States saw a pattern of growth, where the US financial sector grew relative to the non-financial sectors. By the year of global financial crisis, the financial sector alone accounted for more than 20 percent of the national value added and 40 percent of corporate profits.[1] The over-development and malfunction of the US financial sector led to a worldwide financial and economic crisis of unprecedented scale. The world still lives in the shadow of this crisis.

Multilateral agencies who till recently were vigorously pushing financial liberalisation and capital account convertibility have admitted the excesses of the present systems. A recent presentation by a team of economists from IMF asked the question: how much finance is too much?[2] Based on a composite index of financial development to include financial institutions and financial markets of each country, the researchers noted the existence of a trade-off between stability and growth at high levels of financial development. Financial development helps growth, but there is a turning point. Further, not only are the advanced economies like the United States, Japan and Ireland past the turning point, but India – an emerging market economy with high levels of unemployment and poverty – is also past the peak![3] Is it the case of too much finance for India?

Growth of service sector in perspective

One notices in the literature two sets of contrary evidences on the question of growth of the service sector vis-à-vis non-service sectors that coexist for the Indian economy. A set of studies have argued that the Indian economic growth since the 1980s is by and large led by service sector growth, which, not being a commodity-producing sector, depends on both industry and agriculture for its growth. The stylisation of the service sector in macroeconomic models shows the service sector output as dependent on incomes and output in the commodity (goods) sector.[4] Co-integration analysis by Kaur, Bordoloi and Rajesh,[5] among other things, points at the long-term equilibrium relationship of services with agricultural and industrial sectors. Debnath and Roy, examining the growth of the regional economies of the northeast for the period 1981–2007, find a unidirectional causality running from agriculture and industrial sectors to the services sector.[6] The authors conclude that the income of economies of the northeast depend on income generation from the service sector, and income growth of service sector in turn depends on growth of agriculture and industry. More recently, and in the context of the debate on the new GDP series, Goldar relies on the interdependence between services and manufacturing (the so-called absence of divergence in growth over time) to establish higher growth in manufacturing in the new GDP series.[7] It would be an aberration, at best short lived, if services were to move independently of the commodity-producing sector.

On the contrary, a second set of studies has failed to find a convincing link between the service and commodity (non-service) sectors. Among those who pointed to the autonomous nature of the service sector growth, two studies are of particular importance. In 1988, Ashok Mitra noted the disproportionate rise of the service sector in India's national income. 'The explosion in service activities cannot be readily attributed to any impulse transmitted by the sectors engaged in material production. It has an autonomous character and is a kind of superimposition on the natural forces of historical evolution.'[8] Within the services sector, the highest rate of growth at the time was being registered in public administration and defence, that is, in the arena of government activities. Expansion in public administration and defence had little causal relationship with developments in either agriculture or industry.

The issue of disproportionate growth of tertiary sector in the Indian economy was brought up in another paper by B. B. Bhattacharya and Arup Mitra.[9] They found that, except in the case of trade group, commodity output had very little relationship with service income. The broad conclusion was that the growth rate of service income is independent of the growth rate of the income of the commodity sector. Both these studies looked at the components of services to understand the impetus for growth.

The context of the debate provides a useful entry point to examine the present phase of service-led growth, which has seen significant growth in certain types of services.

Trend and pattern of growth in FINREBS

The growing service sector comprises three types of services corresponding broadly to National Accounts classification:

(a) trade, hotel, transport and communications (TRAD&TRAN);
(b) community, social and personal services (COMMUNITY); and
(c) finance, insurance, real estate and business services (FINREBS).

Trends in the growth rates of these services in real terms in the last 15 years are examined below.

Figure 12.1(a) shows the quarter-on-quarter (five years' rolling) growth rate of three components of services (TRAD&TRAN, COMMUNITY and FINREBS) and all goods since the year 2001: Q1. Figure 12.1(b) traces the growth of finance, insurance, real estate and business services (FINREBS) vis-à-vis the rest of the sectors of the economy (GDP excluding FINREBS). Rolling estimates of growth smooth out the short-run fluctuations. The dataset consists of quarterly data from 1996: Q2 to 2014: Q3 (calendar year) at 2004–2005 prices.[10] Since the five-year rolling estimates have been obtained, the rolling growth rates begin from 2001: Q1.

• Between 2001: Q1 and 2007–2008: Q3, the TRAD&TRAN sector was the fastest growing sector among the services (Figure

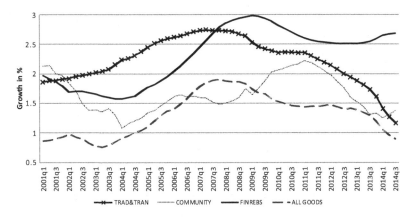

Figure 12.1a Quarterly growth rate (rolling)

Source: RBI, Database on the Indian Economy and authors' calculations.

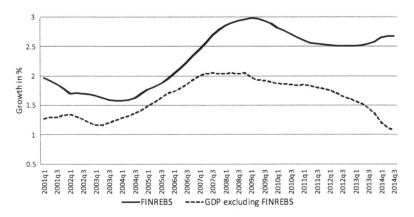

Figure 12.1b Quarterly growth rate (rolling)

Source: RBI, Database on the Indian Economy and authors' calculations.

Note: The rolling estimates were developed using $Lny_t = \beta_t + \beta_t t + \mu_t$ where y represents the different components of GDP. In rolling estimation, the initial period of 20 quarters is taken; each subsequent estimation added one recent quarter and excluded the oldest quarter. Rolling estimates have been used to look at the growth rate as it is less volatile compared to the actual growth rate.

12.1a). Thereafter, the growth of TRAD&TRAN has continuously declined, whereas FINREBS growth shot up. FINREBS has maintained a reasonably high growth rate throughout, except for a small decline from 3 percent to 2.5 percent between 2009: Q1 and 2012: Q4. The growth of the COMMUNITY sector accelerated from 2009: Q1 to 2011: Q1, a reflection of the countercyclical policy; it subsequently fell as the government went for fiscal consolidation via expenditure tightening. Unlike the period Mitra (1988) was referring to, growth of COMMUNITY has been the lowest among the three sub-sectors beyond 2002.

- Across the period, the FINREBS sector has grown at a rate higher than the rest of the sectors of the economy taken together (Figure 12.1b). The growth differential clearly widened since 2007. Even so, the direction of movement of growth of FINREBS and the rest of the sectors of the economy were similar till 2011. As the growth of the economy plummeted further, growth in FINREBS, defying the trend, showed upward movement (but for the last few quarters of the sample period).

- Higher growth of FINREBS compared to the rest of the sectors of the economy is reflected in its rising share in service GDP and overall GDP (Figure 12.2). After 2005, FINREBS has grown phenomenally; its share in GDP has risen to around 22 percent by the 2014: Q3, and its share in service output has increased to around 35 percent from 28 percent in 2005.

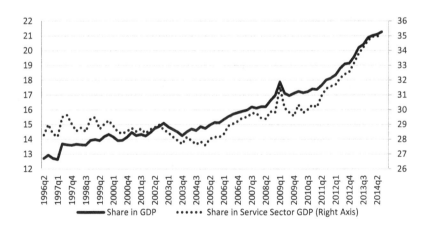

Figure 12.2 Share of finance, insurance, real estate and business services (FINREBS) in percentage

Source: RBI, Database on the Indian Economy and authors' calculations.

Box 1   What constitutes FINREBS?

FINREBS comprises a large number of services that can broadly be clubbed into three components: (a) banking and insurance; (b) ownership of dwellings and real estate; and (c) business services. While the first component relates to finance, the second refers to property and related services, and the third component relates business services. Banking and insurance covers commercial banks, non-banking financial corporations (organised and unorganised), post office savings bank, cooperative credit societies and life and non-life insurance activities. The gross output of banks and similar financial institutions are estimated in two components, namely, actual service charges and imputed service charges. Ownership of dwellings refers to services of occupied residential houses, and real estate services include activities of all types of dealers such as operators, developers and agents connected with real estate. Business services include computer and related activities in the private sector, legal activities, accounting, book-keeping and auditing activities and tax consultancy services. Besides, renting of machinery and equipment without operator, research and development, market research and public opinion polling, business and management consultancy, architectural, engineering and other technical activities and advertising also fall under business services.

Since 2004–2005, banking and insurance sectors have grown at a rapid rate and consolidated their position within FINREBS. In the latest year, banking and insurance comprise 49 percent of the total output of the sector. Ownership of dwellings and real estate comprise another 23 percent; hence, the combined share of these two segments is close to three-fourths of GDP of FINREBS. Business services, which includes the fast growing computer services segment, contributed 28 percent of FINREBS output in 2012–2013 (see Figure 12.3a and 12.3b).

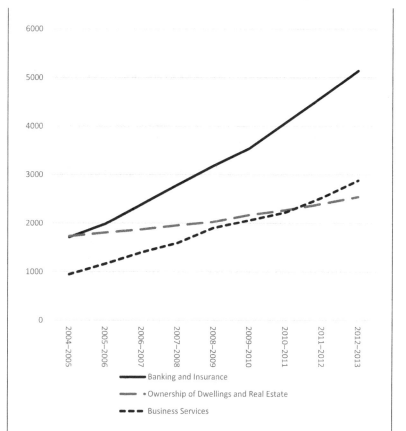

Figure 12.3a Components of FINREBS (Rs Billion) at 2004–2005 prices

Source: Sources and Methods, National Accounts Statistics, 2007 and NAS reports.

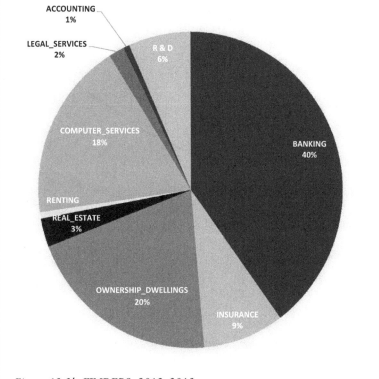

Figure 12.3b FINREBS, 2012–2013

Source: Sources and Methods, National Accounts Statistics, 2007 and NAS reports.

A priori, one would hold that the growth of FINREBS would have a reasonable interlinkage with the rest of the sectors of the economy. For banking, insurance, real estate and business services could all feed into the growth of commodity sectors and vice versa. However, the kind of finance-led growth India has witnessed in the recent period does not seem to be embedded in the real economy. The linkages of finance, insurance, real estate and business services sectors with the other sectors of the economy have probably been weak such that the expansionary phase of this sector has not been accompanied by a revival of overall economic growth.

The next three sections of this essay try to empirically explore this hypothesis. Firstly, we explore intersectoral relations using the input–output matrices for the Indian economy. Secondly, we apply rolling recursive co-integration to study the movement of FINREBS vis-à-vis other sectors using quarterly data. Thirdly, we approach the connectedness question using forecast error variance decomposition of time series data. The results validate low linkages of FINREBS as compared to most other sectors of the economy. Co-integration results substantiate the weak linkages (but for a few exceptions). A large percentage of variation in the growth of FINREBS cannot be explained by other sectors of the economy, which gives FINREBS (and services) an autonomous character. Next, we posit a possible explanation on how this might be possible and connect the weak linkages to the ensuing instability in the system. Finally, we sum up the concluding arguments.

Inter-linkages across sectors: analysis of input–output matrices

In order to understand the nature of relationship between FINREBS and other sectors of the economy, linkage effects provide a useful framework. The structural relationship between sectors can be measured in terms of two types of linkage effects first described by Albert Hirschman.[11] Backward linkage effects are related to derived demand, that is, the provision of input for a given activity. Forward linkage effects are related to output utilisation, that is, the outputs from a given activity will induce attempts to use this output as inputs in some new activities.

The idea underlying the measures of linkages is that industries provide the driving forces for the expansion of the system through their activities or rather through the input demands as well as output production stemming from these activities. Economic systems with a high degree of interrelatedness and strong causal linkage effects are more dynamic than systems with few causal linkages due to few incentive-driving activities in the existing industries. As Drejer notes, what is studied is the systemic character of an economy: no unit – firm or industry – exists in isolation from the other units in the system.[12] Linkage effects have been used extensively to identify the key or the leading sectors of the economy.

Linkage measures are computed using input–output tables for the Indian economy for the three latest years 1998–1999, 2003–2004 and

2007–2008. Industries in the input–output table are aggregated into eight categories corresponding to the NAS classification:

- agriculture and allied activities (AGRI),
- mining (MIN),
- manufacturing (MFG),
- construction (CONSTR),
- electricity, gas and water supply (EG&WS),
- transport, storage and communication and trade, hotels and restaurants (TRAD&TRAN),
- community, social and personal services (including public administration and defence) (COMMUNITY),
- financing, insurance, real estate and business services (FINREBS).

Backward linkage

Backward linkages exist when the growth of an industry leads to the growth of the industries that supply it. Analysis of input–output coefficients (matrix A) of the Indian economy for the year 2007–2008 reveals manufacturing, construction and electricity, gas and water supply (the secondary sector) have the strongest backward linkage, followed by trade and transport among service sector activities. AGRI comes next in terms of demand for inputs from other sectors as a proportion of total output of the AGRI sector. The last two sectors, with regard to backward linkage, are FINREBS and COMMUNITY. FINREBS one of the fastest growing sectors of the Indian economy has one of the lowest backward linkages and ranks seventh amongst the eight sectors of the economy. Backward linkage from FINREBS to each individual sector is maximum to FINREBS itself though, even this coefficient is low. The next three sectors in decreasing order to which FINREBS has a backward linkage are TRADE&TRAN, MFG and CONSTR.

Table 12.1 presents a summary of the backward linkages derived from input–output matrices for the three years, 1998–1999, 2003–2004 and 2007–2008. Backward linkage effects computed using the $(I-A)^{-1}$ matrix gives both direct and indirect backward linkages for the respective years. The inverse matrix coefficients indicate the magnitude of the ultimate direct and indirect production repercussions on the n industrial sectors when there is one unit of final demand for j^{th} sector.

Across the three time points, manufacturing, electricity, gas and water supply and construction have consistently had the strongest backward linkage. This is seen in the backward linkage index (BLI),

Table 12.1 Summary of backward linkage (direct and indirect): inter-sectoral and inter-temporal comparison

YEAR		AGRI	MIN	MFG	CONSTR	EG&WS	TRAD&TRAN	FINREBS	COMMUNITY
1998–1999	Backward linkage (direct and indirect)	1.42	1.41	2.36	2.048	2.177	1.675	1.279	1.606
	Backward linkage index	0.81	0.81	1.35	1.172	1.246	0.959	0.732	0.919
	RANK	6	7	1	3	2	4	8	5
2003–2004	Backward linkage (direct and indirect)	1.67	1.55	2.52	2.289	2.561	1.813	1.366	1.283
	Backward linkage index	0.89	0.82	1.34	1.217	1.362	0.964	0.726	0.682
	RANK	5	6	2	3	1	4	7	8
2007–2008	Backward linkage (direct and indirect)	1.65	1.49	2.61	2.399	2.172	1.814	1.334	1.29
	Backward linkage index	0.89	0.81	1.42	1.3	1.177	0.983	0.723	0.699
	RANK	5	6	1	2	3	4	7	8

Source: Authors' calculation based on input–output tables published by Central Statistical Office.

which gives the backward linkage of the particular sector relative to the average backward linkage of the system as a whole.[13] BLI has a value greater than 1 for the three sectors. After the secondary sector, trade and transport (TRAD&TRAN) has the next highest backward linkage, with BLI close to 1. The rest of the sectors of the economy have BLI less than 1.

Significantly, COMMUNITY has moved down from fifth to eighth rank across the years and pushed FINREBS to the seventh rank. The change in relative ranking between COMMUNITY and FINREBS could partly be because of definitional changes. With re-classification of sectors between COMMUNITY and FINREBS, services that were earlier counted as part of community moved into FINREBS.[14]

Backward linkages from all the sectors of the economy, except community, increased between 1998–1999 and 2003–2004. One may infer that there were growing interlinkages across the sectors, with most sectors moving together between these two time-points. The movements across 2003–2004 and 2007–2008 show different tendencies across sectors. Rising backward linkage is observed for manufacturing, construction, trade and transport and community. Backward linkages from the rest of the sectors declined between 2003–2004 and 2007–2008. FINREBS exhibited a rising trend in backward linkages between 1998–1999 and 2003–2004 and a declining trend in backward linkages between 2003–2004 and 2007–2008.

Forward linkages

It has been argued that the service sector may not have enough backward linkages, but the forward linkages from this sector could be strong.[15] Higher output of the service sector may induce other sectors of the economy to expand production and utilise more of their inputs. Growth in banking activities will induce industry and other production that is dependent on banking services to increase. One expects a fairly high forward linkage in that case.

Analysis of output coefficient matrix for the Indian economy for the year 2007–2008 shows that mining (MIN), electricity, gas and water supply (EG&WS), and manufacturing (MFG) are the top three sectors with the highest forward linkages with the rest of the economy. The high value of forward linkage for the mining sector is due to the high input use of mining industry by the manufacturing sector. Construction is the only secondary sector with low forward linkage. Among the service sectors, trade and transport has the highest forward linkage.

FINREBS has sixth position among sectors, behind agriculture but ahead of construction and community.

Forward linkage from FINREBS to each individual sector is the highest to manufacturing, followed by TRADE&TRAN and FINREBS. Manufacturing uses the maximum share of FINREBS output amongst all the sectors.

For comparison across time, forward linkages (direct and indirect) for the years 1998–1999, 2003–2004 and 2007–2008 are computed using the (I-O) inverse matrix (Table 12.2). Compared to direct linkages, FINREBS moved ahead of AGRI to improve its position from sixth to fifth when ranked in terms of direct plus indirect forward linkages. The forward linkage index (FLI) gives the forward linkage of the particular sector relative to the average forward linkage of the system as a whole.[16] A lower than one figure for FINREBS implies that the forward linkage from FINREBS is lower than the average forward linkage of the system.

Looking at the trends across time, between 1998–1999 and 2003–2004, the forward linkage increased for all sectors, except COMMUNITY. Between 2003–2004 and 2007–2008, the forward linkage increased for all but two sectors electricity, gas and water supply and FINREBS, where it declined.

To sum up, backward and forward linkages from FINREBS has weakened between 2003–2004 and 2007–2008, the period corresponding to the initial boom in this sector. Forward linkage from FINREBS to the rest of the economy is below average compared to the rest of the sectors of the economy, and backward linkage from FINREBS is amongst the lowest. Based on the above, one can infer that FINREBS cannot be a 'leading sector' in the Hirschman sense. Rather finance, real estate and business service seems to have developed as an autonomous sector with limited linkages with other sectors of the economy.

The next section carries forward the enquiry into the relationship between FINREBS and the other sectors of the economy using econometric techniques.

Inter-relationship with FINREBS: co-integration and causality

Input–output tables are available only at discrete time points. Since the latest available table for India is only 2007–2008, the period since the worldwide financial crisis is not captured. In Figure 12.1(b), the quarterly growth rate (rolling) suggests significant divergence in FINREBS

Table 12.2 Summary of forward linkage (direct and indirect): inter-sectoral and inter-temporal comparison

	Forward linkage (direct and indirect)	Rasmussen forward linkage Index	RANK	Forward linkage (direct and indirect)	Rasmussen forward linkage Index	RANK	Forward linkage (direct and indirect)	Rasmussen forward linkage Index	RANK
	1998–1999			2003–2004			2007–2008		
AGRI	1.375	0.919	6	1.845	0.758	6	1.972	0.757	6
MIN	1.989	1.33	1	6.061	2.489	1	7.296	2.801	1
MFG	1.542	1.031	3	2.231	0.916	3	2.282	0.876	3
CONSTR	1.134	0.758	8	1.276	0.524	7	1.333	0.512	7
EG&WS	1.73	1.156	2	3.091	1.269	2	2.887	1.108	2
TRAD&TRAN	1.454	0.972	4	1.957	0.804	4	2.066	0.793	4
FINREBS	1.453	0.972	5	1.872	0.769	5	1.803	0.692	5
COMMUNITY	1.289	0.862	7	1.148	0.471	8	1.202	0.461	8

Source: Authors' calculation based on input–output tables published by Central Statistical Office.

and other sectoral components of GDP. Another problem with the use of input–output tables to compute backward and forward linkages is that 'input–output analysis is by nature synchronic, whereas linkage effects need time to unfold'.[17] The responses to increase in demand or higher availability of inputs may be lagged. Time series econometric techniques can take care of some of these issues and throw additional light on the intersectoral relations.

Co-integration methods have been used by researchers to explore the intersectoral relationship, as noted in the earlier section. Interdependence across sectors, either from demand or supply side or both, is expected to manifest in co-integrating equations. Given the interdependence between sectors, the different components of the economy are expected to move together. However, it is also true that different components may receive different shocks, thus the intersectoral relations may change over time. For example, a global slump may affect tradable goods sector (manufacturing) the most and because of that the long-run relation between manufacturing and other GDP components may suddenly breakdown. Statistically, the identification of long-run relationship through co-integration is therefore sensitive to choice of sample. In recent years, researchers have thus begun to use co-integration in rolling recursive framework. In what follows, Johansen co-integration in a rolling recursive framework has been applied to the quarterly GDP series after testing for stationarity.[18] If the trace statistics is increasing with time, it implies the increasing association of components and vice-versa.

We have noted that FINREBS has low overall linkages. Specifically, what is the nature of relationship between FINREBS and other sectors of the economy, and how has it evolved over time? Co-integration along with causality enables us to understand the evolving nature of relationship between FINREBS and rest of the sectors. COMMUNITY has been excluded as the latter is largely policy determined and there is no a priori reason to expect co-movement of FINREBS and COMMUNITY output.

Figure 12.4 presents the results of Johansen co-integration of FINREBS with the other components of GDP in a rolling recursive framework. Thereafter, causality was tested using the Toda–Yamamoto method.[19]

Overall the association between FINREBS and other sectors seems weak, with trace statistics being statistically insignificant for mining, for construction and, lately, for manufacturing sector also. With respect to two sectors – electricity, gas and water supply and trade and transport – though the trace statistics in the latest period has crossed

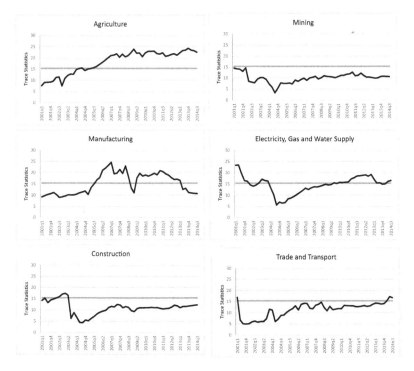

Figure 12.4 Co-integration test with FINREBS rolling recursive trace statistics

Note: Horizontal line denotes critical values at 5 percent. When the trace statistics is higher than the horizontal red line (critical value for null hypothesis of $K_0 = 0$), it denotes the presence of long run relationship. First estimation was done with 20 data points, and in subsequent estimation, one additional data point was added at each step. Results become more robust as sample size increases.

the critical value, it has not been significant in the past/for very long. However, agriculture and FINREBS seem to have a steady and rising association.

The results of co-integration and causality tests are interpreted below:

(a) The trace statistic between agriculture and FINREBS has risen over time and is statistically significant beyond 2005. Beyond 2010, the association although still significant has flattened. Causality in Table 12.3 shows FINREBS causes agriculture.

The link between AGRI and FINREBS is essentially through credit finance (direct and indirect) of agriculture activities.

Agricultural credit growth after severe stagnation and neglect in the 1990s began to revive. Narayanan studying the ground level credit flows finds that institutional credit as a percentage of value of inputs plus compensation to employees in agriculture in India surged from 42 percent in 2004–2005 to 85 percent in 2011–2012.[20] A range of supply side policy measures, including debt waiver and interest subvention contributed to flow of credit to agriculture and allied activities by scheduled commercial banks in the recent years. Short-term credit to agriculture to finance working capital needs increased notably. It appears that agriculture being a supply-constrained sector has benefited from growing FINREBS although after 2010 the relationship has flattened. The latter accords with the observation that agricultural growth flattened in UPA-2 regime compared to UPA-1 years.[21] An in-depth analysis of the sectors would be required to understand the phenomenon fully.

(b) The relationship of FINREBS with manufacturing shows a double dip phenomenon very similar to the movement of growth in manufacturing sector. Before the onset of financial crisis, the trace statistics between manufacturing and FINREBS increased and was statistically significant. It dipped sharply with the crisis and recovered and then again dipped, such that the relationship is statistically insignificant in the latest periods. Prima facie, the relationship between manufacturing and FINREBS is dictated by the former as the causality tests also suggest. Causality is unidirectional running from MFG to FINREBS. Unlike agriculture, where the relationship with FINREBS appeared to be supply driven, movement of FINREBS vis-à-vis manufacturing in particular appears to be demand determined. This is true of mining and construction too (Table 12.3).

(c) A somewhat surprising result is the comparatively low trace statistics between construction and FINREBS. A priori, one would expect construction and FINREBS to move together given the proximity of finance and real estate (further discussed below). One possible reason why that may not be happening is that finance need not automatically translate to construction activities. For instance, finance may be involved in repurchase of property, acquisition and development of land and other real estate activities and need not give rise to new construction activities. In other words, FINREBS may grow by acquisition of assets rather than creating new assets.

(d) The relationship between FINREBS and electricity, gas and water supply has been significant over last few quarters of 2014. Also, vis-à-vis trade and transport, trace statistics lately shows a significant relationship with FINREBS. The indication of these sectors (electricity, gas, water supply and trade and transport) moving

Table 12.3 Causality between FINREBS and other sectors, sample: 1996:Q2–
2014: Q3

	Chi square	Prob> Chi square
Agriculture does not cause FINREBS	0.99	0.3195
FINREBS does not cause agriculture	16.67	0
Mining does not cause FINREBS	2.8	0.0943
FINREBS does not cause mining	0.26	0.6099
Manufacturing does not cause FINREBS	8.59	0.0034
FINREBS does not cause manufacturing	0.42	0.5146
EG&WS does not cause FINREBS	6.55	0.0105
FINREBS does not cause EG&WS	5.96	0.0147
Construction does not cause FINREBS	5.02	0.025
FINREBS does not cause construction	0.4	0.5252
TRAD&TRAN does not cause FINREBS	5.59	0.0181
FINREBS does not cause TRAD&TRAN	3.22	0.0728

together in the last quarters of the sample period with respect to
FINREBS is to some extent due to the growth of FINREBS finally
tapering off. The following section discusses why the tapering of
FINREBS growth is ultimately inevitable.

Growth connectedness: further econometric evidence

The co-integration and causality tests suggest autonomous nature of
growth of FINREBS, with variations across sectors and periods. To
substantiate this point, we do forecast error variance decomposition
(FEVD) of growth of sectoral components. FEVD determines how
much of the forecast error variance of each of the variables can be
explained due to shocks to the other variables. This is another way
to look at the growth connectedness. Similar in format as the input –
output table, FEVD combines two advantages: (a) time series data till
the most recent period can be used; and (b) optimum lag structure
takes care of lagged effect on variables and allows us to explore the
inter-linkages with lagged effects.

A generalised VAR is estimated between GDP components at lag 1
and lag 4, the latter being based on information criterion.[22] After estimation, the forecast error variance is obtained at 10 period (that is,
after 10 quarters). Comparing FEVD with one and four lags, one finds
that as we increase the number of lags from one to four, the variation in growth explained by the other sectors (or components) increase
considerably. It reflects that the linkages need time to take effect and
are not completely instantaneous. Contemporaneous frameworks may

not be able to fully capture the full extent of linkages, such that the relationships can be best understood with an optimum lag length. In understanding the intersectoral relations in the Indian case, this might be an important way forward.

In both the estimations, with 1 and 4 lags, the variation in growth of FINREBS is least explained by the other sectors. At 1 lag, 82 percent of variation in growth of FINREBS is explained by FINREBS itself. Even after allowing for 4 lags, 48 percent variation in FINREBS is explained by FINREBS itself. Agriculture and community are the next two sectors where the interdependence, expectedly, is weak. Variation in agriculture is typically explained by variation in rainfall, whereas in case of community, the growth is policy determined. Analysis of FEVD corroborates the least association of FINREBS with other components of GDP in terms of growth connectedness and suggests that there is significant autonomous component in FINREBS.

Whither FINREBS driven growth?

The foregoing analysis raises some fundamental questions. How did FINREBS within the services sector continue to grow when the other sectors of the economy were performing badly? What are the implications of high growth of FINREBS with weak links to other sectors of the economy? Is it sustainable? While the full range of answers is beyond the scope of the study, a few exploratory arguments are placed here.

As we saw, FINREBS consists of three sets of services: (a) banking and insurance; (b) ownership of dwellings and real estate; and (c) business services. To the extent business services include outsourced services and service exports, one may suggest that business services to have propelled growth through export demand. This is the dominant view prevailing in India, even though the situation on the ground has changed. Nagaraj argues on these lines when he says that higher growth rates between 1992–2003 and 2006–2007, compared to 1980s in services, is due to communication and business services.[23] While this may be one factor, one cannot overlook that in 2012–2013, business services accounted for not more than 28 percent of GDP of the FINREBS, whereas the remaining 72 percent comprised output of banking and insurance and ownership of dwellings and real estate. In other words, while business services which include services like computer services are significant contributors to gross value added and export earnings, growth of FINREBS cannot be wholly or primarily be attributed to business services, at least during the past decade or so.

In fact, the rising importance of finance has forced a methodological shift in the computation of national income. The recent revision of GDP series for India (new GDP series with 2011–2012 base) has reclassified the government and private sectors into financial and non-financial corporations as per SNA, 2008.[24] Estimates of the institutional sectors – financial and non-financial – are shown separately in view of their intrinsic differences in their economic objectives, functions and behaviours. Further, in the new series, the coverage of the financial sector has been expanded to include stock brokers, stock exchanges, asset management companies, mutual funds and pension funds, as well as regulatory authorities, like SEBI, PFRDA and IRDA. As the financial sector grows with a much wider range of players, the activity of all these entities determine the scope of the financial sector. Compared to the 2004–2005 series, the gross value added by financial corporations at current prices for the year 2011–2012 shows higher value added by (a) non-bank financial intermediaries; (b) cooperative credit societies; and (c) unorganised sector. These changes would help in more accurate estimation of the growth of the financial sector and its contribution in future.

Keynes–Minsky framework

To understand fully the nature of growth of FINREBS, one has to turn towards dynamics of finance and investment under uncertainty. From the Keynes–Minsky perspective of financial instability, periods of deep recession associated with financial fragility are an outcome of financial excesses in the preceding booms. The great threat to stability is the boom since it encourages risky behaviour that ultimately leads to the crash – explosive growth that eventually crashes. The underlying theory, known as the investment theory of the cycle and financial theory of investment, ties together insights from Keynes and Minsky.

Investment can proceed only if the demand price, which emerges out of the asset price system, exceeds the supply price, which emerges out of the current output price system.[25] Optimism and reduced uncertainty tend to raise the demand price for capital assets. At the same time, optimism would lower both lender's risk and borrower's risk, which lowers the supply price and reinforces the demand price. This feeds investment and growth. Pessimism and rising uncertainty work in the opposite direction. Lower expected income plus higher borrower's risk mean low demand prices, and high perceived lender's risk means high supply prices so that little investment materialises.

Both lenders and borrowers operate with margins of safety on their balance sheets. Minsky observed that the margin of safety differs across unit types – hedge financing units, speculative financing units and Ponzi-financing units. The risk profile increases across the three types of firms. Further, over the course of expansion, the financial stance of all types of firms – financial and non-financial, as well as households – evolves from largely hedge finance units to include ever-rising proportions of speculative and even Ponzi positions. Debt is issued against debt with little net worth backing it up. When the weight shifts from hedge finance units to speculative and Ponzi finance units, the system becomes unstable and could spin out of control. When the expected revenues are not realised, a snowball of defaults lead to debt deflation, recession and unemployment, unless there are circuit breakers.

Market forces, thus, must be constrained. The countercyclical policies of the government and the Central Bank – BIG government and BIG bank – have an important role in preventing or limiting the instability. Unfortunately, the institutional constraints that had attenuated the instability in the post-Second World War years, like the New Deal reforms of the financial sector and the greater role of the government in managing the economy have been reversed. In the past 20–30 years of money-manager capitalism, the policy response has been in the opposite direction. As institutions found ways around rules, the response was often to deregulate, de facto accepting the innovations.[26]

Market-based financial structures, shadow banking structures and innovations by commercial banks have compounded the fragility of the system. Sen notes how new institutional arrangements have fed instability and driven a wedge between the real economy and the financial sector:

> Financial assets bought and sold in the primary market as initial public offerings of stocks are usually transacted later, in the secondary market, where these are no longer backed by physical assets. In the upswing, finance creates a myriad of financial claims and liabilities, and thus becomes increasingly remote from the real economy, while innovations to hedge and insulate assets continue to proliferate in the financial market, especially in the presence of uncertainty. . . . Further, in the new institutional setting of universal banking and deregulated finance, banks and non-bank financial entities actually follow an 'originate and distribute' model by the repackaging of assets and their sales. In this, the shifting of risks to counterparties can generate more profits than what is possible from the simple 'commitment models', which rely on the spread at the loan officer's desk.[27]

In commodity trading, financial investors looking for short-term gains have a greater presence on commodity future exchanges than genuine market players looking to hedge their positions based on real demand and real supply of commodities.[28]

Sen concludes that 'an expansionary financial market thus does not necessarily generate corresponding expansions in real terms, while the growing disproportion between the two may finally end the financial boom itself, has happened as of late in the world economy'.[29]

The Indian story

The 1991 debt crisis triggered a major reform of the financial sector in India along the neo-liberal lines. External liberalisation to integrate foreign capital flows and internal liberalisation of financial structures went hand-in-hand. Controls on interest rates were loosened, as were the controls on entry and exit promoting price and non-price competition among similarly placed firms. Controls over investments that could be undertaken by financial agents were liberalised, as was the access to funds. Regulatory walls separating banking from merchant banking, investment banking, mutual funds and insurance business were eased along the universal banking model. Development financial institutions that had served long-term credit needs of the economy were dismantled or converted to multipurpose banks. Institutions within the financial system developed very much along Anglo-Saxon lines, with their attendant cycles.

In the past 10 years, the financing regime in India essentially transited from financial relations that make for a stable system to financial relations that make for an unstable system. Sen analysed the transition from boom to panic in the Indian stock markets within Minsky–Kindelberger–Keynes framework.[30] Stock markets in India saw a long period of boom with rising market capitalisation and price/earnings ratio abetted by foreign portfolio flows till the time expectations turned adverse and from a boom period the system transited to panic and crash.

For the banking sector, the most evident symptom of instability is the rise in proportion of distressed and non-performing assets (NPAs) of the Indian banking sector. The stressed asset ratio of the commercial banks defined as the ratio of sum of gross NPAs and restructured standard advances to the gross advances of banks stands at 11.3 percent, as of September 2015. For public sector banks, the ratio is 14.1 percent.[31] Not surprisingly, credit growth in the Indian economy has slowed. All scheduled commercial banks credit growth on a year-on-year basis in 2014–2015 records 9.7 percent, whereas the average credit growth for the past 10 years between 2004–2005 and 2013–2014 was around 22 percent. The health of the banking sector is under serious strain.

A number of tendencies have contributed overtime to the buildup of the vulnerability within the banking system. From exposures to sensitive sectors to government directives on lending to cases of cronyism – all this contributed to the disproportionate growth of banking, as discussed below.

Part reason for the high NPAs lies in bad credit and lax appraisal by the banks as typical of boom periods. Financial instability began there. RBI's Financial Stability Report (2013) acknowledges that credit making during the 2005–2008 boom was associated with less stringent credit appraisal. Moreover, after the slowdown in the rest of the economy, as we have noted, FINREBS continued to grow. In what has now become a universal trend, loans to real estate and other sensitive sectors have increased. Sensitive sectors include the real estate sector, capital markets and commodity trade. RBI's Report on Trend and Progress of Banking notes that growth in credit to sensitive sectors almost doubled in 2012–2013, primarily on account of credit to real estate, whereas in the past, growth in credit to sensitive sectors generally followed a pattern similar to the growth in overall credit.[32]

In a recent paper, Jorda, Schularick and Taylor have compared modern banks to real-estate funds in which long-term mortgage lending is funded by short-term borrowing from the public.[33] Borrowed funds from the banking system drive real-estate prices and prop up the bank balance sheets, until market expectations reverse and boom gives way to panic and crash. For the Indian economy, housing prices galloped upwards steadily for several years before stabilising. Certain large real-estate firms with massive debt exposure to housing finance companies defaulted on their loans.[34] While the main issue with the financial sector in India now is the high defaults on corporate debts, binges in risky lending build vulnerability into the financial sector that could snowball into a crisis at any time.

Economic slowdowns are also periods associated with rise in rent-seeking activities in sectors such as land, gold and spectrum licenses (another finite natural resource), using borrowed funds. When demand for finance from manufacturing sector, or others, falls in downturns, demand from speculative and rent-seeking sectors go up as economic agents try to maximise returns through buying and selling. The rent-seeking sector, however, cannot sustain itself for long periods and, ultimately, demands from the rent-seeking sector would also go down, bringing it in sync with the real sector.

The sectors with the highest level of stressed assets in the Indian economy are the infrastructure, mining, iron and steel, aviation and textile sectors. Government interference in terms of pushing bank finance into avenues that were better served by long-term industrial financing institutions is said to be a major contributing factor. The erstwhile development banks have been eroded by financial reforms. Prodded by the government, commercial banks lent to projects involving lumpy, illiquid investments with long gestation lags and relatively high risks typical of these sectors.[35] Besides, crony capitalism thrived as firms with low capital base managed to get massive loans on the basis of political connections. Transparency and accountability in the system were compromised in the attempts to privilege certain big and powerful borrowers. The result has been concentration of bad debt and a large number of wilful defaulters.

The transition from a stable to unstable financial system was thus brought about in many ways. What one might consider as mitigating circumstances and therefore would have allowed finance and real estate to grow despite overall economic slowdown, essentially added to the fragility in the system. In other words, the forces that make for the autonomous characterisation of FINREBS are the ones that push the economy into an unstable financial regime. In our opinion, this is not sustainable.

Conclusion

After 2005, the FINREBS sector has grown phenomenally with its share in GDP rising to around 22 percent by 2014:Q3. This essay tried to empirically explore the relation of services in terms of the major component of FINREBS with the rest of the sectors of the economy, focusing on the period since the late 1990s. Forward linkage from FINREBS to the rest of the economy is below average compared to the rest of the sectors of the economy, and backward linkage from FINREBS is amongst the lowest. It is difficult, therefore, to imagine FINREBS as a 'leading sector' in the Hirschman sense. Rather, the causality vis-à-vis most of the sectors of the economy run from the other sector to FINREBS, with agriculture and allied being notable exception. A natural corollary of this result should be that as the rest of the sectors of the economy slow down, growth of FINREBS would slow. The fact this has not been the case until recently and several of the co-integrating relations are statistically insignificant mean that other impulses are generated from within FINREBS and elsewhere to support the growth in the sector. The variance decomposition of forecast error corroborates that a large percentage of variation in the growth of FINREBS cannot be explained by other sectors of the economy.

Under deregulated financial regime, growth in finance was made possible through a number of channels, such as real-estate lending and lending to other sensitive sectors, investments in gold, land and others. Lax regulations and supervision at the time of expansion promoted excessive debt creation and encouraged speculative and Ponzi position-taking by firms, which was bound to implode when market conditions and revenue growth turned adverse. Crony capitalism played its part with banks overextending themselves to lend to certain big players. Financialisation of commodity markets provided another avenue for short-term gains. These same forces, however, weakened the system and pushed it from a stable to unstable financial regime. It is the fallout of the imbalance between the real and financial economy that the system today is saddled with huge bad debt, large companies as wilful defaulters and drastic slowdown in credit and investments in the economy. The stylised Minsky cycle played out through financial markets, banking institutions, real estate firms and other institutions affecting the overall economy. The present pattern of finance-driven growth in the current phase of finance capitalism does not appear to be sustainable.

Notes

1 L. Randall Wray, *Why Minsky Matters: An Introduction to the Work of a Maverick Economist*, Princeton, NJ: Princeton University Press, 2015.
2 'How Much Finance Is Too Much: Lessons for Emerging Markets by Ratna Sahay', Presentation at the Indian Council for Research on International Economic Relations, New Delhi, 9 March 2016. This is based on www.imf.org/external/pubs/ft/sdn/2015/sdn1508.pdf (accessed on 5 March 2016).
3 Though still within the 95 percent confidence band around the turning point.
4 See Sabyasachi Kar and Basanta K. Pradhan, 'Shocks, Meltdowns, Policy Responses and Feasibility of High Growth in the Indian Economy', in *Macro-Modelling for the Eleventh Five Year Plan of India*, New Delhi: Academic Foundation, 2009.
5 Gunjeet Kaur, Sanjib Bordoloi and Raj Rajesh, 'An Empirical Investigation of the Inter-Sectoral Linkages in India', *Reserve Bank of India Occasional Papers*, 2009, 30(1): 29–72.
6 Avijit Debnath and Niranjan Roy, 'Structural Change and Intersectoral Linkages: The Case of North-East India', *Economic and Political Weekly*, 2012, 47(6): 72–6.
7 B.N. Goldar, 'Growth in Gross Value Added of Indian Manufacturing: 2011–12 Series vs 2004–05 Series', *Economic and Political Weekly*, 2015, 50(21): 10–13.

8 Ashok Mitra, 'Disproportionality and the Service Sector: A Note', *Social Scientist*, 1988, 179: 3–8.
9 B.B. Bhattacharya and Arup Mitra, 'Excess Growth of Tertiary Sector in Indian Economy: Issues and Implications', *Economic and Political Weekly*, 1990, 25(44): 2445–50.
10 Quarterly data on GDP is available on 1999–2000 base and 2004–2005 base. There is no linking factor available to get a uniform dataset. Data preceding 2004–2005 was transformed in two steps. Quarterly data on 1999–2000 base was deseasonlised using X-12 ARIMA. Using the growth rate of deseasonlised series, deseasonlised quarterly series on 2004–2005 base was extrapolated backwards to create a uniform series.
11 A.O. Hirschman, *Interdependence and Industrialization* in The Strategy of Economic Development, New Haven: Yale University Press, 1958.
12 Ina Drejer, 'Input-Output Based Measures of Inter- Industry Linkages Revisited: A Survey and Discussion', http://iioa.org/conferences/14th/files/Drejer_.pdf (accessed on 12 December 2015).
13 Backward linkage index, originally proposed by Rasmussen in 1957 (who called it the power of dispersion index) may be defined as

$$BLI_j = \frac{\frac{1}{n}\sum_i b_{ij}}{\frac{1}{n^2}\sum_{ij} b_{ij}}$$

where b_{ij} are the coefficients of $(I-A)^{-1}$ matrix, and n is the number of industries. The numerator denotes the average stimulus imparted to other sectors by a unit's worth of demand for sector j. The denominator denotes the average stimulus for the whole economy when all final demands increase by unity. $BLI_j>1$ implies that industry j has higher than average backward linkage.
14 In the 2004–2005 series of NAS, research and scientific services are placed along with the activities 'real estate, ownership of dwelling and business services sector'. In the earlier series, these services were included under 'other services' sector (National Accounts Statistics, Sources and Methods, 2007), Ministry of Statistics and Programme Implementation, Government of India.
15 Sanjay K. Hansda, 'Sustainability of Services-Led Growth: An Input Output Analysis of the Indian Economy', *Reserve Bank of India Occasional Papers*, 2001, 22(1, 2 and 3): 73–118.
16 It is measured in a manner similar to BLI with the coefficients of $(I-O)^{-1}$ matrix replacing the coefficients of $(I-A)^{-1}$ matrix.
17 Hirschman, 'A Generalized Linkage Approach to Development, with Special Reference to Staples', in Manning Nash (ed.), *Essays on Economic Development and Cultural Change – in Honour of Bert F. Hoselitz, Economic Development and Cultural Change*, Vol. 15, Supplement,1977, cited in Drejer, 'Input-Output Based Measures of Interindustry Linkages Revisited'.
18 Bose, Sukanya and Abhishek Kumar (2016) Growth of Finance, Real Estate and Business Services: Explorations in an Inter-Sectoral Framework, NIPFP Working Paper No. 162.
19 For results of causality tests refer to our NIPFP Working Paper no. 162.

20 Sudha Narayanan, 'The Productivity of Agricultural Credit in India', IGIDR Working Paper, 2015, www.igidr.ac.in/pdf/publication/WP-2015-01.pdf (accessed on 1 Dec 2015).

21 Pulapre Balakrishnan, 'The Great Reversal: A Macro Story', *Economic and Political Weekly*, 2014, 49(21) 24 May.

22 Refer to NIPFP Working Paper no. 162 for detailed results.

23 R. Nagaraj, 'India's Recent Economic Growth: A Closer Look', *Economic and Political Weekly*, 2008, 43(15): 55–61.

24 See 'Changes in Methodology and Data Sources in the New Series of National Accounts: Base Year 2011–12', Ministry of Statistics and Programme Implementation, Government of India, March 2015, www.epwrfits.in/Changes_in_Methodology_NS_2011_12_%20June_2015.pdf (accessed on 15 June 2016).

25 Minsky distinguished between a price system for current output and one for asset prices. Current output prices can be taken as determined by 'cost-plus markup' set at a level that generates profits. In the case of investment goods, the current output price is effectively a supply price of capital, which ordinarily would also include the cost of external finance. If the firm has to borrow funds, either from banks or markets, then the supply price of capital also includes external finance costs. In that case, supply price increases because of 'lender's risk' – the additional cost associated with borrowing funds from the lender. Turning to the demand for capital assets, the demand price would be determined by the expectations of the net revenue that the asset can generate. However, if the asset is externally financed, as is often the case, the amount one is willing to pay depends on the amount of external finance required. Greater borrowing exposes the buyer to higher risk of insolvency and bankruptcy. That is why 'borrower's risk' must also be incorporated into demand prices. Note that adding borrower's risk and lender's risk is a way of adding uncertainty to the analysis. These adjustments add margin of safety in case the future turns out to be worse than expected (see L. Randall Wray, *Why Minsky Matters*; Hyman P. Minsky, 'The Financial Instability Hypothesis', The Jerome Levy Economics Institute of Bard College Working Paper, 1992, 74).

26 Wray, *Why Minsky Matters*.

27 Sunanda Sen, 'The Meltdown of the Global Economy: a Keynes-Minsky Episode?' Levy Economics Institute of Bard College Working Paper No. 623, 5 September 2010.

28 Sunanda Sen, 'Uncertainty and Speculation in the Keynesian Tradition: Relevance in Commodity Futures', in Toshiaki Hirai, Maria Cristina Marcuzzo and Perry Mehrling (eds.), *Keynesian Reflections*, Oxford: Oxford University Press, 2013.

29 Sen, 'The Meltdown of the Global Economy', p. 6.

30 Sunanda Sen, 'Panics in India', Triple Crisis Blog, September 2013, http://triplecrisis.com/panics-in-india/ (accessed on 13 February 2013).

31 'As per RBI Financial Stability Report', December 2015, https://rbidocs.rbi.org.in/rdocs/PublicationReport/Pdfs/0FSR6F7E7BC6C14F42E99568A80D9FF7BBA6.PDF (accessed on 5 May 2016).

32 'RBI's Report on Trend and Progress of Banking', 2013, https://rbidocs.rbi.org.in/rdocs/PublicationReport/Pdfs/0FSR6F7E7BC6C14F42E99568A80D9FF7BBA6.PDF (accessed on 5 May 2016).

33 Òscar Jordá, Moritz Schularick and Alan M. Taylor, 'The Great Mortgaging: Housing Finance, Crises, and Business Cycles', NBERWorking Paper, 2014, No. 20501, www.nber.org/papers/w20501September (accessed on 1September 2015).
34 Raghavendra Kamath and Mansi Taneja, 'LIC Housing Finance Takes Over Orbit Corp's Mumbai Property', *Business Standard*, 4 December 2013.
35 C.P. Chandrasekhar and Jayati Ghosh, 'The Looming Banking Crisis', *Macroscan*, 4 September 2013, www.macroscan.org/fet/sep13/fet04092013 Banking_Crisis.htm (accessed on 1 December 2015).

13 Contemporary imperialism and labour

An analytical note

Byasdeb Dasgupta

Capitalism and its contemporary phase

In orthodox Marxist literature, capitalism as a macroeconomic system is defined as one where social relationship of productions is characterised by private ownership of means of production. In this definition, there are two homogeneous classes – bourgeoisie who are the owners of means of production, and proletariat who do not own means of production but own labour power. We beg to differ to define capitalism in this manner, as it does not allow us to view the ground reality.[1] One of the reasons for which we distance ourselves from this definition is the fact that under capitalism, sometimes the means of production may be owned by the state which signifies state ownership of means of production, with other features of capitalism (which we discuss shortly) remaining unaltered. For example, in India, we have public sector enterprises which are capitalist enterprises with state ownership of means of production. To be more close to the ground reality of capitalism, there is need to invoke the Marxian notion of surplus labour as capitalism is necessarily an exploitative economic system and exploitation cannot be understood without understanding what surplus labour is. Following the class-focused Marxist approach,[2] we define a capitalist process as one where appropriation of surplus labour is done by the non-performer(s) of surplus labour. In capitalism, surplus labour takes the money value form – surplus value which is made possible by commodity exchange in the market. This differentiates capitalism from other exploitative production system (for example, feudalism). So, the pertinent question at this point is what are the principal markers of capitalism as a macroeconomic system? The principal markers of capitalism are the following: (a) economic exploitation of labour, (b) money using market and price system, (c) wage labour, and (d) commodity form of the produced staff. Let us begin our analysis with the

Marxian concept of surplus labour. As Marx puts it, surplus labour is labour performed by direct producer(s)[3] beyond the necessary labour. Necessary labour (which takes the value form as necessary value under capitalism) is the labour performed by a direct producer to socially reproduce their labour power. This necessary value is equivalent to wage received by a direct producer in a capitalist production process. It is to be noted that in capitalism labour power (not labour) is also a commodity which is bought and sold in the (labour) market. The basic difference between labour power as a commodity and other commodity is that while the other commodities can only be consumed or used only by buying them in the market first, labour power is consumed first and then its price is the wage paid to the owner of labour power. So, labour in capitalism becomes wage labour. The significant aspect of capitalism is that as an economic system, it is based on market for purchasing the basic resources including labour power for production and, also, for selling the produced goods and services. A good or service takes the commodity form only when it is exchanged for its money value (which Marx and other classical economists including Smith and Ricardo called exchange value) in the market. So, money using market is a basic social institution of capitalist order without which capitalism cannot survive. Keynes dubbed this type of economy as money using entrepreneurial economy. In *Capital* (volume 1), Marx defined surplus value in terms of the M–C–M' circuit. Suppose one productive capitalist[4] begins with M amount of money with which necessary materials are procured, including labour power and a commodity X is produced, which in the market, fetches M' amount of money. Then, M'–M is the surplus value in this production process. Note the essentiality of money using the market for generation of this surplus value. The profit forms a portion of this surplus value, as the latter is distributed to different agents in the process including state,[5] who render the necessary and fundamental conditions of reproduction of this capitalist production process. Exploitation occurs here as the performers of surplus value cannot appropriate and hence, distribute the surplus value. They are performed by the productive capitalist who is a non-performer of surplus value.

As per Marx, capital is viewed in money form as distinct from the notion of capital used in mainstream neoclassical economics. In the above M–C–M' circuit, the initial capital invested in the production is M amount of money with which the productive capitalist buys the means of production, raw materials and labour power from the market.

Now, two types of market are important when one looks at capital accumulation and circulation of capital under global capitalism. One is the market for the final good, which is produced in the capitalist production process. The other is the input market, as the productive capitalist purchases all the means of production and raw materials and labour power from input market. Of the input markets, the most significant is the labour market, as it is labour power which adds value in any capitalist production process. From the inception of global capitalism, what we find is that there is a trenchant need for the productive capitalists to increase the market shares. The history of colonialism is basically the history of expansion of markets by the capitalists a world over.

Contemporary capitalism is no exception, as far as market expansion by the multinational corporate entities is concerned. Today, this expansion does take shape through overt colonial tactics. Three global institutions – International Monetary Fund, the World Bank and the World Trade Organization – play a pivotal role in contemporary capitalism to ensure that all the countries of the world follow laissez faire economic policy under what is known as neoliberalism. There is fierce competition between the top MNCs to capture the market world over. But what is more interesting to note is the fact that this neoliberal economic policy also stresses deregulation of labour in the name of flexible labour rule. This is to ensure more and more control of labour so as to increase surplus accumulation – sometimes even without increasing the market share! Now, let us see the three seemingly different phases of imperialism and the latter's concern for labour control for more capital accumulation.

Phases of imperialism

Imperialism, as noted at the onset, is a political means to ensure expansion of markets for the global capitalists. There are three apparently different phases of this political means to expand both output and input markets.

The first phase is that of the age of colonialism when the imperial powers of the world subjugated the sovereignty of the nation states and imposed the imperial rules for these conquered national territories. The principal objectives of such imperial expansion under the garb of colonialism were to ensure secured market for the products of the capitalists belonging to the empire states and, also, to ensure sourcing of cheap raw materials including labour for the capitalist production processes. This phase continued from the eighteenth century to the end of the Second World War.

The second phase of imperialism beginning from the end of the Second World War, lasts till 1973 when the Bretton Woods System broke down. This phase saw the rise of United States as the greatest imperial power, as well as the rise of multilateral institutions – the International Monetary Fund and the World Bank – to serve the interests of the United States and other imperial powers. This is the phase when US dollar became the reserve currency of the world. Magdoff provides a brilliant exposition of this phase of imperialism.[6]

The third phase of imperialism started from 1973 with the demise of the Bretton Woods System although the US dollar retained its supremacy as the international currency. During this phase, the entire world witnesses the rise of neoliberalism as the economic policy prescribed by the imperial powers, including the United States, through the multilateral organisations – the IMF and the World Bank. From 1995, the World Trade Organisation (WTO) gave further boost to these policies through its stress on 'free trade' world over. One of the key ingredients of neoliberal policies is flexible labour. Rapid financialisation is another phenomenon which took place in this phase leading finally to global crisis in 2007. Dasgupta makes an attempt to decipher the link between financialisation and flexible labour rules as culminating into global crisis of 2007.[7] The imperialist legacy during this phase put stress on labour control so that multinational corporations can accumulate capital at an increasing scale in the face of fierce competition at the global scale. The key features of this labour control is the policies to weaken labour organisations, easy hire and fire and the spate of reserve of army of labour (involuntarily unemployed workers). Except for a few overt coercive operations (military operations) by the imperialist powers including the United States, the main strategy of the imperialism during this phase is to make the different national markets for output and labour open to the multinational corporations without any intervention from the national state power. It was made to believe that without foreign investments (direct as well as portfolio), a national economy cannot grow. And apart from different subsidies to be offered to global capital by the sovereign national state powers, flexible labour is a must. Otherwise, foreign investments would not be forthcoming and the national economic growth is bound to suffer. So, in this phase, we come across a direct interface between imperialism and labour. Let us now see how imperialism tends to work to serve the interest of global capital and capital accumulation at increasing scale.

Contemporary imperialism and labour

This section is largely drawn from Dasgupta.[8] The contemporary phase of imperialism is characterised by neoliberalism, as we have noted in the preceding section. The basic tenets of neoliberalism are the following:

(a) Setting up of free market economy leaving any market including labour market to be regulated in its own terms by itself.
(b) Reshaping the role of the state from being an interventionist one to be a facilitator, namely, making state power serve the interest of global capital and MNCs.
(c) Containing fiscal deficit which ultimately signifies doing away with all kinds of social public expenditure and leaving the social sectors (like health and education) to be exploited for churning surplus and profit by the large capital including the global capital.
(d) Subsidising global capital at any cost and thus making labour the risk-bearing factor of production.

All these have adverse implications for labour, as they signify greater labour control. As far as surplus value generation and thereby the process of capital accumulation is concerned, there are two aspects of living labour (the labour that adds value in current production as per Marx) which must be noted here:

i) What is happening to the social status of living labour which concerns their means of livelihood?
ii) What is happening to the reserve army of labour (involuntary unemployment if we use the Keynesian term)?

Under neoliberalism, the key subsidy given by the third world national state at the direction of the Fund-Bank is that within the geographical boundaries of the country the labour cost would be made as cheap as possible vis-à-vis other third world countries. This has significant implications – (a) for necessary equivalent of the surplus generated and (b) for surplus value generated (both absolute surplus value and relative surplus value). The very idea of a competitive market-driven economy (with efficiency in allocation and production) warrants low cost of production. The market for various commodities today is characterised by cost-effectiveness and labour is the soft target in this respect. The rise of few MNCs during this period world over signifies the weakening bargaining strength of labour and further lowering of labour cost of production. Reshaping of the national state power through the Fund-Bank's conditions facilitated the interest of big business and global capital, which is directed to containment of labour cost of production. Slashing down of fiscal deficit by the neoliberal state is same as doing away with the welfare state and all its programmes for poverty alleviation and employment generation. In this instant also, labour suffers as most of third world labour is poor and unemployed. The job status of a worker is getting continuously weakened, and technology-induced rises in labour productivity have increased the risk and uncertainty in a worker's life. This is happening at a time when some third world countries, including India, are in the process of making few billionaires. Accumulation of wealth by the rich cannot take place without super exploitation in the standard Marxian sense.

In a capitalist class process, the Marxian definition of exploitation is the ratio of the surplus value generated (s) to the variable capital (v), that is, s/v where variable capital in Marxian sense is the wage component given to the labour for using his/her labour power. Let $e = s/v$, where e is the degree of exploitation. There are four possibilities through which super exploitation can take shape as follows:

(a) One can increase e by increasing s, given v. This can happen in either of the two ways as follows. One can increase s by increasing the working hours (this is absolute surplus value as described by Marx in *Capital* [volume I]) presuming no change in the technology of production. One can also increase s given v by increasing labour productivity through technological progress (this is dubbed as relative surplus value by Marx).

(b) One can increase e by decreasing v, given s. This is one of the key ingredients of labour market flexibility as practised today world over. This requires necessary changes in labour laws which permit easy hire and fire along with downward flexibility of real wage.

(c) One can increase e by increasing s and decreasing v at the same time. This means lengthening working hours and technological progress simultaneously. Commodity production in the new economy under neoliberalism, like the IT sector, exemplifies this.

(d) One can increase e by increasing s proportionately more the increase in v. This is the case which points out at the structural change at the enterprise level. This is happening in many private enterprises (of course, large business) which are shedding what they dub as surplus labourers while allowing some increment in v for the retained workers. This also requires technological innovation which would increase what Marx has defined as the intensity of labour in the production process. This warrants that an individual worker must possess multiple skills. For example, the number of workers required in a car manufacturing unit has gone down manifold today than what it was four decades ago.

All the above four possibilities have been ensured by flexible labour regime and the contemporary phase of imperialism remained so far successful in guaranteeing such labour regime in each and every third world country. Of course, the advanced countries of the world are no exception in this regard.

Flexible labour regime under contemporary imperialism

Let us now see how the flexible labour regime works or what does flexible labour regime in reality means? Following Sen and Dasgupta (2009), this is described below.[9] A standard flexible labour regime typically has the following four ingredients which would ensure super exploitation (in terms of our notation introduced in the preceding section a very high e):

(a) Numerical flexibility: Numerical flexibility is the capacity of a firm to easily adjust the number of workers to meet the varying level of effective demand in the market. From the supply side, it also means the capacity of the firm to easily adjust the number of workers to be employed because of continuous technological innovation. The increasing casualisation and contractualisation replacing standard regular workforce in factories is testimony to numerical flexibility under neoliberalism world over.

(b) Functional flexibility: Functional flexibility basically implies a firm's capacity to force its workforce to perform multi-skilling job as opposed to the specialised skill. This an individual worker must do without any resistance, and that is to be ensured legally by the reformulation of labour laws of the land in favour of flexible labour laws.

(c) Wage flexibility: Wage flexibility refers to a firm's ability to adjust wages (in Marxian term variable capital) at its own terms and conditions without resistance from the workers. This suits the capitalists' need for cost-effectiveness so that they survive the competition in the global market. Wage flexibility today is guaranteed by the attempt to do away with minimum wages law in many third world countries. The most important thing is that wages can be changed either way at the will of the capitalists and there should not be any labour resistance when wages are revised downward. In fact, in most the cases, it is the real wages which get downwardly revised, not the nominal wages.

(d) Temporal flexibility: Functional flexibility refers to adjustment capability of a firm in the utilisation of labour hours over time according to temporal and/or seasonal variations in effective demand for commodity in the market. It allows the firms to adapt to the practices of overtime work when required, when the effective demand in the market is high and many firms may not pay the overtime allowances, as happens today in the IT sector. At the same time, it implies utilisation of less labour hours a day (at reduced wage, if possible) when the effective demand is low. It, therefore, signifies temporal involuntary unemployment for some workers, and there should not be any resistance to it which is ensured by the changes in the labour laws in favour of flexible labour laws. When the effective demand is low, the labour demand is also low and business firms can then easily shed off some workers for the time being.

Each one of these four norms of labour flexibility facilitates cheap labour, which is actually facilitated by neoliberal state power. And the neoliberal state power in each third world country is facilitated by the contemporary phase of imperialism through the Fund-Bank's conditions imposed upon the third world. This means greater control of labour and labour power in the face of stiff competition in the final commodity markets. And this can be done in a political climate which speaks the language of global capital in the liberal democratic facade that is ensured by the contemporary phase of imperialism.

Let us now see the ground reality of contemporary imperialism as it works with the aim of controlling labour market through flexible labour rules. For this purpose, we have chosen India as a case study. India is now regarded as one of the important emerging market economies in the world. India remained colonialised for two centuries and is the victim of imperial policies and dictum. At present, India has been under neoliberal grip since 1991. India is both a large market for final commodities and labour. One of the conditions of the neoliberal policies dictated by the Fund-Bank to India is flexible labour laws. There is continuous pressure on India by these multilateral organisations (which act as the agents of the imperial powers, like the United States) to change the labour laws and repeal many of the clauses in the existing labour laws which to some extent provide some voice representation guarantee and certain labour rights (like minimum wages act) to the formal sector workers. It is to be noted that in India, hardly 7 percent of the total workforce is engaged in formal sectors where the existing labour laws are applicable. The majority of the Indian workforce (93 percent of the total workforce) is in the informal sectors, where the existing labour laws do not apply. Although the labour laws in India have not been changed so far owing to the compulsion of political democracy, de facto we find the use of flexible labour norms.[10] The major trends of flexible labour norms, as they exist today in India, as far as the controlling of labour are concerned are the following:

(a) Casualisation and contractualisation: In most firms, including the large ones, permanent and regular workers are now being replaced by casual and/or contractual workers. There are subtle differences between casual and contractual workers. In the case of a casual worker, there is no written contract between the employer and the concerned worker. The particular worker can be absorbed in work and can also be laid off at the will of the employer. During a field survey[11] of the formal manufacturing factory workers, it was found that a casual worker cannot take legal step against the employer if they are sacked.[12] Furthermore, it was also found that these workers are generally not enrolled as labourers of the firms. Rather, they are recruited through some labour contractors and every month or week (as the case may be), they are paid through their concerned labour contractors. These workers do not receive any benefits (like PF, gratuity, paid leaves and like) other than wages. In many instances, we have found that these workers do not even get the minimum wages they are supposed to get. A contractual worker, on the other hand, is one where there is contract between the firm and the worker. The contract is generally a written one. The contract specifies the period up to which the worker can work in the firm. Once the contract period is over, it is up to the firm to decide whether to renew the contract with the worker or not. Apart from the contract, a contractual worker is like a casual worker. They generally receive only wages and no other benefits. In the case of contractual worker, minimum wages are mostly not guaranteed. The increasing casualisation and contractualisation of the workforce in the formal sector is dubbed as informalisation of the formal space. For both casual and contractual workers, there are, in general, no fixed daily working hours. Even if the daily working hours are fixed, the casual and contractual workers do not receive overtime allowance as per law[13] when they work beyond the stipulated working hours. For both casual and contractual workers 'no work, no pay' is the general norm now. Since these types of workers are not generally registered as workers in the factory roll book, they cannot take legal steps. And they even mostly remain outside the grip of any trade unions. This is an era where rampant cost-cutting strategies are adopted by the firms across different sectors which basically stand for slashing down labour cost as far as possible. As the official data shows, labour costs as a percentage of total cost of production in registered manufacturing factories have declined from 7.78 percent in 2000–2001 to 5.63 percent in 2007–2008, which is the obvious result of the cost cutting strategy of the manufacturing firms of late. This means the onus of cost-cutting strategy has fallen on labour.[14] Note further that the number of average worker per factory increased only marginally from 47.81 persons in 2000–2001 to 56.10 persons in 2007–2008 which signifies an increase of 8.30 persons for this seven-year period or on average a rise by 1.19 persons per factory every year. On the other hand, contract workers' proportion in the total workers rose from 20.50 percent in 2000–2001 to 30.96 percent in 2007–2008.[15] Note that this does not include all the casual workers in the registered factories. So, including the casual workforce the proportion of the informal in the formal manufacturing employment would be much higher, no doubt. Surely, labour in casualised and contractualised forms is much more exploited than labour in regularised conditions. Moreover, in this age, even those who are in regular employment conditions are facing some flexibility in terms of undefined working hours and contraction in different non-wage benefits, which used to be the principal features of such employment. In addition, there is a large labour force engaged in informal works (a significant proportion of them being self-employed) with low payments and without any non-wage benefits and labour security. Almost 93 percent of the total labour force in India is in informal activities, as many of them could not find any opportunity in the formal segment of the economy. Finally, a great number is unemployed; some of them may be categorised as discouraged unemployed.[16] The very idea of casualisation and contractualisation corroborates to the four forms of labour flexibility discussed above, namely, numerical flexibility, wage flexibility, functional flexibility and temporal flexibility.

(b) Outsourcing and subcontracting: In the Indian context, as elsewhere in the world, the formal business firms (mostly large firms) try to avoid rigid labour laws and also, try to contain labour cost of production by outsourcing and sub-contracting their production to the workers in the informal sectors. This on the one hand helps to curtail labour cost and on the other renders greater control of labour. There is no guarantee that a firm will continue to outsource the same set of informal workers who are mostly self-employed. This is so because there is a huge reserve army of labour and competition among these labourers to receive job contracts from large enterprises which actually help to slash down the labour cost and also compel labour to follow the dictum of global capital. There is no official data in India regarding outsourcing. However, during our field survey in Delhi and West Bengal during 2012–2013, we found that a significant portion of the total jobs in different production units in these two areas is performed by the informal workers from outside who are mostly paid on piece-rate basis. Marx in *Capital* (volume 1) has shown that the degree of exploitation rises when wage payments are made on piece-rate basis and not on hourly basis. No law exists in India to stop outsourcing of works by large firms to the informal sectors. As we have mentioned earlier, there is statistical evidence that unit labour cost has fallen significantly during the last decade (as can be observed from the Annual Survey of Industries data) in the formal manufacturing sector in India. And outsourcing and sub-contracting, to our understanding, have helped to garner this reduction in unit labour cost of production along with casualisation and contractualisation. One of the greatest advantages of outsourcing is that the formal sector firm has no responsibility towards the labour who, outside the firm, is making actual production. Another significant merit of outsourcing is that it allows the firm to exercise temporal flexibility as we have observed during our field survey in Delhi, Haryana and West Bengal during 2012–2013.[17]

(c) Weakening voice representation of labour in India: The question of voice representation of labour assumes greater significance as the space of labour is continuously squeezed by the (global) capital. Flexible labour rules under neoliberal order warrant less and less scope for voice representation of labour. Labour should not have the chance to organise themselves to represent its voice against global capital. In the context of BPO and ITES sector, Sandhu noted:

> there are real concerns about whether the unions can even organise effectively given the structural organisation of BPO work.

Most of the call centre employees work nights and sleep during day. They even maintain this schedule over weekends, when the only groups that they are able to socialise with are other call centre employees who keep similar schedules. This has given rise to a call centre tribe, which stays up weekend nights and socialises to get rid of the build up of stress much that comes out of the stress at work. How can one approach the workers when they are picked up from home and driven into the innards of the building where they work – and after work, are picked up and dropped outside their home? The tired workers who sleep during the day much rather catch up on sleep them spend time on any other issue.[18]

In fact, the space of voice representations of workers of different varieties in this age of neoliberalism is continuously shrunk even without formal change in the existing 'rigid' labour rules towards more flexible ones. But through the back door already flexibility has engulfed the space of labour without much dissent or resistance. Otherwise, how can one justify the significant rise in the casual workforce in the formal sector? This period is marked by rapid decline in the strength of trade unions (TUs) and other labour organisations. Central TUs in India are sharply losing membership. In a span of 18 years from 1991 to 2008, the total membership of all the TUs in the formal sector has increased from 61,01,000 to 95,74,000, which means a rise of 34,73,000.[19] On average, this means an increase in membership by 1,92,944 only per annum. What is noteworthy is that the average membership of trade unions, calculated as total number of trade union members divided by the manufacturing firms, registered a sharp fall during the last 25 years of neoliberal reforms. This is calculated on the basis of information on trade union membership provided by the Labour Bureau of Government of India. Another noteworthy feature is emergence in some production units independent labour organisations which are not affiliated to any political party, like Hero Honda Theka Majdoor Sangathan (Hero Honda Contract Labour Organisation) at the Hero Honda plant in Dharuhera in Haryana near Delhi. We interviewed some 20 workers there who are contract labourers of the plant and also, the general secretary of the organisation on 20 January 2013. The workers in the plant are mostly contract labourers (95 percent of the total workforce in the plant) who are recruited through the labour contractors of the factory in the area. Almost each one of them has migrated from their native villages in Uttar Pradesh, Bihar, Orissa, Chhattisgarh, Jharkhand, Madhya Pradesh, Rajasthan,

Himachal Pradesh, West Bengal and also from the neighbouring countries like Bangladesh and Nepal. The contract workers' organisation
was formed in 2008 out of the labour agitation in the plant over
higher wages and better working conditions. From its very beginning,
the organisation remained independent (meaning not affiliated to any
political party) and as per the workers, the political party-led TUs
initially tried to mobilise them, but later the workers found them not
working in the interest of the workers. So, they rejected them. After
the 2008 agitation in the plant, an individual contract worker was
recruited for six months only and the contract did not get renewed.
Under such circumstances, they were forced to take up a job in another
factory in the area at a lower wage and bereft of any non-wage benefit
like PF, ESI and leave. They were, in fact, forced to keep changing their
workplaces at regular intervals, and workers' turnover ratio is very
high naturally. The contract workers in the Hero Honda Plant (whose
total number at the time of interview is approximately 5000) are
underpaid, as they are paid below the minimum wage rate stipulated
in the labour law of the state. Also, there is a huge difference in wages
between the permanent workers and contract workers, although both
are performing the same jobs. While a permanent worker in a month
receives Rs 40,000, a contract worker at most receives Rs 8,800.
There is also anomaly in the overtime payment rate. Firstly, as per
law, an individual cannot put in extra work for more than two hours.
However, in reality, they work beyond the stipulated eight hours a
day. Sometimes they work for 12–14 hours a day. Secondly, as per
the statutory requirement of the state, an overtime hour should be
double the normal hour of work, which is known as double-rate. But
the workers are never paid double-rate. They receive only the single-
rate payment, which is the payment on the basis of normal working hours. Thirdly, sometimes the workers are not paid their overtime
hours properly. Some hours of work remain unpaid. When they raise
this problem to their contractors, they assure them that it would be
adjusted in the next month's salary. Needless to say, that 'next month'
never arrives. And if someone protests over this practice then he is
immediately thrown out of the job. The contract workers' organisation is trying to raise these issues along with parity with permanent
workers. However, to date, the plant management has remained successful in crushing their demands. There is a union of the permanent
workers, and the contract labour organisation is in conflict with it, as
the former perceives the latter as threat to their existence. The story of
Hero Honda plant is not a story in isolation in India today. This trend
is observable in many parts of the country as far as labour conditions

are concerned. However, this feature marks the era of economic liberalisation in India when, without making de jure change in the rigid labour laws, a more flexible de facto regime emerged with companies at the shop floor implementing flexible labour rules based on easy hire and fire thereby violating the basic minimum labour conditions as entailed in some of the labour laws of the land.

Conclusion

Summing up the major arguments of this essay, it can be asserted that global capitalism today thrives on capital accumulation and circulation of capital by ensuring greater control of labour through flexible labour regime world over. This is ensured by the contemporary imperial powers to facilitate the interests of the large MNCs and, hence, global capital. Imperialism is the political means to capture both final commodity market and input market including labour market in distant land world over. Contemporary imperialism is no exception in this regard. What is noteworthy of contemporary imperialism is its stress on controlling labour market in distant land by imposing neoliberal flexible labour rules on the sovereign states through multilateral organisations like the International Monetary Fund (IMF) and the World Bank.

Notes

1 It is to be noted that under feudalism the means of production are owned by the feudal lords, not by the feudal serfs. So, this definition does not distinguish capitalism from feudalism. In fact, in any exploitative production process, means of production are not owned by the performers of surplus labour.
2 See Stephen Resnick and Richard D. Wolff, *Knowledge and Class – A Marxian Critique of Political Economy*, Chicago, London: The University of Chicago Press, 1987.
3 We use the term 'direct producer' following Marx to signify the surplus labour (value) performing worker in a capitalist production system.
4 In Karl Marx, *Capital Volume I*, London: Penguin Books in association with New Left Review: London, 1976, reprinted in Penguin Classics in 1990, Marx used the term 'productive capitalist' to signify those capitalists who appropriate, hence, distribute surplus value generated by the direct producers. Unproductive capitalists are those who do not directly appropriate surplus value, hence, also do not distribute surplus value but are receivers of portion of surplus value appropriated by the productive capitalist. For example, a banker exemplifies an unproductive capitalist.
5 A capitalist firm – especially a corporate entity – pays different taxes including corporate tax to the state and these tax payments are made from the surplus value generated by the direct producers.

6 Harry Magdoff, *The Age of Imperialism – The Economics of U.S. Foreign Policy*, New Delhi: Aakar Books for South Asia, 2010, first published in 1968 by Monthly Review Press: New York.

7 Byasdeb Dasgupta, 'Financialization, Labour Market Flexibility and Global Crisis: A Marxist Perspective', in Byasdeb Dasgupta (ed.), *Non-Mainstream Dimensions of Global Political Economy – Essays in Honour of Sunanda Sen*, London: Routledge, 2013.

8 Byasdeb Dasgupta, 'Flexible Labour and Capital Accumulation in a Post-Colonial Country', in Iman Kumar Mitra, Ranabir Samaddar and Samita Sen (eds.), *Accumulation in Post-Colonial Capitalism*, London: Springer, 2016.

9 Sunanda Sen and Byasdeb Dasgupta, *Unfreedom and Waged Work – Labour in India's Manufacturing Industry*, New Delhi: Sage, 2009.

10 Sen and Dasgupta, *Unfreedom and Waged Work*.

11 This field survey was carried out during 2003–2006 among the formal manufacturing sector workers in Delhi, Haryana, Uttar Pradesh, West Bengal, Gujarat and Maharashtra. For details please see Sen and Dasgupta, *Unfreedom and Waged Work*.

12 As is cited in Sen and Dasgupta, *Unfreedom and Waged Work*.

13 Indian labour law specifies that the overtime allowance for a worker will be double the hourly wage rate. For example, if the specific working hour is eight hours a day and for that daily wage rate is Rs 100, then hourly wage rate is Rs 12.50. The overtime allowance per hour should then be twice of this hourly wage rate, namely, Rs 25.

14 These estimates are obtained from the statistics provided by the Labour Bureau, Government of India which is available online at www.labour bureau.nic.in and accessed on 12 November 2012.

15 Sourced from Labour Bureau, Government of India, 2007–2008, www.labourbureau.nic.in (accessed on 12 November 2012).

16 Note that the discouraged unemployed have no place in the of late modern neoclassical theory of search unemployment. Those who are discouraged have given up searching any jobs after getting frustrated of doing so indefinitely. Hence, they cannot be classified as unemployed due to searching jobs, as claimed by the search theory of unemployment. There is no official data on discouraged unemployment in India. However, the official statistics of the United States shows significant presence of discouraged unemployed in the labour force.

17 This field survey was part of the ICSSR Sponsored Research Project on Imperialism – Old and New.

18 See Amandeep Sandhu, 'Why Unions Fail in Organising India's BPO-ITES Industry?' *Economic and Political Weekly*, 2006, 14 October: 4321.

19 This information is obtained from the statistics provided by the Labour Bureau of Government of India.

14 'Emerging' Third World capitalism and the new imperialism

The case of India

Surajit Mazumdar

A somewhat paradoxical phenomenon associated with contemporary globalisation has been that of the 'emergence' of some Third World capitalisms, or what has been described as the 'rise of the rest'.[1] Globalisation emerged and unfolded in an undeniably unequal world where the balance of power – economic, political and military – was and has remained with the advanced countries of the triad which make up the core of the capitalist world economy. At the same time, significant evidence of the rising weight and importance of the Third World and some within the group, in particular, in the world economy, also exists.

In the last few decades, economic expansion in the Third World has outpaced that in advanced capitalist countries, though the average per capita income levels in the two groups of countries remain vastly different.[2] Third World countries have also come to account for a large share of global manufacturing value added and have witnessed a much faster growth of their foreign trade during the period of globalisation. Savings and investment ratios have increased greatly in the Third World, and they have become increasingly important recipients of inward FDI (foreign direct investment). Alongside this, outward FDI from these countries has also grown and their firms have also become transnational in character. Since the late 1990s, the 'capital flows paradox' or the phenomenon of 'capital flowing uphill' also emerged, wherein developing countries became net exporters of capital to the advanced capitalist world mainly by taking the form of accumulation of low return foreign exchange reserves. While there have been significant variations within Third World economies, this overall picture does clearly capture the distinctive nature of contemporary globalisation when compared with earlier phases of capitalist internationalisation. The opening up of Third World economies to global competition has clearly not led to any generalised destruction of the production and industrial base in the Third World. Instead, we see the international division of labour taking a different shape, wherein there is migration or 'relocation' of production in the opposite direction and so-called de-industrialisation in the advanced world. Domestic capital in Third World countries has also not been run over by international capital rooted in the advanced economies; instead, it has internationalised itself.

Though its story is a little less dramatic than that of China, a fellow 'emerging' economy, India has certainly played a major part in the story of the rise of the rest. The question is: does this growth and its nature imply an increase in Indian capitalism's autonomy, its ability to rival the major powers or to play a counter-hegemonic role as a power on the world stage, whether individually and as a member of larger groupings of Third World capitalist nations (like the BRICs)? On that is contingent also the degree to which this 'emergence' can enlarge the democratic space within India (of course within the limits of capitalism). This essay argues, on the basis of an examination of the nature of the accumulation regime of Indian capitalism as it has increasingly integrated with the global economy, that the answers to these questions may be on the negative side. To that extent, the Indian case also illustrates the limits to which 'emergence' signifies a shift in the fundamental iniquities of the world order.

India's 'emergence', divergence and the trap of subordination

India entered into its liberalisation phase in 1991 with a background of a relatively limited industrialisation process and a highly domestic economy-oriented capitalist class. Despite this, as can be seen in Table 14.1, in the last three decades, India has become a larger economy than all the advanced countries barring the United States (in purchasing power parity, or PPP terms though). In the process, it has gone past not only a number of advanced economies whose economic sizes were more than two or three times that of India in 1980, it has also done the same relative to developing economies like Brazil and Mexico. In fact, within the so-called emerging economies, it is only India and China which have achieved a steady and significant rise in their share in world GDP since the turn of the century. Between them, however, there is an important difference – a shift to current exchange rates rather than on a PPP basis as the means for measuring leads to a far sharper drop in India's share in world GDP than that of China. Thus, in 2014, China's share in world GDP at current exchange rates was 13.4 percent, while that of India was a mere 1.6 percent.

Table 14.1 Share of 15 largest economies in world GDP on PPP basis (percentages)

Country/group	1980	1990	2000	2008	2014
United States	21.93	22.15	20.76	17.73	15.9
Japan	7.64	8.74	6.53	5.16	4.36
Germany	6.64	6.06	4.91	3.95	3.43
United Kingdom	3.76	3.66	3.11	2.71	2.38
France	4.43	4.12	3.39	2.79	2.37
Italy	4.55	4.2	3.29	2.55	1.95
Canada	2.2	2.08	1.84	1.6	1.46
Spain	2.27	2.22	1.97	1.84	1.42
Advanced	53.42	53.21	45.79	38.32	33.28
China	2.32	4.11	7.39	12.01	16.46
India	2.93	3.66	4.19	5.25	6.73
Brazil	4.37	3.71	3.19	3.08	3.01
Indonesia	1.41	1.91	1.94	2.13	2.46
Mexico	2.99	2.62	2.44	2.11	1.97
Korea	0.64	1.19	1.56	1.62	1.64
Emerging	14.66	17.19	20.71	26.19	32.27
Russia			3.29	3.97	3.5
All 15 countries	68.08	70.41	69.79	68.47	69.05

Source: World Economic Outlook (WEO) database April 2016 (www.imf.org; accessed 18 April 2017).

Indian growth in the last two decades or so has been, of course, greatly beneficial to some segments of the Indian society, in particular the capitalist class. The corporate sector in India has grown rapidly during this period, and the distribution between its private and public sector components – of both the income generated in it as well as its accumulated capital stock – has moved more decisively in favour of the former (see Table 14.2 and Figure 14.1). As a result, a significant increase has taken place in the share of the private corporate sector in India's national income. This trend was most marked during the period of very high growth rates that began soon after the turn of the century and continued till the global crisis, and after a dip in 2008–2009, it resumed for a short time till a slowdown set in from the second half of 2011–2012. If we consider the new GDP series where the value added in private corporations is being explicitly measured, then the importance of the private corporate sector would appear to be even greater than that emerging from the older series. While the estimated share of the private organised sector in the older series reached a peak which was under 25 percent of net domestic product (NDP), in the new series, the share in gross value added (GVA) and NDP of

Table 14.2 Distribution of net fixed capital stock of the corporate sector between public and private sectors: 1991–2013 (percentage shares)

Sector	1991	2001	2008	2013
At current prices				
Public sector non-departmental enterprises	51.22	40.98	29.89	28.75
Private corporate sector	48.78	59.02	70.11	71.25
At 2004–2005 prices				
Public sector non-departmental enterprises	55.48	41.92	29.57	26.97
Private corporate sector	44.52	58.08	70.43	73.03

Source: Central Statistical Organization (CSO), National Accounts Statistics

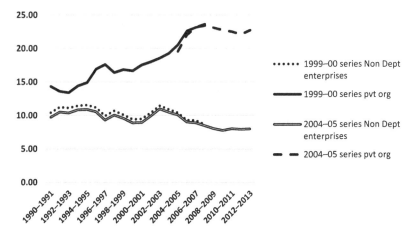

Figure 14.1 Share of private organized sector and public sector non-departmental enterprises in NDP at current prices, 1990–1991 to 2012–2013

Source: CSO, National Accounts Statistics.

private corporations since 2011–2012 is estimated at around 35 percent compared to 20 and 45 percent of the public and household sectors, respectively.

In addition, the distribution of income within the sector has moved very sharply in favour of surplus incomes (see Table 14.3) – the biggest gain of which has been in corporate profits. As a result, corporate

Table 14.3 Distribution of factor incomes in the private organised sector/ private corporations

	1990–1991	2002–2003	2007–2008
Compensation of employees	54.85	35.58	29.08
Operating surplus	45.15	64.42	70.92

2004–2005 base year series (private organized)

	2004–2005	2007–2008	2012–2013
Compensation of employees	32.46	27.69	32.12
Operating surplus	67.54	72.31	67.88

2011–2012 base year series (private corporations)

	2011–2012	2012–2013	2013–2014
Compensation of employees	33.31	33.92	34.45
Operating surplus	66.69	66.08	65.55

Source: CSO, National Accounts Statistics.

savings, which were generally below 2 percent of GDP for more than four decades after independence, climbed to 9.4 percent of GDP by 2007–2008, before declining somewhat thereafter on account of the slowdown.[3] Underlying the process of redistribution within the corporate sector has been the stagnation and depression of the incomes of India's working population, most of which are in agriculture and the informal non-agricultural sectors. This context has enabled real wages in even the regulated and unionised private formal sector to be stagnant for over 20 years and for all productivity gains to be cornered by surplus incomes.[4] Only a small section of white-collar employees has seen increases in compensation levels, and in some cases, this has been very significant, contributing to the enriching of India's middle class.

While wage depression has been a generalised phenomenon, the profits they have enabled remain highly concentrated in a few hands. As Table 14.4 (based on income-tax returns of very large samples of companies)[5] shows, among the large number of registered companies – over 800,000 – a handful of heavyweights dominate. Some of these are, of course, public sector companies, but largely it indicates private corporate profit concentration.[6] Moreover, some individual business groups would often be controlling more than one private sector company with high profits, and many would also have additional group companies outside that set. The actual level of concentration

Table 14.4 Concentration of corporate profits

Year	All sample companies		Companies in sample with profits > Rs. 500 crores		
	Number	Share in gross corporate tax revenue (%)	Number	Share in profits before taxes of all sample cos. (%)	Estimated share in profits before taxes of all cos. (%)
2005–2006	301736	77.72	113	49.87	38.76
2006–2007	328061	79.21	150	54.8	43.41
2007–2008	410451	82.02	190	54.98	45.09
2008–2009	366623	71.36	179	57.54	41.06
2009–2010	427811	79.26	216	55.75	44.19
2010–2011	459270	76.51	239	57.92	44.31
2011–2012	494545	70.03	252	59.49	41.66
2012–2013	618806	68.45	272	61.28	41.95
2013–2014	564787	65.33	263	60.29	39.39
2014–2015	582889	69.52	297	60.63	42.15

Source: Government of India, Ministry of Finance, Union Budget for different years.

in corporate profits, therefore, would be even higher than the figures given would indicate.

The presence of foreign firms in the corporate sector with headquarters in the countries of the Triad (and South Korea) has certainly increased after India's liberalisation. An increasing number of them, including the top ones, now have Indian affiliates who are in a wide variety of activities (see Table 14.5). MNC interests in India have mainly been of the market-seeking variety and in some sectors like passenger cars, scooters, consumer electronics, soft drinks and so on, they completely dominate the Indian domestic market. Yet, in many industrial and service sectors, including very large ones, they are entirely absent or share space with major Indian firms.

MNCs have also played a relatively limited direct role in drawing Indian manufacturing into global production networks. In comparison with many other countries, the scale of presence of foreign affiliates in India's economy has remained restricted, and the degree of their export orientation even lesser.[7] Indeed, Indian firms have played a more important role than MNCs in pushing Indian manufactured exports and also exports of services, though their imports have also risen. This is indicated by the lower than average export intensity of

316 *Surajit Mazumdar*

Table 14.5 Illustrative list of MNCs in different sectors in India

Sector	Prominent MNCs
Financial services	Citigroup, HSBC, Merril Lynch, Goldman Sachs
IT services	Cognizant, IBM, Microsoft, Adobe, Oracle, Cisco, Hewlett-Packard
Media	News Corp, Sony
Electronics, including consumer electronics	Nokia, Whirlpool, Samsung, LG, Motorola, Sony, Hitachi, Canon
Automobiles	Suzuki, Honda, Toyota, Ford, GM, Hyundai Kia Automotive, Daimler Chrysler, BMW
Consumer goods	Unilever, Proctor and Gamble, Colgate-Palmolive, Nestle, Cadbury, Johnson and Johnson, Henkel
Machinery and equipment	Robert Bosch, Siemens, Caterpillar, JCB, SKF, Alfa-Laval, ABB, Cummins
Chemicals	Bayer, Mitsubishi Chemical, Monsanto, Akzo Nobel, BASF
Drugs and pharmaceuticals	Pfizer, Novartis, GlaxoSmithKline, Sanofi-Aventis
Non-metallic mineral products	Holcim, Lafarge, Saint-Gobain
Petroleum and products	ExxonMobil, BP, Royal Dutch Shell, Total
Outsourced services	Convergys, Sykes, Accenture
Contract manufacturers	Flextronics, Jabil Circuits

Source: Author's compilation.

MNC affiliates (see Table 14.6). However, in the IT-BPO (information technology-business process outsourcing) sector, while Indian firms are ahead of foreign affiliates as the main suppliers of services, multinational firms are their major clients and have also set up their own captive units.[8] Such outsourcing to Indian firms by multinational firms has also happened in manufactured products but on a relatively modest scale.[9]

Thus, notwithstanding the greater openness of the economy, Indian firms have been the principal beneficiary of rapid corporate growth in India, and much of the Indian corporate sector has remained in 'national' hands.[10] Rather than any foreign takeover of the Indian corporate sector, it is the lack of FDI into India that has been the chief concern of Indian big business and the state. What has happened instead, in the backdrop of the rapid growth of the Indian corporate

Table 14.6 Export to sales ratios of FDI and non-FDI companies (percentages)

Category	2011–2012	2012–2013	2013–2014
All FDI companies (957)	12.2	12.3	13.6
All non-FDI companies (4578)	18.6	19.3	20.2
Manufacturing FDI companies	*15.1*	*16.4*	*17.1*
Manufacturing non-FDI companies	*23.5*	*24.5*	*26*

Source: Finances of Foreign Direct Investment Companies, 2013–14, Reserve Bank of India (RBI) Bulletin December 2015.

Note: Figures in brackets indicate number of companies in the sample.

sector, is a push of Indian firms in the direction of greater internationalisation, mainly through acquisitions abroad.[11]

Thus, for Indian big capital, increased integration into the global economy measured in pure capitalist terms has been highly successful. The acquisition of new technology development capabilities and a reduction of technological dependence has, however, not been the basis for this success (see Table 14.7). Apart from the pharmaceutical industry, there is little evidence of any such transition.[12] Even in pharmaceuticals, Indian firms lack drug development capabilities and their success instead have been founded on their established strength in generics attributable to India's earlier protective patent regime and the licensing of molecules developed by their own research and development (R&D) efforts.[13] Thus, the Indian capitalist class has retained its limited technology development capability[14] and circumvented this in a variety of other ways, like sourcing technology from specialised technology suppliers, outsourcing to foreign firms, and, wherever possible, through the older traditional routes of technological collaboration and joint ventures with multinational firms. Outside of manufacturing, the technological challenge has been less formidable. In the highly export-oriented software industry, Indian firms have found their niche in a relatively subordinate position to the internationally dominant firms.[15] In many other services and construction activities, the role of self-development of technology, in any case, tends to be limited and increased technological sophistication in these has sectors facilitated by technical equipment suppliers and software service providers.

The Indian growth story is also somewhat unique, and sharply distinct from China's, because it lacks an *industrial* character.[16] High growth in India reflects the steady and growing contribution of services and construction to Indian growth, while manufacturing's share in output has tended to remain low and even decline – leading to

Table 14.7 R&D intensity of Indian business groups and independent companies, 2012–2013* (Rs. million)

R&D expenditure to net sales ratio range (%)	No of groups	No of cos	Net sales	R&D expenditure	R&D expenditure to net income ratio (%)	Share in total net sales (%)	Share in total R&D expenditure (%)
>10	6	12	144751	18192	12.57	0.45	14.27
5–10	7	35	294976	19494	6.61	0.92	15.29
3–5	9	20	245775	10216	4.16	0.77	8.01
2–3	5	17	71951	1570	2.18	0.23	1.23
1–2	19	119	1233594	14955	1.21	3.86	11.73
0.5–1	31	266	3378596	27122	0.8	10.57	21.27
0–0.5	161	852	14497553	15292	0.11	45.35	11.99
0	316	905	5253825	0	0	16.44	0
All groups	554	2226	25121021	106843	0.43	78.59	83.79
Other companies		2740	6845130	20674	0.3	21.41	16.21
All companies		4966	31966151	127517	0.4	100	100

*Excluding foreign companies/groups.

Source: Centre for Monitoring Indian Economy (CMIE), Prowess Database.

India being classed among the countries experiencing *premature* de-industrialisation.[17] Indian business firms have reflected and contributed to this trend by increasingly shifting towards seeking expansion in services and construction activities rather than on manufacturing (see Table 14.8).

Related to the above has also been a clear and decisive trend of a worsening of India's trade deficit in the current century (see Figure 14.2). As India has become more integrated with global networks, Indian exports have diversified and grown, and the share in world exports has increased, but these have been offset by the faster increase in imports.[18] Production itself became more intensive in the use of imported materials and capital goods, a sharp rise in such imports being seen in the period just before the eruption of the global crisis.[19] Manufactured imports thus have been the chief source of the growth of imports reflecting the fact that India is not competitive as a location for production in a sufficiently wide range of

Table 14.8 Share of manufacturing, construction and services in private organized net domestic product (NDP) (percentage shares), 1999–2000 base year series (private organized)

	1990–1991	1995–1996	2002–2003	2007–2008
Manufacturing	47.53	49.32	36.38	31.48
Construction	12.19	10.34	9.28	14.23
Services	27.19	30.73	46.45	49.1

2004–2005 base year series (private organized)

	2004–2005	2007–2008	2010–2011	2012–2013
Manufacturing	29.82	29.08	31.1	30.58
Construction	10.48	14.06	10.72	10.59
Services	55.5	54.52	54.38	57.31

2011–2012 base year series (private corporations)

	2011–2012	2012–2013	2013–2014
Manufacturing	39.29	37.29	36.23
Construction	4.1	3.6	3.28
Services	52.68	55.05	56.51

Note: The figures for manufacturing and construction in the 2011–2012 base year series differ from the previous figures probably because there has been a change from an establishment based method of computing value added to an enterprise based one.

Source: Computed from CSO, National Accounts Statistics.

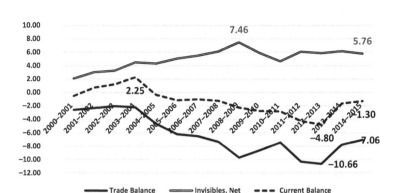

Figure 14.2 India's trade, invisibles and current balances as percentages of GDP, 2000–2001 to 2014–2015

Source: RBI, Handbook of Statistics.

manufactured products – which is the reason India does not get significant efficiency-seeking manufacturing FDI and the exports linked to it. India's exceptional performance in services exports and the large inflow of remittances have not been able to prevent the deterioration of India's current account situation, particularly after the 2008 global crisis. Thus, rather than being a capital exporter like many developing country counterparts, India has ended up becoming excessively dependent on volatile capital flows to finance its deficit and to accumulate foreign exchange reserves. This source of vulnerability has further aggravated on account of the global crisis, and since then, the Indian rupee has been on shaky ground – experiencing successive episodes of depreciation – even though a full-blown currency crisis has not yet happened. A relatively comfortable situation on the external balances front has in fact become contingent on a growth slowdown and a favourable situation with regard to international commodity prices. Indeed, in 2014–2015 and 2015–2016, India's non-oil trade deficit actually increased on account of contracting exports and increased competition from cheap imports but the collapse of oil prices kept the overall deficit in check (see Table 14.9).

The external imbalances arising from the way India has fitted into globalisation's international division of labour has another significant implication, in addition to the dependence on volatile capital flows. This is India's increased dependence on exports to the United

Table 14.9 India's foreign trade (million US dollars)

Year	Exports			Imports			Trade balance		
	Oil	Non-oil	Total	Oil	Non-oil	Total	Oil	Non-oil	Total
2012–2013	60865.1	239535.5	300400.7	164040.6	326696.1	490736.7	–103176	–87160.6	–190336
2013–2014	63179.4	251236.3	314415.7	164770.3	285443.3	450213.7	–101591	–34207	–135798
2014–2015	56794.1	253544.3	310338.5	138325.5	309707.9	448033.4	–81531.4	–56163.6	–137695
2015–2016	29183.9	231953	261136.8	82662.3	296933.9	379596.2	–53478.4	–64981	–118459

Source: Reserve Bank of India, Real Time Handbook of Statistics on the Indian Economy (http://dbie.rbi.org.in/DBIE/dbie.rbi?site=publications#!2) accessed 2 July 2016.

Table 14.10 India's merchandise trade balance with selected countries (million US dollars)

Year	All EU countries	United States	Japan	People's Republic of China
2011–2012	–5803.52	10262.52	–5764.12	–39298.4
2012–2013	–1705.62	10941.53	–6308.88	–38708.4
2013–2014	2089.68	16705.73	–2637.26	–36100.6
2014–2015	304.57	20623.92	–4767.94	–48475.5

Source: Reserve Bank of India, Real Time Handbook of Statistics on the Indian Economy (http://dbie.rbi.org.in/DBIE/dbie.rbi?site=publications#!2) accessed 2 July 2016.

States to offset an increasingly adverse trade balance with China (see Table 14.10). Among the three components of the triad, it is only with the United States that India has enjoyed a significant merchandise trade surplus. The United States also accounts for nearly three-fifths of India's computer services exports with its closest ally, the United Kingdom, accounting for another fifth. The United States is also a major source of remittances to India. In other words, the United States is extremely important to India for keeping its external payments situation within control. Thus, while the reasons for it may be different, India is, like China, quite 'dependent' on the US market, and the difference between the two dependencies in fact also imply that India and China's interests have a somewhat rival character.

The spectacular expansion of Indian big business during the last two decades has heavily depended on, rather than being despite, international integration. Foreign capital flows and access to external capital markets has played an important role in enabling both domestic and overseas expansion of Indian capital. One expression of that has been the increased recourse to foreign financing by Indian firms (see Table 14.11). Capital inflows have also contributed indirectly; given India's current account situation, they were essential requirements for the easing of norms for Indian investment abroad, and they have been important movers of the Indian stock market creating conditions whereby Indian firms could raise cheap capital. Access to technology and imports of capital goods and intermediate products where they are cheaper has contributed to the competitiveness of Indian firms and enabled them to find some niches in which they could grow, often in a collaborative arrangement with foreign capital.

The Indian case, therefore, serves as an illustration of something that perhaps may be common to all the 'emerging' Third World

Table 14.11 Pattern of net issues for financing private corporate business deficit (percentage shares)

Source sector	1994–1995 to 1996–1997	1997–2008 to 2002–2003	2003–2004 to 2007–2008	2008–2009 to 2011–2012
(i) Banking	54.54	35.28	53.83	42.22
(ii) Other financial institutions	3.51	26.54	7.67	15.22
Banking and other FIs	**58.04**	**61.83**	**61.5**	**57.44**
(iii) Government	–14.19	–0.55	–11.69	–5.89
(iv) **Rest of the world**	0.47	8.14	54.72	36.69
(v) Households	48.54	32.97	5.11	3.26
(vi) Others	7.14	–2.39	–9.65	8.51

Source: RBI Bulletin (various issues), Flow of Funds Accounts of the Indian Economy.

capitalisms even if in varied ways, namely, the contradictory nature of their so-called rise. The great divergence between a spectacular aggregative growth performance and international spread of Indian capital co-existing with a colossal 'development' failure – the inability to decisively raise the standards of living of the vast majority of the Indian population – is one important expression of this. The extremely sharp economic polarisation that has accompanied Indian growth, notwithstanding India's long-established political democracy and the repeated expressions of popular discontent with the growth trajectory through the ballot, is not an accident. By creating a cheap labour regime and the conditions for heightened informalisation and casualisation of work, it has instead provided the key foundation for the accumulation process of Indian capitalism under globalisation.

The fountainhead of the cheap labour regime in India has been the agrarian crisis[20] – the depression of agricultural incomes and the consequent reinforcement of a labour-surplus situation creating a strong wage-depressing tendency. The existence of a large labour reserve has meant that increased requirements of labour generated by the accumulation process, which in the Indian case came mainly from rapidly growing construction activities, could be met without exerting any pressure on wages. Wage stagnation enabled intensified exploitation of the working class in the core of the accumulation process, in sectors like manufacturing, as rapid increases in productivity swelled the surplus and profit share. Indeed, the squeezing of the wage share has allowed this result of swelling profits to be achieved alongside a

Table 14.12 Assets, sales and exports of foreign affiliates in selected host countries (millions of dollars)

Economy	Sales ($ million)		Exports ($ million)	
	2004	2005	2004	2005
China	698,718	..	338,606	444,209
India	34,139	41,237	3,798	4,906
Czech Republic	98,681	112,535	35,607	39,682
Ireland	108,393	..	100,301	..
Singapore	79,512	95,922	58,464	67,596
Slovenia	14,345	14,954	6,674	7,229

Source: UNCTAD, World Investment Report 2008.

rising trend in the salaries of white collar employees with higher levels of education in the private corporate sector. This cleavage between two categories of employees has been replicated within the category of self-employed providers of services too (for example, domestic help versus self-employed professionals). In response to these, public sector salaries also eventually went up, and more so at the higher end of the salary range. The cheap availability of a range of labour-intensive services have also effectively raised the real incomes of those with higher incomes. In many cases, where such services are 'produced' on capitalist lines (for example, security, sanitary or courier services or restaurants), it has allowed high incomes to be generated for some by enabling cheap and yet profitable provision of these services domestically.

Wage and income depression, thus, have shaped the sharp tilting of the distribution of income towards facilitating sharply rising corporate profits and an enrichment of a diverse category of high personal income earners deriving their earnings from business and ownership of assets or as salaries and professional incomes. However, cheap labour has also played its role in enabling the activities generating that income to be competitive under conditions of openness. Even if the accumulation regime in India has not been manufacturing export-led and driven by the industrial sector, low wages did limit the extent of loss of competitiveness of Indian manufacturing and contributed to the generation of large services exports. Wage stagnation in organised manufacturing and labour flexibility have held up the profitability of Indian manufacturing at internationally competitive prices even in the face of increasing capital and material costs of manufacturing output. Cheap labour in various supporting activities has served to an extent in compensating for the cost effects of India's large deficits in infrastructure. Via its effects on the prices of non-tradeables, cheap labour has been the principal basis for keeping India's 'national price level' (ratio of PPP conversion factor to market exchange rate) low and sustained the rupee exchange rate at a competitive level. Without this enabling a lowering of the dollar cost of production of exportable labour-intensive tradable services even when they involve large high salary employment, the export success of India's software sector would also not have been possible.

The opening up process of the Indian economy and its important implication – the circumscribed room for manoeuvring in the realm of domestic economic policy – have naturally played an important part in creating and sustaining the cheap labour situation. It is these that were responsible for the agrarian crisis which started pushing people out of agriculture, swelling the labour reserves. The continuing pressure to hold down public expenditures, in turn, limits any possibility of addressing that problem or to ameliorate its consequences through greater social expenditures. This factor indeed has worked even by strengthening the leverage of Indian private capital over the state and contributed towards locking in a particular trajectory over which changes in governments through elections have little influence. Symptomatic of this has been the renewed thrust towards 'austerity' in Indian fiscal policy, which began three years before the 2014 general elections and contributed to the massive defeat of the ruling party government in the elections. The result of the change in government, however, has only been towards a more authoritarian regime doing even more of the same.

Conclusion

Explaining the sharp contrast between this recent trend of global shift of productive activity toward the Third World and that which characterised an earlier era of capitalist imperialism does not require assuming that the world has become flat. All it requires is acknowledging a simple fact that the context after the Second World War engendered some process of capitalist development and diffusion of industrialisation to the Third World. This diffusion meant that by the time contemporary globalisation opened up Third World economic spaces for international capital from the 1980s, they had developed some limited production and industrial base and their own capitalist classes had in the process gained in at least production experience and had access to cheaper labour power. As such, the Third World could perform a role under globalisation that was different from that of classical colonialism, in particular, by becoming important locations for the generation and appropriation of surplus value through a process in which both advanced country and Third World capital participate but in a hierarchical fashion.

Under globalisation, the more concentrated monopoly over technology, finance and markets has been overlaid over a relatively more dispersed monopoly over production. The consequences of any corresponding shifts in the geography of world production and the need to redress that through income flows in the reverse direction in turn only reinforce the striving for dominance. On the other side, this new reality engenders rivalry within the Third World as the space demarcated for their economies and their capitals is more or less common so that the more direct and immediate competition may be between them. This rivalry within the Third World weakens their capacity to alter the balance of power. Thus, both the 'emergence' of Third World capitalism in a background of slow growth of the world economy as well as unevenness in the development of production within the Third World can be consistent with the maintenance of a structure of relative dominance and subordination within the world economy. The Indian case fits in very well with such an interpretation.

By some yardsticks such as GDP growth (absolute and relative), rate of expansion of corporate capital and profits and degree of transnationalisation of domestic firms, Indian capitalism's story in the era of globalisation has been one of 'success'. This was, however, not based on any prior transformation that enabled Indian capitalism to overcome its historical weaknesses as a Third World capitalism. Moreover, no such fundamental transformation of Indian capitalism has been the result of this 'success'. Indian capitalism's technological dependence remains severe. Let alone the elimination of barriers to India achieving a full-fledged industrialisation, it has, in fact, become a prominent case of premature de-industrialisation. The limits to India's ability to be a competitive location for production has in turn meant a persistent structural vulnerability on the external payments front and a great degree of dependence on volatile capital flows as well as on the US market. In such circumstances, to sustain Indian capitalism's accumulation process, adjustments must be made to a pre-existing pattern of dominance, rather than challenging it, and it leverages heavily on the extremely low wage situation. The reliance on low wages has not been without contradictions and underlays the fluctuations characterising the accumulation process;[21] however, these have only reinforced the pressures for lowering wages and adhering to austerity. The only path through which 'success' has been possible has also placed contradictions in the path of Indian capitalism developing deeper alliances with fellow 'emerging' economies. If the room for manoeuvring that these permit to Indian capitalism for dealing with its internal contradictions is extremely limited, the underlying and entrenched vulnerabilities and dependencies inherent in the nature of Indian integration also circumscribe its capacity to play an *autonomous* leading role on the global stage, whether as a partner or as a rival of the advanced capitalisms. The two, in fact, are mutually reinforcing. The palpable erosion of India's foreign policy autonomy in the last two decades exemplifies the second dimension of this reality.

For world capitalism and for Indian society – the so-called rise of Indian capitalism thus does not constitute a process automatically generating significant 'democratising' tendencies in the world order. The only way in which it can do so is if its contradictions spur the development of popular struggles which decisively change the balance of class forces. Such struggles necessarily have to contend with the reality of 'imperialism' and the entrenched inequities of the world order it implies and, therefore, can ill afford to abandon that concept.

Notes

1 Alice Amsden, *The Rise of 'The Rest': Challenges to the West From Late-Industrializing Economies*, Oxford: Oxford University Press, 2001.
2 The extent of the change in the distribution of world production, however, is far less pronounced when we compare GDPs measured on the basis of prevailing exchange rates as against measurement in PPP terms.
3 Data sourced from the National Accounts Statistics.
4 Atul Sood, Paaritosh Nath and Sangeeta Ghosh, 'Deregulating Capital, Regulating Labour: The Dynamics in the Manufacturing Sector in India', *Economic and Political Weekly*, 2014, 49(26/27): 58–68; Kunal Sen and Deb Kusum Das, 'Where Have All the Workers Gone? Puzzle of Declining Labour Intensity in Organised Indian Manufacturing', *Economic and Political Weekly*, 2015, 50(23): 108–15; T. Muralidharan, Bino Paul G. D. and Ashutosh Bishnu Murti, 'Should Real Wages of Workers Go Up in Indian Manufacturing?' *Economic and Political Weekly*, 2014, 49(30): 153–62.
5 Used to estimate revenue losses in an appendix to the Union Budget. Clearly a very small number of companies with large individual profits have accounted for more than half the profits of the sample companies in recent years. Since these sample companies also account for the bulk of corporate taxes (and therefore corporate profits), it follows that the concentration level in the sample reflects a real concentration in corporate profits in a small number of companies.
6 The share in profits of *all* 1800 odd PSUs is in every year significantly lower than of the companies with large profits.

7 The following table is slightly dated but still conveys the picture:
8 An Infosys study of 394 leading global firms engaged in a variety of different services and manufacturing activities showed that as many as 309 of them (78 percent) were offshoring services to India, with 124 of them setting up captives. Meera Rajeevan, Manish Subramanaian, Pramod Beligere and Rohini Williams, 'Research Study of Captives in India and China: a Majority of Parent Organizations also rely on Third-Party Relationships', *Infosys White Paper* June 2007, www.infosys.com/global-sourcing/white-papers/captives-research-study.pdf (accessed on 25 October 2009).
9 A prominent example is the automobile components sector where leading Indian groups like Kalyani (Bharat Forge), TVS, Mahindra, Rane and Amtek have succeeded in establishing themselves as suppliers to the Indian and foreign operations of global auto companies. Even in automobile components trade, however, India has had a deficit.
10 Even a sector like banking, for instance, in many countries dominated by international banks, exhibits this feature in India. It is only Indian private banks that have displaced the public sector to an extent, with foreign banks remaining a somewhat peripheral segment with a share of around 5 percent.
11 Deepak Nayyar, 'The Internationalization of Firms from India: Investment, Mergers and Acquisitions', *Oxford Development Studies*, 2008, 36(1): 111–31; Prema-chandra Athukorala, 'Outward Foreign Direct Investment From India', *Asian Development Review*, 2009, 26(2): 125–53.
12 Sunil Mani, 'Is India Becoming More Innovative since 1991? Some Disquieting Features', *Economic and Political Weekly*, 2009, 44(46): 41–51.
13 Ravinder Jha, 'Options for Indian Pharmaceutical Industry in the Changing Environment', *Economic and Political Weekly*, 2007, 42(39): 3958–67; Sudip Chaudhuri, 'Ranbaxy Sell-out: Reversal of Fortunes', *Economic and Political Weekly*, 2008, 43(29): 11–13.
14 Nasir Tyabji, *Industrialisation and Innovation: The Indian Experience*, New Delhi: Sage, 2000.
15 Anthony P. D'Costa, 'The Indian Software Industry in the Global Division of Labor', in A.P. D'Costa E. Sridharan (eds.), *India in the Global Software Industry: Innovation, Firm Strategies and Development*, Houndmills, Basingtoke: Palgrave Macmillan, 2004, pp. 1–26.
16 Surajit Mazumdar, 'Globalisation and Growth: The Indian Case in Perspective', in Ratan Khasnabis and Indrani Chakraborty (eds.), *Market, Regulations and Finance: Global Meltdown and the Indian Economy*, New Delhi: Springer, 2014, pp. 213–30. India's share in world manufacturing value added in 2014 stood at 2.66 percent, which pales in comparison to China's 24 percent, http://unctadstat.unctad.org (accessed on 30 June 2016).
17 Dani Rodrik, 'Premature Deindustrialization', NBER Working Paper Series, Working Paper 20935, 2015, www.nber.org/papers/w20935 (accessed on 22 March 2015).
18 C. Veeramani, 'Anatomy of India's Merchandise Export Growth, 1993–94 to 2010–11', *Economic and Political Weekly*, 2012, 47(1): 94–104; Malini Chakravarty, 'India's Foreign Trade: Recent Patterns, Challenges and Prospects', in Jayati Ghosh (ed.), *India and the International Economy*:

Vol. 2 of the ICSSR Research Surveys and Explorations in Economics, New Delhi: Oxford University Press, 2015, pp. 65–111; Sudip Chaudhuri, 'Manufacturing Trade Deficit and Industrial Policy in India', *Economic and Political Weekly*, 2013, 48(8): 41–50.

19 Bishwanath Goldar, 'Productivity in Indian Manufacturing (1999–2011): Accounting for Imported Materials Input', *Economic and Political Weekly*, 2015, 50(35): 104–111; Chakravarty, 'India's Foreign Trade'; M. Mohanty, 'India: Globalisation and Growth', Indian Institute of Management, Calcutta, Working Paper Series WPS No. 762, 2015; Chaudhuri, 'Manufacturing Trade Deficit and Industrial Policy in India'; Mazumdar, 'Globalisation and Growth'.

20 D. Narasimha Reddy and Srijit Mishra, 'Crisis in Agriculture and Rural Distress in Post-Reform India', in R. Radhakrishna (ed.), *India Development Report 2008*, New Delhi, Oxford University Press, 2008, pp. 40–53; Utsa Patnaik, 'Food Stocks and Hunger: The Causes of Agrarian Distress', *Social Scientist*, 2003, 31(7/8): 15–41; Utsa Patnaik, 'Neoliberalism and Rural Poverty in India', *Economic and Political Weekly*, 2007, 42(30): 3132–50; R. Ramakumar, 'Economic Reforms and Agricultural Policy in India', Paper presented at the "Tenth Anniversary Conference of the Foundation for Agrarian Studies", Kochi, 9–12 January 2014.

21 Mazumdar, 'Globalisation and Growth'.

Index

Page numbers in italic indicate a figure. Page numbers in bold indicate a table.

accumulation: abstract theory of 15; division of the world 31; through dispossession 31; *see also* capitalism

advanced capitalist countries 6; BRIC *vs.* 124; conflict between 16, 122–123; working class in 62

Africa, slaves from 228, 241

Agrarian History of Western Europe AD 500 to 1850 (van Bath) 201–202

AITUC *see* All India Trade Union Congress (AITUC)

Allende, Salvador 161

All India Trade Union Congress (AITUC) 253–254, 258, 260

All Parties Convention of 1921 259

Andrews, C. F. 258

Anglo-Saxon model of financial organisation 137

anti-imperialism 82–89

Aristotle 205

armed conflicts, post-Second World War 122

arms exports 119

Arrighi, Giovanni 16, 25–26

Asia 208–217

autonomy 5

backward linkage 275–278, **277**

Banerjea, Surendranath 257

banking and insurance 272

banking sector: health 289; NPAs 288–289

Barclays 239

Base Structure Report 118

Basu, Jyoti 260

Bentham, Jeremy 256

Besant, Annie 258

Bhattacharya, Sabyasachi 247

Blyth 239

Bounty scheme 238

bourgeoisie: anti-imperialist stance 124; during colonialism 123–124; nationalist 123–124; newly independent countries 124; third world countries 107, 123

Bretton Woods System 298

BRICS 6, 93–94, 99–100

Britain 8–9; export of capital 32; international dominance 201–222; Slavery Abolition Act 226–227; slave trade and 226; trade balance 207, **214**, 215, **216–217**, 217–218; trade deficit 207, 213–220, **221**; trade pattern 208–217; trade volumes (1750–1754 to 1800–1804) 207, **208**

British Economic Growth 1688–1959, Trends and Structure (Deane and Cole) 206–207, 213

Bukharin, Nikolai 78–79

business bureaucracy 136–137

business services 272

Capital (Marx) 48–54, 296, 300, 305

capital inflows, India 322

Capital in the 21st Century (Piketty) 204–205

capitalism: contemporary phase 295–297; crisis 57; diffusion of 28–29; economic power in 28; immature 57; imperialism under 89–101; Marx on 15; monopoly stage of 19–21; new trends in 133–135; principal markers 295; surplus labour in 295–296
capitalist class, India 317
capitalist relations: diffusion of 33; globalisation and 30–31; imperialist chain in 23
capitalocentrism 86–87
Castro, Fidel 160
casualisation of labour *see* casual workers
casual workers 303–304
centralisation of capital 5, 23, 29, 61, 120–121, 125; *see also* monopoly capitalism
Césaire, Aimé 78, 83, 87, 89
Chaudhuri, B. B. 201
cheap labour 32, 37; in India 254, 302, 323–325
Chelmsford 256–258
child labour 250
China 6; Britain's trade deficit with 217; capitalist development 105–106; richest bourgeoisie 107; share in world GDP 311
Chinese Revolution 62
Churchill, Winston 62
circuits of global capital 82–85, 87–88
class domination-induced imperialism 6
Cole, W. A. 206–207, 213
colonial India: cotton textiles 203, 205; Council Bills 203–204; exchange earnings 204; export earnings 8, 202–204; global trade 201–222; gold and forex earnings 204; invisible liabilities imposed on 204; raw cotton 205
colonialism 3, 297–298; history of 297
colonial transfers 204–206; financing deficits with sovereign regions 217–222
Commerce Constituencies 258
commercial agriculture 201

commercial classes 259
commercial crops 201
commodity trading 288
Communist Girni Kamgar Union 259
Communist Manifesto 57
conflicts of capital 33
conflicts with imperialism 123–124
contractualisation *see* contractual workers
contractual workers 303–304, 306–307
contract workers' organisation 307
contradictions of globalisation 68–71
converse theory of accident 205
coolie trade 238
corporate-led finance 3
cotton textiles 203, 205
Council on Foreign Affairs in the United States 116
Countouris, Nicola 247
crony capitalism 290

Dange, S. A. 252–253, 255
Davis, Kingsley 252
Davis, Ralph 208–209
Deane, Phyllis 206–207, 212–213
debt crisis of 1991, India 288
de Cecco, Marcello 134, 203
decolonisation 2, 62, 71, 105, 113, 124
deflationary policies 3, 121
dependency theory 46–48
deregulation of markets 3
developing countries 6; capitalist development in 105–106; changes in 108–113
Discourse on Colonialism (Césaire) 83
division of world 31
dollar 62; in foreign exchange reserves 116, *117*; maintaining stability 118–120; oil price and 119–120
Dutt, Romesh 203

East India Company 201; taxes raised by 202
Economic and Political Weekly 247
economic polarisation, India 323

elections: labour constituencies 258–260; labour representatives and 258–260
empire with/without imperialism 26–30
entrepreneurial economy 296
epistemic community 67
Europe: Britain's trade deficit 213–215, **214**
European invasions of South America 2
exploitation: Marxian definition of 300; super 300–301; theories of 46–56
export of capital 32
external imperialism 83

Factories Act of 1911 249
Factories Act of 1922 249
Factory Act of 1934 249
FDI *see* foreign direct investment (FDI)
Feinstein, Charles 219–220
FEVD *see* forecast error variance decomposition (FEVD)
finance capital: globalisation of 65–67; international 121–122; Lenin and 63–64, 121; nation state and 65–67, 121–122; nature of 65; then and now 63–65
financial asset: deflationary policies 3; hedging 3
financialisation: beneficiaries of 33; characteristic of 136; concept and operation 135–137; FINREBS 269–275; growth pattern under 267–275; inter-linkages across sectors 275–279; in Latin America 139–141; service sector growth 268–269
Financial Stability Report (RBI 2013) 289
FINREBS (finance, insurance, real estate, and business services) 267; co-integration and causality 279, 281–283; components/services 272–274, 285; GDP 285–286; growth trend and pattern 269–275, *270*; Keynes–Minsky framework 286–288; variation in 285

The First Industrial Revolution (Deane) 212–213
First World War 9
flexible labour regime 301–308; casualisation and contractualisation 303–304; functional flexibility 301; multilateral organisations and 302–303; numerical flexibility 301; outsourcing and subcontracting 304–305; temporal flexibility 302; voice representation of 305–308; wage flexibility 301–302
forecast error variance decomposition (FEVD) 284–285
foreign direct investment (FDI) 39, 42, 45, 106–107
foreign ownership of US assets 116, 118
forward linkages 275, 278–279, **280**
France: export of capital 32
Franchise Committee of 1932 259
free trade 235
Frías, Hugo Chávez 161
functional flexibility 301; *see also* flexible labour regime
Fund-Bank 299–300

G7 124
Gibson-Graham, J. K. 86
Gladstone, John 234
global financial community 67–68
global financial oligarchy 67
global hegemony 31
globalisation 5, 39–46; capitalist relations 30–31; contradictions of 68–71; of finance 65–67; labour arbitrage 43–46; of production 39–43
Government of India Act of 1919 256–257
Government of India Act of 1935 259–260
Great Depression (1929) 61, 252
gross domestic product (GDP): advanced capitalist countries 6, 113–114, *114*; developing and emerging economies 6; share of largest economies in **312**

Growth of Commercial Agriculture in Bengal 1777–1900, The (Chaudhuri) 201
Grundrisse (Marx) 15, 56, 252

Habib, Sayera 203
Hailey, W. M. 257
Hardt, Michael 26–27, 72–74, 76, 104
Harvey, David 16, 24–26, 28, 31
Hero Honda plant, Dharuhera in Haryana 306–308
Hero Honda Theka Majdoor Sangathan, Haryana 306–307
Higginbottom, Andy 55
Hilferding, Rudolph 1, 4, 16, 19, 20–22, 32
Hirschman, Albert 275
Hughes, Steve 247
humbug of finance 67–68

IFTU *see* International Federation of Trade Unions (IFTU)
IGO *see* inter-governmental organisations (IGO)
ILO *see* International Labour Organisation (ILO)
immature capitalism 57
Immigration of Agricultural Labourers from the British Dominion in India and elsewhere 239
imperialism: as arrangement of exploitation 2; characterisation of 16; class domination-induced 6; earlier formulations of 1–2; empire with or without 26–30; interpretations of 1; labour and 299–301; Lenin's theory of 54–56; Marxian literature 16; neoliberal globalisation and global capitalism 89–101; new form of 3; particularity of 82–89; phases of 61–63, 297–298; realisation crisis and 17–19; situating problem of 79–82; war arising from 64–65
Imperialism, the Highest Stage of Capitalism (Lenin) 54–56
Imperialism and World Economy (Bukharin) 78

Imperialism Pioneer of Capitalism (Warren) 28
import substitution industrialisation model (ISI) 145
indentured labour 9; plantation colonies 227–228; shipping industry 241; sugar plantations and flow of 228–231
India: accumulation regime in 324; capital inflows 322; capitalist class 317; capitalist development 105–106; cheap labour in 254, 302, 323–325; colonial state in 9; concentration of corporate profits 314–315, **315**; corporate sector and growth 312–317, **313–314**; debt crisis of 1991 288; dependence on exports to the United States 320, 322; economic polarisation 323; as emerging economy 311–325; exports 319; financial sector 288–289; growth 6; imports 319–320; liberalisation phase 311; manufacturing in 317, 319, **319**; metropolis–colony trade and 203; MNCs in 315–316, **316**; non-oil trade deficit 320; per capita grain output 206; pharmaceuticals 317; R&D intensity of business groups 317, **318**; richest bourgeoisie 107; services and construction 317, 319, **319**; services exports 320, 322, 324; trade balance 322, **322**; trade deficit 319–320, *320*; volatile capital flows 320; wage depression and stagnation 314, 323–325
Indian Emigration Acts of 1922 and 1938 249
Indian Factory Labour Committee 249
Indian Railways 252
Industrial Revolution 241–242
Industrial Revolution and British Overseas Trade, The (Davis) 208–209
In. Pre. Cor. 251
input market 297
inter-governmental organisations (IGO) 251

internal imperialism 82–83
International Association for the
 Legal Protection of Workers 251
international credit system 15
international division of labour 106
International Federation of Trade
 Unions (IFTU) 255
international finance capital
 121–122
International Labour Convention of
 Washington 249
International Labour Office,
 Geneva 248
International Labour Organisation
 (ILO) 9, 247–248; advanced
 industrialised countries 251;
 Indian delegation to 251–252;
 right to strike 249–250
International Monetary Fund (IMF)
 3, 43, 45, 90, 122, 165, 206,
 297–298
International Monetary System 62
intra-imperialist rivalry
 107–108, 120
Iran 62
Ireland: Britain's imports from
 210–212, **212**, 216; Britain's trade
 deficit with 216–217, **217**

Jinnah, M. A. 258

Kautsky, Karl 19, 29, 64
Keynes–Minsky framework
 286–288
Klare, Michael 182
Krishnamurthy, J. 247
Krugman, Paul R. 206

labour 299–308; cheap 254,
 302, 323–325; contemporary
 imperialism and 299–301;
 flexible labour regime 301–308;
 indenturing of 9; international
 division of 106; promoting
 legislation 9–10; super
 exploitation 300–301
Labour Bureau of Government of
 India 306
labour constituencies 258–260
labour contractors 306

labour flexibility *see* flexible labour
 regime
labour laws and legislations
 247–261; Acts 249; class
 representation in 255–260;
 enforcement of 250; ILO norms
 and conventions 250; multilateral
 organisations and 302–303; right
 to strike 249–250
labour market 297;
 internationalisation of 9,
 252; Marx's observations on
 252–253
labour migration 252
labour shortages, end to slavery and
 226–227
LAI *see* League against imperialism
 (LAI)
Latin America 6–7, 131–157;
 capital market operations in
 terms of GDP 141, **142–143**;
 exchange rate 153, *154*; external
 financial channel 149–154; fears
 for 161–163; financial account
 components *150*; financialisation
 in 139–141; GDP 141, **144,
 145**; hope for countries sticking
 to ideals 163–165; income
 distribution by deciles 153–154,
 155; interest rate and sovereign
 bonds in 149, 153, *153*; market
 capitalisation 139–141, **140**;
 neomercantilism in 141, 145–147;
 net income composition from
 direct and portfolio investment
 149, *152*; overview 160–161;
 primary account 149, *151*;
 principal disequilibria in 139;
 trade 145–147, **146**, *148*; US
 imperialism under Obama
 165–167
League against imperialism
 (LAI) 255
Lenin 5; export of capital 32;
 finance capital and 63–64, 121;
 *Imperialism, the Highest Stage of
 Capitalism* 54–6
liberation: worldview of 21–24
Luxemburg, Rosa 16, 206; theory of
 imperialism 17–19

Maclaren, Neil 251
Magdoff, Harry 32, 298
Mandel, Ernest 31
manufacturing: in India 317, 319, **319**
market: for final good 297; input
    297; *see also* labour market
Marx, Karl 15–16; *Capital* 48–54;
    on international credit system 15;
    on labour market 252–253; on
    surplus labour 295–296
Marxists 15
Mauritius, British colony of:
    bankruptcy of sugar estates 239;
    consumption duty on all spirits
    238–239; indentured labour from
    India to 229–231, *230–231*;
    plantation owners 239; rates of
    duties 232; slave population 226;
    sugar production 230–231
Meerut Conspiracy Trial 253
Mezaros, Istvan 34
migration: pull factor 229; push
    factors 229
military expenditure, US 7–8,
    118–119, *119*; as compared
    with other countries 179–181,
    180–181; cost as per budget
    177–179, **179**; current account
    deficit 184–186; employment and
    growth 189, 190; oil and terms
    of trade 186–189, *188*, *189*; tax
    shared by working class 182–183,
    183; trend of 177, *178*
military interventions 122
Mines Act of 1935 249
Mining Act of 1923 249
Minsky–Kindelberger–Keynes
    framework 288
Mitchell, B. R. 207
MNCs *see* multinational
    corporations (MNCs)
mobile capital 3
monopoly capitalism 5, 19–22, 61,
    81, 120–121
Muddiman Committee *see* Reforms
    Enquiry Committee of 1924
multinational corporations (MNCs)
    70, 184, 298; competition
    between 297; in India 315–316,
    316; monopoly stage of capitalism
    20; rise of 299–300

Nagaraj, R. 285
NAIRU *see* Non-Accelerating
    Inflation Rate of Unemployment
    (NAIRU)
Naoroji, Dadabhai 203
nationalist bourgeoisie 123–124
nation states: finance capital
    and 65–67; legitimacy of 33;
    neo-liberalism and 33; oppressed
    classes 33; role of 32–33; trade
    liberalisation 66; transnational
    capitalist class 33
Navigation Law of Britain 202, 241
Negri, Antonio 26–27, 72–74,
    76, 104
Nehru, Jawaharlal 250
Nehru, Motilal 258
neocolonialism 28
neoliberal globalisation 4–5;
    imperialism and 89–101
neoliberalism, tenets of 299
neomercantilism 7; defined 137; in
    Latin America 141, 145–147;
    operation 137–139
Netherlands 202
New Deal reforms 287
Non-Accelerating Inflation Rate of
    Unemployment (NAIRU) 131
non-performing assets (NPAs)
    288–289
North America: production of
    surplus value 31
NPAs *see* non-performing assets
    (NPAs)
numerical flexibility 301; *see also*
    flexible labour regime

Obstfeld, Maurice 206
ODA *see* overseas development
    assistance (ODA)
oil reserves 120
outsourcing 304–305
overcapitalisation 136
overseas development assistance
    (ODA) 2
ownership of dwellings 272

Panitch, Leo 33
particularity of imperialism 82–89
Patel, Vitthalbhai 258
Patnaik, Utsa 203

Payment of Wages Act, 1936 249
per capita grain output, India 206
Phelan, F. J. 250
Piketty, Thomas 204–205
Pinochet, Augusto 161
plantation colonies: abolition of
    slavery and 226–227; finance in
    237–240; imports of processed
    sugar 233; imports of raw sugar
    from 232, *232*; indentured
    labourers 9, 227–231; tariff
    structure 231–236; triangular
    trade 240–242, *241*
political class 259
Pollard, Sidney 219–220
Ponzi-financing units 287
portfolio income 135
post-colonial imperialism 24–26
pre-capital 87–88
pre-capitalist sector 104–105
primitive accumulation 2, 31, 56
production of surplus value 31
pull factor 229
purchasing power parity (PPP)
    311
push factors 229

Rai, Lala Lajpat 258
Ranadive, B. T. 252
real-estate funds 289
real estate services 272
realisation crisis, and imperialism
    17–19
Red International Labour Union
    (RILU) 255
Reforms Enquiry Committee of
    1924 258
relative surplus value 52–53
Reliance 107
resource transfers from colonies
    203
Ricardo, David 205–206
right to strike 249–250
RILU *see* Red International Labour
    Union (RILU)
Robinson, Joan 18
Rodgers, Gerry 247
Roy, M. N. 251

Saul, S. B. 203
Schumpeterian atavism 28

Second World War 2, 298; armed
    conflicts since 122; European
    countries and 138; financial
    oligarchies and 61–62
Sepoy Mutiny of 1857 229
service sector: growth of 268–269
shadow banking 3
Simon Commission 258
slavery, end to 226–227
Slavery Abolition Act 226–227
slave trade 2, 226
Sly, F. G. 257
social democratic governments 2
Southborough, Lord 257
Southborough Committee 257
spatial dimension 104–105
Srinivasan, V. S. 257
stock markets in India 288
subcontracting 304–305
sub-contracting 304–305
sub-prime crisis 3
sugar plantations 227
surplus labour 295–296
surplus value 5, 299–300;
    appropriation and distribution
    of 31; Marx on 296; neoliberal
    globalisation 91; production of
    31; rate of 49–50; relative 52–53;
    surplus labour and 295; third
    form of 52–54, 57; unproductive
    capitalists 92

tariff structure, in British plantation
    colonies 231–236; end to tariff
    protection 235; import duties on
    sugar imports 235–236, *236*
Tata Motors 107
tax collection, East India
    Companies 202
tax or rent extraction 206
temporal flexibility 302; *see also*
    flexible labour regime
Third World 6, 310–325; domestic
    capital 311; economic expansion
    310–311; FDI 310; global
    competition and 310–311; *see
    also* India
third world bourgeoisie 107,
    123
Tilak, B. G. 254
Tory Party 62

trade 2
trade balance 8, 137; Britain 207, 214, 215, **216–217**, 217–218; India 322, **322**; Latin American and Caribbean 145–147, **146**
trade deficit 145; Britain 207, 213–220, **221**; India 319–320, *320*; Latin American and Caribbean 145
trade union movement, international affiliations of 253–255
trade unions (TU) 306; political party-led 307
trade volumes of Britain (1750–1754 to 1800–1804) 207, **208**
trading in indentured labour 9
traditional pre-capitalist formation 86–87
transnational capitalist class 33
triangular trade: defined 240; Industrial Revolution 241–242; plantation colonies 240–242, *241*

ultra-imperialism 64
United Nations 204, 206
United States: arms exports 119; Britain's trade deficit 213–215, **214**; current account deficit 114–116, *115*; de-industrialising process 7; export of capital 32; financial innovations 138; financial system 7; imperialism 6–8; India and 320, 322; measurement of financialisation 135; military expenditure 7–8, 118–119, *119*; oil and 119–120; PL480s 2; strategic commodity and 119
unproductive capitalists 92
US workers, US imperialism (1985–2000) and 171–191; accounting framework 173–175; benefits from iron fist imperialism 184–191; distributional impact 171–172; framework for assessing impact of 171–172; illiberal

imperialism 176–177; welfare of 176–177

van Bath, Bernald Slicher 201–202
van Daele, Jasmien 247
Vietnam War 62

wage flexibility 301–302; *see also* flexible labour regime
Warren, Bill 28, 32
wars 64–65
Western Europe: production of surplus value 31
West Indies 239; Britain's trade balance/deficits with 215, **216**; indentured labour from India 229, *230*, 231; planters from 234; preferential duties 232
Wikipedia 122
Wood, Ellen Meiksins 16, 28
Workers' and Peasants' Party 259
Workers Welfare League of India (WWLI) 251, 254
working class 57, 253; wage depression and stagnation 323–325
working hours: casual and contractual workers 303–304; Factories Act of 1911 249; super exploitation 300
workmen's compensation 250
Workmen's Compensation Act of 1923 249
world, division of 31
World Bank 43, 68, 90, 162, 165, 193, 206, 297–298
World Economic Situation and Prospects Report (UN 2014) 116
world trade: colonial relations between India and Britain and 9; current structure of 5
World Trade Organization (WTO) 298
WTO *see* World Trade Organization (WTO)
WWLI *see* Workers Welfare League of India (WWLI)

Printed in the United States
by Baker & Taylor Publisher Services